The British Army Against Napoleon

Facts, Lists and Trivia 1805–1815

The British Army Against Napoleon

Facts, Lists and Trivia 1805–1815

Robert Burnham and Ron McGuigan

Foreword by Rory Muir

FRONTLINE
BOOKS

*The British Army Against Napoleon
Facts, Lists and Trivia 1805–1815*

This edition published in 2010 by Frontline Books,
an imprint of
Pen & Sword Books Limited, 47 Church Street,
Barnsley, S. Yorkshire, S70 2AS
www.frontline-books.com
email info@frontline-books.com

© Robert Burnham and Ron McGuigan, 2010

The right of Robert Burnham and Ron McGuigan to be identified
as Authors of this Work
has been asserted by them in accordance with the
Copyright, Designs and Patents Act 1988.

ISBN: 978-1-84832-562-3

All rights reserved. No part of this publication may be reproduced, stored in or introduced into a retrieval system, or transmitted, in any form, or by any means (electronic, mechanical, photocopying, recording or otherwise) without the prior written permission of the publisher. Any person who does any unauthorised act in relation to this publication may be liable to criminal prosecution and civil claims for damages.

A CIP data record for this title is available from the British Library.

For more information on our books, please visit
www.frontline-books.com, email info@frontline-books.com
or write to us at the above address.

Typeset by Palindrome

Printed in the UK by CPI Antony Rowe

Contents

List of Illustrations	vi
List of Tables	vii
Foreword	xv
Acknowledgements	xix
Introduction	xxiii
Abbreviations	xxvi

Chapter One
   The British Army — 1

Chapter Two
   Officer Seniority — 21

Chapter Three
   The Regiment — 59

Chapter Four
   Life of an Officer — 140

Chapter Five
   Life of a Soldier — 186

Chapter Six
   British Casualties in the Napoleonic Wars — 211

Chapter Seven
   Sovereign's Honours Awarded for Merit — 235

Chapter Eight
   Campaign Medals for Meritorious
   or Honourable Service — 255

References — 315
Index — 321

Illustrations

Plates may be found between pages 166 and 167

1. Sir David Baird
2. Sir William Beresford
3. Sir Archibald Campbell
4. Sir Galbraith Lowry Cole
5. Charles Marquis Cornwallis
6. Sir Ronald Ferguson
7. Sir Thomas Graham
8. Sir Henry Hardinge
9. Sir Rowland Hill
10. Sir John Hope
11. Edward Duke of Kent and Strathearn
12. Sir James Leith
13. Sir John Moore
14. Sir George Murray
15. Frederick William, Prince of Orange
16. Sir Denis Pack
17. Henry Lord Paget
18. Sir Thomas Picton
19. The Duke of Wellington
20. The guardhouse and gunners' barracks at Fort Cumberland
21. Drum Major and Pioneer of a British Line Regiment
22. A corporal of the 10th Hussars
23. Uniforms of the 42nd Foot
24. Uniform of the 1st Life Guards
25. Army Gold Medal awarded for Maida
26. The medals of Denis Pack
27. Colonel James Bathurst's Army Gold Cross
28. Army Gold Medal Awarded to Major Young
29. Waterloo Medal awarded to Surgeon John Bolton
30. Military General Service Medal

List of Tables

1.1	Effective strength of the rank and file 1805–15	2
1.2	Estimated Strength of the British army 1805–15	2
1.3	Number of men raised for the British army by recruiting and transfers from the militia 1805–12	3
1.4	Location and strength of the British army 1805–9	4
1.5	Authorised establishment of British overseas garrisons in 1814	5
1.6	Principal appointments at the War Department 1805–15	6–7
1.7	Districts in Great Britain and Ireland 1805	8–9
1.8	Districts in Great Britain and Ireland in 1814	10–11
1.9	Commissary equivalent ranks in the army	12
1.10	Deployment of Commissariat officers 1814	13
1.11	Deployment of chaplains in 1814	15
1.12	Nobility in the army 1805–10	16
1.13	Nobility in the army 1811–16	17
1.14	Wellington's promotions	18
1.15	Wellington's theoretical promotion dates, regulations of 1795/6	18
1.16	Wellington's theoretical promotion dates, regulations of 1809	18–19
1.17	Wellington's actual promotions 1787–1813	20
2.1	Officer seniority – Hanover 1805	22–3
2.2	Officer seniority – Cape of Good Hope 1805–6	24
2.3	Officer seniority – Maida and Calabria 1806	25
2.4	Officer seniority – South America 1806–7	26
2.5	Officer seniority – Baltic 1807	27–8
2.6	Officer seniority – Egypt 1807	28–9
2.7	Officer seniority – Baltic 1808	29–30
2.8	Officer seniority in the Peninsula July 1808–April 1809	31–2
2.9	Officer seniority in the Peninsula 1809 – 1814	32–9
2.10	Officer seniority – Martinique 1809	40
2.11	Officer seniority – Bay of Naples 1809	41–2
2.12	Officer seniority – Walcheren 1809	43–4
2.13	Officer seniority – Guadeloupe 1810	44–5
2.14	Officer seniority – Bourbon 1810	46

Tables

2.15	Officer seniority – Mauritius 1810	47
2.16	Officer seniority – Java 1811	48
2.17	Officer seniority in North America during the War of 1812	49–50
2.18	Officer seniority – The Netherlands 1813–14	51
2.19	Officer seniority – Genoa 1814	52
2.20	Officer seniority – The Netherlands March 1815	53–4
2.21	Officer seniority – the Campaign of 1815	54–6
2.22	Officer seniority in the British contingent of the army of occupation 1815	57
2.23	Officer seniority – Guadeloupe 1815	58
3.1	Location of cavalry regiments in 1805	60–1
3.2	Location of foot regiments in 1805	61–6
3.3	Location of miscellaneous infantry units in 1805	66–7
3.4	Location of foreign troops in British service in 1805	67
3.5	Location of the King's German Legion in 1805	68
3.6	Location of cavalry regiments in 1815	68–9
3.7	Location of foot regiments in 1815	69–74
3.8	Location of miscellaneous infantry units in 1815	74–5
3.9	Location of foreign troops in British service in 1815	75–6
3.10	Location of Royal Horse Artillery troops from 1805–10	76
3.11	Location of Royal Horse Artillery troops from 1811–16	76
3.12	Location of Foot Artillery from 1805–10	77
3.13	Location of Foot Artillery from 1811–16	77–8
3.14	Location of the King's German Artillery and foreign artillery 1805–10	78
3.15	Location of the King's German Artillery and foreign artillery 1811–16	78
3.16	Barracks in England in 1809	79–83
3.17	Barracks in Scotland in 1809	83–4
3.18	Establishments of the cavalry regiments in 1812	85–6
3.19	Establishments of the infantry regiments in 1812	86–9
3.20	Establishments of the garrison and veteran battalions in 1812	89
3.21	Establishments of miscellaneous regiments in 1812	89–90
3.22	Establishments of the foreign regiments in 1812	90–1
3.23	Establishments of cavalry regiments in the Peninsular army January 1813	91
3.24	Establishments of foot regiments in the Peninsular army January 1813	92–3
3.25	Regimental colonels of the cavalry regiments 1805–15	94–6
3.26	Regimental colonels of the infantry regiments 1805–15	96–104
3.27	Regimental colonels of garrison battalions disbanded 24 February 1805	104–5
3.28	Regimental colonels of garrison battalions 1805–14	105
3.29	Regimental colonels of garrison battalions 1814–15	105
3.30	Regimental colonels of the Royal Veteran Battalions 1805–14	106
3.31	Regimental colonels of the Royal Veteran Battalions 1815	106
3.32	Regimental colonels of the King's German Legion (KGL) 1805–15	107
3.33	Regimental colonels of the various foreign corps 1805–15	108
3.34	Regimental commanders of the Royal Regiment of Artillery, the Horse Brigade and the Invalid Battalion 1805–15	109
3.35	Regimental facings of the cavalry 1814–15	110–11
3.36	Regimental facings of the infantry and the KGL 1814–15	111–14

3.37	Regimental facings of miscellaneous regiments 1814–15	115
3.38	Battle honours earned from 1805–11	116–17
3.39	Battle honours earned from 1812–13	118–19
3.40	Battle honours earned from 1814–15	120–1
3.41	Nicknames of the cavalry regiments	121–3
3.42	Nicknames of the infantry regiments	123–8
3.43	Regimental agents' addresses in 1812	129
3.44	Regimental agents for the cavalry regiments	129–30
3.45	Regimental agents for the infantry	130–4
3.46	Regimental agents for miscellaneous units	134–5
3.47	Regimental books to be kept by every regiment throughout the army	135–7
3.48	Company books to be kept by every troop and company in the army	137–8
3.49	Quartermaster's books	138–9
3.50	Surgeon's books	139
4.1	Cost to purchase a commission in different regiments	140
4.2	Fees paid for receiving a commission in different regiments	141
4.3	Average cost of initial officer uniforms	141
4.4	Rooms authorised to officers in a barracks	142
4.5	Equipment furnished in an officer's room	142
4.6	Weekly lodging allowance for rooms when no barracks rooms are available	142
4.7	Fuel allowances for cavalry officers' rooms for seven days	143
4.8	Daily and yearly pay for officers	143
4.9	Stoppages or deductions to pay of officers	146
4.10	Income tax paid by officers in an infantry regiment	147
4.11	Deductions for rations in daily and yearly pay for infantry officers	147
4.12	Deductions in yearly pay for an ensign in 1810	148
4.13	Daily expenses of an ensign stationed in Ireland 1807	148
4.14	Deductions for daily subsistence for officers in the Life and Royal Horse Guards	148–9
4.15	Deductions for daily subsistence for officers in a Foot Guards Regiment	149
4.16	Deductions in pay for an ensign in the Foot Guards in 1810	149–50
4.17	Minimum number of years' service before promotion – 1809	150
4.18	The rise through the ranks of George Brown	151
4.19	Price of commissions for the Household troops	152
4.20	Price of commissions for line cavalry and infantry regiments	152
4.21	Number of lieutenancies purchased between September 1810–August 1811 and March 1812–February 1813	153
4.22	Commission fees payable for staff appointments	153–4
4.23	Commission fees payable for Household troops in 1814	154
4.24	Commission fees payable for line cavalry and infantry regiments in 1814	154–5
4.25	Commission fees payable for army rank in 1814	155
4.26	Advance pay issued to officers embarking on foreign service	155–6
4.27	Allowance for officers embarking on foreign service	156
4.28	Allowances for tentage on campaign	156

Tables

4.29	Allowance for infantry officers to purchase a horse when embarking on foreign service	156
4.30	Number of horses authorised for cavalry officers for which forage was provided	157
4.31	Number of horses belonging to officers of the 7th Hussars embarked for the Coruña campaign, October 1808	157–8
4.32	Estimated cost of outfitting an aide-de-camp in November 1813	158
4.33	Items carried on campaign by Lieutenant George Bell, 34th Foot, 1812	159
4.34	Personal baggage of Major Alexander Dickson, February 1810	159
4.35	Items carried on campaign by Captain Dugald Ferguson, 95th Rifles, 1812	160
4.36	Items purchased by an ensign, Coldstream Guards, 1812	161
4.37	Books carried by Major Edward Charles Cocks in the Peninsular War	161–2
4.38	Money spent by a guards officer in 1812 to buy mounts in Lisbon	162–3
4.39	Number of native servants authorised in the Peninsula, 1809	163
4.40	Two hundred days of bât and forage money in the Peninsula	164
4.41	Number of forage rations authorised for officers in the Peninsula	164–5
4.42	Cost of food in the Peninsula 1809–10	165–6
4.43	Cost of food in the Peninsula 1813	166
4.44	Cost of shipping packages from Plymouth to an officer in the Peninsula	167
4.45	Reimbursement for cavalry horses lost in action or shot for glanders	167–8
4.46	Reimbursement for infantry officers' horses lost in action or shot for glanders	168
4.47	Reimbursement for officers' lost baggage and camp equipage on campaign	168
4.48	Types of punishment imposed on officers in the Peninsula	168–9
4.49	Prize money shares for all ranks	169–70
4.50	Prize money paid to the army	170–1
4.51	Average amount of prize money British officers received for each action in the Peninsula	171
4.52	Prize money paid to the army after Waterloo	172
4.53	Daily rates of half pay, 1814	173–4
4.54	Wounds for which pensions were awarded to an officer	176
4.55	Officer annual pensions for wounds	177–8
4.56	Widow's pensions, 1815	180
4.57	Composition of an officer's funeral party	181
4.58	Three unlucky officers	182
4.59	Officers who served in the Peninsula throughout the War	183
4.60	Most common first names among officers serving in the Peninsula	184
4.61	Most common family names among officers serving in the Peninsula	184
4.62	Most common names among officers serving in the Peninsula	185
4.63	Unusual names among officers serving in the Peninsula	185
5.1	Bounty paid to new recruits, June 1804	186–7
5.2	List of necessaries to be paid from the recruit's bounty money	187
5.3	Administrative costs to enlist one recruit in the army, June 1804	188
5.4	Authorised clothing and equipment for infantry	188–9
5.5	Authorised clothing and equipment for cavalry	189–91
5.6	Horse appointments and other items issued	191–3

Tables

5.7	Rooms authorised to enlisted soldiers in a barracks	193
5.8	Equipment furnished in enlisted soldiers room	194
5.9	Equipment for the stables of the cavalry	195
5.10	Equipment for a guard room	195
5.11	Fuel allowances for guard rooms for seven days September–April	195
5.12	Daily rations in garrison	195–6
5.13	Daily and yearly pay for soldiers, 1805	196
5.14	Daily and yearly pay for soldiers, 1806	197
5.15	Yearly pay for an infantry private after deductions	198
5.16	What a soldier in the 7th Fusiliers carried in the Peninsula, 1813	198–9
5.17	What a British rifleman carried in 1809	199
5.18	Amount of daily forage for mules and horses, 1809	201
5.19	Amount of daily forage for mules and horses, 1810	202
5.20	Daily allowances for fire wood in bivouac, 1809	202
5.21	Amount of money set aside out of the pay of guardsmen in the Peninsula, August 1813	203
5.22	Amount of money to be paid daily to guardsmen in the Peninsula, August 1813	203
5.23	Reimbursement for baggage lost on campaign	203
5.24	Types of punishment a general court martial in the Peninsula could impose	204
5.25	Verdicts of courts martial for three infantry regiments over a five-month period	204
5.26	Number of courts martial where a maximum sentence of 300 lashes was given	205
5.27	Number of lashes inflicted versus number sentenced	205
5.28	Number of lashes sentenced versus sentences carried out	205
5.29	Number of lashes inflicted by regimental courts martial in 1st Battalion 23rd Foot, October 1812–February 1813	205–6
5.30	Number of lashes inflicted by regimental courts martial in the 103rd Foot, April–October 1812	206–7
5.31	Number of lashes inflicted by regimental courts martial in the Glengarry Light Infantry, February–July 1815	207–8
5.32	Disability payments for soldiers rendered blind	209
5.33	Annual disability payments – enlisted men unfit for duty	209
5.34	Prize money paid to the army for actions in the Peninsula and Waterloo	209
5.35	Composition of a funeral party for an enlisted soldier	210
6.1	British casualties during the Napoleonic Wars	211
6.2	Number of killed and wounded of all ranks in the British army 1805–15	212
6.3	Casualties among the British officer corps 1805–15	212
6.4	Casualties among the British enlisted soldiers 1805–15	212–13
6.5	Chance of becoming a casualty in Wellington's army, 1811–14	213
6.6	British casualties in the Peninsula, 1808–14	213–14
6.7	British casualties in campaigns and battles in the Peninsula, 1808–12	214
6.8	British casualties in campaigns and battles in the Peninsula, 1813–14	214–15
6.9	Casualties in campaigns and battles other than in the Peninsula, 1806–9	215–16
6.10	Casualties in campaigns and battles other than in the Peninsula, 1810–15	216

Tables

6.11	British casualties during the War of 1812	216–217
6.12	Bloodiest battles of the British army – highest percentage of force lost	217–18
6.13	Bloodiest sieges in the Peninsular War	218
6.14	British Units with the highest casualties at Maida, 4 July 1806	219
6.15	British Units with the highest casualties at Roliça, 17 August 1808	219
6.16	British cavalry regiments with the highest casualties in Sir John Moore's army, October 1808–January 1809	219
6.17	British infantry regiments with the highest casualties in Sir John Moore's army, October 1808–January 1809	219–20
6.18	British regiments with the highest casualties at Talavera, 27–28 July 1809	220
6.19	British regiments with the highest casualties at Busaco, 27 September 1810	221–2
6.20	British regiments with the highest casualties at Barossa, 5 March 1811	221
6.21	British regiments with the highest casualties at Fuentes de Oñoro, 3–5 May 1810	221
6.22	British regiments with the highest casualties at Albuera, 16 May 1810	221–2
6.23	British regiments with the highest casualties at Salamanca, 22 July 1812	222
6.24	British regiments with the highest casualties at Vitoria, 21 June 1813	222
6.25	British regiments with the highest casualties at Nivelle, 10 November 1813	223
6.26	British regiments with the highest casualties at St Pierre, 13 December 1813	223
6.27	British regiments with the highest casualties at Orthez, 27 February 1814	223
6.28	British regiments with the highest casualties at Toulouse, 10 April 1814	223–4
6.29	British regiments with the highest casualties at Quatre Bras, 16 June 1815	223
6.30	British cavalry regiments with the highest casualties at Waterloo, 18 June 1815	224–5
6.31	British infantry regiments with the highest casualties at Waterloo, 18 June 1815	225
6.32	The bloodiest regiments – highest percentage of casualties	225
6.33	British general officers captured during the Napoleonic Wars	226
6.34	Exchange rates for prisoners of war during the Peninsular War	226–7
6.35	Senior British officers captured in the Peninsula	227
6.36	Percentage of the Peninsular army reported sick, 1808–14	228
6.37	Cause of death in British hospitals in the Peninsula, 1812–14	228
6.38	Casualties caused by disease to the Walcheren expedition, 1809	229
6.39	General officers killed in action or died from wounds, 1805–13	230
6.40	General officers killed in action or died from wounds, 1814–15	230
6.41	Leading from the front – casualties among commanding generals, 1805–15	231
6.42	Generals who died from illness, fatigue, accident or drowning, 1805–15	231–2
6.43	British generals in Portuguese service who died on active service 1811–14	232
6.44	British colours lost in combat	233
6.45	Number of deaths in Wellington's army, December 1810–May 1811	234
7.1	Award of baronetcies, 1805–15	236
7.2	Award of peerages 1807–15	237
7.3	Patriotic Fund awards for Dominica, 14 May 1805	238
7.4	Recipients of the Knight Bachelor, 1807–15	239–41

7.5	Knight Grand Cross of the Bath	242–3
7.6	Knight Commander of the Bath	243–6
7.7	Companion of the Bath	246–54
8.1	Gold Medals and Number of Recipients	257
8.2	Number of recipients of a Gold Medal or a Gold Cross	258
8.3	Officers who had six or more clasps on their army Gold Cross	258–9
8.4	Gold Medal recipients for Maida	259
8.5	Gold Medal recipients for Roleia and Vimiera	260–1
8.6	Gold Medal recipients for Sahagun and Benevente	261
8.7	Gold Medal recipients for Corunna	262–3
8.8	Gold Medal recipients for Martinique	263–4
8.9	Gold Medal recipients for Guadaloupe	264–5
8.10	Gold Medal recipients for Talavera	265–7
8.11	Gold Medal recipients for Busaco	268–9
8.12	Gold Medal recipients for Barrossa	269–70
8.13	Gold Medal recipients for Fuentes de Onor	270–2
8.14	Gold Medal recipients for Albuhera	272–3
8.15	Gold Medal recipients for the Java expedition	274–5
8.16	Gold Medal recipients for the Siege of Ciudad Rodrigo	275–6
8.17	Gold Medal recipients for the Siege of Badajoz, 1812	276–8
8.18	Gold Medal recipients for Salamanca	278–82
8.19	Gold Medal recipients for Fort Detroit	282–3
8.20	Gold Medal recipients for Vittoria	283–8
8.21	Gold Medal recipients for the Pyrenees	288–91
8.22	Gold Medal recipients for the Siege of St Sebastian	291–3
8.23	Gold Medal recipients for Chateauguay	293
8.24	Gold Medal recipients for Nivelle	294–7
8.25	Gold Medal recipients for Chrystler's Farm	297
8.26	Gold Medal recipients for Nive	298–301
8.27	Gold Medal recipients for Orthes	301–5
8.28	Gold Medal recipients for Toulouse	305–7
8.29	Recipients of the Waterloo Medal	309–10
8.30	Bars to the Military General Service Medal	311–12
8.31	Military General Service Medal – number of clasps	312
8.32	Military General Service Medal – recipients	313–14
8.33	Recipients of the Military General Service Medal with Benevente clasp	314

Foreword

Two hundred years ago Sir Arthur Wellesley landed in Lisbon and took command of a heterogeneous force consisting of troops left behind when Sir John Moore marched into Spain and several subsequent batches of reinforcements. Within a few weeks Wellesley led this force to its first victory, driving Soult from Oporto and out of Portugal into the mountains of Galicia. The success gave the troops confidence in themselves and in their commander, and enabled him to turn them into an effective functioning army, although some of the support services, such as the Commissariat, were still far from perfect and men and officers alike had much to learn. The Talavera campaign revealed some of these deficiencies, and the long months of quiet that followed saw a considerable improvement in the British army as well as the forging of a Portuguese army that could be relied upon to play its part in the field. Nonetheless Wellington was still careful not to ask too much of his troops: it was much easier to hold and defend a strong position, such as Busaco, than to manoeuvre across rough ground under heavy fire while keeping alert for enemy cavalry. The pursuit of Massena in 1811 offered valuable practice in small-scale attacks against the French rearguard and important lessons were learnt by mid-grade and senior officers as much as by the rank and file and their immediate commanders. Fuentes de Oñoro and El Bodon saw British infantry execute difficult retreats under extreme pressure without the confusion or loss of confidence which would lead to disaster; while amid the hard fighting at Albuera there were signs of improved manoeuvrability, despite the disaster which befell Colborne's brigade. The *esprit de corps* and fighting spirit of the troops had always been good, and it was this and nothing else that ensured success at the storming of Badajoz in April 1812. Three months later, at Salamanca, Wellington reaped the benefits of years of patient training and building up the confidence and skill of his regiments and of his subordinates, when he launched a sudden attack upon the French who had become over-extended while manoeuvring too close to his position. The result was a decisive victory, which left no doubt that the allied army was now just as capable of attacking as defending a position. Subsequent campaigns showed just how far the balance had swung: poorly commanded and deployed, the French made little resistance at Vitoria; and, while they fought much better in subsequent battles in the Pyrenees and the south of France, it was very evident that they lacked confidence and were conscious that Wellington's veterans, Portuguese as well as British, were superior to them. By late in the war Wellington could say with justified pride that his army was the 'most complete machine for its numbers now existing in Europe.'[1]

The Peninsular War as a historical subject has been shaped and defined by the work of William Napier, who served in the campaigns as a young officer and who published his history (6 vols, 1828–40) while many of the principal players were still alive. Napier was diligent in his research and took care to consult French as well as British sources. He was a man of strong views and passionate prejudices. A radical in politics, he was fervent in his admiration for Napoleon; he despised the Tory ministers who governed Britain throughout the war and admired Wellington immensely, but felt a much warmer, more emotional, attachment to the memory of Sir John Moore. A brilliant writer, he could be scathing in his condemnation of mistakes committed by officers in action and, when they attempted to defend themselves, retaliated with biting sarcastic pamphlets and reviews. The controversies he provoked, and the strange twist he gave the politics of the war, caught the public interest, while the high drama of some of his prose set-pieces became established classics for several generations of readers in Victorian England and far beyond.

As the nineteenth century drew to its close two historians tackled the subject again, matching and even surpassing the scale of Napier's six volumes. Sir Charles Oman's *History of the Peninsular War* (7 vols, 1902–30) covered exactly the same ground as Napier, more carefully and coolly, but without the benefit of personal experience. Oman consciously corrected Napier's prejudices: he was much more critical of the French, and less contemptuous of the Spanish role in the war. He had little interest in British politics but gave the ministers some credit, and ventured some mild criticism of Sir John Moore. He also, of course, took advantage of all the sources which had come to light in the eighty years since Napier's work had appeared; and his history is still the most complete and reliable account of the war. He wrote well, although in a much plainer style than Napier's, and was remarkably fair in his judgements.

---

1 Wellington to Bathurst, 21 Nov. 1813, *Wellington's Dispatches*, vol. 7, p. 153.

Foreword

Oman's contemporary, Sir John Fortescue, was engaged on a different but overlapping task: *A History of the British Army* (14 vols with 6 vols of maps, 1899–1930). His accounts of the campaigns of Moore and Wellington are not, generally, quite so full as those of Oman, but form a useful supplement to them, and in the early campaigns, where Oman's volumes were published first, Fortescue offers some valuable corrections. While no admirer of politicians in general, Fortescue has important things to say about the essential support given to Wellington by the Perceval and Liverpool administrations. His attitude to Wellington is curiously ambivalent, occasionally even hostile, while he is sympathetic, even indulgent, towards Moore.

All three works are narratives, with only the occasional section or chapter to examine broader themes or the structure and functioning of the army. Oman also wrote *Wellington's Army, 1809–1814* (1912) a fine study of the organisation of the army, the character and ability of Wellington's subordinates, and related topics such as discipline and logistics. This has been supplemented but not superseded by similar works by later historians including Michael Glover's *Wellington's Army in the Peninsula, 1808–1814* (1977) and Philip Haythornthwaite's *The Armies of Wellington* (1994). A number of important specialist works have also been published on specific aspects of the army, among others *Wellington's Headquarters* by S. G. P. Ward; *Life in Wellington's Army* by Antony Brett-James; *The British Light Infantry Arm* by David Gates; *Wellington's Doctors* by Martin Howard; *Wellington's Navy* by Christopher Hall; and *Rifles* by Mark Urban. Biographies of subordinate and junior officers have added immensely to our knowledge of the war, especially when they include significant new primary material (a good example is *Intelligence Officer in the Peninsula* by Julia Page, but there are too many to attempt to mention them all); while newly discovered letters, diaries and memoirs continue to be published, filling gaps in our coverage and enriching our understanding. There have also been detailed studies of individual battles and campaigns, overviews of the subject, and important work on the French and Spanish side of the war (although less than one would like, and almost nothing on the Portuguese contribution).

What is lacking amid all these riches is some of the basic fundamental information about the army, not just a few examples to illustrate a point, but a comprehensive account in a readily accessible form. It is this lack which *The British Army against Napoleon: Facts, Lists and Trivia, 1805–1815* is designed to address. Other books may tell you how many regiments were sent on the expedition to Hanover in 1805, but *The British Army against Napoleon* will tell you where every single regiment in the British army was stationed and who their honorary colonels were, and it

xvii

Foreword

will give you a list of all the barracks in Britain with the number of men they were designed to hold. Where else will you find, not just the pay of the different rank of officer, but the amount of income tax they had to pay, as well as all the other deductions and stoppages which reduced their actual receipts to a fraction of their nominal (and generally quite low) pay? There are tables that list all the recipients of the honours and awards issued, casualties in action and disease, and the seniority of officers in the numerous expeditions and campaigns (a matter not just of curiosity but of major significance, for the date of rank of an officer determined who commanded the force and all of its subunits).

The material in these tables has all been collected from original primary sources, including official publications such as the *Army List* and the *London Gazette*; advice books for young officers such as Thomas Reide's *A Treatise on Military Finance Containing the Pay and Allowances in Camp, Garrison, and Quarters of the British Army*, and the *Royal Military Calendar*. This is typical of the approach of the two authors who are indefatigable in their pursuit of an authoritative answer to the questions they encounter. I came into contact with them ten years ago when I first ventured on to the internet (this was in the dying days of the second millennium, before it became ubiquitous). An American and a Canadian, they were prominent contributors to *The Napoleon Series* Discussion Forum. Over the years they have been immensely generous with their help and advice, often able to unravel a thorny question or answer a specific query by return of email; and scrupulous in their use of primary sources. In 2006 they, Howie Muir and I collaborated in a book of essays, *Inside Wellington's Peninsular Army*, which tackled neglected aspects of the war such as bridging operations, or the composition of the army which Wellington inherited when he landed in Lisbon in 1809. Other essays uncovered the long-forgotten regulating mechanisms which enabled armies to form and manoeuvre rapidly on the battlefield; explained the significance of seniority, with all its complexities of regimental, army and brevet rank; and gave readers a comprehensive guide to the first hand sources available for each regiment in the army. *The British Army Against Napoleon* grew out of *Inside Wellington's Peninsular Army* and while the demands of a separate large project prevented me from contributing to it more substantially, I was delighted and honoured to be asked to write this foreword, and so have the opportunity to be the first to welcome the publication of this invaluable reference work.

Rory Muir

Acknowledgements

Robert Burnham: Many people throughout the world provided insight and ideas for this book. More importantly, they shared their knowledge and answered what had to appear to be an endless number of questions, on some very obscure topics. They lived on four continents and in seven different countries. Of the fifteen individuals who provided help, I have only met two of them in person. The rest are colleagues with whom I have been corresponding through *The Napoleon Series* website (www.napoleon-series.org). Without their willing assistance, this book would have been near impossible to write. Among those to whom I am indebted are my co-authors from *Inside Wellington's Peninsular Army*, who were not able to participate in the writing of this volume, Rory Muir and Howie Muir. Between them, I think they have every article and book written on the British Army of the Napoleonic era in the past 200 years. Invariably, when I exhausted my own resources, I would ask Rory to check what I refer to as his 'magical filing cabinet' and sure enough he would have it! What Rory didn't have, Howie did! Howie was particular instrumental in digging up information on regimental books and pay. Don Graves, John Grodzinski and Andrew Bamford all provided invaluable assistance on a variety of subjects ranging from courts martial, flogging, the War of 1812, and prize money. Stuart Reid and Gareth Glover opened up their own files to me on everything from officers' pay to medals to regimental agents. Not once did they ignore my appeals for help. John Cook was able to provide detailed information on regimental nicknames and the capture of British colours, while Steven Smith, who is known for his ability to find anything in Google Books, also found items that I had given up on. Vic Powell and the Portsmouth Napoleonic Society were as helpful as always, providing photographs of Napoleonic barracks. Although, I have corresponded with many people whom I have met online, the true sense of community that is *The Napoleon Series* came when I was looking for

Acknowledgements

information on British and Portuguese medals. I posted an enquiry on *The Napoleon Series* History Forum and within a day João Centeno, Jacques Declercq, Michael Crumplin and Chris Earle all not only answered my questions, but sent me photographs of various medals in their collection. Dan Fitzgerald was very helpful on answering what had to seem to him to be my endless questions on the Army Gold Medal and Gold Cross. I must also thank the auction house Spink and Sons Ltd for permitting us to use the picture of Major General Denis Pack's medals; and Oliver Pepys of their medals department who provided background information on the Army Gold Cross.

There are three people I must mention who have assisted me with the running of *The Napoleon Series* over the past thirteen years. Like most of the others, I have never met any of them. The first is Tom Holmberg, the reviews editor for the *The Napoleon Series*. Many years ago, he suggested that we start a Statistical Abstract of the Napoleonic Wars on the *The Napoleon Series*. This book had its genesis in this. The other person is Tony Broughton, who serves as the research editor for *The Napoleon Series*. His personal library is truly phenomenal and he has spent countless hours looking for information for me, that otherwise would have never seen the light of day – and that is just from his books! His collection of uniform prints has to be one of the best in the world and many of the illustrations in this book are from his collection. Finally, there is David McCracken, whose moderating of *The Napoleon Series* History Forum provided me with enough time to write this book. I cannot thank them enough.

This brings me to my co-author, Ron McGuigan. What I can say about someone whom I have never met nor even talked to? Over the years we have developed a friendship that has allowed us to co-author two books and many articles. Disagreements are rare and always minor. It helps that Ron is the leading authority on the British officer corps of the era, with an incredible memory for the most arcane details about the lives and careers of different officers. Many times he has been able to answer my numerous questions on British officers – most of them too junior in rank to be known by anyone but the serious researcher. I stand in awe of his uncanny ability to find anything in the *London Gazette* and the *Army Lists*. This book would have been impossible without him. Finally, it would be remiss of me if I did not thank my wife of thirty-two years, Denah Burnham. For the past five months she has given up our kitchen table, without a complaint, to my piles of books, articles, maps and computer. I suspect that in the back of her mind was the thought that it was a fair trade, since if I was at the kitchen table I would not be dragging her to Waterloo for the fourth time!

Acknowledgements

Ron McGuigan: My co-author, Bob Burnham must be acknowledged as both the inspiration and the driving force behind the project. The book is his achievement. He has also served as the editor formatting my work into a usable presentation for the book. No easy task! It has been a challenging experience writing this over the internet and not working face-to-face. Our friendship allowed us to co-write with minimal references to that War of 1812!

I appreciate that Bob twice asked me to join him, on our previous book *Inside Wellington's Peninsular Army* and this new one. Thank you, Bob.

Michael Leventhal of Frontline Books must be acknowledged and thanked for having faith in the book and giving the go-ahead for it.

Thank you to Deborah Hercun, Senior Editor, Frontline Books, for ensuring that the book moved along and to Paula Turner for her hard work on the text layout and the index.

I wish to thank Rory Muir for his writing the wonderful foreword to the book and Howie Muir for his recommendations on the text, both missed as authors on this book.

Others contributed to the researching and writing of this book and must be thanked: the staff of the Central Library, London Ontario; the staff of the Archives and Research Collections Centre and the staff of the D. B. Weldon Library of the University of Western Ontario, London; John Cook and Steven H. Smith for information on the French Eagles; the contributors to *The Napoleon Series* website where any question is readily answered; Google Book Search and *London Gazette* on-line. Errors and omissions are mine.

A very special thank you goes to my wife Debbie for her encouragement, patience and understanding during my writing of the book and my children, Shannon, Ian and Nikki, for their usual support.

Introduction

Ron McGuigan and I have been collecting information on the British army for many years. Often the discovery of one piece of information would lead us on a tangent looking up something else. This led us to amass data on a wide range of topics, from recruiting to pay to casualties and a host of other things. Most of this information came from sources that have long been out of print and unavailable except for those with access to national libraries. This book is intended to be a fact book. It contains the information that we thought was important to a researcher. Some of it stands alone – such as the list of regimental colonels – while other information is critical for understanding why events unfolded as they did. For example, there is a chapter concerned solely with the dates of rank of the officers at various battles and their commands. Although at times this appears to be too much information, for the historian to completely understand how the chain of command functioned during any given campaign or battle he needs to know the dates of rank of the various officers, for commands were allocated by the seniority of the officers present. In turn, this affected how units were deployed.

Although having all of this data is important to the researcher, it is meaningless if not put into perspective. Much of the data goes a long way to supporting or debunking popular myths about the era. For example there are many stories of junior officers getting into trouble because they were living beyond their means and were forced to have a parent or an older brother pay their bills. If the researcher only looks at the pay charts for the period and finds that an ensign was paid 5 shillings and 4 pence a day, it tells him little. However, when the deductions to his pay – such as income tax and mess fees – are taken out, it is found that the ensign often had no money left over and it becomes very apparent why a young officer could quickly get into financial difficulty. Our research has found that many of the myths about the British army can not be supported by

Introduction

the data. For example, our examination of the records of three regiments' courts martial records shed new light on how often soldiers were flogged. Another enduring myth about the officer corps is that it was filled by the nobility and the upper crust of British society. Yet the data does not support this.

Our goal however was not just to provide raw data. Over 9,000 British officers served in the Peninsular War. But little is known about most of them, apart from the senior officers and the handful of junior officers who wrote memoirs. Although the generals get the credit for winning the battles, it was the junior officers who provided the leadership at the battalion and company level that were so essential to the success of the British army. Throughout the book, you will find the names of many officers who have slipped into the obscurity of time, not because they were undeserving of being remembered, but because they were just too junior for the historian to be recognised. Several chapters in this book are devoted to them.

Additionally, while much is made of how Napoleon created a new nobility for his most deserving officers and the Légion d'Honneur for those individuals who distinguished themselves, one of the common misconceptions about the British army was how their officers and soldiers were never recognised. This was not true. As history has shown, general officers always received their share of recognition, what is not well known is that many British colonels, lieutenant colonels, majors, captains and an occasional lieutenant also received medals and knighthoods for their meritorious service. We provide the most comprehensive list of those officers who received awards from the British government.

Another way of rewarding those who participated in a campaign was the awarding of prize money. Unlike medals, which were only awarded to officers, all soldiers received prize money. How much a soldier received depended on his rank and the battle. For the private or the sergeant this amounted to a few months' pay, while for an officer it could be substantially more. Prize money was paid for five different campaigns in the Peninsular War, but it was especially important for Waterloo, as the prize money was quite high: an ensign received about four months' pay, a captain about six months' pay, while a major or lieutenant colonel received over a year's pay.

Throughout the book, we have included trivial details to bring to life some of the lesser-known events and people of the British army. This 'trivia' includes such things as an aide-de-camp who had the misfortune of having two of his generals die in his arms; the amount of money a major spent on gin in a year; an officer who waited seventy-five years to apply for a medal to which he was entitled; and the unluckiest officer in the Peninsular Army.

Introduction

Our readers may wonder about why we started with the year 1805. Although war between Great Britain and France had been declared in May 1803, we chose to begin our study with 1805, the year that Britain faced its greatest threat of invasion. Further, it was also the year in which the British began to go on the offensive against their enemies, striking at them wherever they could.

Many of our readers will notice that we often use non-standard or modern spellings of various battles and locations, except in chapter three, where battle honours are listed, and chapter eight, which covers the medals that the British government awarded its soldiers. Etched on the medal was the name of a particular battle or campaign. The spelling of the names of these battles has changed since the medals were awarded. To avoid confusion, we have kept with the original names. The more common names and their modern spelling are:

Original spelling	Modern spelling
Roleia	Roliça
Vimiera	Vimeiro
Guadaloupe	Guadeloupe
Barrosa	Barossa
Fuentes d'Onor	Fuentes de Oñoro
Albuhera	Albuera
Vittoria	Vitoria
St Sebastian	San Sebastian
Orthes	Orthez

The spelling of first and family names was also a problem. There were a number of different variations used for some officers. We chose the spelling that is either modern or most used in contemporary works.

A purist will note that we occasionally include information about the Royal Marines. We know that the Royal Marines were not part of the British army. However, we have included them when the information warranted it, as the Royal Marines had served on land under army command in a number of campaigns and officers received rewards for this service.

Abbreviations

AAG	Assistant Adjutant General	HEIC	Honourable East India Company
ADC	Aide-de-Camp		
AG	Adjutant General	JAG	Judge Advocate General
AQMG	Assistant Quartermaster General	KB	Knight of the Bath
		KCB	Knight Commander of the Bath
Bart	Baronet		
BG	Brigadier General	KGA	King's German Artillery
Bn	Battalion	KGL	King's German Legion
Bt	Baronet	KIA	Killed in Action
Capt	Captain	Kt	Knight
CB	Companion of the Bath	£ s d	Pounds, shillings and pence
Col	Colonel	L Bn	Line Battalion
Coldm FG	Coldstream Foot Guards	LCol	Lieutenant Colonel
D	Dragoons	LD	Light Dragoons
DAAG	Deputy Assistant Adjutant General	LG	Lieutenant General
		LGd	Life Guards
DAG	Deputy Adjutant General	LI	Light Infantry
DAQMG	Deputy Assistant Quartermaster General	Lieut	Lieutenant
		Lt Bn	Light Battalion
DG	Dragoon Guards	Maj	Major
DoW	Died of Wounds	MG	Major General
DQMG	Deputy Quartermaster General	N/A	Not Applicable
		NCOs	Non-commissioned Officers
FG	Foot Guards	No.	Number
FI	Fencible Infantry	QMG	Quartermaster General
FM	Field Marshal	R	Regiment
GCB	Knight Grand Cross of the Bath	RA	Royal Artillery
		RE	Royal Engineers
Gen	General	RHG	Royal Horse Guards
H	Hussars	RN	Royal Navy

Chapter One

The British Army

Much has been written about the regiments and soldiers of the British army, but little on its overall structure, where it was deployed or how it filled its ranks.

Effective strength of the British army 1805–15
The British army was small in comparison to the Continental armies fielded during the Napoleonic Wars. It had to provide troops for home defence, garrisons for the colonies and for any overseas expeditions. As the tables show, the army was stretched to provide for all of its commitments as the wars carried on, because as the strength of the army increased, so too did its responsibilities. The regular army was all volunteers; no conscription was used to make up the numbers. Service in the militia was compulsory and maintained by ballot. Yet the militia could not be required to serve outside the United Kingdom: volunteering from the militia into the regular army was finally allowed after being declared illegal for years.[1] Other attempts to maintain its strength included recruiting prisoners-of-war into foreign regiments, allowing Spanish volunteers to join British regiments in the Peninsula and the formation of three provisional battalions of militia from militia men who volunteered for overseas duty.[2] The effective strength was actual numbers compiled from the returns of the army. It would differ from the establishment set for the army overall. The establishment was the authorised strength of officers and men for the army and for which it recruited to attain. The cavalry and infantry include foreign corps in British service. The effective strength is for rank and file only. Returns are dated 1 January for 1805, 1806, 1807, 1808 and 1809; 25 January for 1810, 1811, 1812 and 1813; 25 June for 1814 and 1815.

---

1 Glover, *Wellington's Army*, pp. 30–5. Volunteers were sanctioned in 1805.
2 Muir et al., *Inside Wellington's Peninsular Army*, pp. 210, 221.

Table 1.1 Effective strength of the rank and file 1805–15

Year	Cavalry	Artillery	Infantry	Total	Militia	Grand total
1805	20,316	17,109	124,521	161,946	89,809	251,755
1806	23,396	19,546	142,177	185,119	74,653	259,772
1807	26,261	20,951	152,245	199,457	76,159	275,616
1808	26,402	22,250	177,775	226,427	67,677	294,104
1809	27,391	23,563	183,223	234,177	81,577	315,754
1810	27,740	24,238	185,474	237,452	72,487	309,939
1811	27,410	23,668	183,516	234,594	84,439	319,033
1812	27,638	23,824	192,423	243,885	77,055	320,940
1813	28,931	25,407	201,538	255,876	71,055	326,931
1814	31,056	19,254	203,052	253,362	63,756	317,118
1815	23,660	14,847	166,913	205,420	11,588	217,008

Sources: Fortescue, *The County Lieutenancies*, p. 293; HCPP *Sessional Papers* 1813, 1814–1815, 1816.

About one eighth of the total army were officers and non-commissioned officers. To get the total strength, add 12.5 per cent for officers and non-commissioned officers.

Table 1.2 Estimated strength of the British army 1805–15

Year	Cavalry	Artillery	Infantry	Total	Militia	Grand total
1805	22,856	19,248	140,086	182,190	101,035	283,225
1806	26,321	21,989	159,949	208,359	83,985	292,344
1807	29,544	23,570	171,276	224,390	85,679	310,069
1808	29,702	25,031	199,997	254,730	76,137	330,867
1809	30,815	26,508	206,126	263,449	91,774	355,223
1810	31,206	27,268	208,658	267,132	81,548	348,680
1811	30,836	26,627	206,456	263,919	94,994	358,913
1812	31,093	26,802	216,476	274,371	86,687	361,058
1813	32,547	28,583	226,739	287,869	79,837	367,706
1814	34,938	20,135	228,434	283,507	71,726	355,233
1815	26,618	15,592	187,777	229,987	13,037	243,024

Recruiting

At the beginning of 1805, the British army had over 283,000 men in uniform. By 1813 it had expanded by 25 per cent, adding 76,000 more men to the ranks. The expansion was steady but slow, increasing on average 9,300 soldiers or 4 per cent per year. This figure only tells part of the story. The army lost 10 per cent of its strength every year through combat, disease and desertion.³ So in addition to adding new soldiers, the army had to replace the 18,000–25,000 soldiers, who had died, become unfit for service or deserted, every year. Over 193,000 men had to be replaced between 1805 and 1813. In order to expand by 76,000 soldiers in nine years, the army had to recruit about 270,000 men. The British army did not conscript, but relied on volunteers to fill its ranks. The militia provided a ready pool of trained volunteers, providing over 40 per cent of the recruits. This caused vacancies in the militia, however, which also had to be filled.

Table 1.3 Number of men raised for the British army by recruiting and transfers from the militia 1805–12

	By ordinary recruiting			Raised under the Additional Forces Act	Militia volunteers	Total
Year	Men	Boys	Total			
1805	10,180	1,497	11,677	8,288	13,580	33,545
1806	10,337	1,538	11,875	5,834	2,968	20,677
1807	15,308	3,806	19,114	—	29,108	61,185*
1808	10,477	2,486	12,963	—		
1809	9,675	2,045	11,720	—	23,885	44,700†
1810	7,367	1,728	9,095	—		
1811	9,532	1,940	11,472	—	11,453	22,925
1812	12,563	1,869	14,432	—	9,927	24,359
Total	85,439	16,909	102,348	14,122	90,921	207,391

* Includes both 1807 and 1808.
† Includes both 1809 and 1810.

Source: Fortescue, *The County Lieutenancies*, pp. 303–5.

Location of the British army

Although the British army had an average strength of over 334,000 men from 1805 to 1814, this included 76,000 militia. Given the need to garrison the far reaches of the British Empire, the actual number of men available for operations outside of the British Isles was considerably fewer. By 1809 Great Britain had over 90,000 men deployed in garrisons overseas. In theory this left about 130,000 troops for active service. Portugal and Spain was not even the main theatre of the war for the British in 1809. There were fewer than 23,000 British troops in Portugal, while the Walcheren expedition to destroy the French fleet at Antwerp had almost 40,000 soldiers.

---

3 Fortescue, *The County Lieutenancies*, p. 292; for more information on attrition in the British army, see chapter six.

Table 1.4 Location and strength of the British army 1805–9

Location	1805	1806	1807	1808	1809
Gibraltar	3,318	4,666	5,281	5,328	3,842
Malta	6,680	4,119	5,288	4,047	3,594
Sicily	—	6,647	11,099	14,947	14,716
Egypt	—	—	5,074	—	—
Leeward Islands	11,904	11,093	12,575	12,556	15,011
Jamaica	3,591	3,645	4,680	5,499	4,937
Bahamas, etc.	589	574	673	2,253	1,470
Canada	1,519	1,696	1,539	3,252	3,559
Nova Scotia	2,367	3,002	2,831	4,566	4,501
East Indies	11,998	15,043	14,499	15,131	19,843
Ceylon	6,870	8,739	4,736	4,645	5,115
Madeira	—	—	—	1,612	913
With LG Sir John Moore	—	—	—	10,871	—
With MG Spencer	—	—	—	3,704	—
Portugal	—	—	—	—	22,623
Heligoland	—	—	—	302	270
South America	—	—	5,956	—	—
With BG Robert Craufurd	—	—	4,026	—	—
Goree, Africa	—	—	226	224	283
New South Wales	—	—	490	536	1,317
Cape of Good Hope	—	5,058	4,193	7,042	5,800
On Passage	12,442	13,427	9,366	4,454	4,223
Great Britain	64,614	73,857	62,569	63,355	91,999
Ireland	29,236	21,883	25,089	33,667	15,858
Militia	76,724	77,429	77,872	86,788	65,524
Total	231,852	250,878	258,062	284,779	285,398

Source: Fortescue, *The County Lieutenancies*, pp 303–5.

Trivia: *Wellington's army in the Peninsula did not exceed 50,000 British soldiers until 1813 – even though it had been fighting in Portugal and Spain for five years!*

In 1814, the British Government came up with authorised establishments for the various locations. These garrisons would total over 75,000 men, almost 30 per cent of the total available force.

Table 1.5 Authorised establishment of British overseas garrisons in 1814

Location	Strength
Gibraltar	5,000
Malta & Ionia	5,000
Leeward Islands	10,500
Jamaica	5,000
Bahamas & Bermuda	1,000
Canada & Nova Scotia	8,000
East Indies	25,000
Ceylon	3,000
Africa	800
New South Wales	0
Relief	5,000
Mauritius	3,000
Cape of Good Hope	4,000
Total	75,300

Source: *Supplementary Despatches*, vol. 14.

The army headquarters – Horse Guards 1805–15

The headquarters of the British army was referred to as 'Horse Guards', from its location in Horse Guards Parade in Whitehall, London. The headquarters consisted principally of the commander-in-chief, his military secretary, the adjutant general to the forces and the quartermaster general to the forces. These were all military men. The post of 'Commander-in-Chief of all His Majesty's land forces' was not a government cabinet post, but was responsible for training and disciplining the army (excluding the artillery, engineers and, at first, the militia, yeomanry or the volunteers), for appointing and promoting officers, selecting staff officers at home and abroad, and assigning general officers at home and abroad. He could not name the commander-in-chief of an expedition, for this was a government cabinet responsibility. The military secretary was the principal point of contact between the commander-in-chief and the general officers commanding on the staff. Among his duties, he dealt mainly with issues of the patronage for appointments and promotions in the army and deployment of troops. The adjutant general was responsible mainly for 'The arming and clothing of the troops ... all subjects connected with the discipline, equipment and efficiency of the army.'[4] General Orders

---

4 Glover, *Wellington's Army*, p. 136.

were issued through his office. The quartermaster general was responsible mainly for 'routes, camp equipage, . . . for cantoning and encamping the troops . . . relating to quarters, marches, camps, plans, and dispositions for defence . . . embarking and conveyance of the troops.'[5]

The commander-in-chief worked closely with members of the government such as the Master General of the Ordnance, the Secretary of State for War and the Colonies and the Secretary at War. The Master General of the Ordnance, usually a cabinet post and the government's principal military adviser, was a general officer in the army. He was not, however, under the command of the commander-in-chief of the army. He was a separate commander-in-chief over the Ordnance Corps of the Royal Artillery and Royal Engineers and their supporting services. He was also responsible for manufacturing and supplying cannon to the army and navy, providing arms and ammunition, other supplies such as greatcoats, surveying the United Kingdom, and supplying maps for the army and the navy.[6] The Secretary of State for War and the Colonies in the War Department, a civilian cabinet post, directed grand strategy. He selected the commander-in-chief of any overseas expeditions, gave him the objective for the expedition, and detailed the troops and supplies available to him. The Secretary at War, not usually a cabinet post, was originally the king's personal military secretary. He worked out of the War Office which was also located at the Horse Guards Parade. Made responsible to Parliament he was mostly concerned with presenting the military estimates each year. He also oversaw that the money voted for the army was used properly and kept the register of commissions. He carried the sovereign's orders to his household troops which were not under the commander-in-chief for internal administration.

Table 1.6 Principal appointments at the War Department 1805–15

	Date announced/appointed
Commander-in-Chief	
Prince Frederick, Duke of York	10 February 1795*
David Dundas	25 March 1809†
Prince Frederick, Duke of York	29 May 1811‡
Military Secretary	
James Gordon	4 August 1804
Henry Torrens	2 October 1809
Adjutant General	
Harry Calvert	9 January 1799

---

5   Ibid., p. 137.
6   Ibid., p. 16.

	Date announced/appointed
Quartermaster General	
Robert Brownrigg	15 March 1803
James Gordon	10 August 1811
Master General of the Ordnance	
John, 2nd Earl of Chatham	16 June 1801
Francis, 2nd Earl of Moira	14 February 1806
John, 2nd Earl of Chatham	4 April 1807
Henry, Lord Mulgrave	5 May 1810
Secretary of State for War	
John, 2nd Earl Camden	2 May 1804
Robert, Viscount Castlereagh	10 July 1805
William Windham	14 February 1806
Robert, Viscount Castlereagh	25 March 1807
Robert, 2nd Earl of Liverpool	1 November 1809
Henry, 3rd Earl Bathurst	11 June 1812
Secretary at War	
William Dundas	15 May 1804
Richard Fitzpatrick§	7 February 1806
James Murray Pulteney§	30 March 1807
Lord Granville Leveson-Gower	22 June 1809
Henry, 3rd Viscount Palmerston	27 October 1809

* Initially appointed to command as a field marshal on the Staff on 10 February 1795. Then appointed as commander-in-chief of all His Majesty's land forces in the kingdom of Great Britain on 3 April 1798 and as captain general of all His Majesty's land forces raised or to be raised and employed in Great Britain and on the continent of Europe on 4 September 1799. Finally as commander-in-chief of all His Majesty's land forces in the United Kingdom of Great Britain and Ireland on 9 June 1801.

† Appointed by the king to replace the Duke of York who had resigned on a point of honour. The Duke had been implicated in a scandal involving his mistress who was accused of receiving money to use her influence with the Duke in the sale of army commissions. The Duke was cleared of any wrong-doing.

‡ Reinstated as commander-in-chief of all His Majesty's land forces in the United Kingdom of Great Britain and Ireland.

§ A general officer in the army.

Districts commands in 1805

With the declaration of war in 1793, Great Britain was divided into military districts, commanded by general officers with subordinate generals, which were responsible both for defending against invasion and for training new troops being raised. Each headquarters and district would have a staff which included, officers serving in the adjutant general and quartermaster general departments, brigade majors, inspecting field officers of recruiting and the Commissariat. The districts would also have the militia, yeomanry and volunteers under command. These district commands remained in use during the Napoleonic Wars, although their composition was altered as the war progressed and circumstances changed.

In 1805 Britain face its greatest threat of invasion and the table shows how the country was formed militarily to meet this threat. The column for headquarters shows the number of general officers assigned to command in the district. Where counties are listed under different districts, this means that these counties were divided between these districts. At this time England was referred to as 'South Britain' and Scotland as 'North Britain'. The districts in Ireland are not broken down by county. The district headquarters and headquarters of the subcommands provide a good idea of the districts' compositions.

Table 1.7   Districts in Great Britain and Ireland 1805

District	Headquarters and Generals	Comprising
Great Britain		
London	London (11)	London
Home	London (3)	Middlesex, Kent, Surrey, Berkshire, Hertfordshire, Essex, Westminster
Southern	Canterbury (25)	Kent, Sussex
Isle of Thanet	(1)	Thanet
South, inland	Northampton (7)	Oxfordshire, Bedfordshire, Northamptonshire, Buckinghamshire
South-West	Winchester (8)	Dorset, Hampshire, Wiltshire
Isle of Wight	(1)	Isle of Wight
Eastern	Colchester (16)	Norfolk, Suffolk, Essex, Huntingdonshire, Cambridgeshire, Northamptonshire
Western	Exeter (8)	Devonshire, Dorset, Somerset, Cornwall
Severn	Bath (5)	Somerset, Wiltshire, Gloucestershire, Worcestershire, Herefordshire, Monmouth, Pembroke, Carmarthen, Cardigan, Glamorgan, Radnor, Brecon
Northern	Newcastle (5)	Durham, Northumberland, Cumberland, Westmoreland

District	Headquarters and Generals	Comprising
North, inland	Lichfield (6)	Staffordshire, Derbyshire, Warwickshire, Leicestershire, Worcestershire, Nottinghamshire, Rutland
York	York (6)	Yorkshire, Lincolnshire
North-West	Liverpool (3)	Lancashire, Shropshire, Cheshire, Flintshire, Denbighshire, Montgomeryshire, Merionethshire, Carnarvon, Anglesea
North Britain	Edinburgh (13)	Scotland
Jersey	(1)	Jersey
Guernsey	(2)	Guernsey
Ireland		
Northern	Armagh (7)	Armagh, Enniskilling, Belfast, Bellturbet, Londonderry, Strabane
Centre and South-East	Kilkenny (9)	Kilkenny, Naas, Mullingar, Clonmell, Longford, Wexford, Carlow
South-West	Cork (6)	Cork, Bandon, Fermoy, Limerick, Loaghrea
Western	Ballinasloe (6)	Athlone, Castlebar
Eastern	Dublin (4)	Arklow

Source: Monthly Army List March 1805.

District commands in 1814

By 1814, any threat of invasion by France had all but vanished. The war was now being fought on the Continent. Great Britain, however, was still divided into military districts, although with a reduced staff of general officers assigned to these districts, which would be responsible for the training of the new troops still being raised. The districts also had under their command the militia, local militia, yeomanry and volunteers. Each headquarters and district had a staff that included officers serving in the adjutant general and quartermaster general departments, brigade majors, inspecting field officers of recruiting and the Commissariat. Scotland was not divided into distinct districts, but the station headquarters will give a good idea of how the country was organised for the military. The numbers in brackets show the total number of general officers commanding in the district.

Table 1.8 Districts in Great Britain and Ireland in 1814

District	Headquarters and Generals	Comprising
Great Britain		
Northern	Newcastle (2)	Northumberland, Cumberland, Westmoreland, Durham, Isle of Man
Yorkshire	York (2)	Yorkshire, Lincolnshire
Eastern	Colchester (5)	Norfolk, Suffolk, Cambridge, Huntingdon, Essex (exclusive of the Hundreds of Beacontree, Waltham and Tilbury Fort
Kent	Canterbury (5)	Kent east of the River Cray and Holwood Hill and Tilbury Fort, Essex
Sussex	Brighton (2)	Sussex
South-West	Portsmouth (4)	Wiltshire, Dorset, Hampshire including Portsmouth and its dependencies
Isle of Wight	(1)	Isle of Wight
Western	Exeter (5)	Devon, Cornwall, Somerset exclusive of the vicinity of Bristol
Severn	Bristol (2)	Gloucestershire and the vicinity of Bristol, Worcestershire, Herefordshire, Monmouth, South Wales*
Home	London (4)	Middlesex, Surrey, Hertfordshire, Berkshire, Kent to the River Cray and Holwood Hill inclusive and part of Essex
North-West	Liverpool (2)	Cheshire, Shropshire, Lancashire and North Wales†
Inland	Lichfield (2)	Derbyshire, Nottinghamshire, Staffordshire, Leicestershire, Warwickshire, Rutland, Bedfordshire, Northamptonshire, Oxfordshire, Buckinghamshire
Jersey	St Helier (2)	Jersey
Guernsey	St Peter's Port (3)	Guernsey, Alderney
Scotland	Edinburgh (8)	Scotland with stations at Aberdeen, Dalkeith, Edinburgh, Glasgow, Leith Fort, Perth

* Pembroke, Carmarthen, Cardigan, Glamorgan, Radnor, Brecon.
† Flintshire, Denbighshire, Montgomeryshire, Merionethshire, Carnarvon, Anglesea.

District	Headquarters and Generals	Comprising
Ireland		
Northern	Armagh (5)	Armagh, Monaghan Fermanaghan, Cavan, Donegal, Londonderry, Tyrone, Antrim, Down and the Baronies of Dundalk in Louth and Rossclogher and Drumahaire in Leitrim
Western	Athlone (4)	Mayo, Sligo, Roscommon, Galway, Leitrim except the Baronies of Rossclogher and Drumahaire; and the Town and Liberties of Athlone in the County of Westmeath
Centre	Tullamore (2)	King's, Queen's, Longford, Westmeath except the town and liberties of Athlone
Eastern	Dublin (7)	Dublin, Wicklow, Kildare, Meath, Louth except the Barony of Dundalk
Lower Shannon	Limerick (1)	Limerick, Clare, and that part of the County of Kerry north of the river Fenle and the Baronies of Ownay and Arra, Upper Ormond and Lower Ormond Tipperary
South-East	Kilkenny (3)	Wexford, Waterford, Carlow, Kilkenny and Tipperary except the Baronies of Ownay and Arra, Upper Ormond and Lower Ormond,
South-West	Cork (4)	Cork and Kerry, except that part north of the River Fenle

Source: Monthly Army List March 1805.

Deployment of Commissariat officers 1814

The department responsible for feeding and supplying the army was the Commissariat. It was not controlled by the army, but was under the jurisdiction of the Treasury Board. In peacetime it had a small staff and so, like the army, had to expand rapidly to meets its commitments during wartime. Its duties included: the provision of bread, forage, fuel and light to the troops; supplying barrack stores, the quartermaster general and Inspector of Hospital stores; and supervising the Commissariat on the foreign stations, except India. On active service, commissaries came under the command of the army when they were assigned to armies and expeditions. They would be further assigned to divisions or brigades as necessary. There were two establishments for the Commissariat, one in Britain and one in Ireland.

The Commissariat department for the British establishment consisted of the commissary-in-chief,[7] a principal deputy commissary general, commissaries general, deputy commissaries general, assistant commissaries general, deputy assistant commissaries general and clerks. These men included those who were deployed overseas, except to India.

In 1809 the newly appointed commissary-in-chief recommended reorganising and standardising the department under one uniform system. This was done by a royal warrant of 19 March 1810. It was determined that the commissary officers would be appointed first as clerks and serve a year in that capacity before qualifying for promotion. No one could be appointed a clerk who was not sixteen years of age. Officers would have to serve a set period in a rank on full pay before being eligible for promotion to the next rank.

The Commissariat officers were also given relative rank in the army for the purposes of pay and allowances.

Table 1.9 Commissary equivalent ranks in the army

Commissary Department Rank	Army Equivalent
Commissary General	Brigadier general
Deputy Commissary General of three years standing	Lieutenant colonel
Deputy Commissary General of less than three years standing	Major
Assistant Commissary General	Captain
Deputy Assistant Commissary General	Lieutenant
Clerk	Ensign

The officers of the Commissariat were allowed to retire on half pay, similar to the army.

The best-known commissary general was Sir Robert Kennedy, who had served with Wellington in the Peninsular War. His services were rewarded by his being made a baronet.

The table below shows the deployment of the Commissariat officers at the end of the Napoleonic Wars in 1814. It shows how well dispersed they had become.

---

7 Full appointment was as 'Commissary in Chief of all His Majesty's Forces Home and Abroad (Ireland and the East Indies alone excepted)'.

Table 1.10 Deployment of Commissariat officers 1814

Location	No. deployed	Location	No. deployed
Africa	4	Holland	9
Algiers	1	Ireland*	23
Antigua	1	Jamaica	3
Bahamas	1	Madeira	1
Barbados	7	Malta	4
Berbice	1	Martinique	3
Bermuda	1	Mauritius	4
Britain	16	Mediterranean	12
British Honduras	1	New South Wales	3
Cadiz	8	Newfoundland	1
Canada	39	Nova Scotia	13
Cape of Good Hope	3	Peninsula	133
Cartagena	1	St Croix	1
Channel Islands	2	St Kitts	1
Coruña	1	St Lucia	1
Curaçao	2	St Martin's	1
Demerara	2	St Thomas	1
Germany	3	Scotland	1
Gibraltar	6	Sicily	26
Grenada	1	Stralsund	2
Guadeloupe	1	Surinam	1
Hanover	1	Trinidad	1
Heligoland	1	Unknown – not stated	14

* In Ireland, the Commisariat comprised the commissary general, deputy commissaries general, an acting deputy commissary general, assistant commissaries general, extra assistant commissaries general, an acting assistant commissary general and clerks. These all remained in Ireland.

Source: *Monthly Army Lists*, July 1814.

Trivia: *In September 1809 a military officer Lieutenant Colonel James Gordon was appointed commissary-in-chief. He was appointed quartermaster general to the forces in August 1811. In June 1812 he was sent out to replace George Murray as quartermaster general to Wellington's army in the Peninsula. He proved unsatisfactory in that appointment and returned home before the end of 1812 to resume his duties at the Horse Guards.*

Deployment of chaplains 1814

In 1793 each regiment had a chaplain on its strength. They were paid the princely sum of 6s 8d per day and there was no requirement to attend the men.⁸ When the Duke of York became commander-in-chief, one of his first acts was to establish the Army Chaplain's Department in September 1796 by royal warrant. Each chaplain was given the option of attending the troops with a raise in salary to 10 s per day or retiring on a pension of 4s per day. All but two chaplains took the pension! Few new chaplains joined to replace them.

Regimental chaplains were abolished by the 1796 reorganisation and replaced by general chaplains to the troops. After 25 December 1796, chaplains could no longer sell, exchange or transfer their commissions.⁹ With that reorganisation and an increase in salary to 16s per day in 1808, the numbers in the army did increase slightly. Even then there was a dearth of chaplains attending the army. For example only one chaplain attended either James Craig's force going to Sicily or Lord Cathcart's going to Hanover, while none attended David Baird's force to the Cape of Good Hope. No chaplains attended the Duke of Wellington's army in 1808 until two joined after the battle of Vimeiro. Only five chaplains went with John Moore's army into Spain. At home local civilian chaplains attended the troops in their barracks for £25 per year.¹⁰

Both the Duke of York and the Duke of Wellington complained of the lack of chaplains with the army and from 1810, Wellington tried 'to organize brigade or divisional chaplains to perform regular services for the Peninsular Army'.¹¹ It was not a complete success.

The head of the department was the chaplain general. His second was chaplain to the forces and assistant to the chaplain general. The chaplains were properly called chaplains to the forces.

The spiritual comfort of the men, however, was hardly looked after. In 1814, there were only thirty-seven chaplains in the army lists for the department.¹²

The best-known chaplain was Reverend Samuel Briscall, who had served with Wellington in the Peninsular War since landing five days after Vimeiro. His services were rewarded by his being made Wellington's personal domestic chaplain on 19 January 1814.¹³

Trivia: At the start of the 1815 campaign, only Reverend Samuel Briscall and five other chaplains joined Wellington's army. This number had increased to thirteen by January 1816.¹⁴

---

8   Glover, *Wellington's Army*, p. 130.
9   Chichester, *Records and Badges*, p. 916.
10 Haythornthwaite, *Armies of Wellington*, p. 123.
11 Ibid.
12 *Monthly Army Lists*, July 1814, p. 106.
13 Glover, *Wellington's Army*, p. 132.
14 Haythornthwaite, *Armies of Wellington*, p. 124. *Monthly Army Lists*, January 1816.

The table below shows their deployment at the end of the Napoleonic Wars in 1814; it clearly shows how few and dispersed they were.

Table 1.11 Deployment of chaplains in 1814

Location	No. deployed	Location	No. deployed
Bourbon	1	Malta	1
Cadiz	1	Martinique	1
Cape of Good Hope	1	Mauritius	1
Ceylon	1	Peninsula	15
Gibraltar	2	Portsmouth	1
Guadeloupe	1	Sicily	5
London	2	Unknown – not stated	3
Madeira	1		

Source: *Monthly Army Lists*, July 1814, p. 106.

Nobility in the British army 1805–16
There is an enduring myth that the British army of the Napoleonic Wars was an aristocratic army filled with the nobility who occupied the highest ranks. According to Michael Glover[15] there were about 450 peers who, along with their sons, besides the army, also supplied the Royal Navy (7.3 per cent of the officers), the Church of England, the militia, the volunteers and the two Houses of Parliament. By 1814 there were 10,590 officers on full pay, not including the foreign regiments and the veteran battalions. The Ordnance Corps added another 912 officers.[16] In 1814 there were 224 nobles in the British Army or 2 per cent of all the officers.

The title of prince in the tables was held by members of the royal family who also all carried the additional title of duke. They are counted under prince. The son and heir of a duke, marquess and earl were granted the use of their father's secondary title as their own courtesy title. Thus the son of the Duke of Wellington was the Marquess Douro. The son and heir of a holder of the courtesy title of marquess or earl also held a courtesy title of his grandfather's third title. They are counted here under their title. The other sons of a duke and a marquess were granted the use of a courtesy title of 'Lord' before their name such as Lord William Bentinck, son of the Duke of Portland. They would never be styled, for example, as Lord Bentinck.

Barons were never referred to as such, but were styled as lord with their title (e.g. Thomas, Lord Lynedoch or Lord Lynedoch). They would never be styled, for example, as Lord Thomas Lynedoch. Peer's sons were styled as 'Honourable' if they themselves did not hold a courtesy title. Thus the

---
15 Glover, *Wellington's Army* p. 37.
16 Ibid., p. 36.

Earl of Uxbridge's eldest son and heir was styled Henry Lord Paget, while his younger son was styled the Honourable Edward Paget.

The tables are restricted to the peers of England, Wales, Scotland and Ireland.

During the course of the wars foreign nobles joined the British army or served in foreign regiments in British service. For example. a number of non-British princes also held rank in the British army, they included the Duke of Brunswick Oels, the Hereditary Prince of Orange, Prince Henry of Reuss, and Prince Castelcicala of Naples (as Paul Ruffo).

German officers who had 'von' in their name prior to joining the British army are a bit of a problem owing to the use of 'Baron' as part of their name in the British Army Lists. While they are referred to as Baron (e. g. Charles Baron Alten), they were not ennobled as Barons in the peerage like British barons. When these German officers joined the British service, and received temporary rank in the British army, they were allowed to drop 'von' from their name and add 'baron' if they were of 'noble family' and were landowners or had landowners in their family. The 'baron' was apparently thought to be equivalent in status to the British 'Baronet'. When they left British service they dropped 'baron' from their name.

None of these foreign officers is counted in the tables.

The tables show the titles of nobility and then the number of each who were either general officers (employed on staff or unemployed), regimental officers serving on full pay and those officers who were on half pay but serving with a staff appointment. The numbers for 1816 are correct for January only.

Table 1.12 Nobility in the army 1805–10

Title	1805	1806	1807	1808	1809	1810
Prince	6	5	5	5	5	5
Duke	3	3	2	2	2	2
Marquess	5	6	5	3	4	4
Earl	17	16	21	21	20	22
Viscount	5	6	6	5	6	6
Baron	20	18	21	17	19	20
Courtesy Lord	15	17	16	20	17	13
Honourable	127	113	144	138	146	147
Total	198	184	220	211	219	219

Source: Yearly *Army List* 1805 and 1807; *Army List* for February 1806, March 1808, January 1809 and March 1810.

Table 1.13 Nobility in the army 1811–16

Title	1811	1812	1813	1814	1815	1816
Prince	5	5	5	5	5	5
Duke	2	2	2	2	2	2
Marquess	3	4	6	5	3	4
Earl	22	24	27	28	26	25
Viscount	7	6	5	5	5	4
Baron	18	19	15	18	19	17
Courtesy Lord	17	16	17	17	15	17
Honourable	143	151	138	144	131	131
Total	217	227	215	224	206	205

Source: *Army List* for March 1811, January 1812, February 1813, July 1814, January 1816; *Yearly Army List* 1815.

The Duke of Wellington's promotions 1787–1813

The rapid rise of Arthur Wellesley in the British army has been much remarked upon. There is no doubt that the Duke of Wellington had the advantage of being promoted during the years 1793 to 1795 where the Secretary at War, Sir George Yonge's excesses in allowing the unregulated rapid purchase of commissions in a fast expanding wartime army saw many junior officers quickly promoted to high rank.[17] Rules were, however, put in place by the Duke of York, the new commander-in-chief of the British army in 1795, which regulated commissions for promotion including purchase. He ruled that no officer could be promoted captain until he had served two years as a subaltern and that no officer could be promoted major unless he had six years of service. On 20 March 1809 he further ruled that no officer could be promoted to captain unless he had served three years as a subaltern, no captain could be promoted to major unless he had served for seven years of which two years, at least, were as a captain and no major could be promoted to lieutenant colonel unless he had nine years of service with at least two years as a major.[18]

Let us compare the rise of Wellington under Yonge's regime as opposed to the Duke falling under the regulations of the Duke of York and having to wait for promotional opportunities.

It is evident from table 1.15 that Wellington would have enjoyed the same ranks and seniority dates in the army even with the new regulations in place. In fact, his rise to higher rank was no more spectacular than that of his contemporaries. His career could then have followed the same path as it did historically.

17 Glover, *Wellington's Army*, p. 21.
18 Ibid., p. 76.

Table 1.14 Wellington's promotions

Rank	Date of rank	Comment
Ensign	7 March 1787	
Lieutenant	25 December 1787	
Captain	30 June 1791	
Major	30 April 1793	
Lieutenant colonel	30 September 1793	
Brevet colonel	3 May 1796	
Major general	29 April 1802	
Lieutenant general	25 April 1808	
General	Local rank 31 July 1811	Normal seniority 12 August 1819
Field marshal	21 June 1813	

Table 1.15 Wellington's approximate promotion dates had the new regulations of 1795/1796 been in place in 1793 and had he kept the same promotion dates

Rank	Date of rank	Comment
Ensign	7 March 1787	
Lieutenant	25 December 1787	
Captain	30 June 1791	After 2 years as subaltern
Major	30 April 1793	After 6 years' service
Lieutenant colonel	30 September 1793	No restriction
Brevet colonel	3 May 1796	
Major general	29 April 1802	
Lieutenant general	25 April 1808	
General	Local rank 31 July 1811	Normal seniority 12 August 1819
Field marshal	21 June 1813	

Table 1.16 Wellington's approximate promotion dates had the new regulations of 1809 been in place in 1793 and he kept the same earlier promotion dates

Rank	Date of rank	Comment
Ensign	7 March 1787	
Lieutenant	25 December 1787	
Captain	30 June 1791	After 3 years as subaltern
Major	7 March 1794	After 7 years' service

Rank	Date of rank	Comment
		with 2 years as a captain
Lieutenant colonel	7 March 1796	After 9 years service with 2 years as a major
Brevet colonel	1 January 1805	Actual general brevet
Major general	25 July 1810	Actual general brevet
Lieutenant general	4 June 1814	Actual general brevet
General	10 January 1837	Actual general brevet
Field marshal	9 November 1846	Longevity in the army with contemporaries who were also promoted

If Wellington had still obtained the lieutenant colonelcy of the 33rd Foot and gone out to India with his regiment, he would have been a relatively junior lieutenant colonel and not a colonel in the army and so might not have been given command of the brigades and armies which he later did command there. He would not have reached a general officer's rank until 1810 and so would not have been eligible for the command of the expedition to Portugal in 1808. At best he might have gone out to Portugal as a brigade commander and perhaps risen to command a division by the end of the war.

So while Wellington did enjoy a rapid promotion to lieutenant colonel, in his case and in the case of many others, it was to the benefit of the army and the country that young and able officers rose early to high rank.[19]

No two sources on Wellington's life and career agree on which of his ranks were purchased. Best guesses are those of major and lieutenant colonel. No firm evidence has been brought forward that he purchased his captaincy (cost £1,500), and had he done so, he would have had to pay a further £1,282 10s for his rank in the 18th Light Dragoons (the difference in the price of a captaincy purchased in the cavalry). The purchase price of £3,500 for a lieutenant colonelcy and the commission fees payable for each of his promotions, almost matches the amount of money (£3,776) which Wellington calculated that he owed his brother Richard, Marquess Wellesley in June 1799.[20] Most sources do seem to agree that Wellington purchased the rank of lieutenant colonel at least. The cost of purchasing a majority was £2,600 and to purchase the next rank only required the difference of £900 be paid. The majority would be sold to make up the difference in the purchase price.

---

19 See Glover, *Wellington as Military Commander*, for a fuller look at some of those others who rose rapidly to high rank.
20 Information on debt supplied to the author by Rory Muir, 17 June 2009.

Table 1.17 Wellington's actual promotions 1787–1813

Rank	Position or regiment	Date of rank	How obtained
Ensign	73rd Foot	7 March 1787	Appointed
Lieutenant	76th Foot	25 December 1787	Promoted
Lieutenant	41st Foot	23 January 1788	Exchange
Lieutenant	12th Light Dragoons	25 June 1789	Appointed
Captain	58th Foot	30 June 1791	Promoted
Captain	18th Light Dragoons	31 October 1792	Appointed
Major	33rd Foot	30 April 1793	Purchased
Lieutenant colonel	33rd Foot	30 September 1793	Purchased
Brevet colonel	Army	3 May 1796	Promoted
Brigadier general*	Egypt	17 July 1801	Local rank
Major general	Army	29 April 1802	Promoted
Regimental colonel	33rd Foot	1 January 1806	Appointed
Lieutenant general	Army	25 April 1808	Promoted
General	Spain & Portugal	31 July 1811	Local rank
Regimental colonel	Royal Horse Guards	1 January 1813	Appointed
Field marshal	Army	21 June 1813	Promoted

* Neither brigadier general nor brigadier was a substantive rank at this time, but a rank associated with an appointment on the staff, for example, of an army or to local rank in a specific location only. If the incumbent either resigned the army appointment or left the location, he reverted back to his substantive rank.

Trivia: *Lieutenant Colonel Henry Torrens, the Duke of York's Military Secretary, enjoyed an excellent and familiar working relationship with the Duke of Wellington. This was mainly due to the fact that Torrens had served as Wellington's Military Secretary during the period June to August 1808 while Wellington commanded the expedition to Portugal prior to being superseded in that command. Torrens had also served in India with Wellington. Torrens had been an Assistant Military Secretary to the Duke of York from 1807 and returned to that post in 1808.*

Chapter Two

Officer Seniority

In the British army of the Napoleonic Wars, seniority in the army was paramount and jealously guarded. Seniority as a general officer helped to determine who would command expeditions and who would be placed on the staff to command districts, divisions, brigades, departments, etc. It was very rare indeed for a British officer to agree to serve under his junior in army rank.[1] For general officers, there were only three substantive ranks, those of major general, lieutenant general and general. Promotion to general officer's rank was through progressive promotion in what was termed a general brevet. This was simply the promotion of all officers to the next army rank who had been promoted to their current rank between certain dates. Promotion to field marshal was rarely granted.[2] At this time the rank of brigadier general was not a substantive rank in the army, but a rank associated with an appointment, for example, to command a brigade. The Secretary of State for War and the Colonies, in discussion with the government cabinet, selected the commander-in-chief of any expedition operating outside of Great Britain. The commander-in-chief of the army was responsible to appoint and promote officers, to select staff officers at home and abroad, and to assign general officers at home and abroad, excluding the commander-in-chief of any expedition.

The following is a short concise background to the twenty-one selected expeditions and campaigns carried out by the British army. Not all of the expeditions for 1805–15 are given. The tables list the army ranks to show seniority in the army of the general officers serving on the expedition and during the campaign. They include the senior staff officers. At the time, the usual employment was to assign lieutenant generals to command armies, expeditions, corps and divisions, major generals to command brigades (and

---

1 Glover, *Wellington as Military Commander*, p. 197.
2 Muir et al., *Inside Wellington's Peninsular Army*, pp. 173–4.

divisions as necessary) with brigadier generals on the staff and colonels on the staff also to command brigades. Although there were hundreds of general officers on the army lists, many were unavailable, being too old or infirm or too senior to take a command under their juniors already commanding on the staff. This resulted in some of the expeditions using colonels and lieutenant colonels to command the brigades, as there were not enough general officers on the staff to command them all.

Rank granted 'on the staff' of a particular station or for service with an army or expedition was for the duration of the officer's service with that army.

Special key to tables:
* indicates brigadier generals on the staff
† indicates colonels on the staff
# indicates serving with the Portuguese army

Officer seniority – Hanover 1805

Great Britain decided to assist its coalition partners in the war against France by landing a force in northern Germany. It also wanted to free Hanover from French occupation and recruit the newly formed King's German Legion there – the king of Great Britain was also the elector of Hanover. The command of the expedition was given to Lieutenant General William, Lord Cathcart. The force landed on the Continent in November 1805 and evacuated by February 1806, as the French victory at Austerlitz and the signing of a peace treaty ended the coalition against France. It faced little opposition as the French evacuated Hanover, except for the fortress of Hameln which was invested by the Russians assisted by the British. The recruiting of the King's German Legion was one of the few benefits of this expedition.

> *Trivia:* On the staff of the army was a relatively junior major general, Arthur Wellesley. Wellesley had just recently arrived back from active service in India. He would become better known as the Duke of Wellington. Many of the generals who served in the expedition would become well known in the Peninsula.

Table 2.1   Officer seniority – Hanover 1805

Name	Rank	Date of rank	Command or position
William, Lord Cathcart§	LG	1 January 1801	Commander of the force
George Don	LG	1 January 1805	Second-in-command

§ Local general on the Continent 13 November 1805.

Name	Rank	Date of rank	Command or position
Francis Dundas	LG	29 April 1802	Division
George Ludlow	LG	30 October 1805	Division
Edward Finch	MG	1 January 1801	Guards Brigade
Alexander Mackenzie Fraser	MG	29 April 1802	Brigade
Arthur Wellesley	MG	29 April 1802	Brigade
Charles, Baron Linsingen	MG	18 August 1804	KGL Cavalry Brigade
John Sherbrooke	MG	1 January 1805	Brigade
Edward Paget	MG	1 January 1805	Brigade
Rowland Hill	MG	30 October 1805	Brigade
Ernest, Baron Langwerth†	Col	16 December 1804	KGL Brigade
Adolphus, Baron Barsse†	Col	21 December 1804	KGL Brigade
Charles Baron Alten†	Col	22 December 1804	KGL Light Brigade
John Hope†	Col	1 January 1805	DAG
George Murray	LCol	5 August 1799	DQMG
George Cookson	LCol	20 July 1804	Commander, RA

Officer seniority – Cape of Good Hope 1805–6

In late July 1805 the British were determined to capture the Cape of Good Hope from the Dutch. This would help to secure passage to India. They had previously captured the colony in 1795, but had returned it with the Peace of Amiens in 1802. The command of the expedition was given to Major General David Baird. He was to use troops from Britain, as well as those going out to serve in India. The expedition sailed from Cork on 31 August 1805 and reached Madeira on 28 September. There were delays at Madeira due to bad weather and it sailed on 3 October. It went to South America in late October to replenish supplies, losing some ships in the shoals off Brazil on 1 November 1805 and sailed again for Cape Colony on 28 November 1805. It arrived off Cape Town 3/4 January 1806 and began landing 5/6 January. Marched on Cape Town on 8 January and defeated a Dutch force blocking its way at the Battle of Bleuberg (Blue Mountain) the same day. The town capitulated on 10 January, but a portion of the Dutch army escaped. The colony finally surrendered on 18 January 1806.

Table 2.2 Officer seniority – Cape of Good Hope 1805–6

Name	Rank	Date of rank	Command or position
David Baird‡	MG	18 June 1798	Commander of the force
William Beresford*	Col	1 January 1800	1st Brigade
Ronald Ferguson*	Col	1 January 1800	Highland Brigade
John Henry Yorke*§	Col	20 July 1804	Commander, RA
Joseph Baird¶	LCol	25 November 1799	1st Brigade
Henry Fox Brownrigg	LCol	25 March 1805	DQMG
William Spicer	Maj	13 August 1804	Commander, RA
William Trotter‡‡	Maj	28 August 1804	Acting DAG
George Tucker	Maj	13 January 1805	DAG
James Carmichael Smyth	Capt	1 July 1802	Commander, RE

‡ Promoted lieutenant general 30 October 1805.
§ Drowned in the loss of the *King George* transport off Brazil, 1 November 1805.
¶ Temporarily commanding brigade as Beresford was on detached duty.
‡‡ Replaced Major George Tucker as the DAG, who was ill.

Trivia: News of David Baird's promotion to lieutenant general on 30 October 1805 did not reach him for some time. He continued to sign his despatches as a major general in early 1806.

Officer seniority – Maida and Calabria 1806

In June 1806 it was decided that the British Garrison in Sicily would provide a force to drive the French out of Calabria. The command of the force was given to Major General John Stuart. The force sailed from Sicily on 28 June 1806 and made a landing on 1 July. On 3 July the French arrived and the battle of Maida was fought the next day, 4 July. The battle was a British victory. The British resumed their advance on 6 July, taking Pizzo, Tropea and Monteleone. On 12 July the British arrived before the castle of Scylla which fell on 22 July after a siege. In the meantime, Brigadier General Brodrick had arrived with more troops from Sicily and took the castle of Reggio. It was never the intent of the British to do more than achieve its limited goal of liberating Calabria for the Sicilians to garrison. Therefore in late July they withdrew from the mainland except for a garrison left in Scylla.

Table 2.3 Officer seniority – Maida and Calabria 1806

Name	Rank	Date of rank	Command or position
John Stuart	MG	29 April 1802	Commander of the force
John Brodrick*‡	Col	1 January 1801	Brigade from Sicily
Galbraith Lowry Cole*	Col	1 January 1801	1st Brigade
Wroth Palmer Acland*	Col	25 September 1803	2nd Brigade
John Oswald†	Col	30 October 1805	3rd Brigade
James Kempt	LCol	28 August 1799	Advance Corps
Henry Bunbury	LCol	31 December 1803	DQMG
John Lemoine	Maj	10 March 1805	Commander, RA
Charles Lefebure	Capt	11 June 1800	Commander, RE
Roger Tomlin	Capt	13 February 1805	DAG

‡ Arrived in July after the battle was fought.

Trivia: John Lemoine fought at the battle of Maida as a major. Word of his promotion to lieutenant colonel on 1 June 1806 had not arrived in the Mediterranean. His rank of lieutenant colonel allowed him to receive the Army Gold Medal for Maida, as only lieutenant colonels and above were originally recommended for the award.

Officer seniority – South America 1806–7

After the capture of the Cape of Good Hope, Lieutenant General David Baird was persuaded by Commodore Home Popham RN that the time was right to attack the Spanish colonies in South America. The feeling was that the Spanish colonists would be agreeable to independence and would begin to trade with the British opening up the South American markets. Baird authorised a small force under Brigadier General William Beresford to accompany the Royal Navy in the enterprise. The force quickly captured Buenos Aires on 27 June 1806. But instead of either surrendering or proclaiming independence, the colonists rallied and in turn captured the British force in the city. The news of the capture of the city caused the British to decide to send reinforcements under Brigadier General Samuel Auchmuty. They also decided to increase the force and ordered an expedition under Brigadier General Robert Craufurd, which was planned for another enterprise, to sail there as well. These forces were put under the command of Lieutenant General John Whitelocke on 7 February 1807. Auchmuty landed on 16 January 1807. He assaulted and captured Montevideo on 3 February to use as a base of operations. With the arrival of Craufurd and Whitelocke, it was decided to again assault

Buenos Aires. The attack on 5 July was a fiasco and the British in the city were again forced to surrender. A capitulation on 7 July allowed the British to evacuate the entire Rio de la Plata area and return home.

> *Trivia:* Many of the officers of this expedition would later become well known in the Peninsular War. LG Whitelocke faced a general court martial on 28 January 1808 on four charges for his conduct. He was found guilty and cashiered on 24 March 1808. His sentence included being declared totally unfit and unworthy to serve the King in any further military capacity.

Table 2.4   Officer seniority – South America 1806–7

Name	Rank	Date of rank	Command or position
John Whitelocke	LG	30 October 1805	Commander of the 2nd force
John Leveson Gower	MG	30 October 1805	Second-in-command
William Beresford*‡	Col	1 January 1800	Commander of the 1st force
Samuel Auchmuty*	Col	1 January 1800	Brigade
William Lumley*	Col	29 April 1802	Brigade
Wroth Palmer Acland*	Col	25 September 1803	On staff
Gore Browne†	Col	1 January 1805	Brigade
Thomas Mahon†	Col	30 October 1805	Cavalry Brigade
Robert Craufurd*	Col	30 October 1805	Expedition/Brigade
Evan Lloyd	LCol	11 February 1799	Cavalry Brigade
Thomas Bradford	LCol	1 January 1801	DAG
Richard Bourke	LCol	16 September 1806	DQMG
Augustus Frazer	Capt	16 July 1799	Commander, RA
John Squire	Capt	2 December 1802	Commander, RE

‡ Appointed a local major general while serving in South America by Baird's authority.

> *Trivia:* Baird anticipated that Beresford would have been promoted in the last general brevet promotions to major general in 1805. Unfortunately the promotions ended just above Beresford's name. He would have to wait until 25 April 1808 to become a major general.[3]

---

3   Hook, vol 2, p. 140.

Officer seniority – Baltic 1807

Great Britain, faced with the knowledge that the Royal Navy would be outnumbered in ships of the line if the neutral navies of Sweden, Denmark and Portugal were seized by Napoleon,[4] which they knew he was secretly planning to do, decided to put pressure on Denmark to send its navy to Britain for internment. Denmark opposed this request, so the British decided to send an expeditionary force there to compel Denmark to surrender its fleet under the command of Lieutenant General William, Lord Cathcart. The British fleet arrived and negotiations began on 3 August. Negotiations failed and the British force began landing on 15 August. Only one land engagement was fought, the battle of Kioge, on 29 August, and won by the British. A Danish sortie against the British siege lines on 31 August also failed. After a bombardment of Copenhagen, from 2–6 September, the Danes capitulated and their fleet was seized and taken to Britain. This expedition left Denmark 20 October.

Trivia: Many generals who would later become well known in the Peninsula participated in this expedition, among them Arthur Wellesley.

Table 2.5 Officer seniority – Baltic 1807

Name	Rank	Date of rank	Command or position
William, Lord Cathcart‡	LG	1 January 1801	Commander of the force
Harry Burrard	LG	1 January 1805	Second-in-command
James, Lord Rosslyn	LG	1 January 1805	KGL Division
George Ludlow	LG	30 October 1805	Right Division
David Baird	LG	30 October 1805	Left Division
Edward Finch	MG	1 January 1801	Guards Brigade
Thomas Grosvenor	MG	29 April 1802	Brigade
Arthur Wellesley	MG	29 April 1802	Reserve Brigade
Thomas Blomefield	MG	25 September 1803	Commander, RA
Frederick, Baron Drechsel	MG	14 August 1804	Attached KGL Division
Charles, Baron Linsingen	MG	18 August 1804	KGL Cavalry Division
Brent Spencer	MG	1 January 1805	Brigade
Robert Macfarlane*	Col	1 January 1800	Brigade

‡ Local general on the Continent 13 November 1805.

---

4 Glover, *The Napoleonic Wars*, p. 124.

Table 2.5 continued

Name	Rank	Date of rank	Command or position
Frederick, Baron Decken*	Col	28 July 1803	Attached KGL Division
Richard Stewart*	Col	25 September 1803	Second-in-command, Reserve Brigade
George de Drieberg†	Col	1 April 1804	KGL Brigade
Peter du Plat†	Col	18 September 1804	KGL Brigade
Adolphus, Baron Barsse†	Col	21 December 1804	KGL Brigade
Charles, Baron Alten†	Col	22 December 1804	KGL Light Brigade
John Hope†	Col	1 January 1805	DAG
George Murray	LCol	5 August 1799	DQMG
Robert D'Arcy	LCol	1 March 1805	Commander, RE

Trivia: While at Copenhagen, Thomas Grosvenor discovered that his mare was in foal and sent her home. The colt was named Copenhagen and was bought by the Duke of Wellington, who would ride him in the Peninsula and at Waterloo. Copenhagen died on 12 February 1836.

Officer seniority – Egypt 1807

In late 1806 the British became involved in a dispute with the Ottoman Empire over its sympathy with France. In early 1807 a decision was made to land in Egypt and occupy Alexandria. The expedition sailed on 6 March from the garrison of Sicily under the command of Major General Alexander Mackenzie Fraser and landed in Egypt on 17 March 1807. Alexandria capitulated to the force on 20 March. Two British attempts to take and hold Rosetta (31 March and 3–21 April) both ended in disaster with the eventual retreat of the British force back to Alexandria. Further reinforcements arrived under Major General John Sherbrooke on 29 May. The British remained in Alexandria until 23 September when they finally evacuated Egypt and returned to Sicily.

Table 2.6 Officer seniority – Egypt 1807

Name	Rank	Date of rank	Command or position
Alexander Mackenzie Fraser	MG	29 April 1802	Commander of the force
Patrick Wauchope	MG	25 September 1803	Second-in-command

Name	Rank	Date of rank	Command or position
John Sherbrooke	MG	1 January 1805	Brigade
William Stewart*	Col	2 April 1801	Brigade
Robert Meade*	Col	29 April 1802	Brigade
John Oswald†	Col	30 October 1805	Brigade
George Airey‡	LCol	4 May 1798	DAG
Edwin Green§	Major	4 March 1807	DQMG
Robert Pym	Capt	3 December 1800	Commander, RA
Frederick Thackeray¶	Capt	18 April 1801	Commander, RE
John Fox Burgoyne	Capt	1 March 1805	Commander, RE

‡ Acting in that capacity with the expedition only.
§ Brevet major and captain.
¶ Captain Thackeray joined later and replaced Captain Burgoyne as the commander of the Royal Engineers.

Officer seniority – Baltic 1808

In April 1808 the British were agreeable to sending an army to assist Sweden in its war with Russia. The army was to go to Gothenburg. It was not to place itself under the command of the Swedish king or to operate too far from the coast, keeping open its option for evacuation. The lack of information meant that no plan of operation had been decided upon and any plan would depend upon conditions in Sweden when the army under the command of Lieutenant General John Moore arrived there. It sailed for Sweden on 30 April 1808. Negotiations to decide upon a plan of operation and to assist Sweden against Russia failed and it was decided to return the army to Britain, sailing on 20 July. The army never landed. Meanwhile, a decision had been made to use this army to reinforce another army being sent out to Portugal and Spain to assist with the uprisings there. It sailed for Portugal on 31 July 1808. Upon arriving in August, it joined the army under the command of Lieutenant General Hew Dalrymple.

> *Trivia: Most of the general officers serving in it either went into Spain with Moore's army and were evacuated at Coruña or remained in Portugal to take commands in its British garrison.*

Table 2.7   Officer seniority – Baltic 1808

Name	Rank	Date of rank	Command or position
John Moore	LG	30 October 1805	Commander of the force
John Hope	LG	25 April 1808	Second-in-command

Table 2.7 continued

Name	Rank	Date of rank	Command or position
Alexander Mackenzie Fraser	LG	25 April 1808	1st Division
Edward Paget	MG	1 January 1805	3rd or Reserve Division
John Murray	MG	30 October 1805	2nd KGL Division
Henry Clinton*	Col	25 September 1803	Brigade
John Sontag*	Col	25 September 1803	On Staff
Richard Stewart*	Col	25 September 1803	AG
George de Drieberg†	Col	1 April 1804	KGL Brigade
Ernest Baron Langwerth†	Col	16 December 1804	KGL Brigade
Charles, Baron Alten†	Col	22 December 1804	KGL Light Brigade
Alan Cameron†	Col	1 January 1805	Highland Brigade
George Murray	LCol	5 August 1799	QMG
George A. Wood	LCol	1 February 1808	Commander, RA
John Fox Burgoyne	Capt	1 March 1805	Commander, RE

Officer seniority – the Peninsular War 1808–14

The Peninsular War is too well known to give more than a cursory summary here. In June 1808 the British made the monumental decision to aid the uprisings in Portugal and Spain, against the French, with an army. This force landed in Portugal starting in late July and liberated Portugal by late August. A force sent into Spain to assist the Spanish armies in the field, facing superior numbers of French, had to evacuate through Coruña in January 1809. The British remained in Portugal and in April 1809 sent reinforcements to defend it. This army, now under the Duke of Wellington was to campaign for just over four years, 1809 to 1813, to drive the French out of Spain. It then invaded southern France and was fighting there when news arrived of Napoleon's abdication and an armistice was signed in April 1814 ending the fighting on that front. The French eagles of the 8th Line, 22nd Line and 62nd Line were captured.

The tables list the army promotions granted before and during the Peninsular War 1808–14 to show seniority in the army of the general officers serving there. Only those officers promoted in the British army are given. Those serving in the Portuguese service continued to be promoted according to their rank in the British service.

The tables for seniority 1808–9 refer to the general officers who served from the landing in Portugal in July 1808 until the evacuation of Coruña in January 1809, as well as those general officers who commanded in the garrison of Portugal. The tables show their seniority for that period only.

The tables for 1809 to 1814 refer to the general officers who served under the Duke of Wellington's command from April 1809 to April 1814. They trace the progressive promotion of the officers for the rank of colonel and above. The general officers include those who served at Cadiz, Cartagena and on the east coast of Spain, all under Wellington's command.

The header 'Local' refers to the grant of a higher rank in the army only while serving in the Peninsula and 'Staff' refers to the grant of a higher rank in the army only while serving on the staff.

Table 2.8   Officer seniority in the Peninsula July 1808–April 1809

Name	Rank	Date of rank
Hew Dalrymple	LG	1 January 1801
Harry Burrard	LG	1 January 1805
John Cradock	LG	1 January 1805
John Moore	LG	30 October 1805
David Baird	LG	30 October 1805
John Hope	LG	25 April 1808
Alexander Mackenzie Fraser	LG	25 April 1808
Henry, Lord Paget	LG	25 April 1808
Arthur Wellesley	LG	25 April 1808
John Sherbrooke	MG	1 January 1805
Lord William Bentinck	MG	1 January 1805
Coote Manningham	MG	1 January 1805
Edward Paget	MG	1 January 1805
Brent Spencer	MG	1 January 1805
Stapleton Cotton	MG	30 October 1805
Rowland Hill	MG	30 October 1805
John Murray	MG	30 October 1805
William Beresford	MG	25 April 1808
William Dyott	MG	25 April 1808
Ronald Ferguson	MG	25 April 1808
John Brodrick	MG	25 April 1808
Henry Warde	MG	25 April 1808
James Leith	MG	25 April 1808
John Randoll Mackenzie	MG	25 April 1808
Christopher Tilson	MG	25 April 1808
John Slade*	Col	29 April 1802
Moore Disney*	Col	29 April 1802
Wroth Palmer Acland*	Col	25 September 1803
Miles Nightingall*	Col	25 September 1803

31

Table 2.8 continued

Name	Rank	Date of rank
Henry Clinton*	Col	25 September 1803
John Sontag*	Col	25 September 1803
Henry Campbell*	Col	25 September 1803
Richard Stewart*	Col	25 September 1803
Charles Stewart*	Col	25 September 1803
George de Drieberg*	Col	1 April 1804
Ernest, Baron Langwerth*	Col	16 December 1804
Charles, Baron Alten*	Col	22 December 1804
Alan Cameron*	Col	1 January 1805
Barnard Bowes*	Col	1 January 1805
Henry Fane*	Col	1 January 1805
Robert Anstruther*	Col	1 January 1805
James Catlin Craufurd‡	Col	30 October 1805
Robert Craufurd§	Col	30 October 1805
Robert Long¶	Col	25 April 1808
John Harding	Col	28 June 1808

‡ J. C. Craufurd was a brigadier general on the staff with Wellesley's Corps in 1808; but only appointed as a colonel on the Staff with Moore's army.
§ R. Craufurd was a brigadier general on the Staff in the United Kingdom; but only appointed as a colonel on the Staff with Moore's army.
¶ Robert Long was appointed as a colonel on the Staff with Moore's army.

Trivia: *The highest-ranking officer commanding the Royal Artillery in 1808 was a regimental colonel, John Harding. In 1809 to early 1812 the commanders were general officers: Edward Howorth and his replacement William Borthwick. With Borthwick's departure, the highest-ranking officers were regimental lieutenant colonels: Hoylet Framingham, William Robe, George Fisher and Charles Waller. In early 1813 the command of the Allied artillery with the field army was given to a Portuguese lieutenant colonel, Alexander Dickson, a regimental captain in the British Royal Artillery.*

Table 2.9 Officer seniority in the Peninsula, 1809–14

Name	Rank	Date of Rank	Local	Date
Arthur, Duke of Wellington	FM	21 June 1813		
John Hope	LG	25 April 1808		
Arthur, Duke of Wellington	LG	25 April 1808	Gen	31 July 1811
Thomas Graham	LG	25 July 1810		

Trivia: Between 16 January and 7 February 1815 Lieutenant General John Murray faced a general court martial on three charges for his conduct while commanding on the east coast of Spain in June 1813. He had evacuated the coast outside of Tarragona and left his siege artillery behind on account of perceived enemy action. Murray was found guilty on part of one charge, that of abandoning his artillery and stores. He was sentenced to be admonished by the Prince Regent. The Prince confirmed the sentence and took no further action.

Name	Rank	Date of Rank	Local	Date
John Sherbrooke	LG	4 June 1811		
William Payne	LG	4 June 1811		
Edward Paget	LG	4 June 1811		
Brent Spencer	LG	4 June 1811		
Stapleton Cotton	LG	1 January 1812		
Rowland Hill	LG	1 January 1812		
John Murray	LG	1 January 1812		
Frederick Maitland	LG	1 January 1812		
William Beresford#	LG	1 January 1812		
George, Earl of Dalhousie	LG	4 June 1813		
James Erskine	LG	4 June 1813		
James Leith	LG	4 June 1813		
Christopher Tilson‡	LG	4 June 1813		
James Campbell	LG	4 June 1813		
Thomas Picton	LG	4 June 1813		
Galbraith Lowry Cole	LG	4 June 1813		
Stafford Lightburne	LG	4 June 1813		
William Clinton	LG	4 June 1813		
William Stewart	LG	4 June 1813		
John Hope	MG	29 April 1802		
Duke of Wellington	MG	29 April 1802		
Thomas Graham	MG	25 September 1803	LG	21 February 1810
John Sherbrooke	MG	1 January 1805	LG	12 April 1809
William Payne	MG	1 January 1805	LG	12 April 1809
Edward Paget	MG	1 January 1805	LG	12 April 1809
Brent Spencer	MG	1 January 1805	LG	5 May 1810
Stapleton Cotton	MG	30 October 1805	LG	31 August 1809
Rowland Hill	MG	30 October 1805	LG	31 August 1809
John Murray	MG	30 October 1805		

‡ Major General Christopher Tilson changed his last name to Chowne in January 1812. When he returned to the Peninsula later in 1812, he was known as Lieutenant General Christopher Chowne.

Table 2.9 continued

Name	Rank	Date of rank	Local Date
Frederick Maitland	MG	30 October 1805	
William Beresford#	MG	25 April 1808	LG 16 February 1809
Earl of Dalhousie	MG	25 April 1808	LG 3 September 1812
James Erskine	MG	25 April 1808	
James Leith	MG	25 April 1808	LG 6 September 1811
John R. Mackenzie	MG	25 April 1808	
Christopher Tilson	MG	25 April 1808	LG 11 November 1811
James Campbell	MG	25 April 1808	
Thomas Picton	MG	25 April 1808	LG 6 September 1811
Galbraith Lowry Cole	MG	25 April 1808	LG 6 September 1811
Stafford Lightburne	MG	25 April 1808	
William Erskine	MG	25 April 1808	LG 6 September 1811
William Clinton	MG	25 April 1808	LG 22 December 1812
William Stewart	MG	25 April 1808	LG 3 September 1812
John Hamilton#	MG	25 October 1809	
William Houston	MG	25 October 1809	
John Slade	MG	25 October 1809	
William Lumley	MG	25 October 1809	
Moore Disney	MG	25 October 1809	
John MacKenzie	MG	25 October 1809	
Miles Nightingall	MG	25 July 1810	
Henry Clinton	MG	25 July 1810	LG 8 April 1813
John Sontag	MG	25 July 1810	
James Dunlop	MG	25 July 1810	
Alexander Campbell	MG	25 July 1810	
Henry Campbell	MG	25 July 1810	
Richard Stewart	MG	25 July 1810	
Charles Stewart	MG	25 July 1810	
George, Baron Bock	MG	25 July 1810	
Augustus Honstedt	MG	25 July 1810	
Victor Baron Alten	MG	25 July 1810	
Sigismund, Baron Low	MG	25 July 1810	
Adolphus, Baron Barsse	MG	25 July 1810	
Charles, Baron Alten	MG	25 July 1810	
John Hope	MG	25 July 1810	
Alan Cameron	MG	25 July 1810	
Daniel Hoghton	MG	25 July 1810	
Charles Colville	MG	25 July 1810	
Barnard Bowes	MG	25 July 1810	

Name	Rank	Date of rank	Local	Date
Henry Fane	MG	25 July 1810		
George Anson	MG	25 July 1810		
Kenneth Howard	MG	25 July 1810		
Henry de Hinüber	MG	4 June 1811		
William Dilkes	MG	4 June 1811		
John Oswald	MG	4 June 1811		
John Le Marchant	MG	4 June 1811		
William Anson	MG	4 June 1811		
Robert Craufurd	MG	4 June 1811		
Edward Howorth	MG	4 June 1811		
John Saunders	MG	4 June 1811		
Andrew Hay	MG	4 June 1811		
Warren Peacocke	MG	4 June 1811		
James Kemmis	MG	4 June 1811		
Robert Burne	MG	4 June 1811		
John Vandeleur	MG	4 June 1811		
Alexander Goldie	MG	4 June 1811		
Robert Long	MG	4 June 1811		
Rufane Donkin	MG	4 June 1811		
Edward Stopford	MG	4 June 1811		
George Cooke	MG	4 June 1811		
George Walker	MG	4 June 1811		
Kenneth Mackenzie	MG	4 June 1811		
George de Grey	MG	4 June 1811		
Terence O'Loghlin	MG	1 January 1812		
George Murray	MG	1 January 1812	MG	26 October 1811
James Kempt	MG	1 January 1812	MG	4 November 1811
William Borthwick	MG	1 January 1812	MG	4 November 1811
John de Bernewitz	MG	1 January 1812	MG	23 November 1811
Richard Blunt#	MG	1 January 1812		
Henry Bayly	MG	1 January 1812		
Richard Hulse	MG	1 January 1812	MG	26 October 1811
Francis Rebow	MG	1 January 1812		
Edward Pakenham	MG	1 January 1812	MG	26 October 1811
Henry Mackinnon	MG	1 January 1812	MG	26 October 1811
William Wheatley	MG	1 January 1812		
William Pringle	MG	1 January 1812		
Andrew Ross	MG	1 January 1812		
Frederick Robinson	MG	4 June 1813		
Edward Barnes	MG	4 June 1813		
William Brooke	MG	4 June 1813		

Table 2.9 continued

Name	Rank	Date of Rank	Staff	Date
William Ponsonby	MG	4 June 1813		
Haviland Smith	MG	4 June 1813		
William Inglis	MG	4 June 1813		
William Spry#	MG	4 June 1813		
Daniel Seddon#	MG	4 June 1813		
John Byng	MG	4 June 1813		
Thomas Brisbane	MG	4 June 1813		
Thomas Fermor	MG	4 June 1813		
John B. Skerrett	MG	4 June 1813		
Denis Pack	MG	4 June 1813		
Lord Edward Somerset	MG	4 June 1813		
Thomas Bradford#	MG	4 June 1813		
Robert Ross	MG	4 June 1813		
John Lambert	MG	4 June 1813		
James Gordon	MG	4 June 1813		
Manley Power#	MG	4 June 1813		
Robert Wilson#	MG	4 June 1813		
Matthew, Lord Aylmer	MG	4 June 1813		
John Hope	Col	3 May 1796		
Arthur, Duke of Wellington	Col	3 May 1796		
Thomas Graham	Col	26 January 1797		
John Sherbrooke	Col	1 January 1798		
William Payne	Col	1 January 1798		
Edward Paget	Col	1 January 1798		
Brent Spencer	Col	28 May 1798		
Stapleton Cotton	Col	1 January 1800		
Rowland Hill	Col	1 January 1800		
John Murray	Col	1 January 1800		
Frederick Maitland	Col	1 January 1800		
William Beresford#	Col	1 January 1800		
George, Earl of Dalhousie	Col	1 January 1800		
James Erskine	Col	1 January 1800		
James Leith	Col	1 January 1801		
John R. Mackenzie	Col	1 January 1801		
Christopher Tilson	Col	1 January 1801		
James Campbell	Col	1 January 1801		
Thomas Picton	Col	1 January 1801		
Galbraith Lowry Cole	Col	1 January 1801		

Name	Rank	Date of rank	Local	Date
Stafford Lightburne	Col	1 January 1801		
William Erskine	Col	1 January 1801		
William Clinton	Col	1 January 1801		
William Stewart	Col	2 April 1801		
John Hamilton#	Col	29 April 1802		
William Houston	Col	29 April 1802		
John Slade	Col	29 April 1802	BG	17 August 1809
William Lumley	Col	29 April 1802		
Moore Disney	Col	29 April 1802		
John MacKenzie	Col	29 April 1802		
Miles Nightingall	Col	25 September 1803		
Henry Clinton	Col	25 September 1803		
John Sontag	Col	25 September 1803	BG	6 May 1809
James Dunlop	Col	25 September 1803		
Alexander Campbell	Col	25 September 1803	BG	1 April 1809
Henry Campbell	Col	25 September 1803	BG	1 April 1809
Richard Stewart	Col	25 September 1803	BG	1 April 1809
Charles Stewart	Col	25 September 1803	BG	1 April 1809
George de Drieberg	Col	1 April 1804	BG	1 April 1809
George, Baron Bock	Col	18 August 1804		
Augustus Honstedt	Col	15 December 1804		
Ernest, Baron Langwerth	Col	16 December 1804	BG	1 April 1809
Victor Baron Alten	Col	19 December 1804		
Sigismund, Baron Low	Col	20 December 1804	BG	18 June 1809
Adolphus, Baron Barsse	Col	21 December 1804		
Charles, Baron Alten	Col	22 December 1804		
John Hope	Col	1 January 1805		
Alan Cameron	Col	1 January 1805	BG	1 April 1809
Daniel Hoghton	Col	1 January 1805	BG	14 April 1810
Charles Colville	Col	1 January 1805		
Barnard Bowes	Col	1 January 1805	BG	Unknown 1810
Henry Fane	Col	1 January 1805	BG	1 April 1809
George Anson	Col	1 January 1805	BG	25 May 1809
Kenneth Howard	Col	1 January 1805		
Henry de Hinüber	Col	9 July 1805		
William Dilkes	Col	30 October 1805	BG	24 February 1810
John Oswald	Col	30 October 1805		
John Le Marchant	Col	30 October 1805		
James Catlin Craufurd	Col	30 October 1805	BG	26 July 1809
William Anson	Col	30 October 1805		

Table 2.9 continued

Name	Rank	Date of Rank	Staff Date
Robert Craufurd	Col	30 October 1805	BG 26 July 1809
Edward Howorth	Col	29 December 1805	BG 3 May 1809
John Saunders†	Col	25 April 1808	
Andrew Hay	Col	25 April 1808	BG 6 August 1810
Warren Peacocke†	Col	25 April 1808	BG 23 January 1811
James Kemmis†	Col	25 April 1808	BG 23 January 1811
Robert Burne	Col	25 April 1808	BG 21 January 1811
John Vandeleur	Col	25 April 1808	
Alexander Goldie	Col	25 April 1808	
Robert Long	Col	25 April 1808	BG 21 January 1811
Rufane Donkin†	Col	25 April 1808	
Edward Stopford†	Col	25 April 1808	BG 23 January 1811
George Cooke	Col	25 April 1808	
George Walker	Col	25 April 1808	
Kenneth Mackenzie†	Col	25 April 1808	
George de Grey†	Col	25 April 1808	
Terence O'Loghlin	Col	1 September 1808	
George Murray†	Col	9 March 1809	BG 1 July 1811
James Kempt	Col	9 March 1809	
William Borthwick	Col	30 April 1809	BG 7 October 1811
John de Bernewitz	Col	25 September 1809	
George Drummond†	Col	25 October 1809	BG 23 July 1811
Richard Blunt#	Col	25 October 1809	
Henry Bayly	Col	25 October 1809	
Richard Hulse†	Col	25 October 1809	BG 23 July 1811
Francis Rebow	Col	25 October 1809	
Edward Pakenham†	Col	25 October 1809	BG 23 July 1811
Henry Mackinnon†	Col	25 October 1809	BG 23 July 1811
James Wynch†	Col	25 October 1809	
William Wheatley†	Col	25 October 1809	
William Pringle	Col	25 October 1809	
Andrew Ross	Col	25 October 1809	BG 1 October 1810
Frederick Robinson	Col	25 July 1810	BG 7 October 1812
Edward Barnes	Col	25 July 1810	BG 7 October 1812
William Brooke†	Col	25 July 1810	BG 14 January 1813
William Ponsonby†	Col	25 July 1810	BG 1 October 1812
Haviland Smith	Col	25 July 1810	
William Inglis†	Col	25 July 1810	BG 21 January 1813
William Spry#	Col	25 July 1810	
Daniel Seddon#	Col	25 July 1810	

Officer Seniority

Name	Rank	Date of Rank	Staff	Date
John Byng†	Col	25 July 1810	BG	25 November 1812
Thomas Brisbane	Col	25 July 1810		
Thomas Fermor†	Col	25 July 1810		
John B. Skerrett†	Col	25 July 1810		
Denis Pack	Col	25 July 1810		
Lord Edward Somerset	Col	25 July 1810		
George Wilson†	Col	25 July 1810		
Thomas Bradford#	Col	25 July 1810		
Robert Ross	Col	25 July 1810		
John Lambert	Col	25 July 1810		
James Gordon†	Col	25 July 1810		
Manley Power#	Col	25 July 1810		
Robert Wilson#	Col	25 July 1810		
William Howe Campbell#	Col	25 July 1810		
Matthew, Lord Aylmer	Col	25 July 1810		
James Stirling†	Col	4 June 1811		
Samuel Hinde†	Col	4 June 1811		
Colquhoun Grant†	Col	4 June 1811		
Thomas S. Beckwith†	Col	4 June 1811		
Robert O'Callaghan†	Col	1 January 1812		
John Keane†	Col	1 January 1812		
Colin Halkett†	Col	1 January 1812		
William Harvey#	Col	1 January 1812		
Richard Vivian†	Col	20 February 1812		
Benjamin D'Urban#	Col	4 June 1813		
Frederick de Arentsschildt†	Col	4 June 1813		
Loftus Otway#	Col	4 June 1813		
George Madden#	Col	4 June 1813		

Trivia: *The highest-ranking officer commanding the Royal Engineers in 1808 was a regimental captain and brevet major, Richard Fletcher. Fletcher was again appointed to command the Royal Engineers with the field army in 1809, now as a local lieutenant colonel in Portugal and Spain. He was promoted to regimental lieutenant colonel in June 1809. He commanded until his death in August 1813 and Lieutenant Colonel Howard Elphinstone was appointed to succeed him. Neither a general officer nor a regimental colonel of Royal Engineers ever served in the Peninsula.*

Officer seniority – Martinique 1809

While the war in the Peninsula carried on, the British decided to capture the French colonies in the West Indies. This was to assist with protecting the supply line from its own colonies in the West Indies by reducing the French naval and privateer bases there. The island of Martinique was one of the bases selected for capture. It had been previously taken in 1794 and returned to France at the Peace of Amiens 1802. The expedition was commanded by Lieutenant General George Beckwith, commander-in-chief in the West Indies. The force sailed on 28 January 1809 and landed on Martinique 30/31 January. It advanced on 1 February and fighting began on 2 February. The force took Fort Edward on 8 February with St Pierre capitulating on 9 February. Fighting continued on 10 and 11 February. The British bombarded Bouille Redoubt and Fort Desaix from 19–24 February. The island surrendered on 24 February and the British took possession beginning on 26 February. The three French eagles of the 82nd Line and one of the 26th Line were surrendered to the British.

Trivia: Some of the generals on the staff of this army would become well known in the Peninsular War.

Table 2.10 Officer seniority – Martinique 1809

Name	Rank	Date of rank	Command or position
George Beckwith	LG	30 October 1805	Commander of the force
George Prevost‡	MG	1 January 1805	1st Division
Frederick Maitland	MG	30 October 1805	2nd Division
Albert Gledstanes*	Col	25 September 1803	QMG
Daniel Hoghton*§	Col	1 January 1805	1st Brigade, 1st Division
Charles Colville*	Col	1 January 1805	2nd Brigade, 1st Division
Charles Shipley*	Col	13 July 1805	Commander, RE
Robert Nicholson*	Col	30 October 1805	Reserve Brigade, 1st Division
George Ramsay*	Col	30 October 1805	AG
Edward Stehelin*	Col	1 February 1808	Commander, RA
Edward Barnes	LCol	1 January 1800	3rd Brigade, 2nd Division
Phineas Riall	LCol	1 January 1800	4th Brigade, 2nd Division
John McNair	LCol	1 August 1804	5th Brigade, 2nd Division

‡ Serving with local rank of lieutenant general commanding Nova Scotia 16 January 1808.
§ Serving on the staff of Nova Scotia.

Trivia: Lieutenant General Prevost and a fusilier brigade commanded by Brigadier General Hoghton joined the army in the West Indies from the garrison of Nova Scotia. The brigade originally consisted of the 1/7th Fusiliers, 1/8th Foot and 1/23rd Fusiliers.

Officer seniority – Bay of Naples 1809
In 1809 Britain allied itself with Austria in another coalition against France. A diversionary operation in the Mediterranean to assist the Austrians was decided upon by Lieutenant General John Stuart (Count of Maida in peerage of Sicily) commanding in Sicily and Rear-Admiral George Martin commanding the Royal Navy on the station. Any thoughts of operating in north Italy with the Austrians were dashed by the news of the capture of Vienna (13 May) by the French and the retreat of the Archduke Charles. It was then decided that the force would threaten Naples and draw French/Neapolitan troops away from north Italy. After much vacillation the best idea was to capture the islands of Ischia and Procida in the Bay of Naples.

The expedition was commanded by Lieutenant General John Stuart. A brigade of Sicilians, under the command of Brigadier Marquis Vito Nunziantes, joined the British. Another force of Sicilians under Lieutenant General Emanuel de Bourcard was to also co-operate with it. The expedition sailed on 11 June, arrived off the coast of Calabria by 15 June and off Ischia on 24 June, landing the next day. Ischia was taken that same day, but the enemy forces withdrew into the castle and were besieged until they finally capitulated on 30 June. The island of Procida was offered the chance to surrender on 25 June and did so by capitulation on 26 June. At the same time, enemy lines opposite Messina were taken by the British but not held. A British attempt (13–28 June) to take the castle of Scylla on the mainland was a failure. Lieutenant General Stuart was informed by the British naval commander-in-chief in the Mediterranean, Vice-Admiral Cuthbert, Lord Collingwood, that he could not guarantee the supply and protection of these islands if the French Toulon fleet broke out of the blockade and portions of it sailed for Naples. Lieutenant General Stuart decided that both Ischia and Procida were to be evacuated by 22 July 1809. The expedition was back in Sicily by 26 July.

Table 2.11 Officer seniority – Bay of Naples 1809

Name	Rank	Date of rank	Command or position
John Stuart‡	MG	29 April 1802	Commander of the force
James, Lord Forbes	MG	29 April 1802	Second-in-command

Table 2.11   continued

Name	Rank	Date of rank	Command or position
Alexander Mackenzie§	MG	25 September 1803	On staff
Robert Macfarlane	MG	25 April 1808	Advance Corps
James Campbell	MG	25 April 1808	AG
William Lumley*	Col	29 April 1802	Advance Brigade
Augustus Honstedt*	Col	15 December 1804	KGL - Foreign Brigade
Henry de Hinüber¶	Col	9 July 1805	KGL Brigade
John Oswald*	Col	30 October 1805	Reserve Brigade
George Airey	Col	25 April 1808	Brigade
Haviland Smith	LCol	1 January 1800	Brigade
Henry Bunbury	LCol	31 December 1803	QMG
John Lemoine	LCol	1 June 1806	Commander, RA
Alexander Bryce	LCol	25 April 1808	Commander, RE

‡ Local lieutenant general in the Mediterranean, 11 February 1808.
§ Ordered back to take chief command in Sicily.
¶ Acting as a brigadier with the force, but was not placed upon the staff in Sicily.

Officer seniority – Walcheren 1809

In July 1809 the British decided to close the mouth of the Scheldt river in order to neutralise the port of Antwerp and prevent its use as a naval base against Britain. They also hoped to capture or destroy the French fleet stationed there. For this purpose an army larger than the one deployed in Portugal at this time was assembled, consisting of some 40,000 men. The command of the expedition was given to Lieutenant General John Pitt, Earl of Chatham. He was replaced in September by Lieutenant General Eyre Coote once it was decide to garrison the island of Walcheren. In October Coote was in turn replaced by Lieutenant General George Don. The expedition began with a landing on Walcheren in late July. The only success was the capture of Flushing on 16 August. Unfortunately for the British, an outbreak of 'Walcheren fever' caused more casualties than the fighting and led to the expedition stalling before an attempt was made to try to capture Antwerp. The expedition ended with the final evacuation of the garrison forces in December.

> **Trivia:** Many of the British generals who served in the Walcheren expedition would serve with distinction in the Peninsula.

Table 2.12   Officer seniority – Walcheren 1809

Name	Rank	Date of rank	Command or position
John, Earl of Chatham	LG	29 April 1802	Commander of the force
Eyre Coote	LG	1 January 1805	Second-in-command
George Don	LG	1 January 1805	Commander of the garrison
John Cradock‡	LG	1 January 1805	1st Division
James, Earl of Rosslyn	LG	1 January 1805	Light Division
George, Lord Huntly	LG	25 April 1808	2nd Division
Thomas Grosvenor	LG	25 April 1808	3rd Division
John Hope	LG	25 April 1808	Reserve Division
Alexander Mackenzie Fraser	LG	25 April 1808	4th Division
Henry, Lord Paget	LG	25 April 1808	5th Division
Robert Brownrigg	LG	25 April 1808	QMG
George Moncrieffe§	MG	25 September 1803	Garrison Brigade
Thomas Graham¶	MG	25 September 1803	1st Division
Charles, Baron Linsingen	MG	18 August 1804	Cavalry Brigade
George, Earl of Dalhousie	MG	25 April 1808	Brigade
William Dyott	MG	25 April 1808	Brigade
James Leith	MG	25 April 1808	Brigade
Thomas Picton	MG	25 April 1808	Brigade
William Erskine	MG	25 April 1808	Brigade
William Stewart	MG	25 April 1808	Light Brigade
William Houston*	Col	29 April 1802	Brigade
John Macleod*	Col	29 April 1802	Commander, RA
Moore Disney*	Col	29 April 1802	Guards Brigade
Henry Montresor*	Col	25 September 1803	Brigade
Wroth Palmer Acland*	Col	25 September 1803	Brigade
John Sontag*	Col	25 September 1803	Commandant of Middleburg
Digby Hamilton†‡	Col	5 November 1803	Commander, Waggon Train

‡ Although originally appointed to the army, Cradock could not return from Gibraltar in time to serve.
§ Arrived in October.
¶ In temporary command.
†‡ Temporary rank in the army while commanding the royal waggon train.

Table 2.12 continued

Name	Rank	Date of rank	Command or position
Charles, Baron Alten*	Col	22 December 1804	KGL Light Brigade
Francis, Baron Rottenburg*	Col	1 January 1805	Light Brigade
Gore Browne*	Col	1 January 1805	Brigade
Thomas Mahon†	Col	30 October 1805	Cavalry Brigade
William Fyers†	Col	1 July 1806	Commander, RE
Andrew Hay†‡	Col	25 April 1808	Brigade
Robert Long†	Col	25 April 1808	AG

‡ In temporary command as Major General Graham was commanding the 1st Division. He later commanded a brigade in the garrison.

Officer seniority – Guadeloupe 1810

While the war in the Peninsula carried on, the British continued their campaign to capture the French colonies in the West Indies. The goal was to protect the supply lines from their own colonies in the West Indies by reducing the French naval and privateer bases there. The island of Guadeloupe was another of the bases selected for capture. It had been previously taken in 1794 and returned to France at the Peace of Amiens 1802. The expedition was commanded by Lieutenant General George Beckwith, commander-in-chief in the West Indies. The British force sailed from Martinique on 22 and 26 January and landed on Guadeloupe 28 January. It advanced against the French forces beginning on 29 January until 4 February. There was some heavy fighting at times. The island surrendered on 5 February and it was ratified on 6 February. The island of St Martin's was included in the capitulation. The French eagle of the 66th Line was surrendered.

Table 2.13 Officer seniority – Guadeloupe 1810

Name	Rank	Date of rank	Command or position
George Beckwith	LG	30 October 1805	Commander of the force
Thomas Hislop	MG	25 October 1809	1st Division
Albert Gledstanes*	Col	25 September 1803	QMG
George Harcourt*‡	Col	25 September 1803	2nd Division
Fitzroy Maclean*	Col	25 September 1803	3rd Brigade, 1st Division
Charles Shipley*	Col	13 July 1805	Commander, RE
George Ramsay*	Col	30 October 1805	AG
Thomas Barrow*	Col	25 April 1808	2nd Brigade, 2nd Division

Name	Rank	Date of rank	Command or position
John Skinner*	Col	25 April 1808	4th Brigade, 1st Division
Charles Wale*	Col	25 April 1808	5th Brigade or Reserve
John R. Burton	Col	4 September 1809	Commander, RA
Phineas Riall§	LCol	1 January 1800	1st Brigade, 2nd Division

‡ In temporary command of the 2nd Division.
§ In temporary command of Harcourt's 1st Brigade.

Trivia: Guadeloupe was returned to France at the Peace of Paris 1814. During the 100 Days, it was again captured by British Forces and later returned to France, one last time.

Officer seniority – Bourbon 1810

The French islands in the Indian Ocean had long been used as bases for the French navy and privateers threatening the trade routes to India and the East. Their capture became a priority for the government of India. The British Governor General of India, Gilbert Eliot, 1st Earl of Minto, ordered an expedition against the island of Bourbon (also known as Île Bonaparté and now Réunion). Command of the expedition was given to Lieutenant Colonel Henry S. Keating. The troops were gathered from the British army in India in the Madras and Bombay Presidencies. The expedition set sail on 8 May 1810, arriving at Roderigues Island on 20 June. From there it sailed for Bourbon on 3 July and arrived on 6 July. It landed the next day and attacked St Denis, the capital, on 8 July. The French then asked for terms of surrender. The town and island capitulated the same day. The capital was occupied on 9 July. Some of the officers and troops which had served here would go to join the expedition against Mauritius.

Trivia: Although a private army of the Honourable East India Company (HEIC), the troops of the Bengal, Madras and Bombay Presidencies could be used by the British government in its campaigns. Officers of the HEIC's army always ranked under the king's officers of equal rank and seniority date. To allow company officers to command their juniors in the king's army, however, HEIC officers were granted local rank, of the same rank they held in the HEIC's army, but only in the king's army in the East Indies. This gave them rank in the British army. Officers of the HEIC's army are noted.

Table 2.14 Officer seniority – Bourbon 1810

Name	Rank	Date of rank	Command or position
Henry S. Keating‡	LCol	1 August 1804	Commander of the force
Hastings Fraser	LCol	7 September 1804	1st Brigade
Edward Drummond	LCol	29 December 1804	2nd Brigade
William Macleod	LCol	12 January 1805	3rd Brigade
John Campbell	LCol	6 August 1807	4th Brigade
Joseph M. Vernon§	Maj	25 July 1805	DQMG
John Taynton§	Maj	19 July 1809	Commander, Artillery
Edward Parkinson	Capt	7 March 1805	DAG
John Blakiston§	Lieut	1 January 1806	Commander, Engineers

‡ Serving in the Bombay Presidency.
§ On the Madras establishment, HEIC.

Trivia: The unique fact about this expedition is that no officer ranking higher than lieutenant colonel served in it. Seniority dictated the appointments for the expedition.

Officer seniority – Mauritius 1810

Having easily captured the Île Bourbon in July 1810, the Governor General of India then ordered the capture of Mauritius. Command of the expedition against Mauritius was given to Lieutenant General John Abercromby commanding the Bombay Presidency. The troops were gathered from the British army in India in the Bengal, Madras and Bombay Presidencies. Some of the officers and troops that had served at the capture of Bourbon also joined the expedition. Officers of the HEIC's army are noted. Prior to the arrival of the army, the Royal Navy attempted to take the French ships in the harbour of Grand Port. They landed and captured Île de la Passe on 13 August securing the mouth of the harbour; the attempt to seize the harbour itself on the 26th ended in disaster, however, and four British ships were destroyed or captured. This gave local superiority to the French and they captured the expedition commander's ship, HMS *Ceylon*, on 17 September. The next morning the ship was recaptured. The Madras contingent began to embark on 17 September and sailed by the 24th. It rendezvoused with the Bombay contingent on 6 November, the Bengal contingent arrived on the 21st and on the 29th they reached Mauritius and landed the same day. It then advanced on Port Louis. Fighting occurred on 30 November and 1 December as the British advanced. The French then asked for terms of surrender on 2 December with the island capitulating on 3 December.

Table 2.15 Officer seniority – Mauritius 1810

Name	Rank	Date of rank	Command or position
John Abercromby‡	MG	30 October 1805	Commander of the force
Henry Warde§	MG	25 April 1808	Second-in-command
John Picton¶	LCol	1 January 1801	1st Brigade
Samuel Gibbs¶	LCol	25 December 1801	2nd Brigade
William Nicholson§	LCol	26 May 1803	DAG
Henry S. Keating	LCol	1 August 1804	Reserve Brigade
Robert Kelso	LCol	1 January 1805	3rd Brigade
William Macleod	LCol	12 January 1805	4th Brigade
Lionel Smith	LCol	6 June 1805	5th Brigade
James Caldwell‡‡	Maj	1 January 1806	Commander, Engineers
John Johnson§§	Maj	5 May 1808	DQMG
John Taynton‡‡	Maj	19 July 1809	Commander, Artillery

‡ Local lieutenant general Bombay Presidency, 19 March 1810.
§ On the staff of the Madras Presidency.
¶ Promoted brevet colonel 25 July 1810.
‡‡ On the Madras establishment, HEIC.
§§ On the staff of the Bengal Presidency.

Trivia: John Picton and Samuel Gibbs served in the campaign as lieutenant colonels, as news of their promotion to brevet colonel in the army was not received in India until later.

Officer seniority – Java 1811

The capture of the Dutch held island of Java had long attracted the interest of the government of India. With the capture of the French-held islands in the Indian Ocean finally ending the French naval and privateer threat, the Governor General of India ordered an expedition against Java. Command was given to Lieutenant General Samuel Auchmuty, who commanded the Madras Presidency. The troops were gathered from the British army in India in the Bengal, Madras and Bombay Presidencies. Officers of the HEIC's army are noted. The expedition sailed in late April 1811, landed on 4 August and took Batavia, the capital of Java, on the 8th. On the 11th the Dutch were driven from Weltewreeden. The British won a battle at Cornelis on 26 August and another near Samarang on 16 September. The Dutch surrendered the island on 18 September.

Trivia: William Eden, George Wood and Patrick A. Agnew all served in the early stages of the campaign as colonels and Alexander Adams as a lieutenant colonel. News of their promotion to higher army rank did not arrived in India until sometime later.

Table 2.16 Officer seniority – Java 1811

Name	Rank	Date of rank	Command or position
Samuel Auchmuty‡	MG	25 April 1808	Commander of the force
Frederick Wetherall	MG	25 October 1809	Division
William Eden§	Col	25 April 1808	QMG
George Wood¶	Col	25 April 1808	Reserve Brigade
Patrick A. Agnew‡‡	Col	25 April 1808	AG
Robert Rollo Gillespie	Col	25 October 1809	Advance brigade
Samuel Gibbs	Col	25 July 1810	Right Brigade
Alexander Adams§§	LCol	7 April 1802	Left Brigade
Colin Mackenzie¶¶	LCol	25 October 1809	Commander, Engineers
Alexander Caldwell**	Major	15 May 1807	Commander, Artillery

‡ Local lieutenant general, Madras Presidency 19 March 1810.
§ Promoted to major general 4 June 1811
¶ On the Bengal Establishment HEIC. Promoted to major general 4 June 1811.
‡‡ On the Madras Establishment HEIC. Promoted to major general 4 June 1811.
§§ Promoted to brevet colonel 4 June 1811.
¶¶ On the Madras Establishment HEIC.
** On the Bengal Establishment HEIC.

Officer seniority in North America during the War of 1812
While Britain was fighting the war against Napoleon, she came into conflict with the United States of America. This was mainly due to Britain's action of enforcing the naval blockade of Napoleonic Europe and its policy of stopping American ships and the impressment of British subjects serving on these ships into the Royal Navy. War was declared by the United States on 18 June 1812. The war was ended by the Treaty of Ghent, signed on 24 December 1814 and ratified by Great Britain on the 28th. The United States did not ratify it until 17 February 1815. The treaty came into effect on 18 February. The war was mainly fought in Upper Canada (now Ontario) on the Niagara Peninsula and along the Great Lakes frontier. There were a number of heavily fought battles. Although not on the scale of European battlefields, they were large for North America at the time. While Britain was more successful defending Canada against invasion, it was less so when it invaded the United States. In the end, the peace treaty restored everything to *status quo ante bellum* (the situation before the war).

For the locations, Canada includes Upper and Lower Canada, while Nova Scotia includes New Brunswick, Cape Breton Island and Newfoundland and lastly America refers to the United States of America.

Table 2.17 Officer seniority in North America during the War of 1812

Name	Rank	Date of rank	Command or position
George Prevost	LG	4 June 1811	Governor General and Captain General, Canada
John Sherbrooke	LG	4 June 1811	Lt Governor, Nova Scotia
Gordon Drummond	LG	4 June 1811	Lt Governor, Canada
Francis Moore	MG	25 April 1808	On Staff, Newfoundland
Nicholas Nepean	MG	25 July 1810	On Staff, Cape Breton
Francis, Baron de Rottenburg	MG	25 July 1810	Acting Lt Governor, Canada
Isaac Brock	MG	4 June 1811	Acting Lt Governor, Canada
George Glasgow	MG	4 June 1811	RA, Canada
Thomas Saumarez	MG	4 June 1811	On Staff, Nova Scotia
Roger Sheaffe	MG	4 June 1811	Acting Lieutenant Governor, Canada
Richard Stovin	MG	4 June 1811	On Staff, Canada
George Murray‡	MG	1 January 1812	Commander, Canada
James Kempt	MG	1 January 1812	On Staff, Canada
George S. Smyth	MG	1 January 1812	On Staff, New Brunswick
Edward Pakenham	MG	1 January 1812	Commander, America
Henry Conran	MG	1 January 1812	On Staff, Canada
Gerard Gosselin	MG	4 June 1813	On Staff, Canada and Nova Scotia
Frederick Robinson	MG	4 June 1813	Brigade, Canada
Charles Campbell	MG	4 June 1813	On Staff, Newfoundland
Duncan Darroch§	MG	4 June 1813	On Staff, Canada and Nova Scotia
Phineas Riall	MG	4 June 1813	On Staff, Canada
John Vincent¶	MG	4 June 1813	On Staff, Canada
Henry Procter¶	MG	4 June 1813	On Staff, Canada
Thomas Brisbane	MG	4 June 1813	Brigade, Canada
Hugh Swayne‡‡	MG	4 June 1813	On Staff, Cape Breton
Robert Ross	MG	4 June 1813	Commander, America
Louis de Watteville	MG	4 June 1813	On Staff, Canada
John Lambert	MG	4 June 1813	Brigade, America

‡ Local lieutenant general North America 17 December 1814.
§ Colonel 25 July 1810 and brigadier general on the staff 8 October 1812.
¶ Colonel 25 July 1810 and local brigadier general 8 February 1813.
‡‡ Local lieutenant general 19 December 1814.

Table 2.17 continued

Name	Rank	Date of rank	Command or position
Manley Power	MG	4 June 1813	Brigade, Canada and America
Samuel Gibbs	MG	4 June 1813	Brigade, America
Archibald Stewart†‡	MG	4 June 1814	Brigade, Canada
Edward Baynes§	MG	4 June 1814	AG, Canada
Robert Young†‡	MG	4 June 1814	Brigade, Canada
Thomas S. Beckwith§	MG	4 June 1814	QMG, Canada
John Keane	MG	4 June 1814	Brigade, America
Edward Macdonnell¶	Col	25 July 1810	QMG, Canada
Lewis Grant†	Col	4 June 1813	Brigade, Canada
John Cameron†	Col	4 June 1813	Brigade, Canada
Ralph H. Bruyeres§§	LCol	1 July 1806	RE, Canada
Andrew Pilkington	LCol	2 November 1809	DAG, Nova Scotia
Joseph W. Morrison	LCol	20 November 1809	On Staff, Canada
Alexander Dickson	LCol	27 April 1812	RA, America
John Fox Burgoyne	LCol	27 April 1812	RE, America
Philip Hughes	LCol	14 May 1812	RE, Canada
Frederick Stovin	LCol	26 August 1813	DAG, America
John Bell	LCol	12 April 1814	DQMG, America
Alexander Ligertwood	Maj	25 October 1810	DQMG, Nova Scotia

‡ Colonel 4 June 1811. Left Canada upon promotion to major general.
§ Colonel 4 June 1811.
¶ Served only as a colonel. Died 30 October 1812. Would have been promoted major general 4 June 1813 with seniority after Phineas Riall and before John Vincent in the army list.
§§ Local colonel 1 March 1813.

Officer seniority – The Netherlands 1813–14

With the defeat of Napoleon in central Europe in 1813, many of the countries annexed by France rose in revolt, including Belgium and the Netherlands. The British sent a force to assist them in November and December 1813. The command of the force was given to Lieutenant General Thomas Graham. It comprised the British troops formerly garrisoning Stralsund in Swedish Pomerania, as well as troops available in Great Britain. The force won engagements at Merxem on 13 January 1814 and again on 2 February but failed disastrously at the night assault on Bergen-op-Zoom 8/9 March. It then participated in an Allied blockade and siege of Antwerp, taking Fort Lillo on 21 March. This was followed by an armistice. Antwerp was occupied by the British on 5 May as part of the terms of the Convention of Paris, which was signed on 23 April.

Trivia: This force remained in the Netherlands and formed the base of the Duke of Wellington's army for the Campaign in 1815

Table 2.18 Officer seniority – The Netherlands 1813–14

Name	Rank	Date of rank	Command or position
Thomas Graham‡	LG	25 July 1810	Commander of the force
Ronald Ferguson	LG	4 June 1813	Second-in-command
George Cooke	MG	4 June 1811	Division
William Eden	MG	4 June 1811	Brigade
Kenneth Mackenzie	MG	4 June 1811	Division
John B. Skerrett	MG	4 June 1813	Brigade
Samuel Gibbs	MG	4 June 1813	Brigade
Herbert Taylor	MG	4 June 1813	Brigade
Arthur Gore*	Col	4 June 1811	Brigade
John, Lord Proby*	Col	1 January 1812	Guards Brigade
Colin Halkett*	Col	1 January 1812	Brigade
George A. Wood	LCol	1 February 1808	Commander, RA
James Carmichael Smyth	LCol	20 October 1813	Commander, RE
Archibald Macdonald	LCol	25 November 1813	DAG
Frederick William Trench	LCol	25 November 1813	DQMG

‡ Local general in Holland and adjacent countries 7 December 1813. Raised in the peerage as Baron Lynedoch of Balgowan 3 May 1814.

Officer seniority – Genoa 1814

In February 1814 Lieutenant General Lord William Bentinck, the British commander-in-chief in Sicily, decided to land British led forces on the mainland of Italy and help liberate it from the French. To do this, he assembled an army from the garrison of Sicily and recalled Sicilian forces from the east coast of Spain. He commanded the expedition. A brigade of Sicilians commanded by Brigadier General Filippo Roth joined the British. Part of the expedition sailed from Palermo on 28 February and landed at Leghorn on 9 March 1814. It slowly advanced on Lucca to join a second force which would land in the Gulf of Spezia on the 29th.

Fort Santa Croce was taken by storm on the 24th, Spezia was occupied on the 27th, and Fort Santa Maria capitulated on the 30th. Hearing that Genoa was lightly defended, Lord William Bentinck advanced on that city fighting the French at Sestri on 7 and 8 April and at Sturla on the 12th. The British attacked the French lines at Genoa on 17 April and drove them back. They were assisted by the Royal Navy and Royal Marines under Captain Josias Rowley who attacked from the sea side. The British then prepared to bombard the city when the mayor and the bishop requested that they suspend operations. Bentinck refused and demanded that the city capitulate. The city was close to revolt. The French commander of the garrison agreed to a convention on 18 April with the British occupying part of the city on the 19th and the remainder of the city on the 21st. Genoa was evacuated by the British in December 1814.

Trivia: The announcement of Major Thomas Kenah's promotion to be Deputy AG in Sicily with rank of lieutenant colonel in the army, was not published in the London Gazette until 19 April. Kenah still signed himself as a major in April 1814. As a major, Kenah with date of rank of 5 November 1812, was junior to Major Reade.

Table 2.19 Officer seniority – Genoa 1814

Name	Rank	Date of rank	Command or position
Lord William Bentinck‡	LG	4 June 1811	Commander of the force
Robert Macfarlane	LG	4 June 1813	Division
Henry Montresor	MG	25 July 1810	Division
Augustus Honstedt	MG	25 July 1810	Brigade
Adolphus, Baron Barsse§	MG	25 July 1810	Brigade
Gerard Gosselin	MG	4 June 1813	Brigade
Henry Bruce	Col	1 January 1812	Brigade
William Paterson	Col	4 June 1813	Brigade
John Lemoine	LCol	1 June 1806	Commander, RA
Thomas Kenah	LCol	27 December 1813	Acting DAG
Thomas Reade	Maj	3 January 1811	Acting DQMG
William Tylden	Capt	15 April 1812	Commander, RE

‡ Local lieutenant general in the Mediterranean since 1 March 1811.
§ Appointed commandant of Leghorn.

Officer seniority – The Netherlands 1815
With the defeat and abdication of Napoleon in April 1814, the Allies met at a Congress in Vienna to redraw the map of Europe and settle the land claims of the major powers and also to restore the lands of the rulers who had been deposed by Napoleon during the wars. One such restored country was Holland. At a meeting of sovereigns in London it was agreed that Holland would be expanded to include the former Austrian Province of Belgium to create the new Kingdom of the Netherlands. The son of Prince William V, the last Stadtholder, was crowned King William I.[5] The British stationed a subsidiary army within its borders to ensure its new boundaries while negotiations were continuing at the Congress of Vienna. This army consisted of the force which had been commanded by General Thomas Graham and had operated against Antwerp in 1813 and 1814. It was joined by the King's German Legion, lately returned from the Peninsular War, and the army of Hanover, newly raised in 1813 and 1814, which had also operated in Holland and Belgium in 1814. The army was commanded by General William, the Hereditary Prince of Orange, son of King William I. It was stationed in Flanders. On 28 March 1815 this army was placed under the command of Field Marshal the Duke of Wellington and in a General Order of 11 April 1815 merged with the Netherlands forces to form the army which would fight at Waterloo. The following table show the seniority of the officers for 8 March 1815.

Table 2.20 Officer seniority – The Netherlands March 1815

Name	Rank	Date of rank	Command or position
William, Prince of Orange	Gen	25 July 1814	Commander of the force
Henry Clinton	LG	4 June 1814	Second-in-command
Victor, Baron Alten	MG	25 July 1810	Cavalry Commander, KGL
Henry de Hinüber	MG	4 June 1811	Infantry Commander, KGL
John Vandeleur	MG	4 June 1811	2nd Division
George Cooke	MG	4 June 1811	1st Division
Kenneth Mackenzie	MG	4 June 1811	2nd Brigade, 1st Division
William de Dornberg	MG	1 January 1812	1st Cavalry Brigade KGL
Edward Barnes	MG	4 June 1813	AG
Peregrine Maitland	MG	4 June 1814	Guards Brigade, 1st Division
Colin Halkett	MG	4 June 1814	3rd Brigade, 2nd Division

5 Glover, *The Napoleonic Wars*, p. 208.

Table 2.20 continued

Name	Rank	Date of rank	Command or position
Hudson Lowe	MG	4 June 1814	QMG
Frederick de Arentsschildt	Col	4 June 1813	2nd Cavalry Brigade KGL
Christian, Baron Ompteda	Col	4 June 1813	2nd Infantry Brigade KGL
Charles du Plat	Col	4 June 1813	3rd Infantry Brigade KGL
William Harris	Col	4 June 1814	1st Brigade, 2nd Division
George A. Wood	Col	4 June 1814	Commander, RA
Louis, Baron Bussche	LCol	29 March 1809	1st Infantry Brigade KGL
James Carmichael Smyth	LCol	20 October 1813	Commander, RE

Officer seniority – the campaign of 1815

Britain had to field an army, once again, in 1815 after the return of Napoleon to the throne of France. This army was organised by combining the subsidiary army garrisoning the Netherlands, which was commanded by General the Prince of Orange, with reinforcements sent out from Britain or returned from service in North America. This larger army was formed in a General Order of 11 April 1815. Command was now given to Field Marshal the Duke of Wellington. It fought at Quatre Bras on 16 June, the retreat on the 17th and at Waterloo on the 18th, where the French eagles of the 45th Line and 105th Line were captured. It was involved in the sieges of French fortresses, such as the taking of Cambrai and Peronne, and at the capitulation of Paris on 3 July. Reinforcements for the army continued to arrive until August 1815. It was disbanded in a General Order of 30 November 1815. This order also created the British contingent of the Army of Occupation in France 1815–18. The Duke of Wellington was chosen to command this occupation army.

The tables list only those officers who served under the Duke of Wellington in Flanders and France. It does not include those who either served in the Mediterranean theatre or who landed at Marseilles

Table 2.21 Officer seniority – the campaign of 1815

Name	Rank	Date of rank	Command or position
Arthur, Duke of Wellington	FM	21 June 1813	Commander of the force
William, Prince of Orange‡	Gen	25 July 1814	Corps Commander

Name	Rank	Date of rank	Command or position
Henry, Earl of Uxbridge	LG	25 April 1808	Cavalry Commander
Stapleton, Lord Combermere	LG	1 January 1812	Cavalry Commander
Rowland, Lord Hill	LG	1 January 1812	Corps Commander
Thomas Picton	LG	4 June 1813	5th Division
Galbraith Lowry Cole	LG	4 June 1813	6th Division
Henry Clinton	LG	4 June 1814	2nd Division
Victor, Baron Alten§	MG	25 July 1810	Hanoverian Cavalry
Charles, Baron Alten¶	MG	25 July 1810	3rd Division
Charles Colville‡‡	MG	25 July 1810	4th Division
Kenneth Howard§§	MG	25 July 1810	1st Division
Henry de Hinüber	MG	4 June 1811	4th Division
John Vandeleur	MG	4 June 1811	4th Cavalry Brigade
George Cooke	MG	4 June 1811	1st Division
Kenneth Mackenzie	MG	4 June 1811	7th Brigade
George Murray**	MG	1 January 1812	QMG
James Kempt	MG	1 January 1812	8th Brigade, 5th Division
William de Dornberg	MG	1 January 1812	3rd Cavalry Brigade
Edward Barnes	MG	4 June 1813	AG
William Ponsonby	MG	4 June 1813	2nd Cavalry Brigade
John Byng	MG	4 June 1813	2nd Brigade, 1st Division
Thomas Brisbane	MG	4 June 1813	7th Division
Denis Pack	MG	4 June 1813	9th Brigade, 5th Division
Lord Edward Somerset	MG	4 June 1813	1st Cavalry Brigade
Thomas Bradford	MG	4 June 1813	3rd Division
John Lambert	MG	4 June 1813	10th Brigade, 6th Division
Manley Power	MG	4 June 1813	11th Brigade, 6th Division
Colquhoun Grant	MG	4 June 1814	5th Cavalry Brigade

‡General in Netherlands Service.
§ Serving in the Hanoverian Army.
¶ Serving as a lieutenant general in Hanoverian Army.
‡‡ Local lieutenant general 4 April 1815.
§§ Local lieutenant general 6 July 1815.
** Local lieutenant general 25 June 1815.

Table 2.21 continued

Name	Rank	Date of rank	Command or position
James Lyon‡	MG	4 June 1814	6th Hanoverian Brigade, 4th Division
Peregrine Maitland	MG	4 June 1814	1st Brigade, 1st Division
George Johnstone	MG	4 June 1814	6th Brigade, 4th Division
Robert O'Callaghan	MG	4 June 1814	13th Brigade, 7th Division
John Keane	MG	4 June 1814	8th Brigade, 5th Division
Lord George Beresford	MG	4 June 1814	8th Cavalry Brigade
Colin Halkett	MG	4 June 1814	5th Brigade, 3rd Division
Hudson Lowe	MG	4 June 1814	QMG
Frederick Adam	MG	4 June 1814	3rd Brigade, 2nd Division
Richard Vivian	MG	4 June 1814	6th Cavalry Brigade
John Elley†	Col	7 March 1813	DAG
Alexander Wallace†	Col	4 June 1813	14th Brigade, 7th Division
Charles Belson†	Col	4 June 1813	5th Brigade, 3rd Division
William de Lancey†	Col	4 June 1813	DQMG
Frederick de Arentsschildt†	Col	4 June 1813	7th Cavalry Brigade
Christian, Baron Ompteda†	Col	4 June 1813	2nd KGL Brigade, 3rd Division
Thomas Reynell†	Col	4 June 1813	3rd Brigade, 2nd Division
Charles Greville†	Col	4 June 1813	12th Brigade, 2nd Division
Charles du Plat†	Col	4 June 1813	1st KGL Brigade, 2nd Division
Hugh Mitchell†	Col	4 June 1813	4th Brigade, 4th Division
Andrew Barnard†	Col	4 June 1814	Commandant of Paris
David Walker†	Col	4 June 1814	15th Brigade, 7th Division
John Cameron†	Col	4 June 1814	16th Brigade, 3rd Division
George A. Wood†	Col	4 June 1814	Commander, RA
Louis, Baron Bussche	LCol	29 March 1809	KGL Brigade, 1st Division
Rudolph Bodecker‡	LCol	22 October 1810	1st KGL Brigade, 2nd Division
James Carmichael Smyth§	LCol	20 October 1813	Commander, RE

‡ Also served with Hanoverian army.
§ Promoted colonel in the army and ADC to the Prince Regent 29 June 1815.

Table 2.22 Officer seniority in the British contingent of the army of occupation 1815

Name	Rank	Date of rank	Command or position
Arthur, Duke of Wellington	FM	21 June 1813	Commander of the force
Stapleton, Lord Combermere	LG	1 January 1812	Cavalry Commander
Rowland, Lord Hill	LG	1 January 1812	Infantry Commander
Galbraith Lowry Cole	LG	4 June 1813	1st Division
Henry Clinton	LG	4 June 1814	2nd Division
Charles Colville‡	MG	25 July 1810	3rd Division
George Murray§	MG	1 January 1812	QMG
James Kempt	MG	1 January 1812	7th Brigade, 1st Division
Edward Barnes	MG	4 June 1813	AG
Thomas Brisbane	MG	4 June 1813	5th Brigade, 3rd Division
Denis Pack	MG	4 June 1813	4th Brigade, 2nd Division
Lord Edward Somerset	MG	4 June 1813	1st Cavalry Brigade
Thomas Bradford	MG	4 June 1813	6th Brigade, 2nd Division
John Lambert	MG	4 June 1813	8th Brigade, 1st Division
Manley Power	MG	4 June 1813	2nd Brigade, 3rd Division
Colquhoun Grant	MG	4 June 1814	3rd Cavalry Brigade,
James Lyon¶	MG	4 June 1814	Infantry, Hanoverian Contingent
Peregrine Maitland	MG	4 June 1814	1st Guards Brigade, 1st Division
Robert O'Callaghan	MG	4 June 1814	3rd Brigade, 2nd Division
John Keane	MG	4 June 1814	9th Brigade, 3rd Division
Richard Vivian	MG	4 June 1814	2nd Cavalry Brigade
John Elley	Col	7 March 1813	DAG
George A. Wood	Col	4 June 1814	Commander, RA
James Carmichael Smyth	Col	29 June 1815	Commander, RE
Charles Broke	LCol	27 April 1812	DQMG

‡ Local lieutenant general 4 April 1815.
§ Local lieutenant general 25 June 1815 and chief-of-staff to the army of occupation.
¶ Serving with Hanoverian army.

Officer seniority – Guadeloupe 1815

During the 100 Days when Napoleon once again became emperor of the French, Charles, Comte de Linois, governor of Guadeloupe, declared for him. Even after Napoleon again abdicated on 22 June, the governor would not submit to King Louis XVIII of France. The commander-in-chief in the West Indies, Lieutenant General James Leith, decided to capture the island as the war in Europe also continued. It had been previously taken in 1794 and returned to France at the Peace of Amiens 1802 and taken again in 1810 and returned at the peace in 1814. It would prove to be an easy capture. Part of the British force sailed from Barbados on 31 July and arrived off Guadeloupe on 2 August. The other part sailed from Martinique and other islands. The whole force concentrated on the 7th and completed its landing on the 8th. It advanced against the French forces in two columns beginning on the 9th with only some light fighting, before gaining the heights of Morne Palmiste. That night the French asked for terms. The island surrendered on 10 August. It was once again returned to France at the peace in 1815.

> *Trivia:* This expedition marks one of the rare times, during the Napoleonic Wars, that officers of the Ordnance Corps commanded line regiments. MG Shipley was in the Royal Engineers and MG Stehelin was in the Royal Artillery. It was not the usual practice then in the British army for ordnance officers to command in the line.

Table 2.23 Officer seniority – Guadeloupe 1815

Name	Rank	Date of rank	Command or position
James Leith	LG	4 June 1813	Commander of the force
Charles Shipley	MG	4 June 1811	1st Brigade
Edward Stehelin	MG	4 June 1811	2nd Brigade
William Johnston	MG	1 January 1812	Commander, RE
John Murray‡	MG	4 June 1813	On Staff
Robert Douglass§	MG	4 June 1814	3rd Brigade
Samuel Popham	LCol	4 June 1811	DQMG
Sackville Berkeley	LCol	4 June 1811	DAG
William Cleeve	Major	4 June 1814	Commander, RA

‡ Arrived after expedition landed on Guadeloupe.
§ Adjutant general in the West Indies, he commanded a line brigade.

Chapter Three

The Regiment

The soul of the British army was its individual regiments. Almost everything associated with the army happened at regimental level. For the individual, the regiment *was* the army. Officers would be commissioned and promoted in the regiment, while men would be recruited into the regiment and remained with it until death or discharged. The officers and men strongly identified with their regiment and its achievements, distinctions, and uniforms were a source of pride for them.

In 1805 the highest total number of cavalry, foot guard and line regiments had almost been reached and few new line regiments were raised after that year (the 101st Foot was new in 1806 and the 102nd, 103rd and 104th Foot were all later formed by re-designating existing units). Instead of adding regiments, new battalions were formed as necessary. These were integrated into the regiment and adopted its distinctions, uniforms and traditions. The new battalions also took pride in their parent regiment's achievements as well. There were no permanent higher formations (divisions and corps) formed in the British army at the time. Brigades would be formed within the military districts, but the individual regiments were rotated in out and out of these districts as required for service elsewhere. In some instances, these brigades would go on active service but in other cases the regiments would be drawn from them to form new brigades. The only permanent brigades were the three brigades of Foot Guards formed in 1803. While the system appears haphazard in comparison with the Continental practice of permanent higher formations, it worked for the British army of the Napoleonic wars.

This chapter examines many of the individual components that were so integral to the regiment. Here you will find information on the locations of the regiments, their barracks, regimental colonels, battle honours, parts of the uniform that were unique to the regiment, regimental nicknames and regimental books.

Location of British units in 1805

With the Peace of Amiens in 1802, Britain began the process of disbanding its army. Many battalions raised during the war were disbanded along with émigré and foreign regiments in its service. When Britain declared war against France in May 1803, however, it also began to rebuild its army for home defence, as well as, still providing garrisons for its overseas empire. The year 1805 was when Britain faced its greatest threat of invasion, but it was also the year in which Britain went on the counter-attack against its enemies. The tables show the units in the army list for 1805, where they were located at the start of 1805 and where many were ordered on active service during 1805. For these tables, Britain includes Scotland.

Table 3.1   Location of cavalry regiments in 1805

Unit designation	Location	Ordered to
1st Life Guards	Britain	
2nd Life Guards	Britain	
Royal Horse Guards	Britain	
1st Dragoon Guards	Britain	
2nd Dragoon Guards	Ireland	
3rd Dragoon Guards	Ireland	
4th Dragoon Guards	Britain	
5th Dragoon Guards	Ireland	
6th Dragoon Guards	Britain	
7th Dragoon Guards	Britain	
1st Dragoons	Britain	
2nd Dragoons	Britain	
3rd Dragoons	Britain	
4th Dragoons	Britain	
6th Dragoons	Britain	
7th Light Dragoons	Britain	
8th Light Dragoons	India	
9th Light Dragoons	Britain	
10th Light Dragoons	Britain	
11th Light Dragoons	Britain	
12th Light Dragoons	Britain	
13th Light Dragoons	Britain	
14th Light Dragoons	Britain	
15th Light Dragoons	Britain	
16th Light Dragoons	Ireland	
17th Light Dragoons	Ireland	
18th Light Dragoons	Ireland	

The Regiment

Unit designation	Location	Ordered to
19th Light Dragoons	India	
20th Light Dragoons	Britain	Cape of Good Hope and Sicily
21st Light Dragoons	Britain	
22nd Light Dragoons	India	
23rd Light Dragoons	Ireland	
24th Light Dragoons	India	
25th Light Dragoons	India	

Trivia: *The 5th Dragoons was disbanded in 1799. The regiment had recruited some Irish rebels into its ranks in 1798 and after a plot to kill the officers had been discovered, it was decided to disband the regiment and leave its number unassigned. It would be 1858 before a new regiment would be raised and assigned the number five.*

Trivia: *Although officially numbered as the 2nd Foot Guards, that title was hardly ever used when referring to the Coldstream Foot Guards. Their motto,* Nulli secundus *(Second to none) is in answer to their being senior to the 1st Foot Guards by date of raising, but second in the army list when King Charles II was restored to the throne in 1660.*

Table 3.2 Location of foot regiments in 1805

Unit designation	Location	Ordered to
1st Foot Guards 1st Battalion	Britain	
1st Foot Guards 2nd Battalion	Britain	
1st Foot Guards 3rd Battalion	Britain	
Coldstream Foot Guards 1st Battalion	Britain	Hanover expedition
Coldstream Foot Guards 2nd Battalion	Britain	
3rd Foot Guards 1st Battalion	Britain	Hanover expedition
3rd Foot Guards 2nd Battalion	Britain	
1st Foot 1st Battalion	West Indies	
1st Foot 2nd Battalion	West Indies	
1st Foot 3rd Battalion	Britain	
1st Foot 4th Battalion	Britain	
2nd Foot	Gibraltar	
3rd Foot 1st Battalion	Ireland	Hanover expedition
3rd Foot 2nd Battalion	Britain	
4th Foot 1st Battalion	Britain	Hanover expedition

Table 3.2 continued

Unit designation	Location	Ordered to
4th Foot 2nd Battalion	Britain	
5th Foot 1st Battalion	Britain	Hanover expedition
5th Foot 2nd Battalion	Britain	
6th Foot 1st Battalion	Canada	
6th Foot 2nd Battalion	Britain	
7th Foot 1st Battalion	Bermuda	
7th Foot 2nd Battalion	Britain	
8th Foot 1st Battalion	Ireland	Hanover expedition
8th Foot 2nd Battalion	Britain	
9th Foot 1st Battalion	Ireland	Hanover expedition
9th Foot 2nd Battalion	Britain	
10th Foot 1st Battalion	Gibraltar	
10th Foot 2nd Battalion	Britain	
11th Foot	West Indies	
12th Foot	India	
13th Foot	Gibraltar	
14th Foot 1st Battalion	Britain	Hanover expedition
14th Foot 2nd Battalion	Britain	
15th Foot 1st Battalion	Britain	West Indies
15th Foot 2nd Battalion	Britain	
16th Foot	West Indies	
17th Foot	India	
18th Foot 1st Battalion	Britain	West Indies
18th Foot 2nd Battalion	Britain	
19th Foot	Ceylon	
20th Foot	Malta	Sicily
21st Foot 1st Battalion	Britain	
21st Foot 2nd Battalion	Britain	
22nd Foot	India	
23rd Foot 1st Battalion	Britain	Hanover expedition
23rd Foot 2nd Battalion	Britain	
24th Foot 1st Battalion	Ireland	Cape of Good Hope expedition
24th Foot 2nd Battalion	Britain	
25th Foot 1st Battalion	Ireland	
25th Foot 2nd Battalion	Britain	
26th Foot 1st Battalion	Ireland	Hanover expedition
26th Foot 2nd Battalion	Ireland	
27th Foot 1st Battalion	Malta	Sicily
27th Foot 2nd Battalion	Britain	Hanover expedition

Unit designation	Location	Ordered to
27th Foot 3rd Battalion	Britain	
28th Foot 1st Battalion	Ireland	Hanover expedition
28th Foot 2nd Battalion	Ireland	
29th Foot	Nova Scotia	
30th Foot 1st Battalion	Ireland	Hanover expedition
30th Foot 2nd Battalion	Ireland	
31st Foot 1st Battalion	Britain	
31st Foot 2nd Battalion	Britain	
32nd Foot 1st Battalion	Ireland	
32nd Foot 2nd Battalion	Britain	
33rd Foot	India	
34th Foot 1st Battalion	India	
34th Foot 2nd Battalion	Britain	Hanover expedition
35th Foot 1st Battalion	Malta	Sicily
35th Foot 2nd Battalion	Britain	
36th Foot 1st Battalion	Ireland	Hanover expedition
36th Foot 2nd Battalion	Ireland	
37th Foot	West Indies	
38th Foot 1st Battalion	Ireland	Cape of Good Hope expedition
38th Foot 2nd Battalion	Britain	
39th Foot 1st Battalion	Britain	Sicily
39th Foot 2nd Battalion	Britain	
40th Foot 1st Battalion	Britain	
40th Foot 2nd Battalion	Britain	
41st Foot	Canada	
42nd Foot 1st Battalion	Britain	Gibraltar
42nd Foot 2nd Battalion	Ireland	
43rd Foot 1st Battalion	Britain	
43rd Foot 2nd Battalion	Britain	
44th Foot 1st Battalion	Britain	Sicily
44th Foot 2nd Battalion	Britain	
45th Foot 1st Battalion	Ireland	
45th Foot 2nd Battalion	Britain	
46th Foot	West Indies	
47th Foot 1st Battalion	Ireland	
47th Foot 2nd Battalion	Britain	
48th Foot 1st Battalion	Britain	Gibraltar
48th Foot 2nd Battalion	Ireland	
49th Foot	Canada	
50th Foot 1st Battalion	Ireland	

Table 3.2 continued

Unit designation	Location	Ordered to
50th Foot 2nd Battalion	Ireland	
51st Foot 1st Battalion	India	
51st Foot 2nd Battalion	Britain	
52nd Foot 1st Battalion	Britain	
52nd Foot 2nd Battalion	Britain	
53rd Foot 1st Battalion	Ireland	India
53rd Foot 2nd Battalion	Britain	
54th Foot	Gibraltar	
55th Foot	Jamaica	
56th Foot 1st Battalion	India	
56th Foot 2nd Battalion	Britain	
57th Foot 1st Battalion	Gibraltar	
57th Foot 2nd Battalion	Britain	
58th Foot 1st Battalion	Britain	Sicily
58th Foot 2nd Battalion	Britain	
59th Foot 1st Battalion	Britain	Cape of Good Hope expedition
59th Foot 2nd Battalion	Britain	
60th Foot 1st Battalion	Jamaica	
60th Foot 2nd Battalion	West Indies	
60th Foot 3rd Battalion	West Indies	Britain
60th Foot 4th Battalion	Britain	
60th Foot 5th Battalion	Nova Scotia	Britain
60th Foot 6th Battalion	Jamaica	
61st Foot 1st Battalion	Malta	Sicily
61st Foot 2nd Battalion	Britain	
62nd Foot 1st Battalion	Ireland	
62nd Foot 2nd Battalion	Britain	
63rd Foot 1st Battalion	Ireland	
63rd Foot 2nd Battalion	Britain	
64th Foot	British Honduras	
65th Foot	India	
66th Foot 1st Battalion	Ceylon	
66th Foot 2nd Battalion	Ireland	
67th Foot 1st Battalion	Britain	India
67th Foot 2nd Battalion	Britain	
68th Foot	West Indies	
69th Foot 1st Battalion	Britain	India
69th Foot 2nd Battalion	Britain	
70th Foot	West Indies	

Unit designation	Location	Ordered to
71st Foot 1st Battalion	Ireland	Cape of Good Hope expedition
71st Foot 2nd Battalion	Britain	
72nd Foot 1st Battalion	Ireland	Cape of Good Hope expedition
72nd Foot 2nd Battalion	Britain	
73rd Foot 1st Battalion	India	
73rd Foot 2nd Battalion	Britain	
74th Foot	India	Britain
75th Foot	India	
76th Foot	India	
77th Foot	India	
78th Foot 1st Battalion	India	
78th Foot 2nd Battalion	Britain	Gibraltar
79th Foot 1st Battalion	Ireland	
79th Foot 2nd Battalion	Britain	
80th Foot	India	
81st Foot 1st Battalion	Britain	Sicily
81st Foot 2nd Battalion	Britain	
82nd Foot 1st Battalion	Ireland	
82nd Foot 2nd Battalion	Britain	
83rd Foot 1st Battalion	Ireland	Cape of Good Hope expedition
83rd Foot 2nd Battalion	Britain	
84th Foot	India	
85th Foot	Jamaica	
86th Foot	India	
87th Foot 1st Battalion	Britain	
87th Foot 2nd Battalion	Britain	
88th Foot 1st Battalion	Britain	
88th Foot 2nd Battalion	Britain	
89th Foot 1st Battalion	Ireland	Hanover expedition
89th Foot 2nd Battalion	Britain	
90th Foot 1st Battalion	Britain	West Indies
90th Foot 2nd Battalion	Britain	
91st Foot 1st Battalion	Britain	Hanover expedition
91st Foot 2nd Battalion	Britain	
92nd Foot 1st Battalion	Britain	
92nd Foot 2nd Battalion	Ireland	
93rd Foot	Ireland	Cape of Good Hope expedition

Table 3.2 continued

Unit designation	Location	Ordered to
94th Foot	India	
95th Foot 1st Battalion	Britain	Hanover expedition
95th Foot 2nd Battalion	Britain	
96th Foot 1st Battalion	Britain	West Indies
96th Foot 2nd Battalion	Britain	
97th Foot	Ireland	
98th Foot	Ireland	
99th Foot	Ireland	
100th Foot	Ireland	
Royal Staff Corps	Britain	
New South Wales Corps	Australia	
1st West India Regiment	West Indies	
2nd West India Regiment	West Indies	
3rd West India Regiment	West Indies	
4th West India Regiment	West Indies	
5th West India Regiment	West Indies	
6th West India Regiment	West Indies	
7th West India Regiment	West Indies	
8th West India Regiment	West Indies	
Royal African Corps	Goree, Africa	
1st Ceylon Regiment	Ceylon	
2nd Ceylon Regiment	Ceylon	
3rd Ceylon Regiment	Ceylon	

Table 3.3 Location of miscellaneous infantry units in 1805

Unit designation	Location	Ordered to
1st Garrison Battalion	Britain	To be disbanded February
2nd Garrison Battalion	Britain	To be disbanded February
3rd Garrison Battalion	Britain	To be disbanded February
4th Garrison Battalion	Britain	To be disbanded February
5th Garrison Battalion	Britain	To be disbanded February
6th Garrison Battalion	Britain	To be disbanded February
7th Garrison Battalion	Britain	To be disbanded February
8th Garrison Battalion	Ireland	To be disbanded February
9th Garrison Battalion	Ireland	To be disbanded February
10th Garrison Battalion	Britain	To be disbanded February
11th Garrison Battalion	Britain	To be disbanded February
12th Garrison Battalion	Britain	To be disbanded February
13th Garrison Battalion	Ireland	To be disbanded February

Unit designation	Location	Ordered to
14th Garrison Battalion	Britain	To be disbanded February
15th Garrison Battalion	Britain	To be disbanded February
16th Garrison Battalion	Ireland	To be disbanded February
1st Garrison Battalion (new February)	Britain	
2nd Garrison Battalion (new February)	Britain	
3rd Garrison Battalion (new February)	Britain	
1st Royal Veteran Battalion	Britain	Gibraltar
2nd Royal Veteran Battalion	Britain	
3rd Royal Veteran Battalion	Britain	
4th Royal Veteran Battalion	Britain	
5th Royal Veteran Battalion	Britain	
6th Royal Veteran Battalion	Britain	
7th Royal Veteran Battalion	Britain	
8th Royal Veteran Battalion	Britain	
9th Royal Veteran Battalion	Britain	
Royal Newfoundland Fencible Infantry	Nova Scotia	
New Brunswick Fencible Infantry	New Brunswick	
Nova Scotia Fencible Infantry	Nova Scotia	
Canadian Fencible Infantry	Canada	
Royal Manx Fencible Infantry	Britain	
1st European Garrison Company	Jamaica	
2nd European Garrison Company	Barbados	

Table 3.4 Location of foreign troops in British service in 1805

Unit designation	Location	Ordered To
de Meuron's Regiment	India	
de Roll's Regiment	Gibraltar	
de Watteville's Regiment	Malta	Sicily
Chasseurs Britanniques	Malta	Sicily
Dillon's Regiment	Malta	
York Light Infantry Volunteers	Barbados	
Royal Corsican Rangers	Malta	Sicily
Royal Regiment of Malta	Malta	

Table 3.5 Location of the King's German Legion in 1805

Unit designation	Location	Ordered to
1st KGL Dragoons	Britain	Hanover expedition
1st KGL Light Dragoons	Britain	Hanover expedition
2nd KGL Light Dragoons	Britain	Hanover expedition
3rd KGL Light Dragoons	Britain	Hanover expedition
1st KGL Light Battalion	Britain	Hanover expedition
2nd KGL Light Battalion	Britain	Hanover expedition
1st KGL Line Battalion	Britain	Hanover expedition
2nd KGL Line Battalion	Britain	Hanover expedition
3rd KGL Line Battalion	Britain	Hanover expedition
4th KGL Line Battalion	Britain	Hanover expedition
5th KGL Line Battalion	Britain	Hanover expedition

Location of British units in 1815

With the end of the Napoleonic Wars in early 1814, Britain began the process of reducing its army. Many war-raised battalions were disbanded along with foreign regiments in its service. But Britain was still at war with the United States of America and also had to provide garrisons for its overseas empire which had grown during the wars. When Napoleon once more became the emperor of the French and a new war began, Britain found itself stretched to provide for an immediate army on the continent. As a peace with the United States was only ratified in February 1815, many of its Peninsular battalions were still in North America and had to be recalled home. By the time the fighting ended on the Continent, Britain had sent most of its available army to France.

The tables show the units in the army list for 1815, where they were located at the start of 1815 and where many were ordered to serve during 1815. For table purposes Britain includes Scotland and Ireland.

Table 3.6 Location of cavalry regiments in 1815

Unit designation	Location	Ordered to
1st Life Guards	Britain	Flanders
2nd Life Guards	Britain	Flanders
Royal Horse Guards	Britain	Flanders
1st Dragoon Guards	Britain	Flanders
2nd Dragoon Guards	Britain	Flanders
3rd Dragoon Guards	Britain	Flanders
4th Dragoon Guards	Britain	
5th Dragoon Guards	Britain	

The Regiment

Unit designation	Location	Ordered to
6th Dragoon Guards	Britain	
7th Dragoon Guards	Britain	
1st Dragoons	Britain	Flanders
2nd Dragoons	Britain	Flanders
3rd Dragoons	Britain	Flanders
4th Dragoons	Britain	
6th Dragoons	Britain	Flanders
7th Light Dragoons	Britain	Flanders
8th Light Dragoons	India	
9th Light Dragoons	Britain	
10th Light Dragoons	Britain	Flanders
11th Light Dragoons	Britain	Flanders
12th Light Dragoons	Britain	Flanders
13th Light Dragoons	Britain	Flanders
14th Light Dragoons	North America	Britain
15th Light Dragoons	Britain	Flanders
16th Light Dragoons	Britain	Flanders
17th Light Dragoons	India	
18th Light Dragoons	Britain	Flanders
19th Light Dragoons	Canada	
20th Light Dragoons	Mediterranean	Britain
21st Light Dragoons	Cape Colony	
22nd Light Dragoons	India	
23rd Light Dragoons	Britain	Flanders
24th Light Dragoons	India	
25th Light Dragoons	India	
Staff Corps of Cavalry (new June)	Flanders	

Table 3.7 Location of foot regiments in 1815

Unit designation	Location	Ordered to
1st Foot Guards 1st Battalion	Britain	
1st Foot Guards 2nd Battalion	Flanders	
1st Foot Guards 3rd Battalion	Britain	Flanders
Coldstream Guards 1st Battalion	Britain	
Coldstream Guards 2nd Battalion	Flanders	
3rd Foot Guards 1st Battalion	Britain	
3rd Foot Guards 2nd Battalion	Flanders	
1st Foot 1st Battalion	Canada	
1st Foot 2nd Battalion	India	
1st Foot 3rd Battalion	Britain	Flanders

Table 3.7 continued

Unit designation	Location	Ordered to
1st Foot 4th Battalion	North America	Flanders
2nd Foot	Britain	
3rd Foot 1st Battalion	Canada	Flanders
3rd Foot 2nd Battalion	Britain	
4th Foot 1st Battalion	North America	Flanders
4th Foot 2nd Battalion	Britain	
5th Foot 1st Battalion	Canada	France
5th Foot 2nd Battalion	Britain	
6th Foot 1st Battalion	Canada	France
6th Foot 2nd Battalion	Britain	
7th Foot 1st Battalion	North America	France
7th Foot 2nd Battalion	Britain	
8th Foot 1st Battalion	Canada	Britain
8th Foot 2nd Battalion	Canada	Britain
9th Foot 1st Battalion	Canada	France
9th Foot 2nd Battalion	Britain	
10th Foot 1st Battalion	Mediterranean	
10th Foot 2nd Battalion	Mediterranean	
11th Foot 1st Battalion	Gibraltar	Britain
11th Foot 2nd Battalion	Gibraltar	
12th Foot 1st Battalion	Mauritius	
12th Foot 2nd Battalion	Britain	France
13th Foot	Canada	Britain
14th Foot 1st Battalion	India	
14th Foot 2nd Battalion	Mediterranean	Marseilles, France
14th Foot 3rd Battalion	Britain	Flanders
15th Foot 1st Battalion	West Indies	
15th Foot 2nd Battalion	Britain	
16th Foot	Canada	France
17th Foot	India	
18th Foot	West Indies	
19th Foot	Ceylon	
20th Foot	Britain	
21st Foot 1st Battalion	North America	France
21st Foot 2nd Battalion	Britain	
22nd Foot	Cape Colony	
23rd Foot	Britain	Flanders
24th Foot	India	
25th Foot 1st Battalion	West Indies	
25th Foot 2nd Battalion	Flanders	

The Regiment

Unit designation	Location	Ordered to
26th Foot	Gibraltar	
27th Foot 1st Battalion	North America	France
27th Foot 2nd Battalion	Britain	
27th Foot 3rd Battalion	North America	France
28th Foot	Britain	Flanders
29th Foot	Canada	France
30th Foot 1st Battalion	India	
30th Foot 2nd Battalion	Flanders	
31st Foot	Mediterranean	
32nd Foot	Britain	Flanders
33rd Foot	Flanders	
34th Foot 1st Battalion	India	
34th Foot 2nd Battalion	Britain	
35th Foot 1st Battalion	Mediterranean	
35th Foot 2nd Battalion	Flanders	
36th Foot	Britain	France
37th Foot 1st Battalion	Canada	
37th Foot 2nd Battalion	Flanders	
38th Foot	Britain	France
39th Foot 1st Battalion	Canada	France
39th Foot 2nd Battalion	Britain	
40th Foot 1st Battalion	North America	Flanders
40th Foot 2nd Battalion	Britain	
41st Foot	Canada	France
42nd Foot	Britain	Flanders
43rd Foot 1st Battalion	North America	France
43rd Foot 2nd Battalion	Britain	
44th Foot 1st Battalion	North America	Britain
44th Foot 2nd Battalion	Flanders	
45th Foot	Britain	
46th Foot	Australia	
47th Foot	India	
48th Foot	Britain	
49th Foot	Canada	Britain
50th Foot	Britain	
51st Foot	Britain	Flanders
52nd Foot 1st Battalion	Britain	Flanders
52nd Foot 2nd Battalion	Flanders	Britain
53rd Foot 1st Battalion	India	
53rd Foot 2nd Battalion	Britain	
54th Foot	Flanders	

Table 3.7 continued

Unit designation	Location	Ordered to
55th Foot	Britain	
56th Foot 1st Battalion	Mauritius	
56th Foot 2nd Battalion	India	
57th Foot 1st Battalion	Canada	France
57th Foot 2nd Battalion	Britain	
58th Foot 1st Battalion	Canada	France
58th Foot 2nd Battalion	Britain	
59th Foot 1st Battalion	India	
59th Foot 2nd Battalion	Britain	Flanders
60th Foot 1st Battalion	Cape Colony	
60th Foot 2nd Battalion	West Indies	
60th Foot 3rd Battalion	West Indies	
60th Foot 4th Battalion	West Indies	
60th Foot 5th Battalion	Britain	
60th Foot 6th Battalion	West Indies	
60th Foot 7th Battalion	Canada	
60th Foot 8th Battalion	Gibraltar	
61st Foot	Britain	
62nd Foot 1st Battalion	Britain	
62nd Foot 2nd Battalion	Canada	France
63rd Foot	West Indies	
64th Foot	Canada	France
65th Foot	India	
66th Foot 1st Battalion	India	
66th Foot 2nd Battalion	Britain	
67th Foot 1st Battalion	India	
67th Foot 2nd Battalion	Gibraltar	
68th Foot	Britain	
69th Foot 1st Battalion	India	
69th Foot 2nd Battalion	Flanders	
70th Foot	Canada	
71st Foot 1st Battalion	Britain	Flanders
71st Foot 2nd Battalion	Britain	
72nd Foot 1st Battalion	Cape Colony	
72nd Foot 2nd Battalion	Britain	
73rd Foot 1st Battalion	Ceylon	
73rd Foot 2nd Battalion	Flanders	
74th Foot	Britain	
75th Foot	Mediterranean	
76th Foot	Canada	

The Regiment

Unit designation	Location	Ordered to
77th Foot	Britain	
78th Foot 1st Battalion	Java	
78th Foot 2nd Battalion	Flanders	
79th Foot 1st Battalion	Britain	Flanders
79th Foot 2nd Battalion	Britain	
80th Foot	India	
81st Foot 1st Battalion	Canada	France
81st Foot 2nd Battalion	Flanders	
82nd Foot 1st Battalion	Canada	France
82nd Foot 2nd Battalion	Britain	
83rd Foot 1st Battalion	Cape Colony	
83rd Foot 2nd Battalion	Britain	
84th Foot 1st Battalion	India	
84th Foot 2nd Battalion	Britain	
85th Foot	North America	Britain
86th Foot	India	
87th Foot 1st Battalion	India	
87th Foot 2nd Battalion	Britain	
88th Foot 1st Battalion	Canada	France
88th Foot 2nd Battalion	Britain	
89th Foot 1st Battalion	India	
89th Foot 2nd Battalion	Canada	Britain
90th Foot 1st Battalion	Canada	France
90th Foot 2nd Battalion	Britain	
91st Foot 1st Battalion	Britain	Flanders
91st Foot 2nd Battalion	Britain	
92nd Foot	Britain	Flanders
93rd Foot 1st Battalion	North America	Britain
93rd Foot 2nd Battalion	Britain	
94th Foot	Britain	
95th Foot 1st Battalion	Britain	Flanders
95th Foot 2nd Battalion	Britain	Flanders
95th Foot 3rd Battalion	North America	Flanders
96th Foot	Britain	
97th Foot	Canada	
98th Foot	Canada	Britain
99th Foot	Canada	
100th Foot	Canada	
101st Foot	Canada	
102nd Foot	Canada	
103rd Foot	Canada	

Table 3.7 continued

Unit designation	Location	Ordered to
104th Foot	Canada	
Royal Staff Corps	Britain	
1st West India Regiment	North America	West Indies
2nd West India Regiment	West Indies	
3rd West India Regiment	West Indies	
4th West India Regiment	West Indies	
5th West India Regiment	North America	West Indies
6th West India Regiment	West Indies	
7th West India Regiment	West Indies	
8th West India Regiment	West Indies	
Royal York Rangers	West Indies	
Royal West India Rangers	North America	West Indies
Royal African Corps	Africa	
York Chasseurs	West Indies	
1st Ceylon Regiment	Ceylon	
2nd Ceylon Regiment	Ceylon	
3rd Ceylon Regiment	Ceylon	
4th Ceylon Regiment	Ceylon	To be disbanded in June
Regiment at the Cape of Good Hope	Cape Colony	
Bourbon Regiment	Bourbon Island	

Table 3.8 Location of miscellaneous infantry units in 1815

Unit designation	Location	Ordered to
1st Garrison Battalion	Mediterranean	
2nd Garrison Battalion	Bermuda	Flanders
3rd Garrison Battalion	Heligoland	
1st Royal Veteran Battalion	Britain	
2nd Royal Veteran Battalion	Britain	
3rd Royal Veteran Battalion	Britain	
4th Royal Veteran Battalion	Canada	
5th Royal Veteran Battalion	Britain	
6th Royal Veteran Battalion	Britain	
7th Royal Veteran Battalion	Britain	Flanders
8th Royal Veteran Battalion	Britain	
1st Garrison Company	West Indies	
2nd Garrison Company	West Indies	
3rd Garrison Company	West Indies	

The Regiment

Unit designation	Location	Ordered to
Veteran Company	Cape Colony	
1st Staff Garrison Company	Britain	
2nd Staff Garrison Company	Britain	
3rd Staff Garrison Company	Britain	Flanders
Veteran Garrison Company	Australia	
Royal Newfoundland Fencible Infantry	Canada	
Nova Scotia Fencible Infantry	Canada	
Canadian Fencible Infantry	Canada	
Glengarry Light Infantry Fencibles	Canada	
New Brunswick Fencible Infantry	Canada	

Table 3.9   Location of foreign troops in British Service in 1815

Unit designation	Location	Ordered to
1st KGL Light Dragoons	Flanders	
2nd KGL Light Dragoons	Flanders	
1st KGL Hussars	Flanders	
2nd KGL Hussars	Flanders	
3rd KGL Hussars	Flanders	
1st KGL Light Battalion	Flanders	
2nd KGL Light Battalion	Flanders	
1st KGL Line Battalion	Flanders	
2nd KGL Line Battalion	Flanders	
3rd KGL Line Battalion	Flanders	
4th KGL Line Battalion	Flanders	
5th KGL Line Battalion	Flanders	
6th KGL Line Battalion	Mediterranean	
7th KGL Line Battalion	Mediterranean	
8th KGL Line Battalion	Flanders	
KGL Foreign Veteran Battalion	Flanders	
Duke of Brunswick-Oels's Hussars	Mediterranean	Depot troops in Britain to France
de Roll's Regiment	Mediterranean	
de Meuron's Regiment	Canada	
de Watteville's Regiment	Canada	
York Light Infantry Volunteers	West Indies	
Royal Corsican Rangers	Mediterranean	
Sicilian Regiment	Mediterranean	
1st Greek Light Infantry	Mediterranean	

Royal Artillery deployment 1805–15

The British Artillery was formally known as the Royal Regiment of Artillery. It consisted of the Horse Brigade (i.e. Royal Horse Artillery) and the Foot Artillery (or Marching Battalions of Artillery). Also serving in the British Army were the artillery of the King's German Legion (i.e. the King's German Artillery) and the Corps of Royal Foreign Artillery.

At this time the Horse Brigade consisted of troops, while the Foot Artillery was organised as companies divided into battalions including an invalid battalion. These battalions were administrative only and the companies were the true tactical units of the artillery being deployed independent of their parent battalion. The numbers of troops, companies and battalions grew during this period and are reflected in the increased numbers deployed.

For the tables, Britain includes Britain, Wales, Scotland and Ireland. Canada includes Nova Scotia, New Brunswick and Newfoundland. The year 1816 is for the month of January only.

Trivia: During the Napoleonic Wars, the foot companies were referred to by their commander's name and not by a number. Numbers for companies within the battalions were only assigned in 1825. Horse Artillery troops used a letter for identification, but many still used the troop commander's name instead.

Table 3.10 Location of Royal Horse Artillery troops from 1805–10

Location	1805	1806	1807	1808	1809	1810
Britain	12	12	11	10	9	9
Peninsula				2	2‡	3
South America			1			
Walcheren					1	
Total	12	12	12	12	12	12

‡ Two troops which had arrived in 1808 were evacuated at Coruña and went to Britain.

Table 3.11 Location of Royal Horse Artillery troops from 1811–16

Location	1811	1812	1813	1814	1815	1816
Britain	8	8	7	8	6	11
France					8	3
Netherlands				1		
North Germany			1			
Peninsula	4	4	5	5		
Total	12	12	13	14	14	14

The Regiment

Table 3.12 Location of Foot Artillery from 1805–10

Location	1805	1806	1807	1808	1809	1810
Britain	54	63	53	61	53	58
Canada	6	6	6	8	8	8
Cadiz						6
Cape of Good Hope		3	3	3	3	2
Ceylon	3	3	3	3	3	3
Copenhagen			6			
Gibraltar	7	7	7	5	5	6
Hanover	3					
Ionian Isles					1	1
Madeira				1	1	1
Malta	5	4	4	4	3	3
Mauritius						1
Peninsula				13‡	5§	7
Sicily	3	5	6	4	4	4
South America			3			
Surinam	1	1				
Walcheren					16	
West Indies	10	10	11	10	10	12
Total	92	102	102	112	112	112

‡ Two companies went to Sweden 1808 and then on to the Peninsula.
§ Eleven companies were evacuated at Coruña and went to Britain.

Table 3.13 Location of Foot Artillery from 1811–16

Location	1811	1812	1813	1814	1815	1816
Britain	55	51	48	51	42	44
Canada	9	9	9	15	12	12
Cadiz	6	3	3			
Cape of Good Hope	3	3	3	3	3	3
Ceylon	3	3	3	3	3	3
East Coast of Spain		5	5	4‡		
France/Netherlands				5	24	25
Genoa				2	2	3
Gibraltar	6	6	6	6	6	6
Ionian Isles	1	1	1	1	1	1
Madeira	1	1	1			
Malta	5	4	4	4	4	4
Mauritius	1	1	1	1	1	1

‡The companies remained on the East Coast until mid-1814.

Table 3.13 continued

Location	1811	1812	1813	1814	1815	1816
Peninsula	9	12	14	2‡		
Sicily	3	3	3	1		
United States of America				4	4§	
West Indies	10	10	11	10	10	10
Total	112	112	112	112	112	112

‡ Fourteen companies were in the Peninsula until the army was broken up starting in May.
§ One company went to Britain and three companies went to France/Netherlands sailing in April.

Table 3.14 Location of the King's German artillery and foreign artillery 1805–10

Location	1805	1806	1807	1808	1809	1810
Britain		6	2	2	2	2
Copenhagen			4			
Hanover	5					
Peninsula				3‡	3	3
Sicily				1	1	1
West Indies	4	4	4	4	4	4
Total	9	10	10	10	10	10

‡ Two companies went to Sweden 1808 and then on to the Peninsula.

Table 3.15 Location of the King's German artillery and foreign artillery 1811–16

Location	1811	1812	1813	1814	1815	1816
Britain	2	2				
France / Netherlands				5	5	
Hanover			1	2	2	7
North Germany			3			
Peninsula	3	3	3			
Sicily	1	1	1	1	1	1
West Indies	4	4	4	4	4	4
Total	10	10	12	12	12	12

The Regiment

Barracks in Great Britain

There were numerous barracks throughout the British Isles that housed the regiments stationed there. Regiments recruited from any geographic location or county were not necessarily stationed in that area when in Great Britain. They might be stationed anywhere in the British Isles. If a regiment was on active service – that is, located outside the British Isles – it would maintain a regimental depot at home. Often this depot was located with the regiment's second battalion, but if there was no second battalion or if the second battalion was also on active service, the depot would consist of a few companies, whose mission was to recruit and train replacements for the battalion on active service. In many cases the location of the battalion at home and the regimental depot changed over the years.

Note: The figures in the table are for the number of men and horses that they could hold in accordance with regulations. This does not mean that they did not hold more.

Table 3.16 Barracks in England in 1809

Barracks	District	Infantry Officers & men	Horses	Cavalry Officers & Men	Horses
Alderney	Guernsey	—	—	434	—
Aldwick Green, Bognor	Sussex	—	—	758	—
Arundel	Sussex	342	340	—	—
Ashford	Kent	—	—	2,188	40
Barnstaple	Western	62	63	—	—
Barn Rock	Sussex	—	—	84	—
Battle	Sussex	—	—	943	120
Billericay	Eastern	—	—	206	—
Berryhead	Western	—	—	1,050	20
Bexhill (Old)	Sussex	—	—	939	50
Bexhill (Sod)	Sussex	?	?	?	?
Birmingham	Inland	188	188	—	—
Blatchington	Sussex	234	219	724	—
Bognor	Sussex	?	?	?	?
Bopeep	Sussex	?	?	?	?
Braybourn Lees	Kent	185	170	2265	—
Bridgeport	South West	63	63	—	—
Brighton	Sussex	705	715	752	—
Bristol	Severn	?	?	?	?
Canterbury	Kent	1154	1089	2600	—
Carlisle	Northern	—	—	144	—

Table 3.16 continued

Barracks	District	Infantry Officers & men	Horses	Cavalry Officers & Men	Horses
Chatham	Kent	—	—	2148	—
Chelmsford	Eastern	—	—	4,040	—
Chester	North West	—	—	54	—
Chichester	Sussex	350	340	982	—
Christchurch	South West	62	63	—	—
Colchester	Eastern	480	450	6,785	—
Coventry	Inland	216	193	—	—
Croydon	Home	384	372	—	—
Cuckmere Haven	Sussex	—	—	124	4
Danbury	Eastern	—	—	831	—
Deal	Kent	149	141	2,260	—
Dorchester	South West	395	400	—	—
Dover	Kent	—	—	215	—
Dover, West Height	Kent	?	?	?	?
Dungeness	Kent	—	—	512	33
Eastbourne	Sussex	183	63	668	—
Exeter	Western	416	412	—	—
Feversham and Ospringe	Kent	280	280	2,100	—
Fort Cumberland	Portsmouth	—	—	1,350	—
Fort Monkton	Portsmouth	—	—	503	10
Forton	Portsmouth	—	—	700	—
Fulwell	Northern	—	—	460	—
Gosport (Old)	Portsmouth	—	—	694	—
Gosport (New)	Portsmouth	?	?	?	?
Guernsey	Guernsey	—	—	4,696	59
Guildford	Home	501	537	—	—
Hailsham	Sussex	—	—	982	—
Hampton Court	Home	139	171	—	—
Harwich	Eastern	—	—	1,586	—
Haslar	Portsmouth	—	—	821	—
Hastings & Bopeep	Sussex	187	170	554	—
Herring House	South West	—	—	68	—
Hilsea	Portsmouth	—	—	4,515	—
Honiton	Western	81	85	—	—
Horsham	Sussex	—	—	2,440	—
Hounslow	Home	315	329	—	—
Hull	Yorkshire	—	—	2138	—

The Regiment

Barracks	District	Infantry Officers & men	Horses	Cavalry Officers & Men	Horses
Hurst Castle	South West	—	—	68	—
Hyde Park	Home	292	385	—	—
Hythe	Kent	262	262	3,378	145
Ipswich (New & Old)	Eastern	1,108	1,256	5,911	—
Jersey	Jersey	—	—	5,771	22
Kensington	Home	46	52	—	—
Kew	Home	—	—	67	—
Kingsbridge	Western	—	—	531	—
King Street	Home	39	384	—	—
Knightsbridge	Home	—	—	502	4
Langney Point	Sussex	—	—	278	—
Languard Fort	Eastern	—	—	416	—
Lewes	Sussex	51	510	2,218	—
Littlehampton	Sussex	—	—	379	—
Liverpool	North West	—	—	104	—
Lymington	South West	—	—	934	—
Maidstone	Kent	879	145	2,100	—
Maldon	Eastern	187	180	1,205	—
Manchester	North West	349	353	—	—
Maker	Western	—	—	343	—
Margate and Westgate	Kent	—	—	400	—
Medina Mill	Isle of Wight	—	—	500	—
Modbury	Western	65	63	—	—
Newcastle and vicinity	Northern	—	—	2,500	—
Newport	Isle of Wight	—	—	22	—
Norman Cross	Eastern	—	—	1,266	—
Norwich	Eastern	252	266	750	—
Northampton	Inland	126	124	—	—
Nottingham	Inland	189	186	—	—
Ospringe	Kent	?	?	?	?
Ottery	Western	?	?	?	?
Out Posts	Isle of Wight	—	—	118	—
Parkhurst	Isle of Wight	—	—	1,705	—
Pendennis Castle and St Maws	Western	—	—	1,125	—
Pevensey	Sussex	—	—	757	—
Picquets Essex	Eastern	113	21	—	—
Pleydon	Sussex	?	?	?	?
Plymouth	Western	221	210	7790	—

Table 3.16 continued

Barracks	District	Infantry Officers & men	Horses	Cavalry Officers & Men	Horses
Portchester	Portsmouth	—	—	1,074	—
Portman Street	Home	—	—	571	—
Portsmouth & Portsea	Portsmouth	—	—	2,057	—
Radipole	South West	430	340	—	—
Ramsgate	Kent	169	161	829	—
Riding Street	Kent	—	—	940	12
Ringmere	Sussex	—	—	140	136
Romford	Eastern	364	378	—	—
Romney	Kent	187	172	—	—
Rye & Pleydon	Sussex	187	172	—	—
Sandhurst	Home	—	—	102	—
Sandows	Isle of Wight	—	—	435	—
Savoy	Home	—	—	50	—
Scarborough	Yorkshire	—	—	118	—
Scilly	Western	—	—	108	—
Seaton Sluice & House	Northern	—	—	—	—
Selsea	Sussex	—	—	304	—
Sheerness	Kent	—	—	585	—
Sheffield	Yorkshire	175	182	—	—
Shoreham	Sussex	187	170	616	—
Shorncliffe	Kent	?	?	?	?
Silver Hill	Sussex	—	—	2,132	—
Southampton	South West	62	63	106	—
St Maws	Western	?	?	?	?
Steyning	Sussex	—	—	984	—
Stonar	Kent	157	160	—	—
Sunderland	Northern	—	—	1,563	—
Taunton	Western	62	63	—	—
Tilbury Fort	Kent	—	—	198	—
Totness	Western	62	63	—	—
Tower	Home	—	—	455	—
Trowbridge	Bristol	62	63	—	—
Truro	Western	215	310	—	—
Tynemouth	Northern	—	—	483	—
Upnor	Kent	—	—	93	—
Wareham	South West	62	63	—	—
Weeley	Eastern	374	360	3,925	—
Westgate	Kent	?	?	?	?

The Regiment

Barracks	District	Infantry Officers & men	Horses	Cavalry Officers & Men	Horses
Weymouth	South West	—	—	377	—
Whitburn	Northern	?	?	?	?
Windsor	Home	222	220	642	—
Winchelsea	Sussex	—	—	150	—
Winchester	South West	—	—	3533	—
Woodbridge	Eastern	724	720	4165	—
Woolwich	Home	—	—	215	—
Worthing	Sussex	—	—	158	—
Yarmouth	Eastern	—	—	1020	—
Yarmouth	Isle of Wight	—	—	285	6
Yealm	Western	—	—	190	—
York	Yorkshire	261	266	—	—

Table 3.17 Barracks in Scotland in 1809

Barracks	District	Infantry Officers & men	Horses	Cavalry Officers & Men	Horses
Aberdeen	Northern	—	—	579	4
Ayr	Western	—	—	464	4
Belhaven	Centre	326	320	—	—
Berwick	Southern	—	—	642	—
Blackness Castle	Southern	—	—	51	—
Dalkeith	Southern	—	—	160	—
Dunbar	Southern	—	—	1,129	—
Dunbarton	Centre	—	—	163	—
Dundee	Centre	—	—	538	4
Edinburgh Castle	Centre	—	—	458	—
Eyemouth	Southern	—	—	75	—
Fort Augustus	Northern	—	—	297	2
Fort Charlotte	Northern	—	—	272	—
Fort George	Northern	—	—	1,840	—
Fort William	Northern	—	—	481	—
Glasgow	Western	—	—	1,040	—
Haddington	Southern	326	410	1,128	—
Hamilton	Western	180	202	—	—
Leith	Southern	—	—	136	—
Musselburgh	Southern	—	—	1,728	—
Piers Hill	Southern	?	?	?	?

Table 3.17 continued

Barracks	District	Infantry Officers & men	Horses	Cavalry Officers & Men	Horses
Port Patrick	Western	—	—	24	—
Port Seaton	Southern	—	—	300	—
Preston	Southern	?	?	?	?
Queensbury House	Centre	—	—	800	—
Sterling Castle	Centre	—	—	927	—
Tontine	Centre	?	?	?	?

Source: *Army List*, March 1808, pp. 47–8; *Army List*, May 1809, pp. 100–1.

Trivia: *The early barracks were dreary places allowing about 300 cubic feet of air space per man. Each room provided sleeping quarters for twenty men, being 7 feet high, 30–32 feet long and 20 feet wide. Four men slept in each crib. They all ate at a central table little more than 6 inches from the cribs. Buckets or tubs were used as urinals. Usually a single pump provided drinking water. 'Married quarters' were provided by hanging blankets from ropes and sectioning off parts of the room. Existence in the barracks could not have been a pleasant experience.*[1]

Regimental establishments in 1812

A peculiarity of the British army was in the use of the terms 'regiment' and 'battalion'. The army would refer to a unit as a regiment even if it consisted of only one battalion, unlike Continental powers where a regiment consisted of many battalions. In peacetime most British regiments were single battalions. The British increased the number of battalions only in time of war and then disbanded them at the peace. The terminology also referred to the unit using either regiment or foot, properly as 'Regiment of Foot'. Single battalion regiments were shown as either regiment or foot, for example as 2nd Regiment or 2nd Foot. Multiple battalion regiments were shown as, for example, 2nd Battalion 1st Regiment or 2nd Battalion 1st Foot or more simply as 2/1st Regiment or 2/1st Foot.

The number of battalions in each regiment was not consistent and establishments differed even within the same regiment. Establishment was the authorised strength of officers and men for a unit and for which it recruited to attain. A unit's war establishment was always larger than its peace establishment. The establishments would change during the course of the wars, being increased or decreased as decided by army headquarters. It was rare for a unit on active service to be at its authorised strength because of the attrition caused by combat and campaigning. In theory a system

---

1 Fosten, *Wellington's Infantry* (1) pp. 16–17.

was put into place whereby the 2nd Battalion would remain at home and keep the establishment of the 1st Battalion up to strength by sending drafts of men as replacements. Increased overseas commitments often prevented this from happening and many regiments had two or more battalions on active service overseas. Regiments stationed in India almost always had a higher establishment. This was probably because reinforcements from home depots/battalions would take a considerable length of time to reach India. Compare the tables for 1812 with the establishment of regiments serving with Wellington's army in the Peninsula for January 1813. The following tables show the unit establishments that the army would require for the period 25 December 1811 to 24 December 1812. It does not include any units raised during that period. The simplest form of the unit name has been used. The source for all the tables is HCPP *Sessional Papers*, volume IX for 1812.

Table 3.18   Establishments of the cavalry regiments in 1812

Unit designation	Establishment	Establishment India
1st Life Guards	417	
2nd Life Guards	416	
Royal Horse Guards	655	
1st Dragoon Guards	1,085	
2nd Dragoon Guards	907	
3rd Dragoon Guards	917	
4th Dragoon Guards	917	
5th Dragoon Guards	917	
6th Dragoon Guards	907	
7th Dragoon Guards	907	
1st Dragoons	917	
2nd Dragoons	907	
3rd Dragoons	918	
4th Dragoons	917	
6th Dragoons	907	
7th Light Dragoons	907	
8th Light Dragoons	—	942
9th Light Dragoons	727	
10th Light Dragoons	907	
11th Light Dragoons	917	
12th Light Dragoons	917	
13th Light Dragoons	917	
14th Light Dragoons	917	

Table 3.18 continued

Unit designation	Establishment	Establishment India
15th Light Dragoons	907	
16th Light Dragoons	917	
17th Light Dragoons	—	1,152
18th Light Dragoons	907	
19th Light Dragoons	697	
20th Light Dragoons	917	
21st Light Dragoons	942	
22nd Light Dragoons	—	942
23rd Light Dragoons	697	
24th Light Dragoons	—	1,152
25th Light Dragoons	—	1,152

Table 3.19 Establishments of the infantry regiments in 1812

Unit designation	No. of battalions	Establishment	Establishment India
1st Foot Guards	3	4,302	
Coldstream Foot Guards	2	2,689	
3rd Foot Guards	2	2,689	
1st Foot	4‡	4,033	1,360
2nd Foot	1	1,151	
3rd Foot	2	1,612	
4th Foot	2	2,301	
5th Foot	2	2,033	
6th Foot	2	1,612	
7th Foot	2	2,243	
8th Foot	2	1,822	
9th Foot	2	2,291	
10th Foot	2	2,080	
11th Foot	2	2,301	
12th Foot	2	1,358	
13th Foot	1	941	
14th Foot	2§	1,360	1,385
15th Foot	2	1,170	
16th Foot	1	727	
17th Foot	1	—	1,151
18th Foot	2	1,612	
19th Foot	1	1,151	

‡ 2nd Battalion serving in India.
§ 1st Battalion serving in India.

The Regiment

Unit designation	No. of battalions	Establishment	Establishment India
20th Foot	1	1,127	
21st Foot	2	1,822	
22nd Foot	1	1,151	
23rd Foot	2	1,612	
24th Foot	2‡	930	1,151
25th Foot	2	1,822	
26th Foot	2	1,302	
27th Foot	3	4,081	
28th Foot	2	1,612	
29th Foot	1	907	
30th Foot	2‡	1,150	1,151
31st Foot	2	1,650	
32nd Foot	2	1,612	
33rd Foot	1	—	1,151
34th Foot	2‡	1,150	1,151
35th Foot	2	2,032	
36th Foot	2	1,392	
37th Foot	1	1,127	
38th Foot	2	1,822	
39th Foot	2	2,081	
40th Foot	2	2,032	
41st Foot	1	1,361	
42nd Foot	2	1,822	
43rd Foot	2	2,083	
44th Foot	2	2,080	
45th Foot	2	1,392	
46th Foot	1	727	
47th Foot	2‡	1,150	941
48th Foot	2	1,612	
49th Foot	1	931	
50th Foot	2	1,612	
51st Foot	1	961	
52nd Foot	2	2,131	
53rd Foot	2‡	719	1,151
54th Foot	1	727	
55th Foot	1	727	
56th Foot	2	—	2,721
57th Foot	2	1,612	

‡ 1st Battalion serving in India.

Table 3.19 continued

Unit designation	No. of battalions	Establishment	Establishment India
58th Foot	2	1,870	
59th Foot	2‡	1,126	1,337
60th Foot	6	6,783	
61st Foot	2	1,612	
62nd Foot	2	1,822	
63rd Foot	2	1,402	
64th Foot	1	941	
65th Foot	1	—	731
66th Foot	2	1,870	
67th Foot	2‡	719	1,361
68th Foot	1	961	
69th Foot	2‡	485	1,127
70th Foot	1	516	
71st Foot	2	2,083	
72nd Foot	2	1,612	
73rd Foot	2	1,911	
74th Foot	1	1,361	
75th Foot	1	931	
76th Foot	1	907	
77th Foot	1	1,151	
78th Foot	2‡	695	1,337
79th Foot	2	1,822	
80th Foot	1	—	941
81st Foot	2	1,822	
82nd Foot	2	2,032	
83rd Foot	2	2,081	
84th Foot	2‡	1,336	1,337
85th Foot	1	727	
86th Foot	1	941	
87th Foot	2	2,301	
88th Foot	2	1,822	
89th Foot	2‡	695	1,337
90th Foot	2	1,822	
91st Foot	2	1,612	
92nd Foot	2	1,822	
93rd Foot	1	1,361	
94th Foot	1	931	

‡ 1st Battalion serving in India.

Unit designation	No. of battalions	Establishment	Establishment India
95th Foot	3	3,232	
96th Foot	2	1,170	
97th Foot	1	697	
98th Foot	1	941	
99th Foot	1	727	
100th Foot	1	721	
101st Foot	1	941	
102nd Foot	1	697	
103rd Foot	1	697	
104th Foot	1	1,127	

Table 3.20 Establishments of the garrison and veteran battalions 1812

Unit designation	No. of battalions	Establishment
1st Garrison Battalion	1	907
2nd Garrison Battalion	1	907
3rd Garrison Battalion	1	907
4th Garrison Battalion	1	1,337
5th Garrison Battalion	1	907
6th Garrison Battalion	1	907
1st Royal Veteran Battalion	1	713
2nd Royal Veteran Battalion	1	924
3rd Royal Veteran Battalion	1	713
4th Royal Veteran Battalion	1	713
5th Royal Veteran Battalion	1	713
6th Royal Veteran Battalion	1	713
7th Royal Veteran Battalion	1	714
8th Royal Veteran Battalion	1	914
9th Royal Veteran Battalion	1	914
10th Royal Veteran Battalion	1	713
11th Royal Veteran Battalion	1	1,124
12th Royal Veteran Battalion	1	1,124

Table 3.21 Establishments of miscellaneous regiments 1812

Unit designation	No. of battalions	Establishment
1st West India Regiment	1	1,126
2nd West India Regiment	1	1,126

Table 3.21 continued

Unit designation	No. of battalions	Establishment
3rd West India Regiment	1	916
4th West India Regiment	1	1,126
5th West India Regiment	1	1,126
6th West India Regiment	1	1,126
7th West India Regiment	1	1,126
8th West India Regiment	1	1,126
Royal York Rangers	1	1,236
Royal West India Rangers	1	1,125
Royal African Corps	1	1,237
Royal Staff Corps	1	686
Canadian Regiment of FI	1	904
Newfoundland Regiment FI	1	693
Nova Scotia Regiment FI	1	693

Trivia: All five cavalry regiments serving in India had an additional recruiting troop of twenty-five men stationed in Britain. Fourteen of the nineteen regiments serving in India had an additional recruiting company of 24 men stationed Britain of which the 1/14th Foot had two such companies. Five regiments did not have the extra company — 1/59th Foot, 1/69th Foot, 1/78th Foot, 1/84th Foot, and 1/89th Foot. Recruiting companies were above the regular establishment.

Table 3.22 Establishments of the foreign regiments 1812

Unit designation	No. of battalions	Establishment
2 regiments of KGL Dragoons		1,810
3 regiments of KGL Light Dragoons		2,505
Brunswick Oels Dragoons		676
KGL Infantry‡	10	11,317
Brunswick Oels Infantry	1	1,348
de Meuron Regiment	1	1,128
de Roll Regiment	1	1,604
Dillon Regiment	1	1,469
de Watteville Regiment	1	1,603

‡ Includes a Depot Company and an Independent Garrison Company.

Unit designation	No. of battalions	Establishment
Chasseurs Britanniques	1	1,602
York Light Infantry Volunteers	1	1,599
Royal Corsican Rangers	1	1,601
Sicilian Regiment	1	1,350
Greek Light Infantry Regiment	1	1,129

Regimental establishments in Wellington's Peninsular army in January 1813

Table 3.23 Establishments of cavalry regiments in the Peninsular army January 1813

Unit designation	Troops	Establishment*
Royal Horse Guards	4	300
3rd Dragoon Guards	6	480
4th Dragoon Guards	6	480
5th Dragoon Guards	6	480
1st Dragoons	6	480
3rd Dragoons	6	480
4th Dragoons	6	480
9th Light Dragoons	6	480
11th Light Dragoons	6	480
12th Light Dragoons	6	480
13th Light Dragoons	6	480
14th Light Dragoons	6	480
16th Light Dragoons	6	480
1st KGL Dragoons	6	480
2nd KGL Dragoons	6	480
1st KGL Light Dragoons	6	480
2nd KGL Light Dragoons	6	480

* Establishment is for the troops in the Peninsula only and not for the full regiment.

Source: Supplementary Despatches vol. 7, p. 526.

> *Trivia: Were the Highland regiments really composed of Highlanders? In 1808 in the 1st Battalion 42nd Foot 583 of 826 soldiers (71 per cent) were Highlanders. However, 87 per cent of the 42nd Foot between 1807 and 1812 were Scots; 80 per cent of the 1st Battalion 79th Foot were also Scots.*[2]

---

2 Mackerlie, *An Account*, pp. 10–17.

Table 3.24 Establishments of foot regiments in the Peninsular army January 1813

Unit designation	Battalion	Establishment
1st Foot Guards	1st	1,620
1st Foot Guards	3rd	1,350
Coldstream Foot Guards	1st	1,200
3rd Foot Guards	1st	1,200
1st Foot	3rd	1,200
2nd Foot	—	1,008
3rd Foot	1st	1,000
4th Foot	1st	1,008
4th Foot	2nd	1,008
5th Foot	1st	1,000
6th Foot	1st	1,000
7th Foot	1st	1,000
9th Foot	1st	1,008
11th Foot	1st	1,008
20th Foot	—	1,008
23rd Foot	1st	1,000
24th Foot	2nd	808
27th Foot	3rd	1,208
28th Foot	1st	1,000
30th Foot	2nd	1,008
31st Foot	2nd	808
34th Foot	2nd	1,008
36th Foot	1st	800
38th Foot	1st	1,000
38th Foot	2nd	600
39th Foot	1st	1,200
40th Foot	—	1,200
42nd Foot	1st	1,200
43rd Foot	1st	1,210
44th Foot	2nd	608
45th Foot	1st	800
47th Foot	2nd	1,008
48th Foot	1st	1,000
50th Foot	1st	1,000
51st Foot	—	818
52nd Foot	1st	1,010
53rd Foot	2nd	608
57th Foot	1st	1,000
58th Foot	2nd	608

Unit designation	Battalion	Establishment
59th Foot	2nd	1,008
60th Foot	5th	1,010
61st Foot	1st	1,000
66th Foot	2nd	808
68th Foot	—	818
71st Foot	1st	1,010
74th Foot	—	1,208
77th Foot	—	808
79th Foot	1st	1,200
82nd Foot	1st	1,200
83rd Foot	2nd	808
87th Foot	2nd	1,008
88th Foot	1st	1,200
91st Foot	1st	1,000
92nd Foot	1st	1,200
94th Foot	—	808
95th Foot*	1st	606
95th Foot*	2nd	606
95th Foot†	3rd	505
Staff Corps‡	—	300
1st KGL Light Battalion	—	1,000
2nd KGL Light Battalion	—	1,000
1st KGL Line Battalion	—	1,000
2nd KGL Line Battalion	—	1,000
5th KGL Line Battalion	—	1,000
Brunswick Oels Regiment	—	1,208
Chasseurs Britanniques	—	1,440

* Establishment is for the 6 companies in the Peninsula only and not the full battalion.
† Establishment is for the 5 companies in the Peninsula only and not the full battalion.
‡ Establishment is for the 5 companies in the Peninsula only and not the full corps.

Source: *Supplementary Despatches*, vol. 7, pp. 523–4.

Each regiment in the British Army tried to keep its own unique identity and there were a variety of differences among the regiments. These included regimental colonels, facing colours, battle honours, customs and traditions, and even their regimental agents.

Regimental colonels 1805–15

All British regiments had regimental colonels appointed who were to be responsible for their well-being. The position was for the most part an administrative one, as the day-to-day operations were left to the regimental lieutenant colonels. By 1805 the regimental colonels were mostly general officers, major general and above, who were appointed as a reward for merit or long service. These colonels were to supply their units with uniforms, except greatcoats, and also to confirm exchanges into and out of the regiment. They would also represent the unit to the commander-in-chief on such items as regimental subtitles, awards of battle honours and so on.

Most regiments had only one regimental colonel, but multiple battalion regiments would have a colonel-in-chief and colonel commandants for each battalion. (e.g. 60th Foot, 95th Rifles and the King's German Legion). The tables below detail the names of the regimental colonels and date of appointment of the colonels serving between 1805 and 1815. Those names marked with an asterisk * were colonel commandants. The titles of nobility are the highest ones held by the officers and not necessarily those which were held during the period 1805–15.

For the Royal Regiment of Artillery, the colonel-in-chief and colonel-en-second were also the Master General of the Ordnance and the Lieutenant General of the Ordnance respectively.

Table 3.25 Regimental colonels of the cavalry regiments 1805–15

Regiment	Colonel	Date appointed
1st Life Guards	Charles, 3rd Earl of Harrington	5 December 1792
2nd Life Guards	William, 1st Earl Cathcart	7 August 1797
Royal Horse Guards	Charles, 3rd Duke of Richmond	15 July 1795
	Hugh, 2nd Duke of Northumberland	30 December 1806
	Arthur, 1st Duke of Wellington	1 January 1813
1st Dragoon Guards	William Pitt	18 July 1796
	Frederick 2nd Lord Heathfield	4 January 1810
	David Dundas	27 January 1813
2nd Dragoon Guards	George, 1st Marquess Townshend	15 July 1773
	Charles Craufurd	18 September 1807
3rd Dragoon Guards	Richard Vyse	2 April 1804
4th Dragoon Guards	Miles Staveley	12 March 1803
	Henry Fane	3 August 1814
5th Dragoon Guards	Thomas Bland	18 November 1790

The Regiment

Regiment	Colonel	Date appointed
6th Dragoon Guards	Henry, 2nd Earl of Carhampton	23 June 1788
7th Dragoon Guards	William Medows	2 November 1796
	Richard Wilford	20 November 1813
1st Dragoons	Thomas Garth	7 January 1801
2nd Dragoons	David Dundas	16 May 1801
	William, 5th Marquess of Lothian	27 January 1813
	James Steuart	12 January 1815
3rd Dragoons	Charles, 1st Earl Grey	4 September 1799
	William Cartwright	18 November 1807
4th Dragoons	Guy, 1st Lord Dorchester	14 August 1802
	Francis Hugonin	9 November 1808
6th Dragoons	George, 11th Earl of Pembroke	15 December 1797
7th Light Dragoons	Henry, 1st Marquess of Anglesey	16 May 1801
8th Light Dragoons	John Floyd	13 September 1804
9th Light Dragoons	James, 2nd Earl of Rosslyn	1 August 1801
10th Light Dragoons	HRH The Prince of Wales	18 July 1796
11th Light Dragoons	William, 5th Marquess of Lothian	23 October 1798
	Lord William Bentinck	27 January 1813
12th Light Dragoons	James Steuart	9 November 1791
	William Payne	12 January 1815
13th Light Dragoons	Francis Craig	15 February 1781
	Henry Grey	30 December 1811
14th Light Dragoons	John, 7th Earl of Bridgewater	1 June 1797
15th Light Dragoons	Guy, 1st Lord Dorchester	16 July 1790
	Prince Ernest, Duke of Cumberland	28 March 1801
16th Light Dragoons	William, 3rd Earl Harcourt	20 October 1779
17th Light Dragoons	Oliver de Lancey	20 May 1795
18th Light Dragoons	Charles, 1st Marquess of Drogheda	7 December 1759
19th Light Dragoons	William, 5th Viscount Howe	21 April 1786
	William Payne	13 July 1814
20th Light Dragoons	Francis, 1st Lord Heathfield	23 March 1797
	Lord William Bentinck	4 January 1810

Table 3.25 continued

Regiment	Colonel	Date appointed
20th Light Dragoons	Stapleton, 1st Viscount Combermere	27 January 1813
21st Light Dragoons	Banastre Tarleton	29 April 1802
22nd Light Dragoons	Francis Gwyn	9 March 1794
23rd Light Dragoons	William Cartwright	13 September 1804
	William Payne	14 November 1807
	Henry Fane	13 July 1814
	George Anson	3 August 1814
24th Light Dragoons	William Loftus	14 August 1802
25th Light Dragoons	Richard Wilford	2 April 1804
	Charles, 3rd Marquess of Londonderry	20 November 1813

Table 3.26 Regimental colonels of the infantry regiments 1805–15

Regiment	Colonel	Date appointed
1st Foot Guards	Prince William, 1st Duke of Gloucester	3 April 1770
	Prince Frederick, Duke of York	5 September 1805
Coldstream Guards	Prince Frederick, Duke of York	27 October 1784
	Prince Adolphus, Duke of Cambridge	5 September 1805
3rd Foot Guards	John, 5th Duke of Argyll	9 May 1782
	Prince William, 2nd Duke of Gloucester	26 May 1806
1st Foot	Prince Edward, Duke of Kent	21 August 1801
2nd Foot	James Coates	20 December 1794
3rd Foot	Thomas Hall	18 April 1786
	Charles Leigh	29 December 1809
	Henry Clinton	9 August 1815
4th Foot	John, 2nd Earl of Chatham	5 December 1799
5th Foot	Richard England	21 August 1801
	William Wynyard	7 November 1812
6th Foot	Prince William, 2nd Duke of Gloucester	4 November 1795
	George Nugent	26 May 1806
7th Foot	Alured Clarke	21 August 1801
8th Foot	Ralph Dundas	30 July 1794

The Regiment

Regiment	Colonel	Date appointed
8th Foot	Edmund Stevens	8 February 1814
9th Foot	Albemarle, 9th Earl of Lindsey	31 December 1794
	Peter Hunter	15 June 1804
	Robert Brownrigg	3 October 1805
10th Foot	Henry Fox	23 June 1795
	Thomas Maitland	19 July 1811
11th Foot	James Grant	9 November 1791
	Richard Fitzpatrick	20 April 1806
	Charles Asgill	25 February 1807
12th Foot	William Picton	21 April 1779
	Charles Hastings	15 October 1811
13th Foot	Alexander Campbell	11 July 1804
	Edward Morrison	15 February 1813
14th Foot	George Hotham	18 November 1789
	Harry Calvert	8 February 1806
15th Foot	Henry W. Powell	20 June 1794
	Moore Disney	23 July 1814
16th Foot	Henry Bowyers	15 December 1797
	Charles Green	29 August 1808
	George Prevost	17 February 1814
17th Foot	George Garth	8 August 1792
18th Foot	James Murray Pulteney	26 February 1794
	John, 2nd Earl of Donoughmore	24 July 1811
19th Foot	Samuel Hulse	24 January 1797
	Hew Dalrymple	25 June 1810
	Tomkyns Turner	27 April 1811
20th Foot	Charles Leigh	2 March 1797
	John, Count of Maida	29 December 1809
	William Houston	5 April 1815
21st Foot	William Gordon	6 August 1803
22nd Foot	John Simcoe	18 June 1798
	James Craig	30 October 1806
	Edward Finch	18 September 1809
23rd Foot	Richard Grenville	21 April 1786
24th Foot	Richard Whyte	13 November 1793
	David Baird	19 July 1807
25th Foot	Lord George Lennox	29 December 1762
	Charles Fitzroy	25 March 1805
26th Foot	Andrew Gordon	28 March 1801

Table 3.26 continued

Regiment	Colonel	Date appointed
26th Foot	John, 12th Lord Elphinstone	24 April 1806
	George, 9th Earl of Dalhousie	21 May 1813
27th Foot	Francis, 1st Marquess of Hastings	23 May 1804
28th Foot	Robert Prescott	6 July 1789
	Edward Paget	26 December 1815
29th Foot	Gordon Forbes	8 August 1797
30th Foot	Robert Manners	7 November 1799
31st Foot	Henry, 1st Earl of Mulgrave	8 February 1793
32nd Foot	James Ogilvie	4 September 1802
	Alexander Campbell	15 February 1813
33rd Foot	Charles, 1st Marquess Cornwallis	21 March 1766
	Arthur, 1st Duke of Wellington	30 January 1806
	John Sherbrooke	1 January 1813
34th Foot	George, 2nd Lord Southampton	13 July 1797
	Eyre Coote	25 June 1810
35th Foot	Charles, 4th Duke of Richmond	17 March 1803
36th Foot	Henry St John	27 November 1778
37th Foot	Hew Dalrymple	18 January 1798
	Charles Ross	25 June 1810
	Charles Green	17 February 1814
38th Foot	James Rooke	2 August 1796
	George, 3rd Earl Ludlow	10 October 1805
39th Foot	Nisbett Balfour	2 July 1794
40th Foot	George Osborn	11 August 1786
41st Foot	Thomas Stirling	13 January 1790
	Hay Macdowall	16 May 1808
	Josiah Champagne	22 February 1810
42nd Foot	Hector Munro	1 June 1787
	George, 5th Duke of Gordon	3 January 1806
43rd Foot	Edward Smith	26 April 1792
	John, 1st Lord Howden	7 January 1809
44th Foot	Charles Rainsford	4 May 1781
	Thomas Trigge	27 May 1809
45th Foot	Frederick Lester	22 April 1802
46th Foot	John Whyte	5 January 1804

Regiment	Colonel	Date appointed
47th Foot	William Dalrymple	19 March 1794
	Richard Fitzpatrick	25 February 1807
	Alexander Hope	26 April 1813
48th Foot	Lord Charles Fitzroy	1 January 1805
49th Foot	Alexander Maitland	25 May 1768
50th Foot	James Duff	31 August 1798
51st Foot	William Morshead	9 May 1800
52nd Foot	John Moore	8 May 1801
	Hildebrand Oakes	25 January 1809
53rd Foot	Charles Crosbie	3 January 1798
	John Abercromby	21 March 1807
54th Foot	David Baird	8 May 1801
	Oliver Nicolls	19 July 1807
	Edward Finch	3 August 1808
	James, 18th Lord Forbes	18 September 1809
55th Foot	Loftus Tottenham	9 November 1791
	Donald Macdonald	20 March 1811
	Colin Campbell	10 October 1812
	William Clinton	25 April 1814
56th Foot	Chapple Norton	24 January 1797
57th Foot	John Campbell	2 November 1780
	John, 2nd Earl of Donoughmore	8 September 1806
	Hew Dalrymple	27 April 1811
58th Foot	George Scott	18 April 1787
	Richard, 7th Earl of Cavan	1 July 1811
59th Foot	Alexander Ross	28 March 1801
60th Foot	Prince Frederick, Duke of York	19 August 1797
60th Foot, 1st Battalion	William Gardiner*	12 March 1799
	William Keppel*	24 April 1806
	Arthur Whetham*	7 February 1811
	Henry Clinton*	20 May 1813
	Wroth Palmer Acland*	9 August 1815
2nd Battalion	Thomas Carleton*	6 August 1794
3rd Battalion	William Rowley*	3 October 1787
	Edmund Phipps*	25 August 1807
4th Battalion	Edward Morrison*	1 January 1805
	Charles Hope*	15 February 1813

Table 3.26 continued

Regiment	Colonel	Date appointed
60th Foot,		
5th Battalion	George Prevost*	8 September 1806
	John Robinson*	2 January 1813
6th Battalion	Robert Brownrigg*	25 July 1799
	John, 4th Earl of Hopetoun*	3 October 1805
	Napier Burton*	3 January 1806
7th Battalion	George Murray*	9 August 1813
8th Battalion	James Kempt*	4 November 1813
61st Foot	George Hewett	4 April 1800
62nd Foot	Edward Mathew	17 November 1779
	George Nugent	27 December 1805
	Eyre Coote	26 May 1806
	Samuel Hulse	25 June 1810
63rd Foot	Alexander, 6th Earl of Balcarres	27 August 1789
64th Foot	John Leland	26 June 1790
	William Villettes	4 January 1808
	Henry Wynyard	15 September 1808
65th Foot	Edmund Stevens	11 October 1797
	Thomas Grosvenor	8 February 1814
66th Foot	John, 13th Earl of Clanricarde	27 November 1794
	Oliver Nicolls	3 August 1808
67th Foot	Peter Craig	9 March 1803
	William Keppel	7 February 1811
68th Foot	Thomas Trigge	25 March 1795
	John Sherbrooke	27 May 1809
	Henry Warde	1 January 1813
69th Foot	Cornelius Cuyler	20 June 1794
70th Foot	John, 15th Earl of Suffolk	16 August 1783
	Galbraith Lowry Cole	12 January 1814
71st Foot	John, 1st Lord Howden	6 August 1803
	Francis Dundas	7 January 1809
72nd Foot	James Stuart	23 October 1798
	Rowland, 1st Viscount Hill	29 April 1815
73rd Foot	George, 1st Lord Harris	14 February 1800
74th Foot	John, 2nd Earl of Donoughmore	24 March 1802
	John, Count of Maida	8 September 1806
	Alexander Hope	29 December 1809

The Regiment

Regiment	Colonel	Date appointed
74th Foot	James Montgomerie	26 April 1813
75th Foot	Robert Abercromby	12 October 1787
76th Foot	Thomas Musgrave	12 October 1787
	George Prevost	2 January 1813
	Christopher Chowne	17 February 1814
77th Foot	Albemarle, 9th Earl of Lindsey	15 June 1804
	Richard, 7th Earl of Cavan	25 March 1808
	Charles Hastings	1 July 1811
	Thomas Picton	15 October 1811
	George Cooke	23 June 1815
78th Foot	Alexander Mackenzie-Fraser	3 May 1796
	James Craig	15 September 1809
	Samuel Auchmuty	13 January 1812
79th Foot	Alan Cameron	17 August 1793
80th Foot	Gerard, 1st Viscount Lake	14 February 1800
	Edward Paget	23 February 1808
	Alexander Campbell	26 December 1815
81st Foot	Henry Johnson	18 June 1798
82nd Foot	Henry Pigot	23 October 1798
83rd Foot	James Balfour	18 November 1795
84th Foot	George Bernard	28 February 1794
85th Foot	George Nugent	28 February 1794
	Charles Ross	27 December 1805
	Charles Asgill	30 October 1806
	Thomas Stanwix	25 February 1807
	James Gordon	27 November 1815
86th Foot	James Craig	5 January 1804
	Charles Ross	30 October 1806
	Francis, 1st Earl of Kilmorey	25 June 1810
87th Foot	John Doyle	3 May 1796
88th Foot	John Reid	27 November 1794
	William, 1st Viscount Beresford	9 February 1807
89th Foot	Eyre Coote	4 September 1802
	John Whitelocke	25 June 1806
	Albemarle, 9th Earl of Lindsey	25 March 1808
90th Foot	Thomas, 1st Lord Lynedoch	10 February 1794
91st Foot	Duncan Campbell	3 May 1796
92nd Foot	George, 5th Duke of Gordon	3 May 1796

Table 3.26 continued

Regiment	Colonel	Date appointed
92nd Foot	John, 4th Earl of Hopetoun	3 January 1806
93rd Foot	William Weymss	25 August 1800
94th Foot	Francis Dundas	9 October 1794
	James, 18th Lord Forbes	7 January 1809
	Rowland, 1st Viscount Hill	18 September 1809
	Charles Colville	29 April 1815
95th Foot	Coote Manningham	25 August 1800
	David Dundas	31 August 1809
95th Foot,		
1st Battalion	Forbes Champagne*	31 August 1809
2nd Battalion	Brent Spencer*	31 August 1809
3rd Battalion	William Stewart*	31 August 1809
96th Foot	George, 3rd Earl Ludlow	8 May 1801
	George Don	10 October 1805
97th Foot	John, Count of Maida	26 December 1798
	Thomas Stanwix	8 September 1806
	Thomas Grosvenor	25 February 1807
	Gordon Drummond	8 February 1814
98th Foot	John Burke	22 May 1804
99th Foot	Francis, 2nd Earl Landaff	28 February 1805
	Montagu Matthew	6 June 1811
100th Foot	Frederick Falkiner	28 February 1805
101st Foot	Henry, Viscount Dillon	20 August 1806
102nd Foot	Francis Grose	5 June 1789
103rd Foot	Samuel Auchmuty	25 June 1808
	Galbraith Lowry Cole	13 January 1812
	George Porter	12 January 1814
104th Foot	Martin Hunter	9 July 1803
Royal Staff Corps	John Brown	6 May 1802
1st West India		
Regiment	Lord Charles Somerset	5 January 1804
2nd West India		
Regiment	William Myers	24 April 1795
	Richard, 7th Earl of Cavan	27 September 1805
	Eyre Trench	25 March 1808
	Brent Spencer	25 June 1808
	George Beckwith	31 August 1809
3rd West India		
Regiment	William Keppel	20 May 1795
	Hildebrand Oakes	24 April 1806

Regiment	Colonel	Date appointed
	John Sherbrooke	25 January 1809
	John Murray	27 May 1809
4th West India Regiment	Oliver Nicolls	20 May 1795
	Thomas Maitland	19 July 1807
	James Leith	19 July 1811
5th West India Regiment	Harry Calvert	6 August 1800
	Charles Asgill	8 February 1806
	Alexander Hope	30 October 1806
	John Despard	29 December 1809
6th West India Regiment	John Whitelocke	1 September 1809
	Simon Fraser	26 May 1806
	Edward Pakenham	21 May 1813
	Miles Nightingall	20 March 1815
7th West India Regiment	George Don	25 November 1799
	Isaac Gascoyne	10 October 1805
8th West India Regiment	Thomas Hislop	29 April 1802
Royal African Corps	James Gordon	13 June 1808
	Henry Torrens	27 November 1815
Royal York Rangers	John Fraser	28 August 1800
Royal West India Rangers	William Wynyard	25 October 1806
	William Lumley	7 November 1811
The York Chasseurs	Andrew Hay	5 November 1813
	Hugh M. Gordon	2 May 1814
1st Ceylon Regiment	Josiah Champagne	25 April 1801
	Frederick Maitland	22 February 1810
2nd Ceylon Regiment	William Ramsay	25 April 1801
	John Hamilton	18 January 1813
3rd Ceylon Regiment	Charles Baillie	7 April 1804
	William Thomas	22 February 1810
4th Ceylon Regiment	John Wilson	8 March 1810
Royal Regiment of Malta	William Villettes	7 December 1804
	John Murray	23 February 1808
	John Brodrick	27 May 1809

Table 3.26 continued

Regiment	Colonel	Date appointed
Regiment at Cape of Good Hope	Alexander Hope	26 January 1806
	Donald Macdonald	30 October 1806
	Tomkyns Turner	20 March 1811
	George Moncrieffe	27 April 1811
Bourbon Regiment	Henry Keating	25 January 1812
Royal Newfoundland Fencible Infantry	John Skerrett	9 July 1803
	Albert Gledstanes	21 August 1813
	William Pringle	12 May 1814
New Brunswick Fencible Infantry (old)	Martin Hunter	9 July 1803
Nova Scotia Fencible Infantry	Frederick Wetherall	9 July 1803
Canadian Fencible Infantry	Thomas Peter	16 July 1803
Royal Manx Fencibles	Lord Henry Murray*	12 July 1803
	Lord John Murray*	20 February 1806
Glengarry Light Infantry Fencibles	Edward Baynes	6 February 1812
New Brunswick Fencible Infantry (new)	John Coffin	25 March 1813

Table 3.27 Regimental colonels of garrison battalions disbanded 24 February 1805

Regiment	Colonel	Date appointed
1st Garrison Battalion	Hildebrand Oakes	22 October 1803
2nd Garrison Battalion	Robert 2nd Earl of Roden	9 July 1803
3rd Garrison Battalion	William Lumley	9 July 1803
4th Garrison Battalion	John Sherbrooke	9 July 1803
5th Garrison Battalion	Thomas Maitland	9 July 1803
6th Garrison Battalion	James Durham	9 July 183
7th Garrison Battalion	John Robinson	9 July 1803
8th Garrison Battalion	Robert Blake	9 July 1803
9th Garrison Battalion	William, 1st Earl of Craven	9 July 1803
10th Garrison Battalion	John Leveson Gower	27 August 1803

The Regiment

Regiment	Colonel	Date appointed
11th Garrison Battalion	John Brodrick	9 July 1803
12th Garrison Battalion	George Vansittart	9 July 1803
13th Garrison Battalion	James Leith	9 July 1803
14th Garrison Battalion	William Erskine	9 July 1803
15th Garrison Battalion	George Stapleton	9 July 1803
16th Garrison Battalion	Edmund, 8th Earl of Cork	9 July 1803

Table 3.28   Regimental colonels of garrison battalions 1805–14

Regiment	Colonel	Date appointed
1st Garrison Battalion	George Vansittart	25 February 1805
2nd Garrison Battalion	John Robinson	25 February 1805
	George Porter	2 January 1813
	Frederick Robinson	12 January 1814
3rd Garrison Battalion	Thomas Maitland	25 February 1805
	James, 18th Lord Forbes	19 July 1807
	Rowland, 1st Viscount Hill	7 January 1809
	Baldwin Leighton	18 September 1809
4th Garrison Battalion	Charles Hastings	25 November 1806
	William Houston	1 July 1811
5th Garrison Battalion	Eyre Trench	25 November 1806
	Colin Campbell	25 March 1808
	Charles Colville	10 October 1812
6th Garrison Battalion	George Beckwith	25 November 1806
	George, 9th Earl of Dalhousie	31 August 1809
	Gore Browne	21 May 1813
7th Garrison Battalion	Patrick Wauchope	25 November 1806
	James Drummond	14 June 1807
8th Garrison Battalion	Forbes Champagne	25 November 1806
	John Despard	31 August 1809
9th Garrison Battalion	Brent Spencer	25 November 1806
	Samuel Auchmuty	25 June 1808

Table 3.29   Regimental colonels of garrison battalions 1814–15

Regiment	Colonel	Date appointed
1st Garrison Battalion	Baldwin Leighton	18 September 1809
2nd Garrison Battalion	William Houston	1 July 1811
	Henry Torrens	5 April 1815
3rd Garrison Battalion	John Hodges	25 May 1815

Trivia: Regimental colonels usually kept their regiment until their death or until the regiment was disbanded. The Marquess of Drogheda was the regimental colonel of the 18th Light Dragoons from its formation in 1759 until it was disbanded in 1821. Some officers would change regiments to obtain the colonelcy of the regiment they had spent most of their regimental service in, while others would request a lower numbered regiment as they knew that higher numbered regiments stood a greater chance of being disbanded when peace was declared.

Table 3.30 Regimental colonels of the Royal Veteran Battalions 1805–14

Regiment	Colonel	Date appointed
1st Royal Veteran Battalion	James Stewart	30 June 1804
2nd Royal Veteran Battalion	David Home	25 December 1802
	Anthony Layard	22 February 1810
3rd Royal Veteran Battalion	James Lumsdaine	25 December 1802
	William Maxwell	14 May 1807
4th Royal Veteran Battalion	Grice Blakeney	25 December 1802
5th Royal Veteran Battalion	Francis, 1st Earl of Kilmorey	16 April 1804
	John Kerr	25 June 1810
6th Royal Veteran Battalion	Paulus Irving	25 December 1802
7th Royal Veteran Battalion	Thomas Murray	25 December 1802
8th Royal Veteran Battalion	John Watson	29 December 1804
9th Royal Veteran Battalion	Colin Mackenzie	21 March 1805
10th Royal Veteran Battalion	Lowther, 2nd Lord Muncaster	25 December 1806
11th Royal Veteran Battalion	Andrew Drummond	25 April 1807
12th Royal Veteran Battalion	John Despard	25 June 1808
	George Benson	31 August 1809
13th Royal Veteran Battalion	William Raymond	19 November 1812

Table 3.31 Regimental Colonels of the Royal Veteran Battalions 1815

Regiment	Colonel	Date appointed
1st Royal Veteran Battalion	None appointed	
2nd Royal Veteran Battalion	John Watson	29 December 1804
3rd Royal Veteran Battalion	Paulus Irving	25 December 1802
4th Royal Veteran Battalion	Lowther, 2nd Lord Muncaster	25 December 1806
5th Royal Veteran Battalion	Andrew Drummond	25 April 1807

Regiment	Colonel	Date appointed
6th Royal Veteran Battalion	None appointed	
7th Royal Veteran Battalion	William Raymond	19 November 1812
8th Royal Veteran Battalion	Alexander Mair	15 June 1815

Table 3.32 Regimental colonels of the King's German Legion (KGL) 1805–15

Regiment	Colonel	Date appointed
The KGL	Adolphus, Duke of Cambridge	12 November 1803
1st Light Dragoons†	George, Baron Bock*	18 August 1804
	John, Count Walmoden Gimborn*	17 March 1813
	William de Dornberg*	15 June 1815
2nd Light Dragoons†	Otto, Baron Schutte*	21 January 1806
	Claus Baron Decken*	1 August 1810
	Adolphus, Baron Veltheim*	24 January 1814
1st Hussars‡	Charles, Baron Linsingen*	18 August 1804
2nd Hussars‡	Victor, Baron Alten*	19 December 1804
3rd Hussars‡	John, Baron Reden*	18 December 1804
	Adolphus, Baron Veltheim*	7 May 1810
	Frederick de Arentsschildt*	26 January 1814
1st Light Battalion	Charles, Baron Alten*	22 December 1804
2nd Light Battalion	Colin Halkett	17 November 1803
1st Line Battalion	Adolphus, Duke of Cambridge*	17 November 1803
2nd Line Battalion	Adolphus, Baron Barsse*	21 December 1804
3rd Line Battalion	Henry de Hinuber*	9 July 1805
4th Line Battalion	Ernest, Baron Langwerth*	16 December 1804
	Sigismund, Baron Low*	17 August 1809
5th Line Battalion	George de Drieberg*	1 April 1804
	George Klingsohr*	2 June 1810
	Christian, Baron Ompteda*	17 August 1813
	Louis, Baron Bussche*	20 June 1815
6th Line Battalion	Augustus Honstedt*	15 December 1804
7th Line Battalion	Frederick, Baron Dreschel*	21 January 1806
8th Line Battalion	Peter du Plat*	18 September 1804
Foreign Veteran Battalion	Claus, Baron Decken*	24 January 1814
King's German Artillery	Frederick, Baron Decken*	28 July 1803

† Raised as Dragoons. Renamed 1813.
‡ Raised as Light Dragoons. Renamed 1813.

Table 3.33 Regimental colonels of the various foreign corps 1805–15

Regiment	Colonel	Date appointed
Brunswick-Oels's Corps	Frederick, Duke of Brunswick	25 September 1809
Hussars	William de Dornberg*	25 September 1809
	Vacant	15 June 1815
Roll's Regiment	Lewis, Baron de Roll	9 December 1794
	Francis, Baron de Rottenburg	2 September 1813
Dillon's Regiment	Edward Dillon	1 February 1794
Meuron's Regiment	Pierre Frederick, Count de Meuron	30 March 1795
	George Walker	24 October 1812
Watteville's Regiment	Frederick de Watteville	1 May 1801
	Louis de Watteville	7 May 1812
Chasseurs Britanniques	John Ramsay	10 February 1803
York Light Infantry Volunteers	Charles Green	16 January 1804
	Edwin Hewgill	29 August 1808
	Alexander Campbell	27 December 1809
	John Byng	26 December 1815
Royal Corsican Rangers	Hudson Lowe	25 June 1804
Sicilian Regiment	John Sherbrooke	5 February 1807
	Ronald Ferguson	25 January 1809
1st Greek Light Infantry	John Oswald	25 February 1811
2nd Greek Light Infantry	Richard Church*	27 May 1813

Trivia: *County titles were first awarded as subtitles to regiments in 1782. However there was no real connection with the county to obtain recruits and regiments continued to recruit generally anywhere in Britain and Ireland. When volunteering from the militia was allowed and volunteers could choose their regiment, the county militia did not necessarily choose their county regiment. The Cambridgeshire Militia opted for the 95th Foot or the Royal Marines instead of the 30th (Cambridgeshire) Foot.*

The Regiment

Table 3.34 Regimental commanders of the Royal Regiment of Artillery, the Horse Brigade and the Invalid Battalion 1805–15

Regiment	Colonel	Date appointed
Master General of the Ordnance	John, 2nd Earl of Chatham	16 June 1801
	Francis, 1st Marquess of Hastings	14 February 1806
	John, 2nd Earl of Chatham	4 April 1807
	Henry, 1st Earl of Mulgrave	5 May 1810
Lieutenant General of the Ordnance	Thomas Trigge	6 November 1804
	Hildebrand Oakes	1 February 1814
Horse Brigade	Vaughan Lloyd*	14 October 1801
1st Battalion	Anthony Farrington*	25 April 1796
2nd Battalion	Ellis Walker*	25 September 1796
3rd Battalion	Thomas Davies*	13 July 1799
	John Ramsey*	17 March 1812
4th Battalion	Duncan Drummond*	6 March 1795
	George Fead*	28 June 1805
	William Cuppage*	21 November 1815
5th Battalion	James Pattison*	25 April 1777
	William Huddlestone*	2 March 1805
	Thomas Trotter*	14 February 1814
6th Battalion	Philip Martin*	2 October 1799
7th Battalion	John Stewart*	17 May 1803
	Orlando Manley*	13 January 1807
	Edward Stephens*	16 December 1808
	John Smith*	3 July 1815
8th Battalion	William Congreve*	12 September 1803
	John Macleod*	1 May 1814
9th Battalion	Thomas Blomefield*	1 June 1806
10th Battalion	Robert Lawson*	1 February 1808
Invalid Battalion	William Borthwick*	12 November 1800
	Edward Fage*	28 June 1808
	Robert Douglas*	4 September 1809

Regimental facings in 1814–15

Except as noted all British regiments wore scarlet coats with facings on the collar and cuffs. The facing colour, officers' lace and metal (buttons) style and men's lace buttonhole loops helped to distinguish the different regiments. Royal regiments all had blue facings. If a regiment was granted either the title 'Royal' or a subtitle for a member of the royal family, the regiment would change its facing colour to blue. Only units in the Army Lists for 1814 and 1815 are given.

Key:
B1 = Bastion loops single arranged evenly
B2 = Bastion loops in pairs
S1 = Square end loops single arranged evenly
S2 = Square end loops in pairs
P1 = Pointed loops single arranged evenly
P2 = Pointed loops in pairs
P3 = Pointed loops in sets of three

Table 3.35   Regimental facings of the cavalry 1814–15

Regiment	Facings	Lace/metal
1st Life Guards	Blue	Gold
2nd Life Guards	Blue	Gold
Royal Horse Guards*	Scarlet	Gold
1st Dragoon Guards	Blue	Gold
2nd Dragoon Guards	Black	Silver
3rd Dragoon Guards	White	Gold
4th Dragoon Guards	Blue	Silver
5th Dragoon Guards	Green	Gold
6th Dragoon Guards	White	Silver
7th Dragoon Guards	Black	Gold
1st Dragoons	Blue	Gold
2nd Dragoons	Blue	Gold
3rd Dragoons	Blue	Gold
4th Dragoons	Green	Silver
6th Dragoons	Yellow	Silver
7th Light Dragoons*	Blue	Gold
8th Light Dragoons*	Scarlet	Gold
9th Light Dragoons*	Crimson	Gold
10th Light Dragoons*	Blue	Silver
11th Light Dragoons*	Buff	Silver
12th Light Dragoons*	Yellow	Silver
13th Light Dragoons*	Buff	Gold
14th Light Dragoons*	Orange	Silver
15th Light Dragoons*	Scarlet	Silver
16th Light Dragoons*	Scarlet	Silver
17th Light Dragoons*	White	Silver
18th Light Dragoons*	White	Silver

The Regiment

Regiment	Facings	Lace/metal
19th Light Dragoons*	Yellow	Gold
20th Light Dragoons*	Orange	Gold
21st Light Dragoons*	Black	Silver
22nd Light Dragoons*	White	Gold
23rd Light Dragoons*	Crimson	Silver
24th Light Dragoons*	Light Grey	Gold
25th Light Dragoons*	Light Grey	Silver

* Wore a blue coat.

Table 3.36   Regimental facings of the infantry and the KGL 1814–15

Regiment	Facings	Lace/metal	Men's lace
1st Foot Guards	Blue	Gold	B1
Coldstream Guards	Blue	Gold	P2
3rd Foot Guards	Blue	Gold	P3
1st Foot	Blue	Gold	S2
2nd Foot	Blue	Silver	S1
3rd Foot	Buff	Silver	S2
4th Foot	Blue	Gold	B1
5th Foot	Gosling green	Silver	B1
6th Foot	Yellow	Silver	S2
7th Foot	Blue	Gold	S1
8th Foot	Blue	Gold	S1
9th Foot	Yellow	Silver	S2
10th Foot	Yellow	Silver	S1
11th Foot	Deep green	Gold	B2
12th Foot	Yellow	Gold	B2
13th Foot	Yellow	Silver	S2
14th Foot	Buff	Silver	S2
15th Foot	Yellow	Silver	S2
16th Foot	Yellow	Silver	S1
17th Foot	White	Silver	S2
18th Foot	Blue	Gold	S2
19th Foot	Green	Gold	S2
20th Foot	Yellow	Silver	S2
21st Foot	Blue	Gold	S2
22nd Foot	Buff	Gold	B2
23rd Foot	Blue	Gold	B1
24th Foot	Green	Silver	S2
25th Foot	Blue	Gold	B1
26th Foot	Yellow	Silver	S2

Table 3.36 continued

Regiment	Facings	Lace/metal	Men's lace
27th Foot	Buff	Gold	S1
28th Foot	Yellow	Silver	S2
29th Foot	Yellow	Silver	P2
30th Foot	Pale yellow	Silver	B1
31st Foot	Buff	Silver	S1
32nd Foot	White	Gold	S2
33rd Foot	Red	Silver	B2
34th Foot	Yellow	Silver	S2
35th Foot	Orange	Silver	S2
36th Foot	Gosling green	Gold	S2
37th Foot	Yellow	Silver	S2
38th Foot	Yellow	Silver	S1
39th Foot	Pea green	Gold	S2
40th Foot	Buff	Gold	S2
41st Foot	Red	Silver	B1
42nd Foot	Blue	Gold	B1
43rd Foot	White	Silver	S2
44th Foot	Yellow	Silver	S1
45th Foot	Dark green	Silver	B2
46th Foot	Pale yellow	Silver	S2
47th Foot	White	Silver	S2
48th Foot	Buff	Gold	S2
49th Foot	Green	Silver	B1
50th Foot	Black	Silver	S2
51st Foot	Grass green	Gold	P2
52nd Foot	Buff	Silver	S2
53rd Foot	Red	Gold	S2
54th Foot	Green	Silver	S2
55th Foot	Green	Gold	S2
56th Foot	Purple	Silver	S2
57th Foot	Yellow	Gold	S2
58th Foot	Black	Gold	S1
59th Foot	White	Gold	B1
60th Foot*	Blue/Red	Silver	None
61st Foot	Buff	Silver	S1
62nd Foot	Buff	Silver	S2
63rd Foot	Deep green	Silver	S2
64th Foot	Black	Gold	S2

* Coat was scarlet or green depending upon battalion. Green coats were faced red.

The Regiment

Regiment	Facings	Lace/metal	Men's lace
66th Foot	Gosling green	Silver	S1
65th Foot	White	Gold	S2
67th Foot	Yellow	Silver	S2
68th Foot	Bottle Green	Silver	S2
69th Foot	Green	Gold	S2
70th Foot	Black	Gold	S1
71st Foot	Buff	Silver	S1
72nd Foot	Yellow	Silver	B1
73rd Foot	Dark Green	Gold	B1
74th Foot	White	Gold	S1
75th Foot	Yellow	Silver	S2
76th Foot	Red	Silver	S2
77th Foot	Yellow	Silver	S1
78th Foot	Buff	Gold	B1
79th Foot	Dark Green	Gold	S2
80th Foot	Yellow	Gold	S2
81st Foot	Buff	Silver	S2
82nd Foot	Yellow	Silver	B2
83rd Foot	Yellow	Gold	S2
84th Foot	Yellow	Silver	S2
85th Foot	Yellow	Silver	S2
86th Foot	Blue	Silver	S2
87th Foot	Green	Gold	S2
88th Foot	Yellow	Silver	S2
89th Foot	Black	Gold	S2
90th Foot	Buff	Gold	S2
91st Foot	Yellow	Silver	S2
92nd Foot	Yellow	Silver	S2
93rd Foot	Yellow	Silver	P2
94th Foot	Green	Gold	S2
95th Foot*	Black	None indicated	None
96th Foot	Buff	Silver	S2
97th Foot	Blue	Silver	S2
98th Foot	Buff	Silver	S1
99th Foot	Pale yellow	Silver	S1
100th Foot	Deep yellow	Silver	S2
101st Foot	White	Silver	S2
102nd Foot	Yellow	Silver	S2
103rd Foot†	White	Silver	S1

* Wore a green uniform.
† Although recorded in the army list as white, the facing colour was pale buff.

Table 3.36 continued

Regiment	Facings	Lace/metal	Men's lace
65th Foot	White	Gold	S2
1st West India Regiment	White	Silver	S2
2nd West India Regiment	Yellow	Gold	S2
3rd West India Regiment	Yellow	Silver	S2
4th West India Regiment	Green	Silver	S1
5th West India Regiment	Green	Gold	S1
6th West India Regiment	Yellow	Silver	S1
7th West India Regiment	Yellow	Silver	S1
8th West India Regiment	Grey	Silver	S1
Royal York Rangers*	Blue	Silver	None
Royal West India Rangers*	Scarlet	Not known	None
Royal African Corps	Blue	Not known	Not known
York Chasseurs*	Red	Silver	None
1st Ceylon Regiment	Buff	Gold	S1
2nd Ceylon Regiment	Green	Gold	S1
3rd Ceylon Regiment	Yellow	Gold	S1
4th Ceylon Regiment	White	Gold	S1
Cape Regiment*	Black	Not known	None
Bourbon Regiment*	Black	Not known	None
Garrison Battalions	Blue	Gold	S2
Royal Veteran Battalions	Blue	Gold	S1
Royal Newfoundland FI	Blue	Gold	S1
Nova Scotia FI	Yellow	Gold	B1
Canadian FI	Yellow	Gold	S1
Glengarry Light Infantry FI*	Black	Silver	None
New Brunswick FI	White	Silver	S1
1st KGL Light Dragoons†	Crimson	Gold	N/A
2nd KGL Light Dragoons†	Crimson	Silver	N/A
1st KGL Hussars†	Scarlet	Gold	N/A
2nd KGL Hussars†	White	Gold	N/A
3rd KGL Hussars†	Yellow	Silver	N/A
KGL Light Battalions‡	Black	Silver	None
KGL Line Battalions	Blue	Gold	S2

* Wore a green uniform.
† Wore a blue coat.
‡ Wore a green coat.

Table 3.37 Regimental facings of miscellaneous regiments 1814–15

Regiment	Facings	Lace/Metal	Men's lace
Brunswick Oels's Hussars*	Light Blue	None	N/A
Brunswick Oels's Infantry*	Light Blue	None	N/A
de Roll's Regiment	Sky Blue	Silver	S1
Dillon's Regiment	Yellow	Silver	B1
de Meuron's Regiment	Sky Blue	Silver	B1
de Watteville's Regiment	Black	Silver	B1
Chasseurs Britanniques	Light Blue	Silver	Not known
York Light Infantry Volunteers†	Black	Silver	None
Royal Corsican Rangers†	Scarlet	Not Known	None
Sicilian Regiment	Green	Gold	Not known
1st Greek Light Infantry	Yellow	Not Known	None
2nd Greek Light Infantry	Green	Not Known	None

* Wore a black uniform.
† Wore a green coat.

Trivia: The Royal Artillery wore blue coats faced red, officers had gold lace and the men's lace was B1. The Royal Engineers wore red coats faced blue with gold lace, while the Royal Sappers and Miners wore red coats faced blue with lace of B1. The Royal Waggon Train wore red coats faced blue, officers had silver lace and the men's lace was P1. The KGL Engineers, the KGA and the Royal Foreign Artillery all wore the British regulation uniform.

Battle honours awarded 1805–15

Although distinctions and honours had been awarded to regiments for service before 1805, they were few and far between. Many were granted years after the battle had been fought. For example, the battle honour for Minden 1759 was only awarded on 1 January 1801. The battle honours for the Peninsular War were awarded over a span of some thirty years starting from 1811. These honours were won by the parent regiment, its battalions, or in some cases just its flank companies (and the award subsequently granted to the entire regiment).[3]

The tables list the name of the battle honour and the regiments which received the honour. According to the regulations, only regiments under

---

3 Leslie, *Battle Honours* pp. xi, xii.

fire were awarded the battle honour. The lists are in chronological order by date of the action. Only units in the British service are given. The regiments of the army of the HEIC are not included although they too won battle honours serving alongside of the British army.

In the case of regiments numbered higher than seventeen in the cavalry and ninety-three in the infantry, battle honours were awarded to these higher numbered regiments; however, these regiments were disbanded by 1820. These honours were, in some cases, subsequently granted to the new regiments raised and allotted the same regimental number.

The spellings of the battle honours are as first awarded. Modern spellings are not used. Additional information on the Battle Honours can be found in the notes.

Table 3.38 Battle honours earned 1805–11

Battle honour and date earned
Dominica   22 February 1805
  Awarded to 46th, 1st West India
Cape of Good Hope*   7–9 January 1806
  Awarded to 24th, 59th, 71st, 72nd, 83rd, 93rd
Maida   4 July 1806
  Awarded to 20th, 27th, 35th, 58th, 61st, 78th, 81st, de Watteville's, Royal Corsican Rangers
Monte Video   3 February 1807
  Awarded to 38th, 40th, 87th, 95th
Roleia†   17 August 1808
  Awarded to 5th, 6th, 9th, 29th, 32nd, 36th, 38th, 40th, 45th, 60th, 71st, 82nd, 91st, 95th
Vimiera   21 August 1808
  Awarded to 20th LD, 2nd, 5th, 6th, 9th, 20th, 29th, 32nd, 36th, 38th, 40th, 43rd, 45th, 50th, 52nd, 60th, 71st, 82nd, 91st, 95th
Sahagun   20 December 1808
  Awarded to 15th LD
Corunna   16 January 1809
  Awarded to 1st FG, 1st, 2nd, 4th, 5th, 6th, 9th, 14th, 20th, 23rd, 26th, 28th, 32nd, 36th, 38th, 42nd, 43rd, 50th, 51st, 52nd, 59th, 71st, 76th, 79th, 81st, 82nd, 91st, 92nd, 95th

* Date of 1806 added in 1882.
† Originally awarded as 'Roleia'. Spelling of name changed to Rolica by Army Order in 1911.

Battle honour and date earned

Martinique* 30 January–24 February 1809
 Awarded to 7th, 8th, 13th, 15th, 23rd, 25th, 60th, 63rd, 90th, 1st West India, 4th West India, Royal York Rangers

Douro 10–12 May 1809
 Awarded to 14th LD, 3rd, 48th, 66th

Talavera 27–28 July 1809
 Awarded to 3rd DG, 4th D, 14th LD, 16th LD, 23rd LD, Coldm FG, 3rd FG, 3rd, 7th, 24th, 29th, 31st, 40th, 45th, 48th, 53rd, 60th, 61st, 66th, 83rd, 87th, 88th

Arabia† Sept–Dec 1809
 Awarded to 65th

Guadaloupe‡ 28 January–5 February 1810
 Awarded to 15th, 63rd, 70th, 90th, 1st West India, 4th West India Royal York Rangers

Bourbon 8 July 1810
 Awarded to 69th, 86th

Busaco 27 September 1810
 Awarded to 1st, 5th, 7th, 9th, 24th, 38th, 42nd, 43rd, 45th, 52nd, 60th, 61st, 74th, 79th, 83rd, 88th, 95th

Barrosa 5 March 1811
 Awarded to 2nd KGL H, 1st FG, Coldm FG, 3rd FG, 28th, 67th, 87th, 95th

Fuentes D'Onor 5 May 1811
 Awarded to 1st D, 14th LD, 16th LD, Coldm FG, 3rd FG, 24th, 42nd, 43rd, 45th, 51st, 52nd, 60th, 71st, 74th, 79th, 83rd, 88th, 92nd, 95th

Albuhera 16 May 1811
 Awarded to 3rd DG, 4th D, 13th LD, 3rd, 7th, 23rd, 28th, 29th, 31st, 34th, 39th, 48th, 57th, 60th, 66th

El Bodon 25 September 1811
 Awarded to 1st KGL H

Java 4–26 August 1811
 Awarded to 14th, 59th, 69th, 78th, 89th

Arroyo dos Molinos 28 October 1811
 Awarded to 34th

Tarifa 31 December 1811
 Awarded to 47th, 87th

---

* Battle honour changed to Martinique 1809 by Army Order in 1909.
† Awarded for service in the Persian Gulf for 1809 (and also for 1819 and 1820).
‡ Battle honour changed to Guadaloupe 1810 by Army Order in 1909.

Table 3.39 Battle honours earned from 1812–13

Battle honour and date earned

Ciudad Rodrigo   8–19 January 1812
  Awarded to 5th, 43rd, 45th, 52nd, 60th, 74th, 77th, 83rd, 88th, 94th, 95th

Badajos   17 March to 7 April 1812
  Awarded to 4th, 5th, 7th, 23rd, 27th 30th, 38th, 40th, 43rd, 44th, 45th 48th, 52nd, 60th, 74th, 77th, 83rd, 88th, 94th, 95th

Almaraz   20 May 1812
  Awarded to 50th, 71st, 92nd

Salamanca   22 July 1812
  Awarded to 5th DG, 3rd D, 4th D, 11th LD, 12th LD, 14th LD, 16th LD, Coldm FG, 3rd FG, 1st, 2nd , 4th, 5th ,7th, 9th, 11th, 23rd, 24th, 27th, 30th, 32nd, 36th, 38th, 40th, 42nd, 43rd, 44th, 45th, 48th, 51st, 52nd, 53rd, 58th, 60th, 61st, 68th, 74th, 79th, 83rd, 88th, 94th, 95th

Garcia Hernandez   23 July 1812
  Awarded to 1st KGL D, 2nd KGL D

Detroit   16 August 1812
  Awarded to 41st

Queenstown*   13 October 1812
  Awarded to 41st , 49th

Venta del Pozo   23 October 1812
  Awarded to 1st KGL Lt Bn, 2nd KGL Lt Bn

Miami†   5 May 1813
  Awarded to 41st

Vittoria   21 June 1813
  Awarded to 3rd DG, 5th DG, 3rd D, 4th D, 13th LD, 14th LD, 15th LD, 16th LD, 1st, 2nd, 3rd, 4th, 5th, 6th, 7th, 9th, 20th, 23rd, 24th, 27th, 28th, 31st, 34th, 38th, 39th, 40th, 43rd, 45th, 47th, 48th, 50th, 51st, 52nd, 53rd, 57th, 58th, 59th, 60th, 66th, 68th, 71st, 74th, 82nd, 83rd, 87th, 88th, 92nd, 94th , 95th

Pyrenees   25 July to 2 August 1813
  Awarded to 14th LD, 2nd, 3rd, 6th, 7th, 11th, 20th, 23rd, 24th, 27th, 28th, 31st, 32nd, 34th, 36th, 39th, 40th, 42nd, 43rd, 45th, 48th, 50th,

---

* The battle was actually fought on Queenston Heights and not at some place called Queenstown. There was no Queenstown on the Niagara Peninsula in 1812, although some British and American accounts call it such. This is probably why the Battle Honour was awarded under that name. The town under the heights was and is known as Queenston.

† Refers to the battle near Fort Meigs on the Miami or Maumee River.

Battle honour and date earned
Pyrenees continued
    51st, 52nd, 53rd, 57th, 58th, 60th, 61st, 66th, 68th, 71st, 74th, 79th, 82nd, 88th, 91st, 92nd, 95th
St Sebastian   9 June to 9 September 1813
    Awarded to 1st, 4th, 9th, 38th, 47th 58th
Göhrde   16 September 1813
    Awarded to 1st KGL H
Nivelle   10 to 12 November 1813
    Awarded to 2nd, 3rd, 5th, 6th, 11th, 23rd, 24th, 27th, 28th, 31st, 32nd, 34th, 36th, 39th, 40th, 42nd, 43rd, 45th, 48th, 50th, 51st, 52nd, 53rd, 57th, 58th, 60th, 66th, 68th, 74th, 79th, 82nd, 83rd, 87th, 88th, 91st, 94th, 95th
Nive   9 December 1813
    Awarded to 16th LD, 1st FG, Coldm FG, 3rd FG, 1st, 3rd, 4th, 9th, 11th, 28th, 31st, 32nd, 34th, 36th, 38th, 39th, 42nd, 43rd, 47th, 50th, 52nd, 57th, 59th, 60th, 61st, 62nd, 66th, 71st, 76th, 79th, 84th, 85th, 91st, 92nd, 95th

---

Trivia: The Royal Artillery and Royal Engineers were present at every major action during the wars, yet they did not receive any Battle Honours, except for Waterloo, granted 23 December 1815.[4] However, two units of the Royal Artillery were granted distinctions for their conduct, the Rocket Troop received Leipsic, granted 16 May 1816 and Holcroft's Company, 4th Battalion received Niagara granted 28 September 1816. It was only on 9 July 1832 that the Royal Artillery and Royal Engineers received the distinct mottoes of Ubique *(Everywhere) and* Quo fas et gloria ducunt *(Where right and glory lead) to honour their participation in any actions. Honour titles, granted to individual troops and companies, were only authorised in the twentieth century, but are not considered battle honours.[5]*

---

4 The King's German Artillery was also granted Waterloo.
5 Some units would choose the name of a battle it distinguished itself at, such as the choice of Corunna, Talavera and Martinique 1809; while, other troops and companies chose nicknames and names of battery commanders to commemorate their achievements. These include Chestnut Troop, Rocket Troop, T. Rogers, Lloyd and Lawson, the latter three having served either in the Peninsula or at Waterloo.

Table 3.40 Battle honours earned 1814–15

Battle honour and date earned

Orthes   27 February 1814
  Awarded to 7th LD, 13th LD, 14th LD, 3rd, 5th, 6th , 7th, 11th, 20th, 23rd, 24th, 27th, 28th, 31st, 32nd, 34th, 36th, 39th , 40th, 42nd, 45th, 48th, 50th, 51st, 52nd, 58th, 60th, 61st, 66th, 68th, 71st, 74th, 82nd, 83rd, 87th, 88th, 91st, 92nd, 94th, 95th

Toulouse   10 April 1814
  Awarded to 5th DG, 3rd D, 4th D, 13th LD, 2nd, 3rd, 5th, 7th, 11th, 20th, 23rd, 27th, 28th, 36th, 40th, 42nd, 43rd 45th, 48th, 52nd, 53rd, 60th, 61st, 74th, 79th, 83rd, 87th, 88th, 91st, 94th, 95th

Peninsula*   1809 to 1814
  Awarded to 1st LGd, 2nd LGd, RHG, 3rd DG, 4th DG, 5th DG, 1st D, 3rd D, 4th D, 7th LD, 9th LD, 10th LD, 11th LD, 12th LD, 13th LD, 14th LD, 15th LD, 16th LD, 18th LD, 20th LD, 23rd LD, 1st FG, Coldm FG, 3rd FG, 1st, 2nd, 3rd, 4th, 5th, 6th, 7th , 9th, 10th, 11th, 20th, 23rd, 24th, 27th, 28th, 29th, 30th 31st, 32nd, 34th, 36th, 37th 38th, 39th, 40th, 42nd, 43rd, 44th, 45th, 47th, 48th, 50th, 51st, 52nd, 53rd, 57th, 58th, 59th, 60th 61st , 62nd, 66th, 67th, 68th, 71st, 74th, 76th, 77th, 79th, 81st, 82nd, 83rd, 84th, 85th, 87th, 88th, 91st, 92nd, 94th, 95th, 97th , 13th Royal Veteran Bn, Roll's R, de Watteville's R, Dillon's R, Chasseurs Britanniques, Brunswick H, Brunswick LI, KGL: 1st LD, 2nd LD, 1st H, 2nd H, 3rd H, 1st Lt Bn, 2nd Lt Bn, 1st L Bn, 2nd L Bn, 4th L Bn, 5th L Bn, 6th L Bn, 7th L Bn

Bladensburg   24 August 1814
  Awarded to 4th, 21st, 44th, 85th

Niagara†   1813 to 1814
  Awarded to 19th LD, 1st, 6th, 8th, 41st, 82nd, 89th, 100th, 103rd, 104th, Glengarry Light Infantry Fencibles, Holcroft's Company RA

India‡
  Awarded to 12th, 69th, 84th, 86th

India with Royal Tiger‡
  Awarded to 14th, 65th, 67th, 75th

Hindoostan‡
  Awarded to 8th LD

Hindoostan with Royal Tiger‡
  Awarded to 17th

---

* Awarded for general service in the Peninsula on 29 March 1815.
† Awarded for general service on the Niagara Peninsula including the capture of Fort Niagara 19 December 1813 and Battle of Lundy's Lane 25 July 1814.
‡ Awarded for general service in India for various years 1805 to 1815.

Battle honour and date earned
Hindoostan with Elephant & Howdah*
 Awarded to 76th
Waterloo   18 June 1815
 Awarded to 1st LGd, 2nd LGd, RHG, 1st DG, 1st D, 2nd D, 6th D, 7th LD, 10th LD, 11th LD, 12th LD, 13th LD, 15th LD, 16th LD, 18th LD, 23rd LD, 1st FG, Coldm FG, 3rd FG, 1st, 4th, 14th, 23rd, 27th, 28th, 30th , 32nd, 33rd, 40th, 42nd, 44th, 51st, 52nd, 69th, 71st, 73rd , 79th, 92nd, 95th, RA, RE. KGL: 1st LD, 2nd LD, 1st H, 3rd H, 1st Lt Bn, 2nd Lt Bn, 1st L Bn, 2nd L Bn, 3rd L Bn, 4th L Bn, 5th L Bn, 8th L Bn, KGA

* Awarded for general service in India for various years 1805 to 1815.

Regimental nicknames

Most British regiments of the Napoleonic Wars had earned a nickname. Sometimes they received them for heroic deeds on the battlefield, while other times they earned them through some event that was caused by the misconduct of their soldiers or from their uniforms. Unfortunately over the years, even though the nickname has stuck, for some regiments the reasons why they were given the nickname have been lost.

Table 3.41   Nicknames of the cavalry regiments

Regiment	Nickname	Reason for nickname
Household Cavalry	Unfortunate Gentlemen	Unknown
The Life Guards	The Cheeses or Cheesemongers	Reduction in social qualifications for recruiting officers, made members of the regiment declare they were 'no longer gentlemen but cheesemongers' i.e. tradesmen
	Piccadilly Butchers	Used to quell the Burdett riots
	Roast and Boil	Part of the Guard thought to be better fed than the Line
Royal Horse Guards	The Blues	Colour of uniform
1st Dragoon Guards	The Trades Union	Used to quell trade riots
1st Dragoon Guards	The Royals	Regimental name

Table 3.41   continued

Regiment	Nickname	Reason for nickname
2nd Dragoon Guards	The Bays	Colour of horses
	Rusty Buckles	After a less than spectacular parade in Ireland
3rd Dragoon Guards	The Old Canaries	Colour of facings
4th Dragoon Guards	The Blue Horse	Colour of facings
5th Dragoon Guards	The Green Horse	Colour of facings
	The Green Dragoons	Colour of facings
	The Old Farmers	After 80 years in Ireland
7th Dragoon Guards	The Black Horse	Colour of facings
	The Virgin Mary's Bodyguard	Sent by George II to assist Maria Theresa of Austria
1st Dragoons	The Bird Catchers	Captured eagle at Waterloo
2nd Dragoons	The Greys	Colour of uniforms when first raised. Also colour of horses.
	The Bird Catchers	Captured eagle at Waterloo
6th Dragoons	The Old Inniskillings/ The Inniskillings	Regimental badge had Inniskilling Castle on it
	The Skillingers	Slang for Inniskilling
7th Light Dragoons	The Saucy Seventh	High uniform standards
11th Light Dragoons	The Cherry Pickers	Detachment captured by French while picking cherries
12th Light Dragoons	The Supple Twelfth	High standards of training that led to superb performance at Salamanca
13th Light Dragoons	The Lily-Whites	White stripe on overalls
	The Ragged Brigade	Worn out equipment and clothing
14th Light Dragoons	Hawks	Eagle on shako plate resembled a hawk
	The Emperor's Chambermaids	Captured King Joseph's chamberpot at Vitoria
15th Light Dragoons	Eliott's Light Horse	Reference to George Augustus Eliott, who

The Regiment

Regiment	Nickname	Reason for nickname
		raised them to help quell a strike by journeymen tailors
15th Light Dragoons	The Tabs	Large number recruits who joined the regiment when it was raised who were formerly journeymen tailors
17th Light Dragoons	The Horse Marines	Because a detachment served on the HMS *Hermione*
18th Light Dragoons	Drogheda Light Horse	Originally from Ireland
Light Dragoons	Young Eyes	Given to them by Foot Guards

Table 3.42 Nicknames of the infantry regiments

Regiment	Nickname	Reason for nickname
Foot Guards	Old Eyes	Given to them by Light Dragoons
1st Foot Guards	The Tow-Rows	From the regimental march
	The Coalers	Regiment's officers once hired the men out to heave coal to raise money to refurbish the officers' mess at St James's Palace.
Coldstream Guards	Coldstreamers	Recruited from Coldstream, Scotland
1st Foot	Pontius Pilate's Bodyguards	Oldest regiment in the army
2nd Foot	Kirke's Lamb	Regimental badge is the Paschal Lamb and they were commanded by a Colonel Kirke
3rd Foot	The Buffs	Colour of facings
	The Resurrectionists/ Resurrection Men	Large number of wounded men and those who escaped from the French after Albuera
4th Foot	The Lions	Regimental badge showed a lion
5th Foot	The Fighting Fifth	Wellington's comment: 'The ever-fighting, often tried, but never failing Fifth.'

Table 3.42 continued

Regiment	Nickname	Reason for nickname
5th Foot	The Old and Bold	Service at Roliça
	Wellington's Bodyguard	Often served as army HQ guard
6th Foot	Saucy 6th	High recruiting standards
7th Foot	The Elegant Extracts	Regiment raised with officers from many regiments
8th Foot	The Leather Hats	Used civilian hats during American War of Independence
9th Foot	The Fighting Ninth	Unknown
	The Holy Boys	Spanish thought figure of Britannia on their shako plate was the Virgin Mary
10th Foot	The Yellow Bellies	After Yellow Belly frog of the Lincolnshire Fens
	The Springers	Used as light infantry during the American War of Independence
11th Foot	The Bloody Eleventh	From heavy casualties at Salamanca (340 of 412)
12th Foot	The Old Twelfth	Number of regiment
	The Old Dozen	Number of regiment
14th Foot	Calvert's Entire	Colonel was Sir Harry Calvert and had three battalions from 1813–16
15th Foot	The Snappers	At the Battle of Brandywine, they ran short of ball which was distributed to the best shots, while the rest 'snapped' powder charges.
16th Foot	The Old Bucks	From Buckinghamshire also senior to 85th Foot
17th Foot	The Tigers	Served in India; regimental badge was the Bengal Tiger
18th Foot	Paddy's Blackguards	Irish Regiment
	The Namurs	For service at Namur
19th Foot	The Green Howards	Colour of facings and colonel named Howard
20th Foot	Kingsley's Stand	When stood down by the Duke of Brunswick and placed in reserve due to casualties after Minden, MG Kingsley, also colonel of the regiment, declined to obey the order with the words 'Kingsley's Regiment, at its own request will

The Regiment

Regiment	Nickname	Reason for nickname
20th Foot		resume its portion of duty in the line.'
	The Two Tens	Regimental number always shown in Roman numerals, XX
	The Minden Boys	Service at Minden
	The Young Fusiliers	Possibly because they joined the Fusilier Brigade in 1812
21st Foot	The Grey Breeks	When first raised, wore grey trousers
22nd Foot	The Red Knights	Uniform was entirely red, including trousers
	The Two Twos	Regimental number
23rd Foot	The Nanny Goats	Mascot was a goat
	The Royal Goats	Mascot was a goat
24th Foot	Howard's Greens	To prevent confusion with 19th Foot, who also had green facings and a colonel called Howard
27th Foot	The Skins	Shortening of Inniskilling, where they were recruited
28th Foot	The Slashers	At the Battle of White Plains, the regiment had to leave its muskets behind to climb a cliff and drove the rebels from their positions with their short swords
	The Silver Tailed Dandies	Officers' coat-tails were apparently longer than regulation and had ornate silver decorations
29th Foot	The Firms	For standing firm at Albuera
30th Foot	The Three Tens	Regimental number
31st Foot	The Young Buffs	Colour of facings caused George II to mistake them for 3rd Foot: he greeted them with 'Bravo Buffs' at Dettingen. When told they were not the 'Old Buffs' but the 31st Foot, he replied, 'Then bravo, Young Buffs.'
33rd Foot	Havercake Lads	Corruption of 'have a cake lad', from the promise of oatcake to tempt recruits
34th Foot	Cumberland Gentlemen	Many officers from Cumberland

125

Table 3.42 continued

Regiment	Nickname	Reason for nickname
35th Foot	Prince of Orange's Own	William III (of Orange) gave them their orange facings
36th Foot	The Grasshoppers	Facing colour was grass green
39th Foot	The Green Linnets	Colour of facings
40th Foot	The Fighting Fortieth	Unknown
40th Foot	The Exellers	Regimental number in Roman numerals is XL
41st Foot	The Invalids	Originally raised as an invalid regiment
42nd Foot	The Forty-twa	Regimental number
44th Foot	Little Fighting Fours	Had a large number of short men
45th Foot	Old Stubborns	Because of service at Talavera
46th Foot	The Red Feathers	At Brandywine Creek, the regiment's light company defeated a group of rebels who swore revenge. So that they not be confused with another regiment the 46th stained their plumes red
47th Foot	The Cauliflowers	Colour of facings
	Wolfe's Own	Served under Wolfe at Quebec
50th Foot	The Dirty Half-Hundred	Black facings ran after they got wet
	The Blind Half-Hundred	A large number of ophthalmia cases while serving in Egypt
53rd Foot	Old Five & Threepennies	Regimental number
	The Red Regiment	Name given by Napoleon when they guarded him on St Helena
54th Foot	The Popinjays	Green shade of their faings
	The Flamers	Burned twelve privateers at New London
55th Foot	The Cattle Reavers	Recruited from border region of England and Scotland; reavers (or reivers) were cattle thieves
	The Two Fives	Regimental number
56th Foot	The Pompadours	Colour of facings, purple
57th Foot	The Steelbacks	Considered a flogging regiment
57th Foot	The Diehards	Cry to men of regimental commander as he lay seriously wounded at Albuera

Regiment	Nickname	Reason for nickname
58th Foot	The Honeysuckers	Caught stealing beehives by Wellington
	The Steelbacks	Flogged for stealing beehives
59th Foot	The Lilywhites	Colour of facings
60th Foot	The Jaggers	Regiment was mostly Germans; corruption of *Jaeger*.
61st Foot	The Flowers of Toulouse	Heavy casualties at Toulouse were very apparent due to new uniform coats on the dead
	The Springers	Used as light infantry to pursue rebels at Trois Rivières in Canada
62nd Foot	The Splashers	Had to use their buttons for ammo when they ran out of ball at Carrickfergus; their buttons thereafter had a dent or 'splash' in them.
	The Moonrakers	Nickname for people from the county of Wiltshire
63rd Foot	The Bloodsuckers	The Fleur-de-lys shako badge looked like the mosquitoes in the West Indies that spread the disease which almost wiped out the regiment
64th Foot	The Black Knots	Had black facing colour and regimental badge had heraldic device of Lord Stafford — a knot
69th Foot	The Ups and Downs	Regimental number
	The Old Agamemnons	Served as marines on HMS *Agamemnon*; nickname supposedly given to them by Admiral Nelson
71st Foot	The Assaye Regiment	For service at Assaye
72nd Foot	The Wild Macraes	Originally recruited from the Clan Macrae
76th Foot	The Old Immortals	Because of high casualties during Lake's campaigns in India.
	The Seven & Sixpennies	Regimental number
77th Foot	The Pot Hooks	Their number '7' looked like a pot-hook
78th Foot	The King's Men	Regimental motto 'Cuidich'n Righ' means 'Help to the King'

Table 3.42 continued

Regiment	Nickname	Reason for nickname
83rd Foot	Fitch's Grenadiers	Raised by Lt Colonel Fitch
85th Foot	The Young Bucks	From Buckinghamshire, but junior to the 16th Foot, also from Bucks
	The Elegant Extracts	Large number of officers court-martialled and had to be replaced by officers from other regiments
86th Foot	Royal County Downs	Irish Regiment
87th Foot	Blayney's Bloodhounds	Hunted rebels in Ireland under Lord Blayney
	The Faughs	From their motto 'Faugh-a-Ballagh' (Clear the Way)
	The Aigle Catchers	Captured an eagle at Barossa
	The Aiglers	Captured an eagle at Barossa
88th Foot	The Devil's Own	Unknown
92nd Foot	The Gay Gordon's	Unknown
95th Foot:	The Rifles	Carried rifles
	Manningham's Sharpshooters	When the unit was formed it did not have a regimental number.
	The Sweeps	The uniform was such a dark green they resembled chimney sweeps.
	The Grasshoppers	Green uniform
96th Foot	The Ups and Downs	Regimental number
97th Foot	The Celestials	Colour of facings
99th Foot	The Nines	From the expression 'dressed up to the nines': officers of regiment were well dressed.

Regimental agents

Virtually every regiment in the British army had a regimental agent. This individual served in a variety of roles. Often they would serve as a bank for the officers on active service. They could deposit money with their agent, transfer funds to another officer through them, or use them to pay bills. Additionally, the agent could represent an officer who wished to transfer to another regiment or to purchase a promotion, both in their own regiment and in other regiments. The King's German Legion did not have regimental agents. Although there were over twenty different agents, most regiments were represented by Greenwood, Cox, & Company of

The Regiment

Charing Cross, London. In addition to serving as a regimental agent, in 1812 Greenwood, Cox, & Company also served as the Paymaster for the officers of the Company of Gentlemen Cadets and the Corps of Foreign Artillery! The source for the information on the regimental agents is the *Army List* for January 1812.

Trivia: The most aptly named agent was Mr Graves, who represented the 2nd West India Regiment. Regiments in the West Indies had a high mortality rate among its officers.

Table 3.43   Regimental agents' addresses in 1812

Name	Address
Mr Adair	Chidley Court, Pall Mall, London
Armit & Company	Leinster Street, Dublin
Messrs. Atkinson	Ely Place, Dublin
Mr Bownas	Parliament Street, London
Mr Bruce	Pall Mall Court, London
Mr Cane & Son	Dawson Street, Dublin
Mr Collyer & Son	Lisle Street, Leicester Square, London
Mr Croasdaile	Silver Street, Golden Square, London
Mr Disney	Parliament Street, London
Donaldson & Company	Invalid Office, Whitehall
Mr James Fraser	Cleveland Row, London
Mr Gilpin	432 Strand, London
Greenwood, Cox & Company	Craig's Court, Charing Cross, London
Mr Hopkinson & Sons	Craig's Court, London
Mr Kirkland	8 Bennett Street, St James's Street
Mr Lawrie	Robert Street, Adelphi
Mr MacDonald	Pall Mall Court, London
Mr Reed & Company	Dublin
Mr Ridge	Charing Cross, London
Rolleston & Company	16 Manchester Building, London

Table 3.44   Regimental agents for the cavalry regiments

Regiment	Agent
1st Life Guards	Greenwood, Cox, & Company
2nd Life Guards	Greenwood, Cox, & Company
Royal Horse Guards	Mr Bownas
1st Dragoon Guards	Hopkinson & Sons
2nd Dragoon Guards	Greenwood, Cox, & Company

The British Army Against Napoleon

Table 3.44   continued

Regiment	Agent
3rd Dragoon Guards	Collyer & Son
4th Dragoon Guards	Hopkinson & Sons
5th Dragoon Guards	Collyer & Son
6th Dragoon Guards	Collyer & Son
7th Dragoon Guards	Mr Bownas
1st Dragoons	Greenwood, Cox, & Company
2nd Dragoons	Mr Adair (in Ireland: Reed & Fraser)
3rd Dragoons	Greenwood, Cox, & Company
4th Dragoons	Hopkinson & Sons
6th Dragoons	Messrs. Atkinsons
7th Light Dragoons	Greenwood, Cox, & Company
8th Light Dragoons	Greenwood, Cox, & Company
9th Light Dragoons	Greenwood, Cox, & Company
10th Light Dragoons	Greenwood, Cox, & Company
11th Light Dragoons	Croasdaile
12th Light Dragoons	Greenwood, Cox, & Company
13th Light Dragoons	Collyer & Son
14th Light Dragoons	Collyer & Son
15th Light Dragoons	Greenwood, Cox, & Company
16th Light Dragoons	Collyer & Son
17th Light Dragoons	Greenwood, Cox, & Company
18th Light Dragoons	Greenwood, Cox, & Company
19th Light Dragoons	Messrs Atkinsons
20th Light Dragoons	Collyer & Son
21st Light Dragoons	Greenwood, Cox, & Company
22nd Light Dragoons	Greenwood, Cox, & Company
23rd Light Dragoons	Greenwood, Cox, & Company
24th Light Dragoons	Greenwood, Cox, & Company
25th Light Dragoons	Greenwood, Cox, & Company

Trivia: *Regimental agents were prohibited from operating in both Great Britain and Ireland. This forced regiments that served in Ireland to have a different agent in Ireland from the one they used in the rest of the British Isles.*

Table 3.45   Regimental agents for the infantry

Regiment	Agent
1st Foot Guards	Greenwood, Cox, & Company
Coldstream Guards	Greenwood, Cox, & Company

The Regiment

Regiment	Agent
3rd Foot Guards	Greenwood, Cox, & Company
1st Foot	Mr Kirkland
2nd Foot	Greenwood, Cox, & Company
3rd Foot	Greenwood, Cox, & Company
4th Foot	Greenwood, Cox, & Company
5th Foot	Greenwood, Cox, & Company
6th Foot	Greenwood, Cox, & Company
7th Foot	Greenwood, Cox, & Company
8th Foot	Mr Ridge
9th Foot	Greenwood, Cox, & Company
10th Foot	Mr Bownas
11th Foot	Greenwood, Cox, & Company
12th Foot	Greenwood, Cox, & Company
13th Foot	Hopkinson & Sons
14th Foot	Greenwood, Cox, & Company
15th Foot	Mr Bounor
16th Foot	Greenwood, Cox, & Company
17th Foot	Greenwood, Cox, & Company
18th Foot	Greenwood, Cox, & Company
19th Foot	Mr Croasdaile
20th Foot	Mr MacDonald
21st Foot	Mr Lowrie (in Ireland: Reed & Company)
22nd Foot	Greenwood, Cox, & Company
23rd Foot	Greenwood, Cox, & Company
24th Foot	Mr MacDonald
25th Foot	Mr MacDonald
26th Foot	Collyer & Son
27th Foot	Mr Ridge
28th Foot	Mr MacDonald
29th Foot	Mr MacDonald
30th Foot	Mr Croasdaile
31st Foot	Greenwood, Cox, & Company
32nd Foot	Greenwood, Cox, & Company (in Ireland: Reed & Company)
33rd Foot	Greenwood, Cox, & Company
34th Foot	Mr MacDonald
35th Foot	Mr MacDonald
36th Foot	Mr Croasdaile
37th Foot	Greenwood, Cox, & Company
38th Foot	Greenwood, Cox, & Company

Table 3.45 continued

Regiment	Agent
39th Foot	Greenwood, Cox, & Company
40th Foot	Collyer & Son
41st Foot	Greenwood, Cox, & Company
42nd Foot	Greenwood, Cox, & Company
43rd Foot	Greenwood, Cox, & Company
44th Foot	Greenwood, Cox, & Company
45th Foot	Greenwood, Cox, & Company
46th Foot	Greenwood, Cox, & Company
47th Foot	Mr Ridge
48th Foot	Greenwood, Cox, & Company
49th Foot	Mr Gilpin
50th Foot	Greenwood, Cox, & Company
51st Foot	Greenwood, Cox, & Company
52nd Foot	Greenwood, Cox, & Company
53rd Foot	Greenwood, Cox, & Company
54th Foot	Greenwood, Cox, & Company
55th Foot	Donaldson & Company
56th Foot	Greenwood, Cox, & Company
57th Foot	Greenwood, Cox, & Company
58th Foot	Greenwood, Cox, & Company
59th Foot	Greenwood, Cox, & Company
60th Foot	Greenwood, Cox, & Company
61st Foot	Greenwood, Cox, & Company
62nd Foot	Greenwood, Cox, & Company
63rd Foot	Mr Fowles
64th Foot	Greenwood, Cox, & Company
65th Foot	Greenwood, Cox, & Company
66th Foot	Greenwood, Cox, & Company
67th Foot	Mr Ridge
68th Foot	Greenwood, Cox, & Company
69th Foot	Greenwood, Cox, & Company
70th Foot	Mr MacDonald
71st Foot	Greenwood, Cox, & Company
72nd Foot	Greenwood, Cox, & Company (in Ireland: Armit & Company)
73rd Foot	Greenwood, Cox, & Company
74th Foot	Greenwood, Cox, & Company
75th Foot	Greenwood, Cox, & Company
76th Foot	Croasdaile
77th Foot	Croasdaile

The Regiment

Regiment	*Agent*
78th Foot	Greenwood, Cox, & Company
79th Foot	Mr Lawrie
80th Foot	Mr Watson
81st Foot	Greenwood, Cox, & Company
82nd Foot	Mr Lawrie
83rd Foot	Greenwood, Cox, & Company
84th Foot	Donaldson & Company
85th Foot	Donaldson & Company
86th Foot	Greenwood, Cox, & Company
87th Foot	Greenwood, Cox, & Company
88th Foot	Mr MacDonald
89th Foot	Greenwood, Cox, & Company
90th Foot	Greenwood, Cox, & Company
91st Foot	Mr A. Campbell
92nd Foot	Mr Bruce (in Ireland: Bruce and Zouch)
93rd Foot	Greenwood, Cox, & Company
94th Foot	Greenwood, Cox, & Company
95th Foot	Mr Adair
96th Foot	Greenwood, Cox, & Company
97th Foot	Greenwood, Cox, & Company
98th Foot	Greenwood, Cox, & Company
99th Foot	Greenwood, Cox, & Company
100th Foot	Greenwood, Cox, & Company
101st Foot	Greenwood, Cox, & Company
102nd Foot	Greenwood, Cox, & Company
103rd Foot	Greenwood, Cox, & Company
104th Foot	Mr Gilpin
Royal African Corps	Greenwood, Cox, & Company
Royal York Rangers	Greenwood, Cox, & Company
1st West India	Greenwood, Cox, & Company
2nd West India	Mr Graves
3rd West India	Donaldson & Company
4th West India	Donaldson & Company
5th West India	Greenwood, Cox, & Company
6th West India	Greenwood, Cox, & Company
7th West India	Greenwood, Cox, & Company
8th West India	Greenwood, Cox, & Company
Royal West India Rangers	Greenwood, Cox, & Company
1st Garrison Battalion	Mr Jones (in Ireland: Mr Cane & Son)
2nd Garrison Battalion	Reed & Company
3rd Garrison Battalion	Messrs Atkinsons

Table 3.45 continued

Regiment	Agent
4th Garrison Battalion	Greenwood, Cox, & Company
5th Garrison Battalion	Armit & Borough
6th Garrison Battalion	Reed & Fraser
1st Royal Veteran Battalion	Brookshank & Company
2nd Royal Veteran Battalion	Brookshank & Company
3rd Royal Veteran Battalion	Brookshank & Company
4th Royal Veteran Battalion	Brookshank & Company
5th Royal Veteran Battalion	Brookshank & Company
6th Royal Veteran Battalion	Brookshank & Company
7th Royal Veteran Battalion	Brookshank & Company
8th Royal Veteran Battalion	Brookshank & Company
9th Royal Veteran Battalion	Brookshank & Company
10th Royal Veteran Battalion	Brookshank & Company
11th Royal Veteran Battalion	Brookshank & Company
12th Royal Veteran Battalion	Brookshank & Company

Table 3.46 Regimental agents for miscellaneous units

Unit	Agent
Veteran Company in New South Wales	Greenwood, Cox, & Company
Corps of Military Artificers	Greenwood, Cox, & Company
Permanent Assistants in Quarter Master General Department	Greenwood, Cox, & Company
Royal Artillery Drivers	Hopkinson & Son
Royal Invalid Engineers	Greenwood, Cox, & Company
Royal Staff Corps	Greenwood, Cox, & Company
Royal Waggon Train	Greenwood, Cox, & Company
Royal Newfoundland Fencible Infantry	Greenwood, Cox, & Company
Nova Scotia Fencible Infantry	Greenwood, Cox, & Company
Canadian Fencible Infantry	Greenwood, Cox, & Company
Officers Serving at Depots	Mr Ridge
Duke of Brunswick Oels's Infantry	Greenwood, Cox, & Company
Roll's Regiment	Mr Disney
Dillon's Regiment	Mr Disney
Meuron's Regiment	Mr Disney
de Watteville's Regiment	Mr Ridge

Unit	*Agent*
Chasseurs Britanniques	Mr Ridge
York Light Infantry Volunteers	Greenwood, Cox, & Company
Royal Corsican Rangers	Mr Disney
Sicilian Regiment	Mr Disney
Greek Light Infantry Corps	Mr Disney

The administration of the regiment

The army required all units to keep a set of books that included fifteen books at the regimental level, seven by the company or troop commander, six by the quartermaster and three by the regimental surgeon.

Table 3.47   Regimental books to be kept by every regiment throughout the army

1   *General Order Book*
'is to contain the Entry of all *General* and *Standing* Orders, and of all General Regulations, and Circular Letters.'

2   *Regimental Order Book*
'is to contain the Entry of all Orders issued by the General Officer Commanding the District, Brigade, &c. or by the Commanding Officer of the Regiment.'

3   *Description and Succession of Officers*
'is to contain an Account of the Names of the Officers of each Rank in the Regiment, shewing the Dates of their Appointments, their age, country, the Date of their first Commission in the Army, and the particular Vacancy to which each Officer is appointed. [...] A part of this Book is to be appropriated to the Registry of the *Non-commissioned Officers*, according to Seniority.'

4   *Description of Soldiers*
'is to contain the Registry of the Name of every Non-commissioned Officer, Trumpeter, Drummer, and Private Soldier in the Regiment, shewing the date of his enlistment and terms; or from what Corps received; his Age, Size and Description, and an Account of his former Service, specifying in what Corps he served, and for what period he served in the East or West Indies. [...] It] must likewise shew the manner in which each Man is disposed of, and the Place and Date of his Discharge, Decease, Desertion, or Transfer. [...] The entry of the names is to be made according to Priority of Enlistment.'

5   *Letter Book*
'is to contain the Entry of all Official Letters written by the Commanding Officer to any of the Public Departments, or under his Direction and Authority to any Individual, on Regimental Business.'

Table 3.47 continued
6   *Monthly Return Book*
'is to contain exact Copies of the Monthly Returns which are made up on the 25th of each Month.'
7   *Miscellaneous Return Book*
'is to contain the Entry of the Quarterly Returns of Officers absent without Leave; of the Quarterly Returns of Officers desirous to purchase; and of the Inspection Returns which are prepared for, and under the immediate Direction of the Inspecting General Officers in the Months of May and October in each Year. It is also to contain the Entry of the Embarkation and Disembarkation Returns...'
8   *Effective and Daily States*
'is to contain exact Copies of the *Effective States* which are required to be made up on the *Tenth* of each Month, and of the *Morning States*...'
9   *Registry of Furloughs*
'is to contain an account of all Leaves of Absence granted to Officers, Non-commissioned Officers, Trumpeters, Drummers, and Private Men. [...] The Entries are to shew the Name of the Person to whom Leave of Absence is granted; the period to which it is granted; the particular Place to which he has been permitted to go, and to which any Orders necessary are to be sent to him during his Absence may be addressed; and the date of his returning to the Regiment.'
10 *Description of Deserters*
'is to contain a very full and accurate Description of such Men as may be guilty of the Crime of Desertion, in Order that the Reports required by the Regulations respecting Deserters may be easily made up, and that every possible means may be adopted for apprehending, and bringing to Punishment, the Men who are guilty of this crime.'
11 *Account of Defaulters*
'should contain the Names of such Men as may be guilty of Offences and Irregularities for which they may be reported to the Commanding Officer, and for which it may not be judged necessary to cause them to be tried by Courts Martial : The nature of the Offences must be specified, and the Directions which may be given with a view of preventing a repetition of them...'
12 *Court Martial Book*
'is to contain a correct entry of the Proceedings of every Regimental Court Martial, which is to be signed by the President, and countersigned, as approved, by the Commanding Officer. [...It] is to shew the Name of the Soldier tried; the Troop or Company to which he belongs; the Time and Place at which the Court Martial assembles; the Offence with which the Soldier is charged; the Decision and Sentence of the Court Martial;

the Punishment inflicted and remitted . . .'
13 *Registry of Deceased Soldiers*
'is to contain an Entry of the Name of the Soldier, the Place, Date, and Cause of his Decease, the Amount of his Effects, and the Sums due to him at the period of his Decease.'
14 *Record Book*
'It is of importance that a Book of this nature should be kept in every Corps: It should state the period and circumstances of the original Formation of the Regiment; the means by which it has been from time to time recruited; the Stations at which the Regiment has been from time to time employed: with the periods of its arrival at, and departure from, such stations; it should specify the Battles, Sieges, and other Military operations, in which the Regiment has been engaged, and record any achievement it may have performed : It should contain the Names of any Officers killed or wounded by the Enemy; and the Name of any Officer, Non-commissioned Officer, or Private Soldier, who may have, in a particular manner, distinguished himself in Action, should be recorded in this book. The Badges and Devices which the Regiment may have been permitted to bear, and the Causes on account of which such Badges and Devices, or any other Marks of Distinction, were granted, should be stated, and the Dates of such permission being granted. Any particular Alteration in the Clothing, Arms, Accoutrements, Colours, Horse-Furniture, &c. should be recorded, and a Reference made toe the Dates of the Orders under which such Alterations were made.'
15 *Description of Horses of Cavalry Regiments*
'is to contain a Registry of the Age, Size, and Description, of the Horses of the Regiment; —the names and residence of the Person of whom they are bought; and the Date of their Purchase [. . . and] the manner in which each Horse is disposed of may be shewn.'

Source: *General Regulations* (1811) pp. 291–8.

Table 3.48 Company books to be kept by every troop and company in the army

'The Books of a Troop or Company are to be kept by the Captain, or in his absence by the Officer to whom the care and payment of the Troop or Company is entrusted, and who is of course responsible that the Books are regularly and accurately kept.'
1 *Memorandum or Day Book*
'In [it] each Soldier is to be debited with the several Articles of Regimental Necessaries, &c. which he may have received, and with the cost of such other things with which he is liable to be charged out of his Pay.'

Table 3.48   continued

2   *Ledger*

'The Entries made in the Day Book are to be transcribed into the Ledger on or before the 24th of each month. [...] The Articles with which a Soldier is charged are always to be detailed in the Ledger, and the price of each Article, and the date at which it is supplied, are always to be specified.'

3   *Order Book*

'is to contain a Copy of all General, Garrison, Brigade, and Regimental Orders, which are issued, and which are required to be read to the Soldiers, and an account of the number of Non-Commissioned Officers and Soldiers appointed for duty each Day.'

4   *Description Book, or Size Roll*

'is to contain the name, age, size, date of attestation, and former service of every Non-Commissioned Officer, Trumpeter, Drummer, and Private Soldier, belonging to the Troop or Company.'

5   *Clothing Book*

'is to shew the quantity of Clothing and Accoutrements *annually* delivered to the Men in *Infantry* Regiments (and during *Two Years* in the *Cavalry*), specifying the *Articles* delivered to *each* Man, and the periods at which they were delivered.

6   *Weekly Mess Book*

'is to contain an account of the Expenditure of that part of the Soldier's Pay, which is appropriated to *Messing*. On the left-hand, or debit side, the Sums expended in Vegetables, Washing, &c. are to be regularly entered, and the Quantities, Price, &c. of all Articles, are always to be detailed. On the right-hand, or credit side, the Names of the Non-commissioned Officers, Trumpeters, Drummers, and Private Men, are to be entered, — the Number of Days each Man is messed, and the Amount of the Expences of his Messing at the fixed Rate per Day.

7   *Description of Horses*

'is to contain an entry of the Age, Size, and Description of the Horses of the Troop. It is also to shew the Date of each Horse joining the Troop, and from whence received; a Column is to be appropriated for *Remarks*, in order that the manner in which each Horse is disposed of may be shewn.

Source: *General Regulations* (1811) pp. 291, 299–30.

Table 3.49   Quartermaster's books

1   *Account of Clothing*

'The Books to be kept by the Quarter-Master are [...] to contain correct

accounts of all Articles of Clothing, Accoutrements, Arms, Ammunition, Fuel, Forage, Provisions, &c. which are received for the Service of the Regiment, and to shew the manner in which the same are distributed.'
2   *Account of Accoutrements*
3   *Account of Arms*
4   *Account of Ammunition*
5   *Account of Fuel, Forage, and Provisions*
6   *Letter Book*
'is to contain the entries of all Letters written by the Commanding Officer, or by his Orders, on the foregoing subjects.'

Source: General Regulations (1811) pp. 291, 302.

Table 3.50   Surgeon's books

1   *Medical Diary*
'is to contain the Name of every Soldier who is admitted into Hospital, shewing the Date of his Admission;—the Nature of his Complaints;—the Means use to effect his Cure;—and the Date of his quitting the Hospital for the Purpose of returning to his Duty.'
2   *Medical Registry*
'is to contain an Account of all serious Cases of Sickness which occur among the Soldiers:—The Date at which each Man is admitted into the Hospital is to be stated, and the Nature of his Complaints, the Means used to effect his Cure, and the Result of the Medical Prescriptions, are to be fully detailed in this Book.'
3   *Hospital Accounts*
'is to contain an exact Account of all the Sums paid into the Hands of the Surgeon, on Account of Men in Hospital, and is to shew the Manner in which such Sums are expended.'

Source: General Regulations (1811) pp. 291, 303.

Chapter Four

Life of an Officer

Traditionally, among the gentry and upper classes of British society, the eldest son would inherit the family estates and business. Younger sons would often become officers in the army or the navy or a member of the clergy. The qualifications for an initial commission were few, just that the candidate be 16 years of age, be eligible in terms of health, education and character, and be prepared to join any regiment. His letter of recommendation was to be signed by a field officer or higher rank.[1] A son who wanted to join the army could try to obtain a commission either by purchase or by an appointment. The cost of purchasing a commission remained the same throughout the Napoleonic Wars. As the army expanded, commissions could be obtained without purchase in many of the regiments. However, it was close to impossible to receive a commission in a fashionable regiment (e.g. the Guards, the 52nd Foot, or the light dragoons) unless the individual was willing to purchase his commission. Commissions in the Royal Veteran Battalions, the Royal Artillery and the Royal Engineers were by appointment only.

Table 4.1 Cost of purchasing a commission in different regiments

Regiment	Cornet	Ensign	2nd Lieutenant
Life Guards	£1,600[2]	–	–
Royal Horse Guards	£1,050	–	–
Foot Guards	–	£900	–
Dragoon Guards	£735	–	–
Dragoons	£735	–	–
Foot	–	£400	–
Fusilier and rifle	–	–	£450

1 Glover, *Wellington's Army*, p. 36.
2 By 1816, the cost of a commission for a cornet had dropped to £1,260.

In addition to paying for the commission, the new officer had to pay a fee for having the King sign his commission. This fee was the same throughout the Napoleonic Wars.

Table 4.2 Fees paid for receiving a commission in different regiments

Regiment	Cornet £ s d	Ensign £ s d	2nd Lieutenant £ s d
Life Guards	8 0 6	– – –	– – –
Royal Horse Guards	6 12 6	– – –	– – –
Foot Guards	– – –	4 16 2	– – –
Dragoon Guards	6 0 6	– – –	– – –
Dragoons	6 0 6	– – –	– – –
Foot	– – –	4 11 10	– – –
Fusilier and Rifle	– – –	– – –	6 11 10

Another expense the new officer had to pay was buying his uniforms. The cost of the initial uniform as well as the type of uniform items needed varied by regiment. The following is what the typical new officer in an infantry regiment was expected to have. The cost is what was considered a standard quality uniform.

Table 4.3 Average cost of initial officer uniforms

Item	Price £ s d
Regimental hat	2 16 0
Regulation sword	2 8 0
Regulation sword knot	0 9 0
Long path silk sash	2 0 0
Regulation gorget with rosettes	0 10 6
Bleached sword belt	0 12 0
Officer's coat	0 10 6
Waistcoat	0 3 6
Breeches	0 3 6
Total	9 13 0

Source: James, *The Regimental Companion*, vol. 1, pp. 66–7, 71.

The new officer would report to his regimental depot for his initial training. Although British regiments recruited from certain geographic areas, there was no permanent location for the regimental depot. If it was a two battalion regiment, it would be where the home battalion was stationed. The officer would be assigned a room in the barracks. His rank determined the number of rooms he was authorised. If he was a cavalry officer, he would have his own room.

Table 4.4 Rooms authorised to officers in a barracks

Rank	Cavalry officers	Infantry officers
Field Officer	2	2
Captain	1	1
Subalterns	1	1 per two officers
Staff and Quartermaster	1	1
Officers' Mess	2	2

Source: Reide, *A Treatise on Military Finance*, vol. 2, p. 513.

The rooms were furnished, but the officer had to provide his own bed.

Table 4.5 Equipment furnishing an officer's room

Rank	Cavalry officers	Infantry officers
Closet	1	1
Table	1	1
Chairs	2	2
Coal Box	1	1
Coal Tray	1	1
Bellows	1	1
Fire Irons	1	1
Fender	1	1

Source: Reide, *A Treatise on Military Finance*, vol. 2, p. 516.

Should rooms not be available in the barracks, an officer would receive a housing allowance.

Table 4.6 Weekly lodging allowance for rooms when no barracks rooms available

Rank	£	s	d
Field Officers	0	10	6
Captain	0	8	0
Subalterns	0	6	0
Staff	0	6	0

Source: Reide, *A Treatise on Military Finance*, vol. 2, p. 232.

An officer also received an allowance for fuel to heat his room.

Table 4.7 Fuel allowances for officers' rooms for seven days

Item	April, September, October	May–August	November–March
Cavalry			
Coal	2½ bushels	1¾ bushels	3¼ bushels
Candles	2 pounds	1½ pounds	2½ pounds
Infantry			
Coal	2½ bushels	1¾ bushels	3¼ bushels
Candles	1 pound	¾ pound	1¼ pounds

Source: Reide, *A Treatise on Military Finance*, vol. 2, p. 514.

Pay and allowances

Pay day was the 25th of each month. An officer's pay was dependent on his regiment. Officers in Guards regiments received better pay than the line and cavalry more than infantry. The following are the pay rates for 1810. Officer pay would remain the same during the Napoleonic Wars. All pay tables are from the July 1810 *Army List*, p. 107.

Table 4.8 Daily and yearly pay for officers

Rank	Daily £ s d	Yearly £ s d
Life Guards		
Colonel	1 16 0	652 0 0
Lieutenant Colonel	1 11 0	565 16 0
Major	1 6 0	474 10 0
Captain	0 16 0	292 0 0
Lieutenant	0 11 0	200 15 0
Cornet	0 8 6	155 2 6
Adjutant	0 13 0	237 5 0
Surgeon	0 12 0	219 0 0
Assistant Surgeon	0 8 6	150 11 6
Veterinary Surgeon	0 8 0	146 0 0
Royal Horse Guards		
Colonel	2 1 0	748 5 0
Lieutenant Colonel	1 9 6	538 7 6
Major	1 7 0	492 15 0
Captain	1 1 0	383 5 0
Lieutenant	0 15 6	282 17 6
Cornet	0 14 6	264 12 6
Adjutant	0 10 0	182 0 0

Table 4.8 continued

Rank	Daily £ s d	Yearly £ s d
Surgeon	0 12 0	219 0 0
Assistant Surgeon	0 8 6	150 11 6
Veterinary Surgeon	0 8 0	146 0 0
Foot Guards		
Colonel	1 19 0	611 15 0
Lieutenant colonel	1 8 6	520 2 6
Major	1 4 6	442 2 6
Captain	0 16 6	301 2 6
Lieutenant	0 7 10	142 19 2
Ensign	0 5 10	106 9 2
Adjutant	0 10 0	182 10 0
Quartermaster	0 6 6	109 10 6
Surgeon major	1 0 0	365 0 0
Battalion Surgeon	0 12 0	219 0 0
Assistant Surgeon	0 7 6	136 19 6
Infantry		
Colonel	1 2 6	410 2 6
Lieutenant Colonel	0 17 0	310 5 0
Major	0 16 0	292 0 0
Captain with brevet rank of major or higher	0 12 6	228 2 6
Captain	0 10 6	191 12 6
Lieutenant with 7 years' service	0 7 6	136 17 6
Lieutenant	0 6 6	119 2 6
Ensign or 2nd Lieutenant	0 5 3	95 16 3
Paymaster, general service	0 15 0	273 15 0
Paymaster, limited service	0 10 0	182 10 0
Adjutant	0 8 6	155 2 6
Quartermaster	0 6 0	109 10 0
Surgeon with 20 years' service	0 18 10	343 14 3
Surgeon with 7 years' service	0 14 1	256 2 5
Surgeon	0 11 4	206 16 8
Assistant Surgeon	0 7 6	136 17 6
Dragoon Guards or Dragoons		
Colonel	1 12 10	599 4 2
Lieutenant Colonel	1 3 0	404 15 0
Major	0 19 3	351 6 3
Captain	0 14 7	266 2 11

Rank	Daily £ s d	Yearly £ s d
Lieutenant	0 9 0	164 5 0
Cornet	0 8 0	146 0 0
Paymaster, general service	0 15 0	273 15 0
Paymaster, limited service	0 10 0	182 10 0
Adjutant	0 10 0	182 10 0
Quartermaster	0 8 0	146 0 0*
Surgeon with 20 years' service	0 18 10	343 14 3
Surgeon with 7 years' service	0 14 1	256 2 5
Surgeon	0 11 4	206 16 8
Assistant surgeon	0 7 6	136 17 6
Veterinary surgeon with 20 years' service	0 15 0	273 15 0
Veterinary surgeon with 10 years' service	0 12 0	219 0 0
Veterinary surgeon with 3 years' service	0 10 0	182 10 0
Veterinary surgeon	0 8 0	146 0 0

* Includes 2s per day and £36 10s per year for a horse.

Royal Horse Artillery

	Daily	Yearly
Colonel commandant	2 19 3	1081 6 3
Colonel	1 12 0	584 0 0
Lieutenant colonel	1 6 9	488 3 9
Major	1 2 8	413 13 4
Captain with brevet rank of major or higher	0 17 11	326 19 7
Captain	0 15 11	266 2 11
Lieutenant with 7 years' service	0 10 10	197 14 2
Lieutenant	0 9 10	179 9 2
Adjutant	0 10 6	191 12 6
Quartermaster	0 10 9	196 30 9

Royal Artillery Drivers

	Daily	Yearly
Major	1 0 9	378 13 9
Captain	0 14 10	270 14 2
Lieutenant	0 9 0	164 5 0
2nd Lieutenant	0 8 0	146 0 0
Adjutant	0 10 0	182 10 0
Quartermaster	0 7 10	142 19 2
Veterinary surgeon with 20 years' service	0 15 0	273 15 0

Table 4.8 continued

Rank	Daily £ s d	Yearly £ s d
Veterinary surgeon with 10 years' service	0 12 0	219 0 0
Veterinary surgeon with 3 years' service	0 10 0	182 10 0
Veterinary surgeon	0 8 0	146 0 0
Royal Engineers on Home Service		
Colonel commandant	2 14 4	988 10 10
Colonel	1 3 9	433 8 9
Lieutenant colonel	0 17 11	326 19 7
Captain with brevet rank of major or higher	0 13 0	237 5 0
Captain	0 11 0	200 15 0
Lieutenant with 7 years' service	0 7 10	142 19 2
Lieutenant	0 6 10	124 14 2
2nd Lieutenant	0 8 0	146 0 0
Adjutant	0 6 0	109 10 0
Quartermaster	0 6 10	124 14 2

Note: Royal Engineers received double pay when on foreign service.

Pay stoppages

The pay tables above show what an officer was due prior to various deductions. These included poundage, which was a commission paid to the regimental agent; agency, which covered the cost of running the regiment; income or property tax; and the Chelsea Hospital. Stoppages accounted for 15–20 per cent of annual pay. The following tables show deductions.

Table 4.9 Stoppages or deductions to pay of officers

Stoppage item	Amount
Poundage – commission paid to the regimental agent)	This varied, but usually 5% of pay; only paid by captains and above
Agency	Usually 5%
Income Tax	10% for those officers making more than £150 per year; 5% for those making less than £150 per year
Chelsea Hospital	1 day's pay

Source: Reide, *A Treatise on Military Finance*, vol. 2, p. 171–2.

Life of an Officer

Table 4.10 Income tax paid by officers in an infantry regiment

Rank	Yearly pay £ s d	Income tax £ s d
Colonel	410 2 6	41 0 3
Lieutenant colonel	310 5 0	31 0 6
Major	292 0 0	29 0 4½
Captain with brevet rank of major or higher	228 2 6	22 1 1½
Captain	191 12 6	19 1 1
Lieutenant with 7 years' service	136 17 6	6 1 8½
Lieutenant	119 2 6	5 1 0
Ensign or 2nd Lieutenant	95 16 3	4 1 9½
Paymaster, General Service	273 15 0	27 2 1
Paymaster, Limited Service	182 10 0	18 1 5
Adjutant	155 2 6	15 1 1½
Quartermaster	109 10 0	5 1 5
Surgeon with 20 years' service	343 14 3	34 2 0
Surgeon with 7 years' service	256 2 5	25 1 10
Surgeon	206 16 8	20 2 2
Assistant surgeon	136 17 6	6 1 1

These deductions did not include the cost of food. Its cost and method of deduction depended on the regiment and location. In some regiments, the officer had his pay deducted, while in others he received a separate mess bill. A typical deduction in an infantry regiment for food was:

Table 4.11 Deductions for rations in daily and yearly pay for infantry officers

Rank	Yearly pay £ s d	Income tax £ s d
Colonel	0 18 0	328 10 0
Lieutenant colonel	0 13 0	237 5 0
Major	0 11 6	209 17 6
Captain	0 8 0	146 0 0
Lieutenant	0 5 0	91 5 0
Ensign	0 4 3	77 11 3
Surgeon	0 8 10	161 4 2

Source: Reide, *A Treatise on Military Finance*, vol. 1 page 205

For a newly commissioned infantry officer, the amount of pay he actually saw was very small... about 5 pence per day! Out of this, he had to pay for his servant, washing and mending, and miscellaneous sundries!

Table 4.12 Deductions in yearly pay for an ensign 1810

	£	s	d
Daily pay	0	5	3
Yearly pay	95	16	3
Regimental agent (5%)	4	1	9½
Agency (2.5%)	2	5	0
Income tax (5%)	4	1	9½
Chelsea Hospital (1 Day's Pay)	0	5	3
Rations (4s 3d per day)	77	11	3
Total yearly deductions	88	5	1
Yearly net pay	7	11	2
Total daily deductions	0	4	10
Daily net pay	0	0	5

John Patterson listed his daily expenses as an ensign when he was stationed in Ireland in 1807.

Table 4.13 Daily expenses of an ensign stationed in Ireland 1807

	£	s	d
Daily pay	0	5	3
Breakfast	0	0	6
Dinner at the mess	0	2	0
Wine at dinner	0	1	0
Servant and sundries	0	0	6
Washing and mending	0	0	6
Total deductions for living expenses	0	4	6
Deductions for Taxes, Agency, etc.	0	0	7
Net Pay after Deductions	0	0	0

Source: Patterson, *Camps and Quarters*, vol. 1, p. 144.

When the deductions to his pay were made, Ensign Patterson had no pay left over for spending money. For an officer of the Household Troops, the deduction for rations was even more.

Table 4.14 Deductions for daily subsistence for officers in the Life and Royal Horse Guards

Rank	Life Guards			Royal Horse Guards		
	£	s	d	£	s	d
Colonel	1	7	0	1	11	0
Lieutenant colonel	1	3	3	1	2	6

Life of an Officer

Rank	Life Guards			Royal Horse Guards		
	£	s	d	£	s	d
Major	0	19	6	1	1	6
Captain	0	12	0	0	16	6
Lieutenant	0	8	3	0	11	6
Cornet	0	7	3	0	11	0
Adjutant	0	13	0	0	10	0
Surgeon	0	9	0	0	9	0
Assistant surgeon	0	8	6	0	8	6
Veterinary surgeon	0	8	0	0	8	0

Table 4.15 Deductions for daily subsistence for officers in a Foot Guards regiment

Rank	£	s	d
Colonel	1	10	0
Lieutenant colonel	1	1	6
Major	0	18	6
Captain	0	12	6
Lieutenant	0	6	0
Ensign	0	4	6
Adjutant	0	10	0
Quartermaster	0	6	6
Surgeon major	0	16	8
Battalion surgeon	0	10	0
Assistant surgeon	0	7	6

Source: *Army List*, July 1810, p. 107.

For an ensign in the Foot Guards, the pay situation was similar to that of an ensign in a line regiment.

Table 4.16 Deductions in pay for an ensign in the foot guards in 1810

	£	s	d
Daily pay	0	5	10
Yearly pay	106	9	2
Regimental agent (5%)	5	6	5½
Agency (2.5%)	2	13	2¾
Income tax (5%)	5	6	5½
Chelsea Hospital (1 day's pay)	0	5	10
Rations (4s 6d per day)	82	2	6
Total yearly deductions	95	14	5¾

Table 4.16 continued

	£	s	d
Yearly net pay	13	14	8¼
Total daily deductions	0	5	3
Daily net pay	0	0	7

If the ensign in the Foot Guards had the same 1 shilling a day expenses for his servant and other miscellaneous things that Ensign Patterson of the 50th had, then the ensign in the foot guards was spending 5 pence a day more than he was receiving in pay.

> ***Trivia:*** *Lieutenant General John Moore stated that a junior officer could not be expected to live on his pay and that he would need an outside income of about £100 per year. Often this would be an allowance from the ensign's father or older brother, who had inherited the family estate.*

Promotions

Before 1795 there were no restrictions on how long an officer had to serve before he could purchase a new rank. This resulted in some very young majors and lieutenant colonels. Wellington himself, through the judicious use of the purchase system, was a lieutenant colonel at the age of 23. However, rules were put in place by the Duke of York, the new commander-in-chief of the British army in 1795, which regulated commissions for promotion including purchase. He ruled that no officer could be promoted captain until he had served two years as a subaltern and that no officer could be promoted major unless he had six years of service. By 1809 he further ruled that no officer could be promoted to captain unless he had served three years as a subaltern, no captain could be promoted to major unless he had served for seven years of which two years were as a captain and no major could be promoted to lieutenant colonel unless he had nine years of service.[3]

Table 4.17 Minimum number of years' service before promotion 1809

Rank	Minimum years in previous rank	Minimum no. of years of service
Lieutenant	None	None
Captain	3 years as a subaltern	3
Major	2 years as a captain	7
Lieutenant colonel	2 years as a major	9

Source: Glover; *Wellington's Army*, p. 83.

---

3 Glover, *Wellington's Army*, p. 76.

Life of an Officer

George Brown's early career is a good example of this.

Table 4.18 **The rise through the ranks of George Brown**

Rank	Regiment	Date of rank	Time in rank	Time in service
Ensign	43rd Foot	23 January 1806	–	–
Lieutenant	43rd Foot	18 September 1806	8 months	8 months
Captain	3rd Garrison Bn	30 June 1811	5 years	5 years
Captain	85th Foot	2 July 1812	–	–
Major	85th Foot	26 May 1814	3 years	8 years
Lieutenant colonel	Half pay	17 July 1823	9 years	17 years

Source: Burnham et al.

He went on to command the Light Division during the Crimean War.

The process of applying to purchase a rank was simple enough. An officer would place his name on the regimental list for promotion, which was compiled by regimental seniority. He would then deposit the necessary funds with the regimental agent or some other person that was made known to the military secretary to the commander-in-chief. Every quarter, on 25 March, 25 June, 25 September and 25 December, these regimental lists were sent to the military secretary to be correlated with those of the whole army. Normally the purchase would go to the senior officer in the regiment on the list by regimental seniority. The commander-in-chief could allow an officer from another regiment to purchase the rank, however, if he was senior in army rank to the senior officer of the regiment concerned.[4]

An officer who had purchased his previous commissions only had to pay the difference between the price of the ranks and not the full price of the next higher rank. Thus an infantry captain, for example, who wished to purchase a majority only needed to deposit the £1,100 difference between the ranks. The seller would receive the rest of the regulation price of the majority from the other officers who would purchase the succeeding promotions selling their commissions in turn and the seller received the difference for each commission (a lieutenant would pay £950 to become a captain, the ensign would pay £150 to become a Lieutenant and a gentleman would pay £400 to become an ensign for a total of £1,500 and with the captain's £1,100 adds up to £2,600 or the cost of a majority). Officers had to swear that only the regulation price was paid, since

---

4 Glover, *Wellington's Army*, p. 76–7.

151

The British Army Against Napoleon

paying a higher price for the commission than was authorised was against regulations.

An officer had to pay the difference in the cost of his commission if he exchanged into a regiment where the cost of a commission was higher, the other officer receiving the difference. For example, an infantry captain who exchanged as a captain into a cavalry regiment had to pay the £1,282 10s difference. An officer who died forfeited the purchase price of his commission. Any promotion to fill a vacancy caused by death was a non-purchase one controlled under the patronage of the commander-in-chief. The following are the cost of purchasing a commission or the next higher rank in the various regiments of the army. It was a considerable outlay of money!

Table 4.19   Price of commissions for the Household troops

Rank	Life Guards	Royal Horse Guards	Foot Guards
Lieutenant Colonel	£5,200	£4,950	£6,700
Major	£4,250	£4,050	£6,300
Captain	£3,100	£2,950	£3,500
Lieutenant	£1,750*	£1,350	£1,500
Cornet	£1,600†	£1,050	–
Ensign	–	–	£900

* By 1816 the cost of a lieutenancy had risen to £1,785.
† By 1816 the cost of a commission for a cornet had dropped to £1,260.

Table 4.20   Price of commissions for line cavalry and infantry regiments

Rank	Dragoon Guards £ s		Dragoons £ s		Foot £
Lieutenant colonel	4,982	10	4,982	10	3,500
Major	3,882	10	3,882	10	2,600
Captain	2,782	10	2,782	10	1,500
Lieutenant	997	10	997	10	550
2nd Lieutenant in fusiliers and rifles	–		–		450
Cornet	735	0	735	0	–
Ensign	–		–		400

Although much has been written about the purchase system, in reality most officers did not purchase their ranks. Michael Glover did a study of the promotions of junior officers between September 1810 and August 1811, and March 1812 and February 1813 appearing in the *London Gazette*. He discovered that only 16 per cent purchased their lieutenancy.

Life of an Officer

Table 4.21 Number of lieutenancies purchased September 1810–
August 1811 and March 1812–February 1813

Unit	No. promoted	No. purchased	% purchased
Foot regiments	975	120	12.3%
Cavalry	206	88	42.7%
Colonial corps	111	1	0.95%

Michael Glover also noted that during the Napoleonic Wars, purchased commissions only made up a fraction of the commissions granted to officers. In fact, only two in ten promotions went by purchase. The remainder were by seniority (seven in ten) and patronage of the commander-in-chief (one in ten).[5]

Regardless of whether he purchased his rank or not, the newly promoted officer would have to pay commission fees, including when he received a staff appointment. The source for the commission fee tables is the January 1814 *Army List*.

Table 4.22 Commission fees payable for staff appointments 1814

Staff Position	£	s	d
Commander of the forces	29	19	6
Brigadier general	11	17	6
Adjutant general	10	17	6
Deputy adjutant general	9	12	6
Quartermaster general	11	17	6
Deputy quartermaster general	9	12	6
Inspecting field officer of militia	10	2	6
Commissary-in-chief	15	7	6
Commissary general	15	7	6
Deputy commissary general	11	17	6
Assistant commissary general	10	2	6
Deputy assistant commissary general	5	12	6
Paymaster of a recruiting district	10	2	6
Adjutant of a recruiting district with rank of lieutenant	7	9	6
Adjutant of a recruiting district already at rank of lieutenant	5	9	6
Adjutant of militia	6	0	6
Adjutant of local militia	4	10	6
Inspector of hospitals	12	17	6
Deputy inspectors of hospitals	11	7	6

5 Glover, *Wellington's Army*, p. 82.

Table 4.22 continued

Staff Position	£	s	d
Physicians	10	17	6
Surgeons	10	2	6
Assistant surgeons	5	7	6
Surgeon of a recruiting district	9	12	6
Purveyor	10	17	6
Deputy purveyor	9	12	6
Apothecary	9	12	6
Hospital assistant	4	19	6
Chaplain general	13	14	6
Chaplain to the forces	10	4	6

Table 4.23 Commission fees payable for Household troops 1814

Rank	Life Guards			Royal Horse Guards			Foot Guards		
	£	s	d	£	s	d	£	s	d
Colonel	12	9	6	12	19	6	12	15	6
Lieutenant colonel	11	6	6	11	3	6	11	1	6
Major	10	16	6	10	18	6	10	13	6
Captain	9	16	6	10	7	6	9	17	6
Lieutenant	8	6	6	8	14	6	9	0	2
Cornet	8	0	6	6	12	6	—	—	—
Ensign	—	—	—	—	—	—	4	16	2
Adjutant	8	6	6	4	14	6	4	12	6
Quartermaster	—	—	—	6	1	6	4	13	10
Surgeon	5	7	2	5	7	2	5	7	2
Assistant surgeon	4	19	6	4	19	6	4	19	6
Veterinary surgeon	5	0	6	5	0	6	—	—	—
Solicitor	—	—	—	—	—	—	5	0	6

Table 4.24 Commission fees payable for line cavalry and infantry regiments 1814

Rank	Dragoon Guards			Dragoons			Foot		
	£	s	d	£	s	d	£	s	d
Colonel	12	7	6	12	7	6	11	5	6
Lieutenant colonel commandant	—			—			10	6	6
Lieutenant colonel	10	13	6	10	13	6	9	18	6
Major commandant	10	13	6	10	13	6	—		
Major	10	5	6	10	5	6	9	14	6

Life of an Officer

Rank	Dragoon Guards £ s d	Dragoons £ s d	Foot £ s d
Captain	9 15 6	9 15 6	9 4 6
Lieutenant	8 2 6	8 2 6	6 13 6
2nd Lieutenant	—	—	6 11 10
Cornet	6 0 6	6 0 6	—
Ensign	—	—	4 11 10
Paymaster	10 2 6	10 2 6	10 2 6
Adjutant	4 14 6	4 14 6	4 12 6
Adjutant with rank of ensign	8 12 0	8 12 0	7 8 0
Quartermaster	5 0 6	5 0 6	4 13 10
Surgeon	5 7 2	5 7 2	5 7 2
Assistant surgeon	4 19 6	4 19 6	4 19 6
Veterinary surgeon	5 0 6	5 0 6	—
Solicitor	—	—	5 0 6

Table 4.25   Commission fees payable for army rank 1814

Rank	£ s d
Field marshal	37 7 0
General	22 9 6
Lieutenant general	17 7 6
Major general	12 17 6
Colonel	11 5 6
Lieutenant colonel	10 6 6
Major	10 2 6

Trivia: A purchase officer retired by sale of his commission, a non-purchase officer resigned his commission. However, after twenty years of service, a non-purchase officer was allowed to sell his commission upon application and approval.

Preparing for campaigning

When an officer was notified that he was going on active service he received several different allowances to help him prepare for the deployment. The first allowance was an advance on his pay, the size of which was dependent on where he was going to.

Table 4.26   Advance pay for officers embarking on foreign service

New duty location	Months of advance pay
East Indies	6
Cape of Good Hope	4

Table 4.26 continued

New duty location	Months of advance pay
North America	3
West Indies	3
The Mediterranean	3
Portugal	2
Gibraltar	2

Source: Reide, *A Treatise on Military Finance*, vol. 1, p. 228.

In addition to the advance pay, he also received an allowance that would permit him to buy the necessary food and supplies for the sea voyage.

Table 4.27 Allowance for officers embarking on foreign service

Rank	£	s	d
Lieutenant colonel	30	0	0
Major	25	0	0
Captain	20	0	0
Subalterns	20	0	0
Staff	20	0	0

Source: Reide, *A Treatise on Military Finance*, vol. 1, p. 227–8.

The officers could expect to maintain some level of comfort while on campaign and were given money to buy a tent and a horse.

Table 4.28 Allowances for tentage on campaign

Rank	£
Field officer	29
Captain	21
Subaltern (1 tent for 2 officers)	21

Source: Reide, *A Treatise on Military Finance*, vol. 1, p. 224.

Table 4.29 Allowance for infantry officers to purchase a horse when embarking on foreign service

Rank	£	s	d
Lieutenant colonel	18	18	0
Major	18	18	0
Captain	18	18	0
Subalterns (every two)	18	18	0
Staff	18	18	0

Source: Reide, *A Treatise on Military Finance*, vol. 1, p. 224.

Life of an Officer

When a cavalry regiment went on active service, its officers were authorised more horses than the infantry. Should the officer have more horses than he was authorised, he would have to pay to feed his extra mounts.

Table 4.30 Number of horses authorised for cavalry officers for which forage was provided

Rank/position	No. authorised	Rank/position	No. authorised
Colonel	8	Adjutant	3
Lieutenant colonel	7	Quartermaster	1
Major	6	Surgeon	1
Captain	4	Assistant surgeon	1
Subaltern	3	Veterinary surgeon	1
Paymaster	2	Sutler	2

Source: Reide, *A Treatise on Military Finance*, vol. 1, p. 260.

Colonel Richard Hussey Vivian of the 7th Hussars left a detailed list of the number of horses his officers took with them when they went to the Peninsula in 1808.

Table 4.31 Number of horses belonging to officers of the 7th Hussars embarked for the Coruña campaign, October 1808

Individual	No. of horses
Lieutenant Colonel Richard Hussey Vivian	5
Lieutenant Colonel Edward Kerrison	5
Major Berkeley Paget	4
Major George Cavendish	4
Captain Charles Denshire	3
Captain George Cholmley	3
Captain Edward Hodge	3
Captain George Treweike	3
Captain William Thornhill	3
Captain Samuel Dukenfield	3
Captain Charles Lovelace	3
Captain Thomas Pipon	3
Captain William Verner	3
Lieutenant Edmund Long	2
Lieutenant Robert Craufurd	2
Lieutenant Edward Waldegrave	2
Lieutenant George Stone	2
Lieutenant John Robeck	2
Lieutenant Henry Lowther	2

Table 4.31 continued

Individual	No. of horses
Lieutenant Thomas Wildman	2
Cornet Robert Champion	2
Cornet Francis Goodwin	2
Cornet Arthur Meyer	0*
Paymaster Henry Keppel	2
Surgeon David Irwin	2
Assistant Surgeon William Drayson	1
Veterinary Surgeon John Parker	1

* Cornet Meyer was so poor he could not afford a horse. Colonel Vivian provided a horse for him.

Source: Vivian, *Richard Hussey Vivian*, p. 65.

Trivia: You might not want this man to be your aide-de-camp... When Major General Robert Ross was mortally wounded at the battle of North Point in 1814, he died in the arms of his ADC, Major Duncan Macdougall, 85th Foot. In January 1815, when Major General Sir Edward Pakenham fell from his horse after being shot a third time at the battle of New Orleans, he was caught by his ADC, Major Duncan Macdougall, and died in his arms shortly afterwards.[6]

Preparing for active service could be quite expensive. In November 1813, Captain Charles Kinloch of the 52nd Foot, was appointed as extra aide-de-camp to Lieutenant General John Hope, commander of the 1st Corps in the Peninsula. He wrote to his father asking for help defraying the costs, which were equivalent to eighteen months' pay!

Table 4.32 Estimated cost of outfitting an aide-de-camp, November 1813

Expense	£	s	d
Horses	160	0	0
Bed, portmanteau, etc.	37	0	0
Sword	7	17	6
Hat	4	4	0
Servants' clothes	10	10	0
Mules	40	0	0
Total	289	11	0

Source: Kinloch, *A Hellish Business*, pp. 176–7.

---

6 Pickles, *New Orleans 1815*, p. 75.

Life of an Officer

The typical officer had a high standard of living and tried to ensure that he had a variety of things to make his life more comfortable in the field. The following is a list of items carried by Lieutenant George Bell, 34th Foot, in 1812. He was fortunate, because he had a donkey to carry his baggage.

Table 4.33   Items carried on campaign by Lieutenant George Bell, 34th Foot, 1812

Item	Quantity
Old leather trunk to carry clothes	1
Sack	1
Tin plates and dishes	
Silver spoon and fork	1 each
Tins for salt, pepper, tea, and sugar	
Frying-pan	1
Camp kettle	1
Reaping hook	1

Source: Bell, *Soldier's Glory*, pp. 35, 41.

Major Alexander Dickson, Royal Artillery, carried quite a bit more, since he had access to carts to carry his baggage.

Table 4.34   Personal baggage of Major Alexander Dickson, February 1810

Item	Quantity
Large chest	1
Portmanteau	2
Carpet bag to hold liquor canteens	1
Canteen baskets	2
Tent with poles	1
Bag with papers and orderly books	1
Box with papers	1
Sword	1
Cheese in a bag	1
Cot and bedding	1
Camp kettles	1

Source: Dickson, *The Dickson Manuscripts*, vol. 2, p. 156.

Captain Dugald Ferguson of the 2nd Battalion 95th Rifles carried an extensive amount of clothing and other items. He died from the wounds received at Salamanca and the contents of his baggage were auctioned off to his fellow officers. (This was a common practice to raise money for the family of the deceased. It also gave the other officers a chance to replenish their own personal items.)

Table 4.35 Items carried on campaign by Captain Dugald Ferguson, 95th Rifles, 1812

Item	Quantity
Tarpaulin bed	1
Saddle and bridle	1
Saddle bags	1 pair
Portmanteau	1
Gloves	2 pair
Braces	1 pair
Morning gown	1
Handkerchiefs	1 set
Towels	6
Trousers	2 pair
Boots	3 pair
Waistcoat	1
Boat cloak	1
Flannel drawers	
Shirts	6
Sash	1
Socks	11 pair
Silk handkerchiefs	8
Spurs and hooks	1 pair
Writing case	1
Canteen	1
Sword	1
Looking-glass	1
Dressing brushes	
Shaving case	1
Silver watch	1
Spy glass	1

Source: Brett-James, *Life in Wellington's Army*, p. 71.

Ensign John Lucie Blackman of the Coldstream Guards found that he was short many essential items and purchased them from a local merchant in Lisbon. The final bill was close to £80 or almost 9 months pay!

Life of an Officer

Table 4.36 Items purchased by an ensign, Coldstream Guards, 1812

Item	Quantity
Keg of port wine	1
Bed	1
Bedding sheets and blankets	
Tent with inside marquise	1
Prog basket with food	1
Cheese	
Hams	
Wax candles and candlesticks	
Tea, sugar and chocolate	
Brandy	
Vinegar, pickles, and other groceries	
Silver tablespoons	2
Teaspoons	3
Mugs	2
Knives and forks	6
Other necessaries	

Source: Blackman, 'It All Culminated at Hougoumont', p. 42.

The officers also carried items to keep themselves entertained, when not on duty. Chess sets and decks of cards were popular. In the field, newspapers were highly sought after, and the smart officer brought a portable library. Major Edward Charles Cocks left a list of the books he carried.

Table 4.37 Books carried by Major Edward Charles Cocks in the Peninsular War

Ralph Adye	*The Little Bombardier and Pocket Gunner*
Archibald Alison	*Essays on the Nature and Principles of Taste*
Hugh Blair	*Sermons and Lectures on Rhetoric*
Julius Caesar	*Commentaries*
Thomas Campbell	*Gertrude of Wyoming*
Alphonse de Beauchamp	*Histoire de la Guerre de la Vendée*
de Beaurzan	*Histoire de Cartes denier de M. de Turenne*
Daniel Defoe	*Robinson Crusoe*
Jacques de Saint Pierre	*Theory of the Tides*
Maurice de Saxe	*Reveries on the Art of War*
Maurice de Saxe	*Essai General de Fortification*
Dulles	*Mathematics*
James Ferguson	*Ferguson's Lectures on Select Subjects in Mechanics, Hydrostatics, Hydraulics, etc.*

Table 4.37 continued

Author	Work
Lewis Goldsmith	*Grecian History from the Earliest State to the Death of Alexander the Great*
Lewis Goldsmith	*Secret History of the Cabinet of Bonaparte*
James Hammond	*Love Elegies*
Hassell's	*Statistique Europienne*
William Hooper	*Rational Recreations*
Antoine Henri Jomini	*Traité de la Grand Tactique*
Henry Lloyd	*History of the Seven Years War*
M. B.	*Memoir sur la guerre de Pyrenée*
John Milton	*Paradise Lost*
Thomas Percy	*Ancient Ballads*
Alexander Pope	
Jean-Jacues Rousseau	*Nouvelle Eloise*
Sir Walter Scott	*The Lady of the Lake* and *Sir Roderick's Vision*
William Shakespeare	
Edmund Spenser	*Faerie Queen*
Dugald Stuart	*Elements of Philosophy of the Human Mind*
Tacticus and Virgil	
Thomas Warton	*History of English Poetry*

Source: Cocks, *Intelligence Officer*, p. 211.

Trivia: *The book most frequently mentioned in British memoirs was* Gil Blas *by Alain-René Lesage. It is about a young man's misadventures in Spain. It was first published around 1730.*

Life on campaign

Once the officer arrived in country, he had to buy any equipment or animals that he needed. For those going to Portugal and Spain, many infantry officers waited until they were in country before they bought their animal. Although they received an allowance for purchasing a horse, it was only fraction of what the actual cost of buying a horse in Portugal. Lieutenant John Rous of the Coldstream Guards, found this out in the summer of 1812, when he spent 516 dollars (£118 13s) for a horse, two mules, and a pony! This was £109 over his allowance or ten months' pay!

Table 4.38 Money spent by a guards officer in 1812 to buy mounts in Lisbon

Type of animal	Cost in dollars*
Strong Spanish horse	200
Mule	130

Life of an Officer

Type of animal	Cost in dollars*
Mule	140
Pony	46
Total	516

* 1 Portuguese Dollar = 4s 6d
Source: Rous, *A Guards Officer*, p. 31.

Trivia: *By 1812, horses were becoming scarce in Lisbon. Ensign John Lucie Blackman, also of the Coldstream Guards, paid 230 dollars (£51 15s) for two mules and a donkey. He could not find a horse and ended up riding one of the mules.*[7]

Additionally, if the officer did not bring a servant with him, he would have to hire one locally. Traditionally, the officer could choose a trustworthy soldier for his servant, but for those officers going to the Peninsula, enlisted servants were forbidden in 1809. It took too many soldiers out of the ranks. One officer calculated that 30 soldiers would be returned to the ranks and this could mean as many as 1,000 more soldiers in the firing line.[8] To compensate for this, officers received an allowance for hiring a servant.

Table 4.39 Number of native servants authorised in the Peninsula, 1809

Rank	No. of servants
Commander-in-chief	4
Lieutenant general	3
Major general	2
Brigadier general	2
Heads of departments	2
Regimental or staff officer	1
Captain	1
Subaltern, adjutant, and assistant surgeon	1
Surgeon and paymaster	1
Quartermaster	1

Note: Native servants would be paid one dollar (4s 6d) a week and a daily ration. These servants would replace enlisted soldiers who were acting as a servant.
Source: *General Orders*, 3 May 1809, pp. 265–6.

Officers did receive money every 200 days to maintain their baggage and to feed their horses. This was known as a *bât* (French for pack or pack saddle) and forage allowance.

---

7 Blackman, 'It All Culminated at Hougoumont', p. 23.
8 Aitchison, p. 31.

Table 4.40 Two hundred days of bât and forage money in the Peninsula

Rank	Forage money £ s	Bât money £ s
Colonel commanding a battalion	7 10	10 0
Colonel not commanding	7 10	10 0
Lieutenant Colonel commanding	7 10	10 0
Lieutenant Colonel not commanding	7 10	10 0
Major commanding	7 10	10 0
Major not commanding	7 10	10 0
Captain commanding	7 10	10 0
Captain with company	7 10	10 0
Company captain absent	7 10	10 0
Captain without a company	7 10	– –
Subalterns each	3 15	– –
Adjutant	5 0	– –
Quartermasters of Cavalry	– –	– –
Quartermasters of Infantry	5 0	– –
Surgeon	7 10	1 0
Assistant Surgeon	3 15	– –
Paymaster	7 10	10 0

Source: *General Orders*, 19 June 1809, p. 27.

In addition to a bât and forage allowance, officers in the Peninsula also received a forage ration of 6d per day. The number of rations authorised varied according to rank. Theoretically, this allowed the officer to maintain that many animals at the army's expense. For example, a lieutenant colonel commanding a battalion was authorised ten animals, while a subaltern was authorised only one. A lieutenant who had a horse and a baggage mule could only draw rations for one of them.

Table 4.41 Number of forage rations authorised for officers in the Peninsula

Rank	No. forage rations[*]
Colonel commanding a battalion	11
Colonel not commanding	9
Lieutenant colonel commanding	10
Lieutenant colonel not commanding	8
Major commanding	9
Major not commanding	7
Captain commanding	7
Captain with company	5

Rank	No. forage rations*
Company captain absent	2
Captain without a company	3
Subaltern	1
Adjutant	1
Quartermasters of cavalry	1
Quartermasters of infantry	1
Surgeon	5
Assistant surgeon	1
Paymaster	5

* Authorised at 6d per day.
Source: *General Orders, Spain and Portugal 1809*, 1 September 1809, pp. 143–5.

> **Trivia:** *Junior officers would often pool their resources when hiring servants. According to Harry Smith, the officers would often buy goats, chickens, geese and other animals. They would even take them on campaign and 'every [company] mess had a boy, who was in charge of them on the march and in quarters, and milked them. On the march the flock of each Regiment and Brigade assembled and moved with their goat-herds, when each drove his master's goats to his quarters. We observed extraordinary regularity with these goats, and upon inquiry we found out the little fellows organized themselves into regular guards. They had a captain; . . . their time of duty was as regular as our soldiers;' they had sentries with long white sticks in their hands, and Mein's little boy held a sort of court-martial, and would lick a boy awfully who neglected his charge.'9*

Food on campaign

In general, officers in the Peninsula were responsible for providing their own food. Junior officers would often form a company mess that helped them share their expenses. The price of food rose over the years and by 1813 it became quite expensive.

Table 4.42 Cost of food in the Peninsula 1809–10

Item	Amount	Cost s	d	Year
Tea, sugar, butter		3	5	1809
Anchovies	10 dozen	9	0	1809
Gin	3 bottles	16	2	1809
Ham	1	5	2	1809
Ham	17 pounds	14	4	1809
Turkeys	2	1	3	1809

9 Smith, *The Autobiography of Sir Harry Smith*, p. 129.

Table 4.42 continued

Item	Amount	Cost s	d	Year
Fowls	4	9	0	1809
Tea	1 pound	13	6	1810
Rum	2 bottles	2	1	1810
Gin	6 bottles	31	6	1810
Tongues	2	9	6	1810
Salmon	1	4	6	1810
Fowl	1	2	6	1810
Brandy	16 bottles	27	0	1810
Tea	2 pounds	18	9	1810
Holland Dutch gin	8 bottles	36	0	1810
Anchovies	10 dozen	9	1	1810
Gin	3 bottles	14	1	1810
Tea	2 pounds	9	0	1810
Ducks	3	4	7	1810
Gin	4 bottles	13	9	1810
Salt, refined	2 pounds	5	0	1810
Pepper	¼ pound	0	3	1810
Ham	1	9	10	1810

Note: Items listed more than once were purchased by the officer several times.

Table 4.43 Cost of food in the Peninsula 1813

Item	Amount	Cost s	d
Butter	1 pound	4	0
Bread	1 pound	1	6
Gin	1 bottle	12	0
Pepper and mustard	1 small bottle	7	0
Tea	1 pound	13	6
Cheese	1 pound	4	0
Gin	1 bottle	7	6
Brandy	1 bottle	7	6
Porter (beer)	1 bottle	5	0
Milk	1 quart	1	0
Salt-butter	1 pound	3	0
Pork	1 pound	1	8
Oil	1 bottle	5	0
Port	1 bottle	6	6

Sources: Dickson, *The Dickson Manuscripts*, vols 1, 2, and 3; Larpent, *Private Journals*, pp. 50, 52.

1 Sir David Baird

2 Sir William Beresford

3 Sir Archibald Campbell

4 Sir Galbraith Lowry Cole

5 Charles Marquis Cornwallis

6 Sir Ronald Ferguson

7 Sir Thomas Graham

8 Sir Henry Hardinge

9 Sir Rowland Hill

10 Sir John Hope

11 Edward, Duke of Kent and Strathearn

12 Sir James Leith

13 Sir John Moore

14 Sir George Murray

15 Frederick William, Prince of Orange

16 Sir Denis Pack

17 Henry, Lord Paget

18 Sir Thomas Picton

19 (Left) The Duke of Wellington

20 (Above) The guardhouse and gunners' barracks at Fort Cumberland, about 1800, is one of the few Napoleonic period barracks still standing. From the collection of the Portsmouth Napoleonic Society.

21 Drum Major and Pioneer of a British Line Regiment by Charles Hamilton Smith. From the collection of Tony Broughton.

22 A Corporal of the 10th Hussars by Charles Hamilton Smith. From the collection of Tony Broughton.

23 Uniforms of the 42nd and 92nd Foot by Charles Hamilton Smith. From the collection of Tony Broughton.
24 Uniform of the 1st Life Guards by Charles Hamilton Smith. From the collection of Tony Broughton.

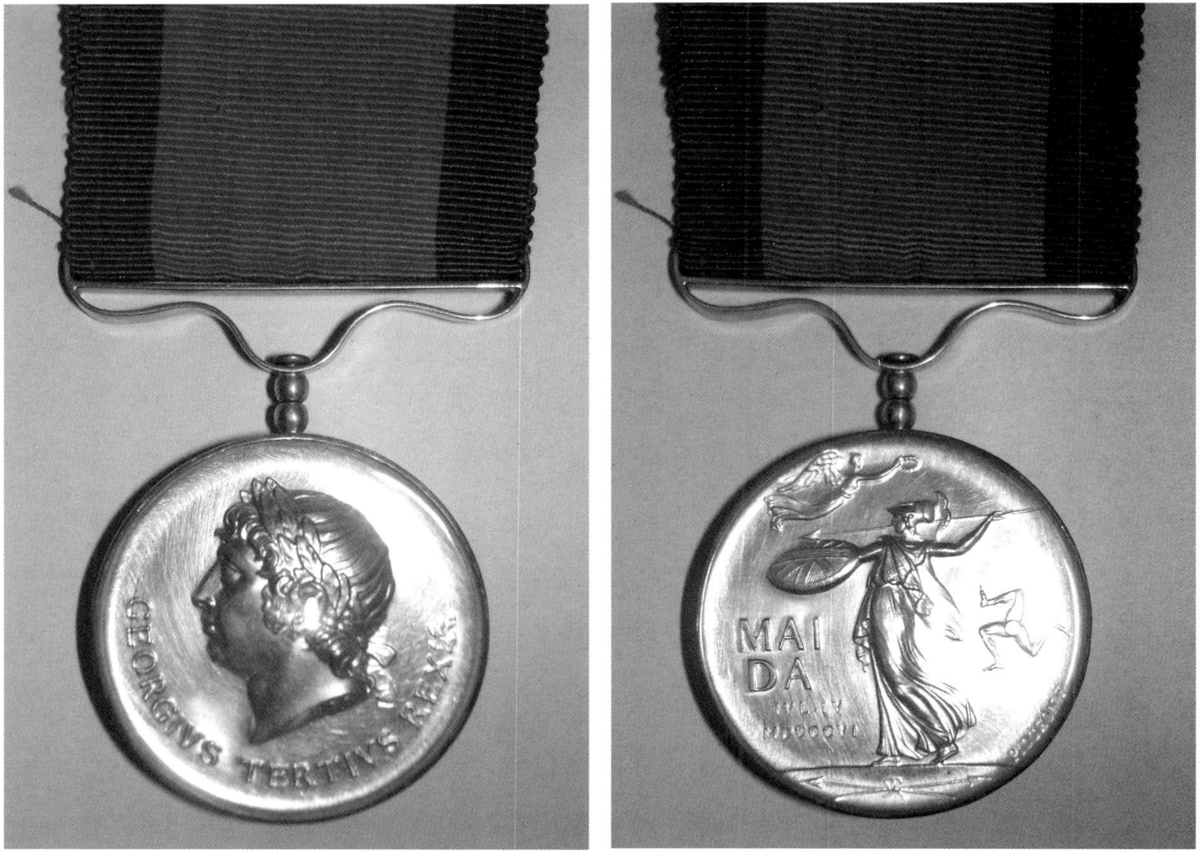

25 Army Gold Medal awarded for Maida. From the collection of Jacques Declercq.

26 (Far left) The medals of Denis Pack: the medal on the left is the Peninsular Gold Cross; top right is the Badge of the Order of the Bath; centre is the Star of the Order of the Bath; bottom centre, the Waterloo Medal, bottom right a Army Gold Medal with Roleia, Vimiera and Corunna engraved on the back. The collection of medals sold for £115,000 in 2003. Photo courtesy of Spink and Sons Ltd.

27 (Left) Colonel James Bathurst's Army Gold Cross engraved with Roleia & Vimiero, Corunna, Talavera and Busaco. Photograph by Dan FitzGerald.

28 The Army Gold Medal Awarded to Major Aretas William Young, 97th Foot. It is engraved 'Talavera'. Photograph by D.M. FitzGerald.

29 (Far left) Waterloo Medal awarded to Surgeon John Bolton, 6th Inniskilling Dragoons. From the collection of Michael Crumplin.

30 (Left) Military General Service Medal with clasps for Busaco, Fuentes D'Onor, Ciudad Rodrigo, Badajoz, Vittoria, Pyrenees, Orthes, and Toulouse. It was awarded to J. Maxwell, 7th Foot. From the collection of Michael Crumplin.

Life of an Officer

Replacing equipment, uniforms, and horses while on campaign
One of the things about campaigning that has not changed over hundreds of years is that the officer brought what he thought he would need. If he was missing something or a uniform item or piece of equipment wore out, he would have to procure locally or send for a replacement from home. This was true during the Peninsular War and the British Army set up a system for the officers to receive packages from home.

There were several rules that had to be followed:
1 The sender was responsible for paying shipping costs to the embarkation point.
2 The name of the officer and his unit had to be on the package.
3 All items were to be sent to John Trotter, Esq., Storekeeper General at Plymouth.
4 The Storekeeper General had to be notified in advance that the package was coming and whether it was coming by coach or waggon.

Once in Plymouth, shipping costs to the Peninsula, were fairly inexpensive.

Table 4.44 Cost of shipping packages from Plymouth to the Peninsula

Weight	Shipping cost s	d
Under 250 pounds	1	0
250 pounds	2	6
251–500 pounds	5	0
501–1,000 pounds	10	0
1,001–1,500 pounds	15	0
1,501–2,000 pounds	20	0

Source: *General Orders*, 13 October 1813, pp. 25–6.

Campaigning was hard on the officers, their equipment and their horses. If an officer lost his horse in action or it had to be destroyed because it had glanders, the officer would be reimbursed for his loss, though the amount received rarely covered the cost of replacing the animal. An officer was not reimbursed if the horse died from fatigue or from sickness other than glanders. Not surprisingly, a cavalry officer's horse was worth more than an infantry officer's horse.

Table 4.45 Reimbursement for cavalry horses lost in action or shot for glanders

Type of horse	£	s
Heavy dragoons, 1st charger	47	0
Heavy dragoons, 2nd charger	31	10
Light dragoons, 1st charger	36	0

The British Army Against Napoleon

Table 4.45	continued		
Type of horse		£	s
Light dragoons, 2nd charger		31	10
Quartermaster		20	8
Bât horses		18	18

Source: Reide, *A Treatise on Military Finance*, vol. 1, p. 216.

Table 4.46 Reimbursement for infantry officers' horses lost in action or shot for glanders

Rank	£	s
Field officer's charger	31	10
Adjutant's charger	31	10
Captain's horse	18	18
Subaltern's horse	18	18
Staff officer's horse	18	18
Bât horses	18	18

Source: Reide, *A Treatise on Military Finance*, vol. 1, p. 227.

An officer was also reimbursed for any baggage he lost on campaign.

Table 4.47 Reimbursement for officers' lost baggage and camp equipage on campaign

	Cavalry officer's		*Infantry officer's*	
Rank	Baggage	Camp equipage	Baggage	Camp equipage
Colonel	£140	£90	£120	£80
Lieutenant colonel	£120	£90	£100	£60
Major	£120	£90	£100	£60
Captain	£90	£45	£80	£35
Subaltern	£70	£45	£60	£35
Quartermaster	£40	—	£60	£35

Source: Reide, *A Treatise on Military Finance*, vol. 1, pp. 215–16; 226.

Discipline and courts martial in the Peninsula

Courts martial of officers in Wellington's army were rare. Four levels of punishment could be imposed, ranging from a reprimand to cashiering.

Table 4.48 Types of punishment imposed on officers in the Peninsula

Punishment	*Description*
Reprimand	Published in the General Orders and read to the regiment

Punishment	Description
Suspension	Suspension of pay and rank; could not be promoted or advanced in seniority.
Displacing	Transfer to another regiment; loss of seniority in rank.
Cashiering	Removal from the army; loss of all rank.

Source: Thomas, *The Local Military Paymaster*, p. 100; Oman, *Wellington's Army*, pp. 237–42.

Trivia: Thirty officers were cashiered in the British army in the Peninsula. Their offences include cowardice in the face of the enemy, swindling merchants, embezzlement, insubordination, public brawling and flagrant immorality. No officer was ever court-martialled for desertion.

Prize money

Although the awarding of prize money to officers and sailors of the Royal Navy is common knowledge, it is less known that soldiers also received prize money for the capture of enemy stores, fortresses, artillery, etc. The individual was authorised a share of the money based on his rank and position in the army. The higher the rank and position, the more shares the individual received. The worth of a one share was determined by the total amount of prize money divided by the total number of shares. An individual had to be present at the battle or action in order to be eligible to receive the prize money. Prize money was also awarded to the families of soldiers who were killed.

Table 4.49 Prize money shares for all ranks

Rank	Shares
Field marshals	2,000
Generals	1200
Lieutenant generals	800
Major generals and commissary general	450
Brigadier generals and commissary general in an army commanded by a major general	300
Colonels, quartermaster general, adjutant general	150
Director general, superintendant general and inspector general of medical department	150
Lieutenant colonels	100
Deputy quartermaster general when chief of the department	100
Deputy adjutant general when chief of the department	100
Deputy commissaries when head of the department	100
Deputy paymasters general	100

Table 4.49 continued

Rank	Shares
Superintendant and inspector general when not head of medical department	100
Majors, deputy quartermasters generals, deputy adjutants generals	80
Deputy inspectors general, assistant inspectors generals	80
Captains, brigade majors, aides-de-camp, judge advocates	50
Military secretary, physicians, purveyors, field inspectors	50
Hospital surgeons, apothecaries, commissaries of stores	50
Paymasters of civil department, chief surveyor and draughtsman	50
Commissaries and paymasters attached to the engineers	50
Lieutenants, provost marshals	20
Assistant quartermasters general, assistant adjutant general	20
Deputy purveyors of hospitals, assistant commissary general	20
Waggon master general, assistant paymasters general	20
Assistant commissaries of stores, assistant draughtsmen	20
Second lieutenants, cornets, ensigns, quartermasters	16
Assistant surgeons, veterinary surgeons, hospital mates	16
Clerks of stores, draughtsmen, clerks of works	16
Quartermaster of dragoons	12
Staff sergeants	8
Sergeants, conductors of stores, and master artificers	3
Corporals, bombardiers, and foreman of artificers	1½
Privates, drummers, trumpeters, drivers, artificers, and servants	1

Source: Reide, *A Treatise on Military Finance*, vol. 1, pp. 237–40.

On 27 January 1816, *London Gazette* announced that the prize money would be paid for six different actions and campaigns.

Table 4.50 Prize money paid to the army

Class	Rank	£	s	d
For Coimbra and Douro				
1	General officers	106	10	11½
2	Field officers and colonels	63	14	7
3	Captains	11	2	1
4	Subalterns	4	17	10
For the French retreat from Portugal, Fuentes d'Oñoro and Albuera				
1	General officers	132	14	10½
2	Field officers and colonels	61	18	11
3	Captains	8	16	11½
4	Subalterns	3	16	7

Class	Rank	£	s	d
For the capture of Ciudad Rodrigo and Badajoz				
1	General officers	134	9	10
2	Field officers and colonels	68	8	8
3	Captains	11	2	10
4	Subalterns	4	14	1½
For the campaign in Spain in 1812				
1	General officers	142	5	7½
2	Field officers and colonels	55	8	10½
3	Captains	9	19	3
4	Subalterns	4	0	0½
For the campaign in Spain in 1813				
1	General officers	164	17	0½
2	Field officers and colonels	75	16	3
3	Captains	11	19	8
4	Subalterns	4	17	2½
For the campaign in Southern France in 1814				
1	General officers	682	18	3½
2	Field officers and colonels	272	8	11½
3	Captains	50	15	8
4	Subalterns	19	16	4

The average amount of prize money was a considerable bonus for the officer – ranging from a month's pay for a subaltern to four months' pay for a lieutenant colonel!

Table 4.51 Average amount of prize money British officers received for each action in the Peninsula

Rank	Average amount received	No. of month's pay
Colonel	£100	3
Lieutenant colonel	£100	4
Major	£100	4
Captain	£17	1
Lieutenant	£7	1
Ensign	£7	1

Prize money awarded after the Waterloo campaign was even greater. In the infantry regiments, an ensign received the equivalent of five months' pay, a captain 6½ months' pay, a major 18 months' pay, while a lieutenant colonel received 17 months' pay!

171

Table 4.52 Prize money paid to the army after Waterloo

Class	Rank	Recipients	£	s	d
	Commander-in-chief	1	61,000	0	0
1	General officers	48	1,274	10	10¾
2	Field officers and colonels	565	433	2	4¼
3	Captains	1,354	90	7	3¾
4	Subalterns	3,522	34	14	9½

Source: Booth, *Battle of Waterloo*, p. 427; *Supplementary Despatches*, vol. 10, p. 750.

Trivia: All prize money awarded to soldiers for actions during the Peninsular War had to be claimed by 31 May 1816. Any unclaimed money was donated to the Chelsea Hospital.

The Duke of Wellington donated over two-thirds of his Waterloo prize money – more than £40,000 – to the British Treasury. This did not leave him a pauper. Parliament had already voted to give him £200,000 for his victory there, in addition to the £500,000 they gave him for his Peninsula victories![10]

When the fighting ended

What happened to the officers when the fighting was over? Some continued to serve on active duty. Others were placed on half pay. Some received pensions for wounds and the widows received pensions too. Eventually, all would die and as with everything else the British army had a set of regulations that showed how they could be buried!

Rates of half pay 1814

British Army regulations allowed for a full-pay officer to be placed on the half pay of his substantive regimental rank up to and including the rank of colonel. This was referred to as retiring on half pay. It was not, however, the same as retiring by sale of a commission as this would entail the officer leaving the army outright. An officer on half pay remained in the service but not regimentally employed. He could still be employed on the staff of an army, district or station in a non-regimental appointment.

Half pay was not a right and was only allowed if the royal warrant raising a new unit specified that the officers would be allowed half pay upon its being reduced. Officers went on half pay for a number of reasons, including disbanding of the regiment or battalion, the reduction of the establishment of the regiment, by exchanging to half pay with an officer who was desirous of going back on full pay or by being medically certified as unfit due to active service. Half pay by disbandment or reduction was

---

10 Adkin, *The Waterloo Companion*, p. 421.

Life of an Officer

by strict regimental seniority, i.e. the junior officer(s) in each rank would go half pay. It did not matter if a commission was purchased or not.

An officer who wished either to exchange to half pay or to go back on full pay had to inform the commander-in-chief's military secretary, in order for the commander-in-chief to recommend him as a vacancy occurred.[11] In some instances, a half-pay officer would be recalled back to full pay if a new unit was formed which required a number of officers on half pay be appointed to serve in it.

In 1814, the *per diem* rates of half pay changed and officers were paid the old or new rate depending upon when they went on the half pay; those receiving the new rate were those who will be reduced upon the formation of a peace establishment for the army, those who went on half pay during the war due to wounds or infirmaries contracted during the war or those who were reduced commencing 25 June 1814.[12]

Half pay was payable every quarter without any deductions. It allowed for a pool of officers to be created from which to draw in time of war. Regulations required an officer to go back on full pay if recalled; many officers, however, remained on half pay for years. Regulations at the time did not allow for an officer to sell a half-pay commission.

Any unit or corps with full-pay officers could see them placed upon half pay (e.g. Royal Artillery and Royal Engineers) Britain also allowed half pay for certain officers of the Foreign Corps in its service.

There were always exceptions to the rules in the British army and one such was the granting of what was called retired full pay to the officers of the reduced Veteran Battalions, Invalid, Garrison, and Veteran Companies and the Royal Irish Artillery. This was essentially the same as being on half pay but receiving the full pay for their substantive rank. These officers, except in the Irish Artillery, being mostly those with infirmaries and wounds contracted while on active service were not subject to recall to duty except to serve again in Royal Veteran Battalions.[13]

Table 4.53 Daily rates of half pay, 1814

Rank	Old rate s	d	New rate s	d
Line cavalry				
Colonel*	13	0	15	6
Lieutenant colonel	10	0	12	6
Major	8	0	10	0

---

11 *General Regulations and Orders for the Army*, 1811.
12 *Monthly Army List*, December 1814, p. 101.
13 *General Regulations*; Haythornthwaite, *The Armies of Wellington*, pp. 40–2; *Monthly Army Lists*, December 1814.

Table 4.53 continued

Rank	Old rate	s	d	New rate	s	d
Captain		5	0		7	6
Lieutenant		3	0		4	8
Cornet		2	6		3	6
Paymaster		7	6		–	–
Adjutant		2	0		–	–
Quartermaster		2	0		4	0
Surgeon†		6	0		7	0
Assistant surgeon†		2	6		4	0
Line infantry						
Colonel*		12	0		14	6
Lieutenant colonel		8	6		11	0
Major		7	6		9	6
Captain		5	0		7	0
Lieutenant		2	4		4	0
Lieutenant of above 7 years' standing in the line		–	–		4	6
Ensign, 2nd lieutenant		1	10		3	0
Paymaster		7	6		7	6
Adjutant		2	0		2	0
Quartermaster		2	0		2	0
Surgeon*		6	0		7	0
Assistant surgeon*		2	6		4	0

Staff	Rate‡	
Commissary general	30	0
Deputy commissary general	15	0
Assistant commissary general	7	6
Deputy assistant commissary general	15	0
Inspector of hospitals	20	0
Deputy inspector of hospitals	12	6
Physician	10	0
Surgeon and assistant surgeon	liable to variation	
Apothecary	5	0
Hospital mate	2	0
Purveyor	10	0
Deputy purveyor	5	0
Chaplain to the forces	liable to variation 5	0

* The new rate applied only to colonels who were not general officers.
† The new rate applied also to a staff surgeon and an assistant staff surgeon.
‡ Rates for officers on staff (not regimental) appointment did not change at this time.

Life of an Officer

> *Trivia:* By an act of Parliament, in time of war, officers on the half pay could serve as a subaltern in the militia, local militia, fencibles or volunteers and continue to receive their half pay in addition to the full pay of holding such a commission in that regiment. In peacetime officers faced no such restriction and when called out for 28 days of training they could receive the full pay of any rank, in the militia, in addition to their half pay for those 28 days. With special permission, a half-pay officer holding a staff or garrison appointment could also receive his half pay.[14]

Officer's pensions for wounds

An officer could receive an annual pension for being seriously wounded. The awarding of pensions for wounds was authorised by the 'Regulation for Granting Pensions to Officers of His Majesty's Land Forces Losing an Eye or Limb on Service'.[15] The regulation stated:

> If an Officer shall be wounded in action and it shall appear upon an inspection made of him by the Army Medical Board, at any period, not sooner than a year and a day after the time he was wounded, that he has in consequence of his wound lost a limb, or an eye, or has totally lost the use of a limb or that his wound has been equally prejudicial to his habit of body with the loss of a limb – such Officer shall be entitled to a pension, commencing from the expiration of one year and a day after the time when he was wounded; and depending as to the amount upon the rank he held at that period according to the scale annexed.
>
> This pension being granted as compensation for the injury sustained is to be held together with any other pay and allowance to which such Officer may be otherwise entitled, without any deduction on account thereof. Officers who shall have lost more than one limb or eye shall be entitled to the pension for each eye or limb lost.
>
> And as the pension is not to commence till the expiration of a year and a day from the date of the wound, it is independent of the allowance of a year's pay or the expences attending the cure of wounds granted under the existing regulations.
>
> All officers who may have sustained such an injury as would entitle them to this pension by any wounds received since the commencement of hostilities in the year 1793, will, upon the production of the proper certificate from the Army Medical Board,

---

14 *Monthly Army List*, December 1814, p. 101.
15 *The Times*, Saturday 27 June 1812.

be allowed a pension proportioned, according to the scale, to the rank they held at the time when wounded, and commencing from the 25th of December, 1811.

A pension was awarded for the following classes of wounds:

Table 4.54 Wounds for which pensions were awarded to an officer

Loss of a leg or the use of a leg
Loss of an arm or the use of an arm
Loss of an arm and other wounds
Loss of the use of a hand
Loss of sight
Loss of an eye or both eyes
Impaired vision in consequence of ophthalmia
For a wound or wounds
For wounds more than equal to loss of limb
For injury sustained in the performance of military duty

The most common ones were 'For a wound' and 'For Wounds'.

Some officers did receive two pensions, such as the poor soul who had a pension for loss of right eye and impaired vision of the left eye and received £100 for each wound. Those wounds which occurred before 1811 and applied for were all awarded dated 25 December 1811 and so a majority of the awards are so dated. There was another amendment to the regulation. Circular Letter No. 287 of 31 July 1815 stated:

> First, That the regulation under which pensions are granted to wounded officers shall be revised and that the pensions which have been, or shall be granted to Officers for the actual loss of eye or limb, or for wound certified to be equally injurious with the loss of limb shall not be continued to the amount attached by the scale of rank which the officer held at the time when he was wounded, but, shall progressively increase according to the rank to which the officer may, from time to time, be promoted; the augmentation with regard to pensions of such officers now upon the list being to take date from the 18th of June 1815, inclusive.

This was ordered by HRH the Prince Regent both in honour of former occasions but also to celebrate the Battle of Waterloo. This regulation also allowed for volunteers wounded before being appointed to army rank and who were subsequently promoted in the army to receive a pension of their then rank. The pensions were payable half-yearly. Some pensions were only awarded for two years and by 1822 many were only temporary.

Life of an Officer

Trivia: Parsimonious as all governments are, the provision outlined in Circular Letter No. 287 was rescinded by Circular Letter No. 362, 30 July 1817, for all officers who were subsequently wounded.

Table 4.55 Officer annual pensions for wounds

Rank	Rate of pension
Field marshal commanding in chief at the time	to be specially considered
General commanding in chief at the time	to be specially considered
Lieutenant general commanding in chief at the time	to be specially considered
Lieutenant general	£400
Major general	£350
Brigadier general commanding a brigade	£350
Commissary general commanding department	£350
Colonel	£300
Lieutenant colonel	£300
Adjutant general*	£300
Quartermaster general*	£300
Deputy adjutant general If chief of the department*	£300
Deputy quartermaster general, If chief of the department*	£300
Commissary general Not at head of department	£300
Deputy commissary general At head of department	£300
Inspector of hospitals	£300
Major commanding	£250
Major	£200
Deputy adjutant general*	£200
Deputy quartermaster general*	£200
Deputy inspector of hospitals	£200
Deputy commissary general Not at head of department	£200
Captain	£100
Assistant adjutant general*	£100
Assistant quartermaster general	£100
Deputy assistant adjutant general	£100
Deputy assistant quartermaster general	£100
Secretary to the commander of the forces*	£100
Aides-de-camp*	£100

Table 4.55 continued	
Rank	Rate of pension
Major of brigade*	£100
Assistant commissary general	£100
Judge advocate*	£100
Chaplain	£100
Paymaster	£100
Physician	£100
Staff surgeon	£100
Surgeon regimental	£100
Purveyor	£100
Lieutenant	£70
Adjutant	£70
Deputy assistant commissary general	£70
Cornet	£50
Ensign	£50
2nd lieutenant	£50
Regimental quartermaster	£50
Assistant surgeon	£50
Apothecary	£50
Hospital mate	£50
Veterinary surgeon	£50
Deputy purveyor	£50

* The officer was permitted to have the allowance according to their army rank, if they preferred.

Sources: *Monthly Army Lists*, January 1816. HCPP *Sessional Papers*; *The Times*, 27 June 1812.

Trivia: *Lieutenant Colonel George Napier, 52nd Foot, received a £300 pension for the lost of an arm at Ciudad Rodrigo in 1812. Major General Sir George Cooke received a £350 pension for the lost of an arm at Waterloo.*

John Kincaid left the following description of wounded officers of the 95th Rifle after the battle of Waterloo.

> At the close of the war, when we returned to England, if our battalion did not show symptoms of its being a well-shot corps, it is very odd: nor was it to be wondered at if the camp-colours were not covered with that precision, nor the salute given with the grace usually expected from a reviewed body, when I furnish the following account of the officers commanding companies on the day of the inspection, viz.:
>
> Beckwith with a cork-leg – Pemberton and Manners with a

shot each in the knee, making them as stiff as the other's tree one – Loftus Gray with a gash in the lip, and minus a portion of one heel, which made him march to the tune of dot and go one – Smith with a shot in the ankle – Eeles minus a thumb – Johnston, in addition to other shot holes, a stiff elbow, which deprived him of the power of disturbing his friends as a scratcher of Scotch reels upon the violin – Percival with a shot through his lungs. Hope with a grape-shot lacerated leg – and George Simmons with his riddled body held together by a pair of stays, for his is no holiday waist, which naturally required such an appendage lest the burst of a sigh should snap it asunder; but one that pertained to a figure framed in nature's fittest mould to 'brave the battle and the breeze!'[16]

Of these only two officers received pensions for their Waterloo wounds: Lieutenant Colonel Charles Beckwith, a £300 pension for the lost of his leg, and Lieutenant George Simmons, a temporary pension of £70.

Pension for an officer's widow

At this time, the British government did not provide a pension for an officer who retired from the service. The sale of his commission was to provide funds in lieu of such a pension. If an officer died while in the service, however, his purchase price was forfeited to the government. In many cases this left his family in dire straits, so previous governments had instituted a pension for an officer's widow to help alleviate distress. In some situations, the government would allow a commission to be sold and the proceeds given to a deserving widow, especially if the widow's husband had been a non-purchase officer.

There was also a special fund, known as the Compassionate Lists, set up under the authority of the king whereby the relatives of an officer who died while on full-pay service received a special payment. It was usually reserved for the dead officer's children, but it was also awarded to widows who were not eligible for a regular widow's pension and to the mothers and sisters of the officer if they were in particular distress. The rate of pension was based upon the individual case. The yearly estimates for the Compassionate Lists presented to Parliament give the names and circumstances of any award made from this fund.

The pensions were not based upon brevet army rank. The army pensions were paid every four months, while those for the commissariat were paid every three months. Pensions from the Compassionate Lists were also paid every four months, in April, August and December. Those for the Commissariat were payable every three months.

---

16 Kincaid, *Adventures in the Rifle Brigade*, p. 258.

Table 4.56 Widow's pensions, 1815

Rank	Annual pension
Regimental officers	
General	£120
Lieutenant general	£120
Major general	£120
Colonel of a regiment, not a general officer	£90
Lieutenant colonel	£70
Major	£50
Captain	£50
Lieutenant	£40
Cornet	£36
Ensign	£36
2nd lieutenant	£36
Paymaster, previous to 24 August 1811	£40
Paymaster, subsequent to 24 August 1811	£50
Adjutant	£40
Surgeon regimental	£40
Regimental quartermaster	£36
Assistant surgeon	£36
Veterinary surgeon	£30
Staff officers	
Commissary general	£120
Deputy commissary general	£60
Deputy commissary general after 7 years on full pay	£70
Assistant commissary general	£50
Deputy assistant commissary general	£40
Inspector of hospitals in certain circumstances	£60
Deputy inspector of hospitals in certain circumstances	£50
Physician after serving abroad as such	£50
Physician not having served abroad	£40
Purveyor	£40
District paymaster	£40
Staff surgeon	£40
Deputy purveyor	£30
Apothecary	£36
Hospital mate having served abroad as such	£30
Chaplain general	£90
Chaplain	£30

Trivia: By 13 August 1807, the British were paying out £38,510 in total widows' pensions. The Compassionate Fund paid a further £12,480 for 1,381 persons on the list.[17]

Funerals

If an officer died on active duty and circumstances permitted, he was entitled to a military funeral. The composition of the funeral party depended on his rank.

Table 4.57 Composition of an officer's funeral party

Rank of deceased	Composition of party	No. of rounds fired
General	4 battalions and 6 squadrons	3 rounds of 11 cannon
Lieutenant general	3 battalions and 4 squadrons	3 rounds of 9 cannon
Major general	2 battalions and 3 squadrons	3 rounds of 7 cannon
Brigadier general	1 battalion and 2 squadrons	3 rounds of 5 cannon
Colonel	his regiment	3 rounds of small arms
Lieutenant colonel	300 men	3 rounds of small arms
Major	200 men	3 rounds of small arms
Captain	his company	3 rounds of small arms
Lieutenant	lieutenant and 36 men	3 rounds of small arms
Ensign	ensign and 27 men	3 rounds of small arms
Adjutant	ensign and 27 men	3 rounds of small arms
Surgeon	ensign and 27 men	3 rounds of small arms
Quartermaster	ensign and 27 men	3 rounds of small arms

Source: Thomas, *The Local Military Paymaster*, p. 103.

Unlucky officers

There were times when no matter how many months an officer served in combat or how conspicuous his conduct was, he just could not get himself promoted. Whether it was because he was not in the right place at the right time in order to have his deeds recognised or because he did not have the money to purchase his next step in rank, some of these officers remained junior officers for many years. The following table shows three officers who served in the Peninsula for an average of five years (sixty months) of unbroken service and had ten clasps on their Military General Service Medal. All had been wounded at least once, Lieutenant Cornell Baldwin four times! None of them was promoted to captain while they served in the Peninsula.

---

17 HCPP *Sessional Papers* 1807

Table 4.58 Three unlucky officers

Name	Rank	Regiment	MGSM clasps	Months in Peninsula	No. of wounds
Francis Armstrong	Lieutenant	48th Foot	10	60	2
Cornell J. Baldwin	Lieutenant	83rd Foot	10	60	4
Charles O'Neill	Lieutenant	83rd Foot	11	60	1

Yet those three were not the unluckiest.

At least nine officers landed in Portugal in August 1808 and would serve with Wellington's Army until the end of the war; each served sixty-nine months on active service without a break! Among them was Lieutenant Theobald O'Dogherty, 40th Foot, who would fight in twelve battles, including the first of the war, Roliça, and one of the last of the war, Toulouse. He would be wounded twice and receive the Military General Service Medal with ten clasps. Yet he was never promoted in his whole time in the Peninsula. He was promoted to lieutenant on 28 August 1807, and when the war ended in April 1814 he was still a lieutenant. He was not the only one in his regiment. Lieutenant John Thoreau, who was three months senior to Lieutenant O'Dogherty, also had sixty-nine months of uninterrupted service in the Peninsula. He fought in thirteen battles and was wounded twice. Yet by the end of the Peninsular War, he was still junior to one other lieutenant in the regiment.

Lieutenant William Irwin, 28th Foot, also had sixty-nine months of unbroken service. He was something of a legend throughout the army and was known as the 'strongest man in the regiment'. He fought in seventeen battles and campaigns during the Peninsular War and was wounded three times. Although only a lieutenant, he commanded the 28th Foot's Grenadier Company much of the time – including at Campo Mayor, Albuera, Arroyo dos Molinos, Almaraz, Vitoria, the Nivelle, Nive, Orthez and Toulouse. He commanded the Light Company at Quatre Bras, where he was severely wounded, but still managed to fight at Waterloo. Despite serving as a company commander for four years, he was not promoted to captain until 1816. William Irwin died in 1840 in Australia. If he had lived long enough to receive it, he would have had ten clasps on his Military General Service Medal.

The unluckiest officer in Wellington's army

Although these three soldiers received very little recognition for their service, they do not qualify as the unluckiest officer in the Peninsular War. This distinction goes to John Cameron of the 79th Foot. Lieutenant Cameron landed in Portugal in August 1808 and served in the Peninsula for the whole war – a total of sixty-nine months. During that time he would fight in ten campaigns and battles without being wounded. Unlike the other three officers, Lieutenant Cameron was promoted to captain in January 1814, eight years after being promoted to lieutenant! Unfortunately for him, his luck ran out in the last major battle of the war. On 10 April 1814, Captain Cameron was killed in action at Toulouse – four days before the war ended.

Officers who served in the Peninsula throughout the war
The Peninsular War lasted sixty-nine months. Owing to the evacuation from Coruña in January 1809, few officers served in the Peninsula during the whole war. The following officers are among those who did:

Table 4.59 Officers who served in the Peninsula throughout the war

Name	Rank	Regiment
Thomas Canch	Lieutenant	5th Foot
William Irwin	Lieutenant	28th Foot
Robert Prescott Eason	Lieutenant	28th Foot
Theobald O'Dogherty	Lieutenant	40th Foot
John Thoreau	Lieutenant	40th Foot
Thomas Lightfoot	Major	45th Foot
John Williams	Surgeon	52nd Foot
James Holmes Schoedde	Major	60th Foot
John Cameron	Captain	79th Foot

Major James Holmes Schoedde, 60th Foot, fought in twenty-two different battles and actions during the Peninsular War. He would receive an Army Gold Medal for commanding at Nivelle and became KCB in 1842 after commanding a brigade in China. He received the Military General Service Medal with fourteen clasps – thirteen for battles in the Peninsular War and one for Egypt!

Names of officers
The names of officers reflected society as a whole. The following are taken from Lionel Challis's 'Peninsula Roll Call' and pertain to those officers who served in the British army in the Peninsula. The 'Peninsula Roll Call' contains biographical data on over 9617 British officers who served in the Peninsular War. The following lists are for all officers who served with British units in the Peninsular War, but excludes those who served with the King's German Legion, the Brunswick Light Infantry, and the Brunswick Hussars, which are included in the Challis index. The total

number of officers for the study below is 8,861. Of these officers 6,503 or 73 per cent of all officers had one of these first names. Of the top five names 46 per cent of all officers had these names.

Table 4.60   Most common first names among officers serving in the Peninsula

First name	No. of officers with name	Percentage of officers with name
John	1,305	14.7%
William	1,024	11.6%
James	605	6.83%
Thomas	598	6.75%
George	524	5.91%
Charles	424	4.69%
Robert	395	4.46%
Henry	376	4.24%
Edward	290	3.72%
Richard	241	2.71%
Alexander	195	2.2%
Francis	149	1.68%
Samuel	148	1.67%
Joseph	128	1.44%
Frederick	101	1.13%

The most common family names among officers in the Peninsular army, were:

Table 4.61   Most common family names among officers serving in the Peninsula

Family name	No. of officers with name
Campbell	105
Smith	58
Stewart	57
Jones	54
Fraser	39
Gordon	39
Hamilton	39
Scott	38
Thompson	37
Cameron	36

Life of an Officer

The most common names among officers were:

Table 4.62   Most common names among officers serving in the Peninsula

Name	No. of officers with name
Alexander Campbell	9
Archibald Campbell	9
John Campbell	9
John Clarke	8
William Jones	8
William Smith	8
William Williams	8
John Armstrong	7
Duncan Campbell	7
John Fraser	7
John Hamilton	7
James Stewart	7
John Stewart	7
William Stewart	7
John Evans	6
John Grant	6
John Hay	6
John Ross	6
John Taylor	6
John Wilson	6
John Wood	6

Although over 26 per cent of all officers were named either William or John, there were also some very unusual names.

Table 4.63   Unusual names among officers serving in the Peninsula

Name	Regiment
Hoylet Framingham	Royal Artillery
Sholto Douglas	4th Light Dragoons
Alured Dodsworth Faunce	4th Foot
Sempronius Stretton	40th Foot
Christmas Knight	61st Foot

185

Chapter Five

Life of a Soldier

There are many misconceptions and myths concerning the life of a soldier, both in garrison and on campaign. Many writers tell of substandard quarters, inedible rations, brutal discipline, and uncaring officers. Although there is some truth in these stories, they need to be placed in the proper context. The soldier's life was hard, but it was probably no worse than what he had experienced before joining the army.

The recruit
All British soldiers were volunteers. The British army of the Napoleonic Wars did not conscript, so recruiting parties were sent out to fill its ranks. On joining, the new soldier had to take an oath stating that he was physically fit, not an apprentice and not already in the military. On taking this oath, the recruit received a bounty. The amount of the bounty depended on whether the new recruit would be joining an infantry or cavalry regiment and his age.

Table 5.1 Bounty paid to new recruits, June 1804

Event	£	s	d
Infantry			
On being attested in, money	2	2	0
On intermediate approval, in money	4	4	0
On intermediate approval, in necessaries	0	12	0
On final approval, in money	7	16	0
On final approval, in necessaries	2	2	0
Total bounty to the recruit	16	16	0
Cavalry			
On being attested in, money	1	1	0

Event	£	s	d
On intermediate approval, in money	3	3	0
On intermediate approval, in necessaries	0	12	0
On final approval, in money	5	9	0
On final approval, in necessaries	3	3	0
Total bounty to the recruit	13	8	0
Boys for general service			
On being attested in, money	1	1	0
On intermediate approval, in money	1	10	0
On intermediate approval, in necessaries	0	12	0
On final approval, in money	3	3	0
On final approval, in necessaries	2	2	0
Total bounty to the recruit	8	8	0

Source: Reide, *A Treatise on Military Finance*, vol. 2, p. 382.

On paper, this was more money than the average recruit had ever seen in his life. The new infantryman may have been authorised £13 18s, but in reality he saw very little of this. His initial outfitting of uniforms, other than his jacket and shako, was paid for from his bounty payment.

Table 5.2 List of necessaries to be paid from the recruit's bounty money

Item	When issued	Quantity	£	s	d
Shirt	Intermediate approval	1	0	5	6
Shoes	Intermediate approval	1 pair	0	6	6
Shirts	Final approval	3	0	18	0
Shoes	Final approval	1 pair	0	6	0
Pack	Final approval	1	0	6	0
Leggings	Final approval	1	0	3	4½
Brushes and black-ball	Final approval	1 set	0	1	1
Stockings	Final approval	2 pair	0	1	10
Combs	Final approval	2	0	0	4
Straps, great coat	Final approval	1 set	0	2	4
Stock and clasp	Final approval	1	0	0	9
Sundries	Final approval	1 set	0	1	3½
Total money			2	14	0

Source: Reide, *A Treatise on Military Finance*, vol. 2, p. 387.

The total cost of recruiting one soldier was quite high. In addition to the money paid to the recruit, there were expenses of the recruiting party. The magistrate who took the soldier's oath and the surgeon who ensured he was healthy enough to serve were all paid for their services. Additionally, the recruiter party's expenses had to be paid, as well as an incentive bonus for finding the new recruit.

Table 5.3 Administrative costs to enlist one recruit in the army June 1804

Expense	£	s	d
Recruiting officer: for attesting	0	1	0
Recruiting officer: surgical examination	0	2	6
Recruiting officer: postage, stationery, etc.	0	7	0
Recruiting officer: other expenses	0	10	6
Recruiting party: reward	1	1	0
Recruiting party: bringing recruit to final approval	0	5	0
Recruiting party: final approval	0	16	0
Total	3	3	0

Source: Reide, *A Treatise on Military Finance*, vol. 2, p. 382.

By June 1804 the British army was spending £16 11s to recruit one cavalryman, £19 19s to recruit one infantryman, and £10 15s to recruit one boy for general service.

The new recruits would be escorted to the regimental depot, where they would learn the basics of soldiering. They would be issued uniforms, paid for either from regimental or public funds or from their enlistment bonus. The infantryman's clothing and equipment was fairly basic.

Table 5.4 Authorised clothing and equipment for infantry

Item	Quantity	Provided by
Regimental cap	1	Colonel
Cockade and feather or tuff	1 each	Colonel
Regimental coat	1	Colonel
Waistcoat	1	Colonel
Breeches	1 pair	Colonel
Shoes	1 pair	Colonel
Necessaries		
Great coat	1	Public
Turnscrew, brush and worm	1 each	Public
Oil, emery and brick-dust	1 each	Public

The Life of a Soldier

Item	Quantity	Provided by
Shoes	1 pair	Soldier
Back cloth gaiters	1 pair	Soldier
Shirts	3	Soldier
Socks, worsted or yarn	3 pair	Soldier
Mitts, worsted or yarn	1 pair	Soldier
Stock, black	1	Soldier
Foraging cap	1	Soldier
Knapsack	1	Soldier
Brush, clothes	1	Soldier
Brush, shoe	3	Soldier
Black ball	1	Soldier
Hair ribbon and leather	1 each	Soldier
Combs	2	Soldier
Straps for carrying great coat	Set	Soldier

Source: Reide, *A Treatise on Military Finance*, vol. 2, pp. 476–7.

Trivia: According to legend, in the regiment of the Isles Highlanders, a fencible regiment, there were so many Donald Macdonalds that when '. . . the sergeants of companies called over the muster-rolls, there having been so many Donald Macdonalds in each, that they had to be numbered. The sergeants, therefore, used to commence in the Gaelic pronunciation and accent with Tonald Mactonald, No. 1; Tonald Mactonald, No. 2; Tonald Mactonald, No. 3, and so on, until the Tonalds were exhausted in each company, the voice being raised to a higher pitch, very amusingly, as they called out the name of each man.'[1]

The clothing and equipment for a cavalryman was more extensive. Additionally, the type of clothing he received depended on his regiment.

Table 5.5 Authorised clothing and equipment for cavalry

Item	Quantity	Provided by	How often
Dragoons and dragoon guards			
Hat	1	Colonel	Yearly
Gloves	1 pair	Colonel	Yearly
Coat	1	Colonel	Every 2 years
Waistcoat	1	Colonel	Every 2 years
Breeches	1 pair	Colonel	Every 2 years
Necessaries			
Breeches	1 pair	Soldier	

---

1 Mackerlie, *An Account*, pp. 45–7

Table 5.5 continued

Item	Quantity	Provided by	How often
Breeches slings	1 pair	Soldier	
Stable jacket	1	Soldier	
Stable trousers	1 pair	Soldier	
Foraging cap	1	Soldier	
Nose bag	1	Soldier	
Watering bridle and log	1	Soldier	
Shirts	3	Soldier	
Night cap	1	Soldier	
Stock and clasps	1	Soldier	
Stockings, worsted	3 pair	Soldier	
Gaiters, long black	1 pair	Soldier	
Shoes	2 pair	Soldier	
Shoe clasps	1 pair	Soldier	
Shoe brushes	3	Soldier	
Combs	2	Soldier	
Razor and soap	1	Soldier	
Clothes brush	1	Soldier	
Worm & picker	1 each	Soldier	
Mane comb & sponge	1 each	Soldier	
Horse picker	1	Soldier	
Scissors	1	Soldier	
Emery oil	1	Soldier	
Pipe clay, whiting & blacking	1 each	Soldier	
Powder bag, powder & puff	1 each	Soldier	
Carbine lock case	1	Soldier	
Saddle bags	1	Soldier	
Light dragoons			
Gloves	1 pair	Colonel	Yearly
Upper jacket	1	Colonel	Every 2 years
Under jacket	1	Colonel	Every 2 years
Waistcoat, flannel	1	Colonel	Every 2 years
Breeches, leather	1 pair	Colonel	Every 2 years
Helmet	1	Colonel	Every 3 years
Watering cap	1	Colonel	Every 4 years
Necessaries:			
Breeches	1 pair	Soldier	
Breeches slings	1 pair	Soldier	
Stable jacket	1	Soldier	

Item	Quantity	Provided by
Light dragoons		
Stable trousers	1 pair	Soldier
Foraging cap	1	Soldier
Nose bag	1	Soldier
Watering bridle & log	1	Soldier
Shirts	3	Soldier
Night cap	1	Soldier
Stock and clasps	1	Soldier
Stockings, worsted	3 pair	Soldier
Gaiters, long black	1 pair	Soldier
Shoes	2 pair	Soldier
Shoe clasps	1 pair	Soldier
Shoe brushes	3	Soldier
Combs	2	Soldier
Razor and soap	1	Soldier
Clothes brush	1	Soldier
Worm & picker	1 each	Soldier
Mane comb & sponge	1 each	Soldier
Horse picker	1	Soldier
Scissors	1	Soldier
Emery oil	1	Soldier
Pipe clay, whiting & blacking	1 each	Soldier
Powder bag, powder & puff	1 each	Soldier
Carbine lock case	1	Soldier
Saddle bags	1	Soldier

Source: Reide, *A Treatise on Military Finance*, vol. 2, pp. 473–5.

The cavalry soldier was also responsible for his horse and its equipment.

Table 5.6 Horse appointments and other items issued

Item	Amount	Duration
Dragoons and dragoon guards		
Boots shod with iron and nails at the toe	1 pair	6 years
Cloak with sleeves	1	12 years
Saddlery:		
Saddle with pannel and pad	1	16 years
Web-girth with 6 roller buckles	1	6 years
Strap flaps	1 pair	6 years
Martingale, breast plate with roller buckles	1	6 years

Table 5.6 continued

Item	Amount	Duration
Stirrup leathers with roller buckles	1 pair	16 years
Stirrup irons	1 pair	16 years
Bit & bridoon with head reins & nose band	1	12 years
Double forage straps with roller buckles	1 pair	6 years
Single forage straps with roller buckles	1 pair	6 years
Firelock strap with roller buckles	1	6 years
Holster straps with roller buckles	1 pair	6 years
Holster and shoe case with roller buckles	1	6 years
Carbine bucket with picket ring	1	16 years
Carbine bucket strap	1	6 years
Cover for holsters	1	6 years
Leather cloak cover	1	6 years
Horse collar with iron chain	1	6 years
Buff accoutrements:		
Pouch curved for thirty rounds	1	20 years
Pocket behind for thirty rounds	1	20 years
Roller buckles	1	20 years
Carbine belt, 3 inches wide	1	20 years
Buckles with two brass tongues & tip	1	20 years
Straps for the pouch to hang by	1 pair	20 years
Brass slider and swivel	1	20 years
Sword waist belt, 2 ½ inches wide	1	20 years
Brass plate & slide with bar & double tongue	1	20 years
Bayonet frog with buff leather	1	20 years
Sword knot of buff leather	1	20 years
Light dragoons		
Boots shod with iron and nails at the toe	1 pair	6 years
Cloak with sleeves	1	12 years
Saddlery:		
Saddle with pannel and pad	1	16 years
Web-girth with 6 roller buckles	1	6 years
Strap flaps	1 pair	6 years
Martingale, breast plate with roller buckles	1	6 years
Stirrup leathers with roller buckles	1 pair	16 years
Stirrup irons	1 pair	16 years
Bit & bridoon with head reins & nose band	1	12 years
Double forage straps with roller buckles	1 pair	6 years
Single forage straps with roller buckles	1 pair	6 years
Firelock strap with roller buckles	1	6 years

Item	Amount	Duration
Holster straps with roller buckles	1 pair	6 years
Holster and shoe case with roller buckles	1	6 years
Light dragoons		
Carbine bucket with picket ring	1	16 years
Carbine bucket strap	1	6 years
Cover for holsters	1	6 years
Leather cloak cover	1	6 years
Horse collar with iron chain	1	6 years
Pouch curved for thirty rounds	1	20 years
Pocket behind for thirty rounds	1	20 years
Roller buckles	1	20 years
Carbine belt, 2 ½ inches wide	1	20 years
Buckles with two brass tongues & tip	1	20 years
Straps for the pouch to hang by	1 pair	20 years
Brass slider and swivel	1	20 years
Sword waist belt, 1 ¼ inches wide	1	20 years
Sword carriage	1	20 years
Bayonet frog of buff leather	1	20 years
Sword knot of buff leather	1	20 years

Source: Reide, *A Treatise on Military Finance*, vol. 2, pp. 461–4.

Life in the barracks

While stationed in the British Isles, the soldiers lived in a variety of different barracks. According to regulations, each cavalry troop or infantry company was allocated rooms based on the number of men assigned to it. NCOs were in separate rooms from the privates.

Table 5.7 Rooms authorised to enlisted soldiers in a barracks

Rank	Cavalry	Infantry
NCOs	1 for each troop	1 for every 12 men
Privates	1 for every 8 men	1 for every 12 men

Source: Reide, *A Treatise on Military Finance*, vol. 2, pp. 513.

Each room was supposed to be equipped with a variety of items including beds with sheets and blankets, a table, and rugs. Soldiers would cook their food and eat their meals in their rooms.

Table 5.8 Equipment furnished in enlisted soldiers room

Item	Cavalry	Infantry
Bedsteads	8 single or 4 double	12 single or 6 double
Mattresses or palliasses	8 single or 4 double	12 single or 6 double
Bolsters	8 single or 4 double	12 single or 6 double
Blankets, pairs	8 single or 4 double	12 single or 6 double
Sheets, pairs	8 single or 4 double	12 single or 6 double
Rugs	8 single or 4 double	12 single or 6 double
Round towel	1	1
Closet or shelves	1	1
Table	1	1
Rack for arms	1	1
Fire irons	1	1
Fender	1	1
Forms	3	3
Iron pots	2	2
Wooden lids	2	2
Pair of iron pot hooks	2	2
Iron trivets	2	2
Wooden ladles	2	2
Iron flesh fork	1	1
Frying pan	1	1
Large bowls or platters	2	2
Small bowls or porringers	8	12
Trenchers	8	12
Spoons	8	12
Water bucket	1	1
Coal tray	1	1
Candlesticks	1	1
Tin can for beer	1	1
Large earthen pan for meat	1	1
Box or basket for carrying coals	1	1
Drinking horns	2	2
Wooden urinal	1	1
Broom	1	1
Mop	1	1

Source: Reide, *A Treatise on Military Finance*, vol. 2, pp. 516–18.

The amount of fuel authorised for the enlisted soldiers' rooms was the same as for the officers' rooms: see table 4.7.

Table 5.9 Equipment for the stables of the cavalry

Item	For 8 Horses	Every 16 Horses
Pitchfork	2	4
Shovel	2	4
Lanthorn	1	2
Wheelbarrow	1	2
Water Bucket	2	4
Broom, per month	4	8

Source: Reide, *A Treatise on Military Finance*, vol. 2, p. 519.

Every regiment mounted a guard and in garrison, the guard room was supplied with the following equipment:

Table 5.10 Equipment for a guard room

Item	Cavalry	Infantry
Water bucket	1	1
Candlestick	1	1
Tin Can for Beer	1	1
Drinking Horn	1	1
Fire Irons	1	1
Coal Tray	1	1

Source: Reide, *A Treatise on Military Finance*, vol. 2, p. 518.

The guard room also received a fuel allowance to heat it during the winter:

Table 5.11 Fuel allowances for guard rooms for seven days, September–April

Item	Officer's Guard	NCO's Guard
Coal	7 bushels	3½ bushels
Candles	4 pounds	2 pounds

Source: Reide, *A Treatise on Military Finance*, vol. 2, pp. 514.

The soldiers were fed quite well by the standard of the day.

Table 5.12 Daily rations in garrison

Item	Amount
Flour or bread	1½ pounds
Beef	1 pound
Pork (if beef is not available)	½ pound
Pease	¼ pint

Table 5.12 continued

Item	Amount
Butter or cheese	1 ounce
Rice	1 ounce
Beer	5 pints

When the above is not available, the following is considered a daily ration:

Bread	1½ pounds
Beef	3 pounds
Pork (if beef is not available)	10 ounces

If the above is not available, then any of the following is also considered a daily ration:

Bread	3 pounds
Beef	3 pounds
Cheese	2 pounds
Rice	1½ pounds

Source: Reide, *A Treatise on Military Finance*, vol. 1, p. 249; vol. 2, p. 520.

Pay

The amount of a pay a soldier received was dependent on whether he was in the cavalry, infantry, artillery, etc.; plus his rank. A cavalry trooper received over £4 a year more than a infantry private, while a cavalry sergeant received £11 more a year than a sergeant in the infantry.

Table 5.13 Daily and yearly pay for soldiers, 1805

Rank	Daily £	Daily s	Daily d	Yearly £	Yearly s	Yearly d
Infantry						
Sergeant	0	1	6¾	28	10	3¼
Corporal	0	1	2¼	21	13	5¼
Drummer	0	1	1¾	20	18	2¼
Private	0	1	0	18	5	0
Cavalry						
Sergeant	0	2	2	39	10	10
Corporal	0	17	½	29	13	1½
Trumpeter	0	1	7	28	17	11
Private	0	1	3	22	16	3

Source: Reide, *A Treatise on Military Finance*, vol. 2, appendix 1.

Table 5.14 Daily and yearly pay for soldiers in 1806

Rank	Daily £ s d	Yearly £ s d
Royal Artillery		
Sergeant major	0 3 7⅛	65 13 6
Quartermaster sergeant	0 3 7⅛	65 13 6
Sergeant	0 2 5¼	43 19 8¼
Bombardier	0 2 0	36 0 0
1st Gunner	0 1 7	28 19 11
Gunner	0 1 3¼	23 3 10¼
Drum Major	0 2 2	39 0 10
Fife Major	0 2 2	39 0 10
Drummer	0 1 3¼	23 3 10¼
Fifer	0 1 3¼	23 3 10¼
Royal Horse Artillery		
Sergeant major	0 3 9¼	68 16 4¼
Quartermaster sergeant	0 3 9¼	68 16 4¼
Sergeant	0 2 7¼	47 0 6¼
Bombardier	0 2 0	36 0 0
Gunner	0 1 5¼	26 4 8¼
Driver	0 1 3¼	23 3 10¼
Trumpeter	0 2 1¼	37 19 0¼
Staff farrier and smith	0 3 4¾	61 19 5¾
Staff wheeler	0 3 4¾	61 19 5¾
Staff collar maker	0 3 4¾	61 19 5¾
Farrier and Smith	0 3 4¾	61 19 5¾
Shoeing smith	0 2 3¼	40 18 10¼
Collar maker	0 2 0¾	37 2 9¾
Wheeler	0 2 0¾	37 2 9¾

Source: Kane, *List of Officers of the Royal Regiment of Artillery*, p. 216.

Like officers, enlisted soldiers had stoppages taken out of their pay. These included messing at 4s per week (6d per day) and necessities at 1s 6d (2½d per day). Necessities were those uniform items that were not issued by the regiment and that the soldier had to pay for himself. Necessities were only deducted for the first twenty-four days of the month.[2]

---

2 Fortescue, *A History of the British Army*, vol. IV, part II, p. 935.

Table 5.15 Yearly pay for an infantry private after deductions

	£	s	d
Yearly pay	18	5	0
Deductions for food	9	2	6
Deductions for necessities	3	2	9
Deduction for Chelsea Hospital	0	1	0
Net pay after deductions	4	18	9

Weekly net pay was 1s 6d per week, from which washing and cleaning was deducted.

Trivia: Pay day for the British army of the Napoleonic Era was on the 25th of the month.

Life on campaign

A soldier's life on campaign was much harder than when stationed in the British Isles. Everything he needed, he carried. He often slept under the stars, in crude huts or in civilian homes. Although theoretically his rations were the same as in garrison, in reality rations were neither of the same quality or quantity. Furthermore, while on campaign, the soldiers often out-marched their supplies and did not receive their daily food.

Several soldiers left accounts of what they carried on campaign.

Table 5.16 What a soldier in the 7th Fusiliers carried in the Peninsula, 1813

Item	Amount	Weight (lb)
Fusilee and bayonet	1	14
Ammunition pouch and 60 rounds	1	6
Canteen and belt	1	1
Mess tin	1	1
Knapsack, frame, and belts	1	3
Blanket	1	4
Great coat	1	4
Dress coat	1	3
White jacket	1	½
Shirts	2	2½
Shoes	2 pair	3
Trousers	1 pair	2
Gaiters	1 pair	¼
Stockings	2 pair	1
Brushes, button, stick, and comb	4	3

The Life of a Soldier

Item	Amount	Weight (lb)
Cross belts	2	1
Pen, ink, and paper		¼
Pipe clay, chalk, etc.		1
Tent pegs	2	½
Bread	3 days	3
Beef	2 days	2
Water		3
Total		61

Source: Cooper, *Rough Notes of Seven Campaigns*, p. 81.

Table 5.17 What a British rifleman carried in 1809

Item	Quantity
Knapsack	1
Shirts	2
Stockings	2 pair
Shoes	2 pair
Extra pair of soles and heels for shoes	
Trousers	2
Greatcoat	1
Blanket	1
Brushes	3
Box of blacking	1
Razor	1
Soap box and strap	1 each
Mess tin, centre tin and lid	1 each
Powder flask	1
Ball bag containing 30 loose balls	1
Small wooden mallet	1
Belt and ammunition pouch	1
Sword belt and sword bayonet	1
Baker's rifle	1
Haversack	1
Canteen	1
Shako	1
Jacket	1
Total weight	80 lb

Source: Costello, *The Peninsular and Waterloo Campaigns*, p. 18.

It should be noted that Sergeant Costello, who left the above list, wrote that his unit was fresh from England. By the end of the war five years later he did not think there was a man in the regiment who '. . . could show a single shirt or a pair of shoes in his knapsack.'

Trivia: In addition to his own personal equipment, a rifleman also was required to help carry the four billhooks assigned to his squad. These billhooks were used for cutting brush and weighed about 6 lb. A squad had a complement of eight riflemen, so each man had to carry the extra 6 lb every other day.

Rations

Theoretically, the soldier was supposed to receive the same rations on campaign as he did in garrison. This rarely happened. When Wellington's army marched, a soldier's daily ration of food was supposed to be 1 lb beef and 1½ of bread or flour. This ideal was rarely achieved. Beef was easier to supply than the bread because immense herds of cattle followed the army. When bread was scarce, 2 oz of rice was authorised as a substitute. If no bread was available, the meat ration was raised to 2 lb per day.[3] The British supply system was notorious for breaking down during retreats. When no food was available, the soldiers either went hungry or foraged for themselves. Often it was either feast or famine. The retreat from Burgos saw many soldiers surviving on acorns.

Trivia: Regardless of the quality or quantity of their rations, the soldier still had 4s a week taken out of his pay to cover the cost of feeding him – even if the soldier received no food owing to supply problems. In 1809 Wellington recognised the inequity of this and ordered that until the food supply returned to normal, the soldiers would only have 3d per day deducted from their pay for rations instead of 6d per day.

Trivia: Idle soldiers tend to get themselves into trouble. In the 45th Foot, one soldier was known for the amount of food he could eat in one sitting. The soldier was asked by his sergeant:

> 'How many of these loaves could you eat if you had your will of them?' The loaves were three pound weight each, and David eyeing them very eagerly, said, 'It is not long since I got my breakfast, still I think I could yam a few of them.' 'Well,' said the sergeant, 'I will give you a quart of wine to each loaf, to wash it down; so begin, and let us see what you can do.' Upon this David commenced the game, which proved dear to him, although most excellent sport to the bystanders.

---

3   *General Orders*, 19 May 1809, p. 37.

In rather more than an hour he finished four loaves, and swallowed as many quarts of wine, which, with his breakfast amounted to thirteen pounds and a half of bread, four quarts of, and one of chocolate, all swallowed in the course of two hours. When he had done, he sat and stared as if his eyes would have started out of their sockets, and was totally unable to rise. The bread he had eaten being made of rye, and newly baken, swelled him to such a degree, that he was in great danger of bursting, and made him groan both long and loud. Some spoke of rolling him, which was immediately commenced on a green in front of the barn, but he roared so loud and hideously, calling upon God, and Pharaoh, King of Egypt, alternately, to assist and save him, it was dropped. His belly was then rubbed with grease and oil, but not producing the desired effect; he was carried to the hospital, where he lay several days before recovering.'[4]

Trivia: William Grattan stated that after the retreat from Burgos in 1813, a man in his company ate an ox head everyday for a week – in addition to his regular rations. It caused a 'violent inflammation of the bowels... and the poor fellow died in the most excruciating agonies'.[5]

Forage for horses and mules

In addition to feeding himself, the cavalry trooper was also responsible for ensuring his mount was fed. The following is what was authorised for daily fodder for a horse or a mule.

Table 5.18   Amount of daily forage for mules and horses 1809

Type of forage	Amount allowed
Hay or straw	14 lb
Oats	12 lb
Barley or Indian corn if oats are not available	10 lb

Source: *General Orders*, 30 May 1809, p. 113

As time went by, the amount of forage available to the army decreased, as was the amount the troopers received. It should be noted that this is what was authorised in a garrison situation. During the initial days of a campaign, the troopers may have received this amount, but the further they went from their supply depots, the less there was available. By the end of the campaigns, the troopers were feeding their mounts anything they could find, including green corn and gorse.

4 Brown, *With the 45th at Badajoz, Salamanca, and Vittoria*, p. 3.
5 Grattan, *Adventures with the Connaught Rangers*, p. 315.

Table 5.19 Amount of daily forage for mules and horses 1810

Type of forage	Amount allowed
Hay or straw	10 lb
Oats	12 lb
Barley or Indian corn if oats are not available	12 lb

Source: *General Orders*, 31 January 1810, p. 115.

Lodging

The British army had no formal barracks in the Peninsula. When not campaigning, the regiments were spread over a fairly large area to reduce the impact on the local economy, particularly on the crops and farmlands. In large towns and cities the troops were quartered in public buildings, convents and even churches whenever possible. In smaller towns and villages the troops would be billeted in houses, stables, barns or any other available building. One of the major problems was the scarcity of fuel for cooking and heating the buildings. When firewood was not available, the soldiers were known to use furniture, roofs, doors and shutters and olive trees. In order to prevent wholesale destruction to areas where soldiers needed to find something to cook their food with, Wellington had his commissaries issue firewood to the units.

Table 5.20 Daily allowances for fire wood in bivouac 1809

Rank	Allowance per person (lb)
Private	3
Non-commissioned officer	3
Subaltern	12
Regimental staff	12
Captain	21
Field officer	30
General officer	unlimited

Source: *General Orders*, 29 November 1809, page 111.

Finding fuel was a constant battle for the soldier and on campaign it was even worse. Whole towns would be stripped of anything flammable and olive orchards were often destroyed by troops passing through.

Pay on campaign

Wellington's army was constantly behind in paying the troops, sometimes by as much as six months. By the time money was available to pay the troops, their net pay was more than some soldiers had ever had in their lives at one time. In August 1813, to prevent the soldiers from spending all their money at once and the ensuing discipline problems that went with it, Wellington ordered the company commanders to divide the sum of money by thirty and dole it out on a daily basis.

For the Guards, the amount of money owed was considerably more and a different system had to be used initially. A certain amount of each soldier's pay was set aside and would be paid later. Any money in excess of what was set aside was immediately paid to the soldier. After that, the soldier would receive the money that had been set aside as daily payments given over thirty days.

Table 5.21 Amount of money set aside out of the pay of guardsmen in the Peninsula August 1813

Regiment	Corporal s d	Trumpeter/drummer s d	Trooper s d
Life Guards	45 0	45 0	30 0
Horse Guards	37 6	22 6	22 6
Foot Guards	20 0	15 0	15 0

Table 5.22 Amount of money to be paid daily to guardsmen in the Peninsula August 1813

Regiment	Corporal s d	Trumpeter/drummer s d	Trooper s d
Life Guards	1 6	1 0	1 0
Horse Guards	1 3	0 9	0 9
Foot Guards	1 0	0 8	0 6

Source: *General Orders*, 3 August 1813, pp. 229–30.

Replacing lost equipment

Life on campaign was hard on the soldier's equipment. He was authorised an allowance to replace items lost or destroyed while on campaign.

Table 5.23 Reimbursement for baggage lost on campaign

Rank	£ s d
Sergeant	2 13 0
Corporal	2 10 0
Trumpeter	2 10 0
Private	2 10 0
Servant, not a soldier	3 8 0

Source: Reide, *A Treatise on Military Finance*, vol. 1, p. 216.

Discipline and courts martial

Discipline in the British army in the Peninsula was often brutal and quick. There were no military prisons, so the offender was returned to his unit after the punishment was inflicted. Flogging was the most frequent punishment. There were different levels of courts martial: the general court martial which tried serious offences and the regimental court martial which handled minor offences. A regimental court martial was restricted to imposing flogging as a punishment, while a general court martial could impose the death penalty. By 1812 the maximum penalty a regimental court martial could impose was 300 lashes.

Trivia: A general court martial had a minimum of thirteen members. The death penalty could only be imposed if nine of the thirteen voted for it, or two-thirds of the members if there were more than thirteen.[6]

Table 5.24 Types of punishment a general court martial in the Peninsula could impose

Crime	Punishment
Desertion to the enemy	Death by firing squad
Desertion	Up to 1200 lashes
Murder	Hanging
Violence against a civilian	Hanging
Violence against a civilian while plundering	Hanging
Grand theft	Hanging
Sodomy	Hanging
Theft or plundering	Transportation to a colony or up to 1,200 lashes

Source Oman, *Wellington's Army*, pp. 237–45.

A study of the inspection returns from three regiments during the Napoleonic Wars, shows that the most common form of punishment given by a regimental court-martial was the lash. A sentence of flogging was given in 70–85 per cent of all verdicts.

Table 5.25 Verdicts of courts martial for three infantry regiments over a five-month period

Regiment	Cases tried	Acquittals	Sentence Other	Lashes	% lashes
1st Battalion 23rd Foot	33	2	3	28	85%
103rd Foot	35	6	1	28	80%
Glengarry Light Infantry	53	4	11	38	72%

6 Thomas, *The Local Military Paymaster*, p. 100.

The Life of a Soldier

The three regiments were consistent with the number of verdicts where the maximum sentence of 300 lashes was given, though the maximum sentence was rarely carried out in two regiments.

Table 5.26 Number of courts martial where a maximum sentence of 300 lashes was given

Regiment	Cases	Times given	%	Times carried out	%
1st Bn 23rd Foot	28	11	39%	1	9%
103rd Foot	28	10	36%	1	10%
Glengarry L.I.	38	15	39%	7	47%

The average number of lashes sentenced was also consistent, ranging from 197 to 236. Rarely were these sentences fully carried out. In the 94 courts-martial that were held by the three regiments, in which the sentence was flogging, the sentence was reduced in 72 (77%) of them.

Table 5.27 Number of lashes inflicted versus number sentenced

Regiment	Cases	Average no. of lashes	Average no. inflicted	No. reduced	% reduced
1st Battalion 23rd Foot	28	236	78	26	93%
103rd Foot	28	197	59	18	64%
Glengarry Light Infantry	38	230	94	28	74%

The average number of lashes inflicted was seventy-eight. Furthermore, thirty-seven (39 per cent) of the sentences were never carried out.

Table 5.28 Number of lashes sentenced versus sentences carried out

Regiment	Cases	Average no. of lashes	No. not carried out	% not carried out
1st Battalion 23rd Foot	28	236	10	37%
103rd Foot	28	197	8	29%
Glengarry Light Infantry	38	230	19	50%

Table 5.29 Number of lashes inflicted by regimental courts martial in 1st Battalion 23rd foot, October 1812–February 1813

Offence	Lashes: sentenced	inflicted
Taking items belonging to Major Beatty (7th foot)	300	300
Drunk and absent from parade	300	100
Drunk and absent on the march	100	0

The British Army Against Napoleon

Table 5.29   continued

Offence	Lashes: sentenced	inflicted
Drunk and disorderly on the march – 6 cases, each	250	0
Neglect of duty on the march	100	0
Losing ammunition	100	0
Destroying a pig – 3 cases, each	200	170
Threatening the master of the band	100	0
Suspicion of theft	200	200
Suspicion of theft	200	160
Suspicion of theft	200	100
Making away with his blanket	200	100
Absent without leave	300	100
Theft – 7 cases, each	300	75
Total	6,600	2,170

Source: TNA WO 27/1021 Inspection Return, 1/23rd Foot, Algodras, Portugal 12 April 1813.

Of the twenty-eight cases where the soldiers received a sentence of lashing, ten were not carried out. Only twice did a soldier receive the full sentence. The average number of lashes received was seventy-eight. Crimes against property were punished the most severely.

Crimes against someone in another regiment were punished the most severely. Twice a soldier was sentenced to 300 lashes and received them. Theft and crimes against property were also punished harshly.

Table 5.30   Number of lashes inflicted by regimental courts martial in 103rd Foot, April–October 1812

Offence	Lashes: sentenced	inflicted
Theft	300	200
Suspicion of theft	300	15
Insolence to a non-commissioned officer	100	100
Absent without leave	300	0
Absent without leave	200	0
Having someone else's property and damaging it	100	75
Suspicion of theft	100	100
Having someone else's property	50	0
Unsoldierlike conduct	300	0
Disobedience of orders	100	100
Unsoldierlike conduct	200	100
Suspicion of theft	300	50
Disrespect to non-commissioned officer	50	50

The Life of a Soldier

Offence	Lashes: sentenced	inflicted
Drunk on parade and disrespect to non-commissioned officer	100	100
Suspicion of theft	25	0
Suspicion of theft – 2 cases, each	200	50
Lost of necessaries	300	7
Knocking down sentry of the 8th regiment and suspicion of theft	300	300
Lost of necessaries	200	50
Lost of necessaries	200	12
Suspicion of theft	200	50
Suspicion of theft	200	37
Insolence to a non-commissioned officer and rioting in barracks room	300	0
Absent from duties	200	100
Drunk on guard	300	0
Insolence to a non-commissioned officer	100	0
Drunk and absent from guard	300	100
Total	5,525	1,646

Of the twenty-seven convictions where the sentence was lashing, the average sentence was 197 lashes. The full punishment was carried out only five times. The average number of lashes inflicted was fifty-six lashes. The maximum sentence of 300 lashes was only inflicted once. This was for assault on a sentry of another regiment and the suspicion of theft.[7]

Trivia: During the Peninsular War, 78 soldiers in the British army were shot for desertion to the enemy. Of them, 52 were British soldiers and 26 were foreigners.

Table 5.31 Number of lashes inflicted by regimental courts martial Glengarry Light Infantry, February–July 1815

Offence	Lashes: sentenced	inflicted
Unsoldierlike conduct	300	300
Unsoldierlike conduct	150	0
Disobedience of an officer	250	125
Disobedience of an officer	150	50
Disobedience of an officer	150	0
Unsoldierlike conduct	200	0

---

7 Library and Archives of Canada, Record Group 8.1, vol. 165, p. 56.

Table 5.31 continued

Offence	Lashes: sentenced	inflicted
Unsoldierlike conduct	100	0
Disobedience of orders – 2 cases, each	300	300
Disobedience of orders	100	0
Neglect of duty	200	100
Unsoldierlike conduct – 2 cases, each	300	300
Unsoldierlike conduct	100	0
Drunk and insolent	200	0
Unsoldierlike conduct	100	100
Theft	300	300
Neglect of duty	200	200
Unsoldierlike conduct	300	100
Quitting his post	250	100
Absent without leave	300	300
Taking a prisoner to get liquor	200	0
Unsoldierlike conduct	250	0
Drunk on duty – 5 cases, each	300	0
Having a blanket that was government property	300	0
Drunk on duty	300	0
Refusing to mount guard	200	0
Drunk when ordered for duty	150	0
Refusing to mount guard	150	50
Refusing to mount guard	150	0
Attempting to strike sergeant mckeon	200	200
Drunk and disorderly	200	150
Disrespectful language	200	100
Making away with cap covers	200	100
Total	8,750	3,575

Trivia: *Being drunk on duty was not severely punished. During a five-month period, the 23rd Foot, 103rd Foot and the Glengarry Light Infantry courts martial convicted nineteen soldiers of being drunk on duty. The two sergeants were reduced in rank and the other seventeen were sentenced to be flogged an average of 265 lashes each. Only three (18 per cent) of the soldiers were flogged and each of them had a charge in addition to being drunk. Only the soldier, who threatened a sergeant while drunk, received his full sentence of 100 lashes.*

After the war was over

There are many horror stories of how blind and severely injured soldiers were discharged and left to survive with no assistance from the government.

But soldiers who were discharged for medical reasons could be placed in Chelsea Hospital, in one of the 13 Royal Veteran Battalions, or given a pension. These pensions could be quite generous – the equivalent to their daily pay.

Table 5.32 Disability payments for soldiers rendered blind

Rank	Daily payment £ s d	Yearly payment £ s d
Sergeant	0 1 6	27 7 6
Corporal	0 1 2	21 5 10
Drummer	0 1 0	18 5 0
Private	0 1 0	18 5 0

Source: Reide, *A Treatise on Military Finance*, vol. 1, p. 246.

Table 5.33 Annual disability payments: enlisted men unfit for duty

Disability	£ s d
1st Class	18 5 0
2nd Class	13 13 0
3rd Class	7 12 6

Source: Reide, *A Treatise on Military Finance*, vol. 1, p. 246.

Prize money
Like officers, enlisted soldiers also received prize money.

Table 5.34 Prize money paid to the army for actions in the Peninsula and Waterloo

Action	Sergeants £ s d	Other ranks £ s d
Coimbra and Douro	2 19 7½	0 7 2½
French Retreat from Portugal, Fuentes de Oñoro, and Albuera	2 3 6½	0 6 3½
Capture of Ciudad Rodrigo & Badajoz	2 3 6½	0 6 3½
Campaign in Spain, 1812	2 3 8	0 6 4
Campaign in Spain, 1813	2 14 3½	0 8 3½
Campaign in Southern France, 1814	10 0 7	1 14 3½
Waterloo campaign	19 4 4	2 11 4

Source: *London Gazette*, 27 January 1816, pp. 153–4; Booth, *The Battle of Waterloo*, p. 427; *Supplementary Despatches*, vol. 10, p. 750.

Trivia: Prize money was a significant bonus for the soldier. For an infantry sergeant, the prize money paid after Waterloo was the equivalent of eight months' salary, for a corporal it was equivalent to a month-and-a-half's salary and for a private it was two months' salary!

Funerals

Soldiers who died on active duty were entitled to a military funeral if circumstances permitted. The funeral would be attended by the members of the soldier's company.

Table 5.35   Composition of a funeral party for an enlisted soldier

Rank of deceased	Composition of party	No. of rounds fired
Sergeant	Sergeant and 18 men	3 rounds
Corporal	Sergeant and 12 men	3 rounds
Musician, Drummer, or Fifer	Sergeant and 12 men	3 rounds
Private	Sergeant and 12 men	3 rounds

Source: Thomas, *The Local Military Paymaster*, p. 103.

Chapter Six

British Casualties in the Napoleonic Wars

Overview of British casualties from 1805–15

Between 1805 and 1813, the British army had almost 200,000 casualties as a result of combat, disease, accident or desertion. This averaged about 21,500 men or 10 per cent of the total army per year. The primary killer of the army was not combat but disease. One study states that the number of British soldiers killed in battle from 1805 to 1815 was less than 14,000.[1] The number killed by disease, however, was at least twice that. For an army that depended on recruitment, rather than conscription, this was a considerable drain. The following table provides an overview of attrition in the British army. Casualties fall into three categories: dead (regardless of combat, accident, or disease), discharged due to wounds or sickness that made the soldier incapable to perform his duties, and desertion.

Table 6.1 British casualties during the Napoleonic Wars

Year	Casualties, British	Casualties, foreign	Total	% of force
1805	15,800	2,443	18,243	11.3%
1806	13,856	3,075	16,931	9.1%
1807	14,570	2,968	17,538	8.8%
1808	17,183	3,703	20,886	9.2%
1809	21,630	2,937	24,567	10.5%
1810	19,498	3,455	22,953	9.7%
1811	19,019	3,441	22,460	9.8%
1812	20,313	5,185	25,498	10.5%
1813	19,653	4,802	24,455	9.6%
Total	161,522	32,009	193,531	

Source: Fortescue, *The County Lieutenancies*, p. 291; Hodge, 'On the Mortality, pp. 264–5; HCPP, *Accounts and Estimates, Army Return*, vol. 8 (1810) p. 435.

---

1 Hodge, 'On the Mortality', p. 266.

The British Army Against Napoleon

Although the disease and desertion caused the most casualties, the number of killed and wounded was immense. These figures are for all of the British army, including those stationed in the British Isles.

Table 6.2   Number of killed and wounded of all ranks in the British army 1805–15

Year	Strength of army	Killed	Wounded	Total	%
1805	198,701	166	902	1,068	0.5%
1806	219,137	145	595	740	0.3%
1807	234,522	703	1,701	2,404	1.0%
1808	258,646	248	1,026	1,274	0.5%
1809	267,135	1,380	5,487	6,867	3.0%
1810	265,158	292	1,305	1,597	0.6%
1811	270,443	1,628	6,816	8,444	3.0%
1812	280,864	1,998	8,789	10,787	4.0%
1813	289,248	2,972	14,913	17,885	6.0%
1814	288,941	1,578	7,822	9,400	3.0%
1815	241,040	2,512	9,685	12,197	5.0%
Total		13,622	59,041	72,663	

Table 6.3   Casualties among the British officer corps 1805–15

Year	No. army officers	Killed	Wounded	Total	%
1805	9,101	9	47	56	0.6%
1806	10,037	4	31	35	0.3%
1807	10,722	32	125	157	1.5%
1808	11,846	9	59	68	0.6%
1809	12,235	63	302	365	3.0%
1810	12,158	19	108	127	1.0%
1811	12,043	80	434	514	4.3%
1812	12,864	131	640	771	6.0%
1813	13,248	168	955	1,123	8.5%
1814	13,241	90	604	694	5.2%
1815	11,040	171	680	851	7.7%
Total		776	3,985	4,761	

Table 6.4   Casualties among British enlisted soldiers 1805–15

Year	No. soldiers	Killed	Wounded	Total	%
1805	189,600	157	855	1,012	0.5%
1806	209,100	141	564	705	0.3%

British Casualties in the Napoleonic Wars

Year	No. soldiers	Killed	Wounded	Total	%
1807	223,800	671	1,576	2,247	1.0%
1808	246,800	239	918	1,157	0.5%
1809	254,900	1,317	5,185	6,502	2.6%
1810	253,000	273	1,197	1,470	0.6%
1811	258,400	1,548	6,382	7,930	3.0%
1812	268,000	1,867	8,149	10,016	3.7%
1813	276,000	2,804	13,958	16,762	6.0%
1814	275,700	1,488	7,218	8,706	3.0%
1815	230,000	2,341	9,005	11,346	5.0%
Total		12,846	55,007	67,853	

Source for above tables: Hodge, 'On the Mortality, p. 266.

Trivia: *Between 1807 and 1809, the regiments stationed in the British Isles had about 5 per cent of its soldiers per year desert. The worst year was 1808, when 4,564 soldiers were listed as deserters.*[2]

The largest number of British soldiers serving overseas during 1805–14 was in the Iberian Peninsula. By 1813 over 50,000 British troops were in Portugal or Spain. During the six years of the Peninsular War, the British army fought in over forty-five battles in Portugal, Spain and France. In those battles, over 8,500 British soldiers were killed, while another 40,000 were wounded. About 10 per cent of the officers and 16.5 per cent of the enlisted soldiers became casualties during the latter years of the war.

Table 6.5 Chance of becoming a casualty, Wellington's army, 1811–14

Type of casualty	For officer	For enlisted
Wounded	29.0%	18.0%
Killed or Died of Wounds	6.5%	5.2%
Disease or Accident	3.6%	11.3%

Source: Hodge, 'On the Mortality, p. 285.

The following table includes only casualties in British regiments and does not include Portuguese or Spanish soldiers.

Table 6.6 British casualties in the Peninsula, 1808–14

Year	Killed	Wounded	Missing	Total
1808	221	1,026	132	1,379
1809	791	4,430	653	5,874
1810	136	673	80	869

2 HCPP, *Accounts and Estimates*, vol. 8 (1810), p. 381.

The British Army Against Napoleon

Table 6.6 continued

Year	Killed	Wounded	Missing	Total
1811	1,324	5,196	843	7,363
1812	1,888	8,983	2,663	13,534
1813	3,145	13,854	1,475	18,474
1814	673	3,603	310	4,586
Total	8,178	37,765	6,156	59,114*

* Includes the Coruña campaign with 7,035 casualties in total spread over 1808–9.

Table 6.7 British casualties in campaigns and battles in the Peninsula, 1808–11

Battle or campaign	Killed	Wounded	Missing	Total
Roliça 1808	70	335	81	486
Vimeiro 1808	135	593	51	779
Sahagun 1808	4	21	—	25
Benevente 1808	12	77	—	89
Coruña campaign 1808–9	—	—	—	7,035
Coruña 1809	137	497	—	634
Oporto campaign 1809	13	18	6	37
Talavera 1809	641	3,915	647	5,203
River Coa 1810	32	182	29	243
Busaco 1810	104	491	51	646
Barossa 1811	192	990	—	1,182
Pombal 1811	1	5	—	6
Redinha 1811	9	60	—	69
Sabugal 1811	16	130	5	151
Fuentes de Oñoro 1811	177	1,056	264	1,497
Albuera 1811	882	2,733	544	4,159
El Bodon 1811	27	92	22	141
Aldea da Ponte 1811	13	66	8	87
Arroyo dos Molinos 1811	7	64	—	71

Table 6.8 British casualties in campaigns and battles in the Peninsula, 1812–14

Battle or campaign	Killed	Wounded	Missing	Total
Siege of Cuidad Rodrigo 1812	98	720	5	823
Siege of Badajoz 1812	836	3,477	11	4324
Almaraz 1812	33	156	—	169
Castrejon and Castrillo 1812	24	450	52	526
Salamanca 1812	388	2,667	74	3,129

British Casualties in the Napoleonic Wars

Battle or campaign	Killed	Wounded	Missing	Total
Siege of Burgos 1812*	509	1,513	42	2,064
Retreat from Burgos 1812	?	?	2,479	2,479
Biar and Castalla 1813	70	297	42	409
Vitoria 1813	509	2,941	223	3,673
Maya 1813	144	994	350	1,488
Roncesvalles 1813	30	175	11	216
1st Sorauren 1813	197	1,139	22	1,358
2nd Sorauren 1813	67	490	20	577
Beunza 1813	26	95	35	156
Venta de Urroz 1813	41	239	35	315
Echalar 1813	32	319	7	358
Siege of San Sebastian 1813	1,228	2,210	60	3,498
Salain 1813	40	275	30	345
Vera 1813	19	54	2	75
Ordal 1813	75	109	333	517
Villafranca 1813	25	68	34	127
Passage of the Bidassoa 1813	82	486	5	573
Nivelle 1813	281	1,779	56	2,116
Nive 1813	279	2,184	210	2,673
Orthez 1814	211	1,373	61	1,645
Toulouse 1814	312	1,775	16	2,103
Bayonne 1814	150	455	233	838

* Includes both British and Portuguese casualties.

Between 1805 and 1815, the British Army also fought on every continent. Although the main focus was Portugal and Spain, there were numerous minor campaigns on every continent. These campaigns not only diverted troops from the Iberian Peninsula, they also caused numerous casualties.

Table 6.9 Casualties in campaigns and battles other than in the Peninsula, 1806–9

Battle or campaign	Killed	Wounded	Missing*	Other†	Total
Cape of Good Hope 1806	15	197	–	–	212
South America 1806–1807	449	761	1,935	–	3,145
Maida 1806	45	282	–	–	327
Egypt 1807	185	282	–	–	467
Copenhagen 1807	42	145	24	221‡	432

* Including prisoners
† Deaths caused by disease and accidents
‡ Drowned when transport sunk returning to England in November 1807.

Table 6.9 continued

Battle or campaign	Killed	Wounded	Missing*	Other†	Total
Martinique 1809	166	566	4	1,700	2,436
Naples 1809	6	17	110	-	133
Walcheren 1809	106	-	84	3,960	4,150

* Including prisoners
† Deaths caused by disease and accidents.

Table 6.10 Casualties in campaigns and battles other than in the Peninsula, 1810–15

Battle or campaign	Killed	Wounded	Missing*	Total
Guadeloupe 1810	52	250	-	302
Bourbon 1810	18	79	-	97
Mauritius 1810	28	94	45	167
Java 1811	75	566	-	641
Bergen-op-Zoom 1814†	387	533	2,263	3,183
Genoa 1814	37	174	-	211
Quatre Bras 1815	317	2,154	32	2,503
Waterloo 1815	1,783	5,944	819	8,546
Guadeloupe 1815	16	51	4	71

* Including prisoners.
† Bamford, 'The British Army in the Low Countries'.

The number of British casualties during the War of 1812 is open to debate. Donald Graves estimated that from the Canadian theatre of war alone there were about 2,700 dead from battle and disease. Bamford compiled the returns from the various regiments serving in North America – but not the West Indies – and determined that the War of 1812 cost the British army 5,048 dead and 3,026 deserters.[3] The following table shows only casualties caused in combat and not by disease or desertion while on garrison duty.

Table 6.11 British casualties during the War of 1812

Battle or campaign	Killed	Wounded	Missing	Total
Queenston 13 October 1812	14	77	28	119
Raisin River 22 January 1813	24	161	-	185
York 27 April 1813	67	82	17	166
Fort Meigs 5 May 1813	14	47	40	101
Fort George 27 May 1813	60	55	262	377

3 Personal communication from Andrew Bamford, 27 July 2009.

British Casualties in the Napoleonic Wars

Battle or campaign	Killed	Wounded	Missing	Total
Sacketts Harbour 29 May 1813	39	188	–	227
Stoney Creek 6 June 1813	32	137	57	226
Fort Stephenson 2 August 1813	26	41	29	96
Thames 5 October 1813	12	36	477	525
Chateauguay 26 October 1813	2	16	4	22
Crysler's Farm 11 November 1813	22	148	9	179
Fort Niagara 19 December 1813	5	3	—	8
Longwoods 4 March 1814	14	52	1	67
Oswego 6 May 1814	15	62	—	77
Chippawa 5 July 1814	148	321	46	515
Lundy's Lane 25 July 1814	84	559	235	878
Fort Erie Assault 15 August 1814	57	309	539*	905
Bladensburg 24 August 1814	64	185	—	249
Hampden Maine 3 September 1814	1	8	1	10
Plattsburgh 6-14 September 1814	37	150	55	242
North Point 12 September 1814	39	251	—	290
Fort Erie Sortie 17 September 1814	115	178	316	609
Cook's Mills 19 October 1814	1	35	—	36
New Orleans 8 January 1815	285	1,186	484	1,955
Fort Bowyer 8-12 February 1815	13	18	—	31
Total	1,190	4,305	2,600	8,095

* Most of these were supposedly killed in the explosion of the magazine.

As shown above, the number of casualties in each battle varied considerably. Most were less than 10 per cent of the troops, though some battles were noted for the extremely high casualties. The following table shows the ten battles that had highest percentage of casualties among British troops.

Table 6.12 Bloodiest battles of the British army – highest percentage of force lost

Battle	Strength*	Casualties	% of strength
Bergen-op-Zoom 9 March 1814	4,150	3,183	76%
Albuera 16 May 1811	10,449	4,159	40%
New Orleans 8 January 1815	7,000	1,955	28%
Buenos Aires 2 – 5 July 1807	8,384	2,325	28%
Talavera 27 – 28 July 1809	20,641	5,203	25%
Waterloo 18 June 1815	36,874	8,546	23%

Table 6.12 continued

Battle	Strength*	Casualties	% of strength
Barossa 5 March 1811	5,217	1,182	23%
Quatre Bras 16 June 1815	13,000	2,504	19%
St Pierre 13 December 1813	5,540	916	17%
Salamanca 22 July 1812	30,562	3,129	10%

* Does not include Spanish or Portuguese forces.

It should be noted that the majority of casualties at Bergen-op-Zoom and Buenos Aires were prisoners who were taken when the attacking force was surrounded and had to surrender.

Trivia: At the battle of Toulouse, the Highland Brigade (42nd, 79th, and 91st Foot) suffered 739 casualties, 16 per cent of all Allied soldiers at the battle, including Portuguese! Their casualties were a staggering 35 per cent of all British casualties in the battle.

Sieges could be particularly vicious, with total casualties disproportionate to the number of troops involved.

Table 6.13 Bloodiest sieges in the Peninsular War

Siege	Casualties
Siege of Badajoz April 1812	4,670
San Sebastian August – September 1813	2,376
Burgos September – October 1812	2,064
Ciudad Rodrigo January 1812	1,121
Siege of Badajoz May – June 1811	485

Trivia: Lieutenant Colonel Richard Fletcher commanding the Royal Engineers in the Peninsula was killed in action at the siege of San Sebastian 31 August 1813.

Casualties among individual regiments

Every battle was different and the casualties were not equally distributed among regiments. Some units appear to be always in the thick of the fight. In two battles the 42nd Highlanders had the highest percentage of casualties in the army. They lost 68 per cent of their effectives at Toulouse and 47 per cent at Quatre Bras. The 61st Foot lost 67 per cent of its men at Salamanca and 40 per cent at Toulouse. In 1813 and 1814 the 2nd Battalion 87th Foot was particularly hard hit. Its average losses in three battles (Vitoria, Nive and Orthez) were 35 per cent. After Orthez the regiment had less than 200 men.

The following tables show which regiments had the heaviest casualties in the major battles during the Napoleonic Wars.

Table 6.14 British units with the highest casualties at Maida, 4 July 1806

Unit	Strength	Casualties	% of strength
1st Battalion 81st Foot	603	84	14%
2nd Battalion 78th Foot	738	85	12%
Light Battalion	694	51	7%
1st Battalion 27th Foot	781	53	7%
Grenadier Battalion	485	31	6%

Source: Oman, *Studies in the Napoleonic Wars*, p. 70.

Table 6.15 British units with the highest casualties at Roliça, 17 August 1808

Unit	Strength	Casualties	% of strength
29th Foot	874	190	22%
2nd Battalion 95th Foot	400	42	11%
9th Foot	833	72	9%
5th Battalion 60th Foot	936	66	7%
5th Foot	990	46	5%

Source: Oman, *History of the Peninsular War*, vol. I, pp. 230, 240.

Table 6.16 British cavalry regiments with the highest casualties in Sir John Moore's army October 1808–January 1809

Unit	Strength	Casualties	% of strength
3rd KGL Light Dragoons	433	56	13%
18th Light Dragoons	624	77	12%
7th Light Dragoons	672	40	6%

Source: Oman, *History of the Peninsular War*, vol. I, pp. 646.

Table 6.17 British infantry regiments with the highest casualties in Sir John Moore's army October 1808–January 1809

Unit	Strength	Casualties	% of strength
6th Foot	882	391	44%
9th Foot	945	373	39%
2nd Battalion 43rd Foot	598	230	38%
81st Foot	719	241	34%

Table 6.17 continued

Unit	Strength	Casualties	% of strength
28th Foot	926	302	33%
2nd Foot	666	205	31%
50th Foot	863	264	31%
36th Foot	804	243	30%
1st Foot	723	216	30%
23rd Foot	590	172	29%

Source: Oman, *History of the Peninsular War*, vol. I, pp. 646, 647.

Trivia: Of the ten regiments with the heaviest casualties in Sir John Moore's army that went into Spain in 1808, four (6th, 9th, 23rd, & 43rd Foot) were part of Major General Beresford's brigade. Three of them (6th, 9th, & 43rd Foot) suffered the heaviest casualties of any unit in the army.

Table 6.18 British regiments with the highest casualties at Talavera, 27–28 July 1809

Unit	Strength*	Casualties	% of strength
2nd KGL Line Battalion	678	390	58%
2nd Battalion 83rd Foot	535	283	53%
1st KGL Line Battalion	604	300	50%
5th KGL Line Battalion	610	296	49%
7th KGL Line Battalion	557	256	46%
23rd Light Dragoons	459	207	45%
1st Battalion of Detachments	609	273	45%
2nd Battalion 24th Foot	787	352	45%
2nd Battalion 87th Foot	599	258	43%
1st Battalion 61st Foot	778	275	35%

* Strength figures are from 25 July 1809 Morning Report.
Source: Oman, *History of the Peninsular War*, vol. II, pp. 645–51.

Trivia: At the battle of Talavera in 1809, four of the five British infantry battalions with the highest percentage of casualties were from the King's German Legion. The 1st, 2nd, 5th, and 7th KGL Line Battalions average 50 per cent casualties!

Table 6.19 British regiments with the highest casualties at Busaco, 27 September 1810

Unit	Strength	Casualties	% of strength
1st Battalion 45th Foot	595	150	25%
1st Battalion 88th Foot	719	134	19%

British Casualties in the Napoleonic Wars

Unit	Strength	Casualties	% of strength
KGL Light Companies	96	15	16%
1st Battalion 79th Foot	923	56	6%
95th Foot	766	41	5%

Source: Oman, *History of the Peninsular War*, vol. III, pp. 544–51.

Table 6.20 British regiments with the highest casualties at Barossa, 5 March 1811

Unit	Strength	Casualties	% of strength
Browne's Flank Battalion*	536	236	44%
1st Battalion 1st Foot Guards	611	219	36%
1st Battalion 3rd Foot Guards	322	102	32%
2nd Battalion Coldstream Guards	211	54	27%
2nd Battalion 87th Foot	696	173	25%

* Flank companies from the 1st/9th Foot, 1st/28th Foot, and 2nd/82nd Foot.
Source: Oman, *History of the Peninsular War*, vol. IV, p. 612.

Table 6.21 British regiments with the highest casualties at Fuentes de Oñoro, 3–5 May 1810

Unit	Strength	Casualties	% of strength
1st Battalion 71st Foot	497	178	36%
1st Battalion 79th Foot	922	281	30%
85th Foot	387	95	25%
3rd Battalion 95th Foot	76	16	21%
5th Battalion 60th Foot	311	36	12%

Source: Oman, *History of the Peninsular War*, vol. IV, pp. 618–24.

Table 6.22 British regiments with the highest casualties at Albuera, 16 May 1810

Unit	Strength	Casualties	% of strength
1st Battalion 3rd Foot	755	643	85%
2nd Battalion 48th Foot	452	343	79%
1st Battalion 57th Foot	647	428	66%
29th Foot	507	336	66%
2nd Battalion 66th Foot	441	272	62%
2nd Battalion 7th Foot	568	349	61%
1st Battalion 48th Foot	497	280	56%
1st Battalion 7th Foot	714	357	50%
1st Battalion 23rd Foot	733	339	46%

Table 6.22 continued

Unit	Strength	Casualties	% of strength
2nd Battalion 31st Foot	418	155	37%
2nd Battalion 28th Foot	519	164	32%

Source: Oman, *History of the Peninsular War*, vol. IV, pp. 632.

Trivia: *At Albuera the 1st and 2nd Battalions 48th Foot lost 623 men out of 949 present for duty – an incredible 66 per cent casualties!*

Table 6.23   British regiments with the highest casualties at Salamanca, 22 July 1812

Unit	Strength*	Casualties	% of strength
1st Battalion 61st Foot	546	366	67%
1st Battalion 11th Foot	516	340	66%
2nd Battalion 53rd Foot	341	142	42%
1st Battalion 7th Foot	495	195	39%
2nd Foot	408	109	27%
1st Battalion 23rd Foot	446	106	24%
1st Battalion 36th Foot	429	99	23%
1st Battalion 40th Foot	582	132	23%
1st Battalion 32nd Foot	609	137	22%
1st Battalion 88th Foot	663	135	20%

* Strength figures are from 15 July 1812 Morning Report.
Source: Oman, *History of the Peninsular War*, vol. V, pp. 595–8.

Table 6.24   British regiments with the highest casualties at Vitoria, 21 June 1813

Unit	Strength*	Casualties	% of strength
2nd Battalion 87th Foot	501	244	49%
1st Battalion 71st Foot	873	316	36%
1st Battalion 5th Foot	510	163	32%
68th Foot	419	125	30%
1st Battalion 88th Foot	732	215	29%
1st Battalion 39th Foot	768	215	28%
2nd Battalion 47th Foot	406	112	28%
1st Battalion 28th Foot	818	199	24%
2nd Battalion 59th Foot	759	149	20%
1st Battalion 3rd Foot	587	111	19%

* Strength figures are from 29 April 1813 Morning Report.
Source: Oman, *History of the Peninsular War*, vol. VI, pp. 757–9; Fortescue, *A History of the British Army*, vol. IX, pp. 521–4.

Table 6.25 British regiments with the highest casualties at Nivelle, 10 November 1813

Unit	Strength	Casualties	% of strength
51st Foot	343	92	27%
1st Battalion 52nd Foot	928	240	26%
2nd Battalion 87th Foot	500	103	21%
94th Foot	428	75	18%
1st Battalion 5th Foot	744	130	17%

Source: Oman, *History of the Peninsular War*, vol. VI, pp. 637–44.

Table 6.26 British regiments with the highest casualties at St Pierre 13 December 1813

Unit	Strength	Casualties	% of strength
1st Battalion 92nd Foot	531	185	35%
1st Battalion 57th Foot	416	128	31%
1st Battalion 50th Foot	494	130	26%
1st Battalion 71st Foot	621	122	20%
1st Provisional Battalion	658	108	16%

Source: Oman, *History of the Peninsular War*, vol. VI, pp. 537–48.

Table 6.27 British regiments with the highest casualties at Orthez 27 February 1814

Unit	Strength*	Casualties	% of strength
1st Battalion 88th Foot	738	269	36%
2nd Battalion 87th Foot	305	109	36%
1st Battalion 45th Foot	496	132	27%
1st Battalion 20th Foot	395	123	31%
1st Battalion 6th Foot	709	145	20%

* Strength figures are from 16 January 1814 Morning Report.
Sources: Oman, *History of the Peninsular War*, vol. VII, pp. 537–48; Fortescue, *A History of the British Army*, vol. X, pp. 421–5.

Table 6.28 British regiments with the highest casualties at Toulouse 10 April 1814

Unit	Strength*	Casualties	% of strength
1st Battalion 42nd Foot	609	414	68%
1st Battalion 36th Foot	365	152	42%
1st Battalion 61st Foot	431	171	40%
1st Battalion 79th Foot	594	214	36%

Table 6.28 continued

Unit	Strength	Casualties	% of strength
1st Battalion 11th Foot	477	142	30%
1st Battalion 74th Foot	404	113	28%
1st Battalion 45th Foot	364	93	26%
1st Battalion 91st Foot	446	111	25%
3rd Battalion 27th Foot	558	106	19%
1st Battalion 40th Foot	463	86	19%

* Strength figures are from 16 January 1814 Morning Report, minus casualties at Orthez.

Sources: Oman, *History of the Peninsular War*, vol. VII, pp. 551–9; Fortescue, *A History of the British Army*, vol. X, pp. 421–5.

> **Trivia:** The 61st Foot had received new jackets a short time before the battle. Its large number of fallen on the battlefield was marked by their bright red jackets. Because of this, the regiment received the nickname of the 'Flowers of Toulouse'.

Table 6.29 British regiments with the highest casualties at Quatre Bras, 16 June 1815

Unit	Strength	Casualties	% of strength
1st Battalion 42nd Foot	617	288	47%
2nd Battalion 79th Foot	744	304	41%
1st Battalion 92nd Foot	708	286	40%
3rd Battalion 1st Foot	671	218	32%
1st Battalion 32nd Foot	699	196	28%
2nd Battalion 1st Foot Guards	1166	285	24%
3rd Battalion 1st Foot Guards	1122	262	23%
2nd Battalion 44th Foot	618	138	22%
2nd Battalion 69th Foot	696	155	22%
2nd Battalion 33rd Foot	682	106	16%

Sources: Dalton, *The Waterloo Roll Call*, pp. 233–47; Smith, *The Greenhill Napoleonic Data Book*, pp. 537–8.

Table 6.30 British cavalry regiments with the highest casualties at Waterloo, 18 June 1815

Unit	Strength	Casualties	% of strength
2nd Life Guards	235	155	66%
6th Dragoons	445	217	49%
1st Dragoon Guards	595	275	46%

Unit	Strength	Casualties	% of strength
1st Dragoons	428	196	46%
2nd Dragoons	442	199	45%
7th Light Dragoons	362	155	43%
Royal Horse Guards	251	98	39%
1st KGL Light Dragoons	534	154	29%
1st Life Guards	245	64	26%
12th Light Dragoons	427	111	26%

Sources: Dalton, *The Waterloo Roll Call*, pp. 233–47; Smith, *The Greenhill Napoleonic Data Book*, pp. 541–5; Fortescue, *A History of the British Army*, vol. X, pp. 431.

Table 6.31 British infantry regiments with the highest casualties at Waterloo, 18 June 1815

Unit	Strength	Casualties	% of strength
1st Battalion 27th Foot	750	478	64%
2nd Battalion 73rd Foot	498	280	56%
2nd KGL Light	437	202	46%
3rd Battalion 1st Foot Guards	847	342	40%
1st Battalion 79th Foot	440	175	40%
2nd Battalion 95th Foot	655	247	38%
1st Battalion 95th Foot	418	156	37%
2nd Battalion 30th Foot	635	230	36%
1st Battalion 32nd Foot	503	174	35%
5th KGL Line	503	162	32%
2nd Battalion 33rd Foot	576	185	32%

Sources: Dalton, *The Waterloo Roll Call*, pp. 233–47; Smith, *The Greenhill Napoleonic Data Book*, pp. 537–8; Fortescue, *A History of the British Army*, vol. X, pp. 431.

Table 6.32 The bloodiest regiments – highest percentage of casualties

Regiment	Battle	Strength	Casualties	% of strength
1st Battalion 3rd Foot	Albuera	755	643	85%
2nd Battalion 48th Foot	Albuera	452	343	79%
1st Battalion 42nd Foot	Toulouse	609	414	68%
1st Battalion 61st Foot	Salamanca	546	366	67%
1st Battalion 57th Foot	Albuera	647	428	66%
29th Foot	Albuera	507	336	66%
2nd Life Guards	Waterloo	235	155	66%
1st Battalion 11th Foot	Salamanca	516	340	66%
1st Battalion 27th Foot	Waterloo	750	478	64%
2nd Battalion 66th Foot	Albuera	441	272	62%

Prisoners of war

The number of British soldiers captured was probably fewer than any other army. Most British soldiers were captured during retreats. Several hundred wounded left in hospitals at Talavera in 1809 were also captured. A large number of British prisoners were taken at Buenos Aires in 1807 and Bergen-op-Zoom in 1814. Between 1805 and 1815, ten general officers were captured.

Table 6.33 British general officers captured during the Napoleonic Wars

Name	Rank	Date captured	Place captured
John Abercromby	LG	17 September 1810	At sea off Mauritius
Edward Paget	LG	17 November 1812	Retreat from Burgos
Thomas Hislop	LG	29 December 1812	At sea off Brazil
John Hope	LG	14 April 1814	Bayonne
William Beresford	MG	12 August 1806	Buenos Aires
Andrew Lord Blayney	MG	13 October 1810	Fuengirola
George Cooke	MG	8 March 1814	Bergen-op-Zoom
John B. Skerrett	MG	8 March 1814	Bergen-op-Zoom
Phineas Riall	MG	25 July 1814	Lundy's Lane
Robert Craufurd	BG	5 July 1807	Buenos Aires

In the Peninsula, far more French soldiers were captured by the British, than British soldiers were captured by the French. Wellington set up a mechanism for the exchange of prisoners and even had a formula for calculating the worth of a prisoner. The exchange was based on a one for one exchange between equivalent ranks or using Wellington's formula for the number of enlisted soldiers to make up the rank. For example a major could be exchanged for eight privates.

Table 6.34 Exchange rates for prisoners of war during the Peninsular War

Rank	No. of men to be exchanged for
Marshal	60
General commanding	60
General or general of division	40
Lieutenant general	30
General of brigade	30
Major general inferior to above	20
Brigadier-general	15
Colonel	15

Rank	No. of men to be exchanged for
Adjutant general	15
Lieutenant colonel	8
Major	8
Chief-of-battalion	8
Captain	6
Lieutenant	4
Ensign	3
Non-commissioned officer	2
Private	1

Source: *Supplementary Despatches*, vol. 6, p. 366.

The British Army in the Peninsula had several senior officers captured. Twice, the second-in-command of the army was captured; in 1812 during the retreat from Burgos and at the battle of Bayonne in 1814.

Table 6.35 Senior British officers captured in the Peninsula

Name	Rank	Date captured	Place captured
Edward Paget	LG	17 November 1812	Retreat from Burgos
John Hope	LG	14 April 1814	Battle of Bayonne
Andrew Lord Blayney	MG	13 October 1810	Fuengirola
Francis Larpent	JAG	30 August 1813	The Pyrenees
William Cox	Col	28 August 1810	Surrender of Almeida
John Waters	LCol	3 May 1811	Battle of Sabagul
Raymond Pelly	LCol	23 October 1812	Battle of Venta del Pozo
William Brooke	Maj	16 May 1811	Battle of Albuera
Colquhoun Grant	Maj	July 1812	Central Spain

Trivia: The Duke of Wellington was almost captured by a French patrol while he was on a reconnaissance two days before the battle of Talavera in 1809. Marshal Beresford, who was captured at Buenos Aires in 1806, had to engage in hand-to-hand combat to avoid being captured at the battle of Albuera in 1811.

Disease

Most British casualties were not caused by combat, but by disease. The Peninsular army averaged 21 per cent of its soldiers being too sick to fight at any given time. At the end of campaign this number could be as high as 25–30 per cent. One soldier in four was not fit to fight!

Table 6.36 Percentage of the Peninsular army reported sick, 1808–14

Date	Strength of the army	No. of sick	%
1 October 1808	33,129	3,470	10.5%
22 April 1809	21,597	2,038	9.4%
1 May 1809	24,227	2,357	9.0%
25 June 1809	26,995	3,246	12.0%
1 July 1809	35,410	4,827	13.6%
25 September 1809	35,018	8,827	25.3%
11 October 1809	33,000	7,800	23.6%
14 November 1809	30,000	9,000	30.0%
20 January 1811	39,454	6,715	17.0%
25 April 1811	37,813	9,298	24.6%
25 July 1811	56,933	12,277	21.6%
1 October 1811	57,781	19,088	33.0%
8 January 1812	50,994	12,255	24.0%
25 January 1812	58,664	13,405	22.9%
5 April 1812	46,751	12,016	25.7%
25 July 1812	62,087	17,033	27.4%
25 January 1813	65,644	17,513	26.7%
25 July 1813	63,868	12,698	19.9%
25 January 1814	67,121	14,144	21.1%
Average	44,600	9,300	20.9%

Source: Hodge, 'On the Mortality, p. 269.

According to Sir James McGrigor, the senior medical officer in Wellington's army, the number of soldiers hospitalised between January 1812 to April 1814 was 352,272. This was equivalent of every soldier being admitted to the hospital twice a year! Almost 17,000 soldiers who entered the hospital during those twenty-eight months died – 5 per cent of those sick.

Table 6.37 Causes of death in British hospitals in the Peninsula, 1812–14

Cause of death	Deaths	% of deaths	% per admittance
Diarrhoea and Dysentery	4,940	29%	1%
Fever	6,761	40%	2%
Catarrh, Pneumonia, Bronchitis	606	4%	0.1%
Wounds	3,411	20%	1%
Other Causes	785	5%	0.2%
Not Specified	467	3%	0.1%
Total	16,970		

Source: Hodge, 'On the Mortality, p. 250.

Trivia: The 1st Guards Brigade of the 1st Division had so many sick in early 1813 it was ordered to Oporto to speed its recovery. The brigade missed the Vitoria campaign due to the number of men in the hospital.

The Peninsula was not the only place where disease caused such a high percentage of casualties. In 1809 the British committed a larger force than they had in the Peninsula to the Walcheren expedition to capture Flushing and Antwerp. It was a distance of less than 200 miles from London. The expedition ended in disaster when almost 40 per cent of the army was struck down by fever – most likely malaria. Furthermore, the West Indies was a graveyard for many regiments because of yellow fever.

Table 6.38 Casualties caused by disease – Walcheren expedition, 1809

	Officers	Enlisted	Total	%
Total troops on expedition	1,738	37,481	39,219	
Died of disease on campaign	40	2,041	2,081	5%
Died after returning to Great Britain	20	1,859	1,879	5%
Troops still on sick list: 1 February 1810	217	11,296	11,513	29%
Casualties caused by Walcheren fever	277	15,196	15,473	39%

Source: Fortescue, *A History of the British Army*, vol. VII, p. 91.

Trivia: The British Walcheren expedition to the Netherlands in 1809 lost less than 1 per cent of its force (106 men) in combat, but 10 per cent of the army (3,960 men) died from Walcheren Fever. Another 29 per cent of the force (11,513 men) were too sick to fight months after the force returned to England.

General officers' deaths 1805–15

During the Napoleonic Wars, it was natural that general officers would lead from the front. This placed them in jeopardy and a number of British general officers were killed in action or died of their wounds. Additionally, despite having better living conditions then the men, these generals also died from illness or from the effects of campaigning. The Peninsular War was particularly deadly. Of 135 general officers who served there, 21 (15 per cent) were either killed, died of wounds, sickness or accident. A general officer had a 60 per cent greater chance of dying in the Peninsula than a junior officer. In the following tables only those generals serving on active service or returning from active service are given.

Table 6.39 General officers killed in action or died from wounds, 1805–13

Name	Rank	Cause	Location	Date
Patrick Wauchope	MG	KIA	Egypt	31 March 1807
Ernest Baron Langwerth	BG	KIA	Talavera	28 July 1809
John Randoll Mackenzie	MG	KIA	Talavera	28 July 1809
John Moore	LG	DoW	Coruña	16 January 1809
Daniel Hoghton	MG	KIA	Albuera	16 May 1811
Barnard Bowes	MG	DoW	Salamanca Forts	23 June 1812
Isaac Brock	MG	KIA	Queenston Heights	13 October 1812
Robert Craufurd	MG	DoW	Ciudad Rodrigo	24 January 1812
John Le Marchant	MG	KIA	Salamanca	22 July 1812
Henry Mackinnon	MG	KIA	Ciudad Rodrigo	19 January 1812

Table 6.40 General officers killed in action or died from wounds, 1814–15

Name	Rank	Cause	Location	Date
Robert Rollo Gillespie	MG	KIA	Kalunga Fort, India	31 October 1814
Arthur Gore	BG	KIA	Bergen-op-Zoom	8/9 March 1814
Andrew Hay	MG	KIA	Bayonne	14 April 1814
Robert Ross	MG	KIA	North Point	12 September 1814
John Skerrett	MG	DoW	Bergen-op-Zoom	10 March 1814
Charles du Plat	Col*	DoW	Waterloo	21 June 1815
Samuel Gibbs	MG	KIA	New Orleans	8 January 1815
Christian, Baron Ompteda	Col*	KIA	Waterloo	18 June 1815
Edward Pakenham	MG	KIA	New Orleans	8 January 1815
Thomas Picton	LG	KIA	Waterloo	18 June 1815
William Ponsonby	MG	KIA	Waterloo	18 June 1815

* Appointed on staff as colonel on the staff commanding a brigade when killed.

British Casualties in the Napoleonic Wars

Six British generals, who were the senior officer present at a battle, became casualties.

Table 6.41 Leading from the front – casualties among commanding generals, 1805–15

Name	Rank	Cause	Location	Date
Patrick Wauchope	MG	KIA	Egypt	31 March 1807
John Moore	LG	DoW	Coruña	16 January 1809
Isaac Brock	MG	KIA	Queenston Heights	13 October 1812
John Hope	LG	Captured	Bayonne	14 April 1814
Robert Ross	MG	KIA	North Point	12 September 1814
Edward Pakenham	MG	KIA	New Orleans	8 January 1815

Note: In March 1801 Lieutenant General Ralph Abercromby, commander of the British forces in Egypt, was killed in action at the battle of Alexandria, Egypt.

Generals were not immune to the hardship of campaigning or disease. They died in about the same portion as the soldiers did.

Table 6.42 Generals who died from illness, fatigue, accident or drowning, 1805–15

Name	Rank	Cause	Location	Date
John Henry Yorke	BG	Drowned	At sea off Brazil	1 November 1805
Robert Anstruther	BG	Pneumonia	Spain	14 January 1809
Alexander M. Fraser	LG	Illness	Britain*	13 September 1809
Coote Manningham	MG	Fatigue	Britain†	26 August 1809
James Catlin Craufurd	BG	Illness	Peninsula	25 September 1810
Richard Stewart	MG	Fall	Lisbon	October 1810
George Drummond	BG	Illness	Peninsula	8 September 1811
James Wynch	Col‡	Illness	Portugal	6 January 1811

* Although he died in Great Britain, Lieutenant General Fraser died of illness from the Walcheren campaign.
† Although Major General Manningham died in Great Britain, the cause of death was fatigue from serving in the Coruña campaign.
‡ Appointed on staff as colonel on the staff commanding a brigade when he died.

Table 6.42 continued

Name	Rank	Cause	Location	Date
Richard Hulse	MG	Fever	Peninsula	7 September 1812
Andrew Ross	MG	Illness	Spain	26 September 1812
William Wheatley	MG	Illness	Peninsula	1 September 1812
William Erskine	MG	Suicide	Lisbon	13 February 1813
George Wilson	Col*	Illness	Peninsula	5 January 1813
George, Baron Bock	MG	Drowned	At sea off France	21 January 1814

* Appointed on staff as colonel on the staff commanding a brigade when he died.

Table 6.43 British generals in Portuguese service who died on active service 1811–14

Name	Rank	Cause	Location	Date
William Campbell	BG	Illness	Trocifal, Portugal	2 January 1811
Francis Colman	BG	Fever	Portugal	12 December 1811
Charles Millar	BG	Illness	Portugal	February 1811
Richard Collins	BG	Illness	Portugal	17 February 1813
William Harvey	BG	Illness	At sea enroute to England	10 June 1813
William Spry	MG	Illness	Spain	16 January 1814

Source: McGuigan, personal research; Hall, *The Biographical Dictionary*, pp. 617–24, Challis, 'The Peninsular Roll Call'.

Trivia: The Deadliest Battles for Generals: *There were two battles where 75 per cent of the general officers became casualties. On 8 March 1814 during the assault on Bergen-op-Zoom three of the four generals present became casualties. Brigadier General Arthur Gore was killed, Major General John Skerrett was mortally wounded and captured, while Major General George Cooke was captured. Only Lieutenant General Thomas Graham, the overall commander of the force, who did not take part in the actual assault, was not a casualty. Exactly ten months later, on 8 January 1815 at the battle of New Orleans, three of the four British generals also became casualties. Major Generals Edward Pakenham and Samuel Gibbs were both killed, while Major General John Keane was seriously wounded in the groin.*

Loss of colours

One of the most disgraceful moments in the eyes of the officers and men of a regiment was the lost of their colours in combat. The stigma would take years to erase. Fourteen British colours were captured by the enemy between 1805 and 1815.

Table 6.44 British colours lost in combat

Battle	Date	Notes
2nd Battalion 71st Foot		
Buenos Aires	1806	Lost both colours
1st Battalion 3rd Foot		
Albuera	16 May 1811	Lost part of regimental colours*
2nd Battalion 48th Foot		
Albuera	16 May 1811	Lost both colours
2nd Battalion 66th Foot		
Albuera	16 May 1811	Lost king's colours
2nd Battalion 53rd Foot		
Salamanca	22 July 1812	Lost part of king's colours†
2nd Battalion 1st Foot Guards		
Bergen-op-Zoom	8 March 1814	Lost 'colours'
4th Battalion 1st Foot		
Bergen-op-Zoom	8 March 1814	Lost both colours
2nd Battalion 69th Foot		
Bergen-op-Zoom	8 March 1814	Lost regimental colours
2nd Battalion 69th Foot		
Quatre Bras	16 June 1815	Lost king's colours
5th KGL Line Battalion		
Waterloo	18 June 1815	Lost king's colours
8th KGL Line Battalion		
Waterloo	18 June 1815	Lost king's colours

* 'Lost the staff, cords, and part of the clothe.' Sorando, 'Trophies of Albuera'.
† 'Lost the staff and part of the clothe.' Muir, *Salamanca 1812*.

> 'I made a computation of all the men I lost in Spain – killed, prisoners, deserters, everything – it amounted to 36,000 in six years.'
>
> The Duke of Wellington, 10 October 1836[4]

The Duke of Wellington was slightly out on the number of casualties the Peninsular army sustained in six years. From December 1810 until May

---

4 Stanhope, *Notes of Conversations*, p. 86.

1814, a period of forty-one months, he lost 35,690 men – 100 short of his estimate. Although he was close, his estimate includes casualties from the early days of the war. The following table includes casualties for both the British and the Portuguese soldiers in his army – perhaps, therefore, he was referring only to British troops!

Table 6.45   Number of deaths in Wellington's army December 1810–May 1814

Cause of death	Officers	Enlisted	Total
Killed in action	399	6,335	6,734
Died of wounds	184	3,778	3,962
Died from disease	357	23,696	24,053
Estimate for death among missing	—	861	861
Total	940	34,690	35,690

Source: Hodge, 'On the Mortality, p. 237.

Chapter Seven

Sovereign's Honours Awarded for Merit

While it is true that the British did not, as a matter of course, award officers and men for meritorious service in the early days of the Revolutionary Wars, they did reward some officers, especially senior officers, at first during the Revolutionary Wars and Napoleonic Wars. Those who had distinguished themselves were given a variety of awards, including investiture as Knight Bachelors or into the Order of the Bath. This was later to include awards of a baronetcy or a peerage. Junior officers and enlisted soldiers, however, rarely received any form of recognition because the prevailing attitude at the time that doing their duty was a reward in itself. By 1815 it was recognised that officers did appreciate receiving some symbol of reward for their services and so the government did look at ways to do so. One such way was to expand the Order of the Bath to include greater numbers receiving recognition including down to the rank of field officer. The tables list those officers who were awarded a knighthood, a baronetcy or a peerage from 1805 to 1815.

Baronets 1805–15
During the course of the wars, the British rewarded a number of officers by making them baronets. Baronet was a hereditary title of honour, for commoners, ranking below a baron. It was not a title of nobility. The title ranked above all orders of knighthood except for the Most Noble Order of the Garter. Being made a baronet entitled the officer to be styled as 'Sir' and to have his rank included after his name. In the army lists a baronet would be shown as either Sir John Doyle, Bt or Sir John Doyle, Bart. While a number of officers were created baronets years after the end of the Napoleonic Wars, the table lists only those created during and immediately after the wars ended.

Table 7.1 Award of baronetcies, 1805–15

Recipient	Date	Reason
John Doyle	29 October 1805	For services
Charles Green	5 December 1805	For services and capture of Surinam
George Prevost	6 December 1805	Defence of Dominica
Charles Hastings	25 February 1806	
George Nugent	11 November 1806	For services
Harry Burrard	3 November 1807	For services Copenhagen
Thomas Blomefield	14 November 1807	For services Copenhagen and Royal Artillery
George Pigot	3 October 1808	
David Baird	13 April 1809	For services India, Egypt, Cape Colony, Peninsula
William Payne	8 December 1812	Commander, Cavalry Peninsula
Richard Fletcher	14 December 1812	Commander, Royal Engineers Peninsula
Roger Sheaffe	16 January 1813	Commander, Upper Canada
Hildebrand Oakes	2 November 1813	For services
Thomas Hislop	2 November 1813	For services
George Hewett	6 November 1813	For services and commander-in-chief India
John Hamilton*	21 December 1814	Division Commander, Peninsula
Howard Elphinstone	3 April 1815	Commander, Royal Engineers Peninsula
Hew Dalrymple	6 May 1815	For Services in Peninsula and Gibraltar
Alexander Campbell	6 May 1815	Division Commander, Peninsula

* In Portuguese service, also as Inspector General of Infantry.

Peerages awarded 1807–15

During the Napoleonic Wars the British government rewarded some officers for their miltary or political services with a peerage. Those already holding a title were elevated in the peerage. It also decided to reward some of the senior officers who had served in the Peninsular War with a peerage. They chose those officers who had commanded either independently or formations larger than a division. The table lists the general officers so rewarded with their title of nobility.

Table 7.2   Award of peerages, 1807–15

Date and title
Gerard, 1st Baron Lake*
    31 October 1807, Viscount Lake of Delhi and Laswary and Aston Clinton in Buckinghamshire
William, 10th Baron Cathcart
    3 November 1807 , Viscount Cathcart of Cathcart in Renfrew
Arthur Wellesley
    4 September 1809 Viscount Wellington of Talavera and Wellington in Somerset
Arthur, Viscount Wellington
    28 February 1812 Earl of Wellington in Somerset
Arthur, Earl of Wellington
    18 August 1812 Marquess of Wellington in Somerset
Henry, 1st Baron Mulgrave
    7 September 1812, Earl of Mulgrave in York
Arthur, Marquess of Wellington
    3 May 1814 Duke of Wellington in Somerset
John Hope
    3 May 1814, Baron Niddry of Niddry in Linlithgow
Thomas Graham
    3 May 1814, Baron Lynedoch of Balgowan in Perth
Stapleton Cotton
    3 May 1814, Baron Combermere in Chester
Rowland Hill
    3 May 1814, Baron Hill of Almaraz and Hawkestone in Shropshire
William Beresford†
    3 May 1814, Baron Beresford of Albuera and Dungarvon in Waterford
Charles Stewart
    1 July 1814, Baron Stewart of Stewart Court and Ballilawn in Donegal
William, 1st Viscount Cathcart
    16 July 1814, Earl Cathcart of Cathcart in Renfrew
Henry 2nd Earl of Uxbridge
    23 June 1815, Marquess of Anglesey in Wales
George Harris
    11 August 1815, Baron Harris of Seringapatam and Mysore and Belmont in Kent

---
* Created Baron Lake 13 September 1804.
† Created Conde de Trancozo and Marquez de Campo Maior in the peerage of Portugal.

Rewards for the defence of Dominica 1805

In 1805, as part of the strategy to draw the Royal Navy away from the English Channel, the French sent a fleet to the West Indies. They were to strike at the islands held by the British. One such island was Dominica.

On 22 February a French fleet arrived off the island. It made a landing under British fire and advanced against the town of Roseau. The British conducted a fighting withdrawal to Fort Prince Rupert. The town of Roseau then capitulated. The French summoned the British to surrender, but this was declined. From 25 February until 1 March the British defended the fort. On the morning of 1 March, the French embarked for Guadeloupe without taking the fort or the garrison.

For some reason, the defence caught the attention of the British government and people. Perhaps it was the small number of men (335 regular infantry and artillery, 340 militia and 30 merchant seamen manning the guns) who defended against an estimated 4,000 enemy. The governor of the island, Brigadier General George Prevost, was awarded a baronetcy for his conduct in the defence. The 46th Foot and 1st West India Regiment were awarded the battle honour 'Dominica'.

The Patriotic Fund at Lloyd's made awards to wounded officers and men.

Table 7.3   Patriotic Fund awards for Dominica, 14 May 1805

Recipient	Rank	First Award	Second Award
George Prevost	BG	Sword worth £100	Plate worth £200
Abraham Nunn*	Maj	Sword worth £50	Plate worth £100
Maurice O'Connell†	Capt	Sword worth £50	Plate worth £100
Colin Campbell†	Capt	£100 for wound	
Soldiers disabled/loss of limb		£40	
Soldiers severally wounded		£20	
Soldiers slightly wounded		£10	

* Mortally wounded in the fighting.
† Slightly wounded.
Source: *United Service Journal*, pp. 281–2.

Trivia: The Patriotic Fund was created in July 1803 at Lloyd's of London as a private means to reward meritorious officers and men. Subscribers were anyone who wished to donate money to the fund. Along with providing rewards for merit such as at Dominica in 1805, the Patriotic Fund also provided £50 to an officer newly promoted from the ranks to help defray the cost of his outfitting himself.[1]

---

1   Glover, *Wellington's Army*, p. 39.

Knight Bachelor 1807–15

The rank of Knight Bachelor was the lowest rank of knighthood. It entitled an officer to be styled as 'Sir' and to have his rank included after his name. Knighthoods were not hereditary and were awarded to the individual only. In the army lists a knight would be shown as Sir Richard Fletcher, Kt. A number of the officers received Foreign Orders of Knighthood. These carried no equivalent British rank of knight unless the king or prince regent knighted the recipient as a British knight. If the officer was not knighted, he was not styled as 'Sir' nor shown as such in British army lists, etc., of the period. A number of the officers who were made British knights were so knighted as they had been awarded a knighthood of the Royal Portuguese Order of the Tower and Sword and had received His Majesty's permission to accept it. Another way to be knighted was to stand in, at the installation ceremony, as a proxy to an officer who had been awarded an Order of Knighthood (usually the Order of the Bath). The king would knight the proxy during the ceremony.

Table 7.4   Recipients of the Knight Bachelor 1807–15

Name	Rank	Date	Reason
George Smith	LCol	9 December 1807	ADC to the King
Charles Imhoff	LCol	1807	Unknown
Charles Shipley	BG	11 March 1808	Royal Engineers
Mark Gerard	Capt	30 August 1809	Royal Marines
William Wynn	Capt	2 May 1810	Governor of Sandown Fort
Richard Fletcher	LCol	18 April 1812	Royal Engineers
George A. Wood	LCol	22 May 1812	Proxy for John Sherbrooke
John Tylden	Maj	22 May 1812	Proxy for Samuel Auchmuty
Charles Gordon	Capt	29 May 1812	Proxy for John Hope
Thomas S. Beckwith	Col	29 May 1812	Proxy for George Beckwith
Robert C. Hill	LCol	29 May 1812	Proxy for Rowland Hill
Alexander Campbell	LG	29 May 1812	Proxy for Duke of Wellington
John Hamilton	LG	15 July 1813	Portuguese Tower and Sword
George Elder	Col	11 November 1813	Portuguese Tower and Sword
John Wilson	BG	16 April 1814	Portuguese Tower and Sword

The British Army Against Napoleon

Table 7.4 continued

Name	Rank	Date	Reason
John Browne	LCol	16 April 1814	Portuguese Tower and Sword
Hudson Lowe	Col	26 April 1814	Royal Corsican Rangers
Archibald Campbell	LCol	7 May 1814	Portuguese Tower and Sword
Albert Gledstanes	LG	May 1814	Unknown
Freeman Barton	Capt	25 June 1814	2nd Foot
Charles Sutton	Col	13 July 1814	Portuguese Service
Tomkyns Turner	LG	28 July 1814	Lieutenant Governor of Jersey
Gregory Way	LCol	28 July 1814	Portuguese Tower and Sword
Thomas Noel Hill	LCol	28 July 1814	Portuguese Tower and Sword
John Milley Doyle	LCol	28 July 1814	Portuguese Tower and Sword
Neil Campbell	Col	7 October 1814	54th Foot
Charles F. Smith	LCol	10 November 1814	Royal Spanish Order of Charles III
Edward Kerrison	Col	5 January 1815	7th Light Dragoons
Loftus Otway	MG	15 January 1815	Unknown
Henry Pynn	LCol	23 February 1815	Portuguese Tower and Sword
John Campbell	LCol	9 March 1815	Portuguese Tower and Sword
Charles Greville	Col	20 April 1815	38th Foot
Victor von Arentsschildt	LCol	20 April 1815	Portuguese Tower and Sword
Samuel F. Whittingham	Col	3 May 1815	ADC to the Prince Regent
Richard Williams	LCol	25 May 1815	Royal Marines
James Malcolm	LCol	25 May 1815	Royal Marines
James Hope	LCol	25 May 1815	Unknown
Hew Ross	LCol	25 May 1815	Royal Artillery
William O. Hamilton	LCol	25 May 1815	Meritorious Service on Heligoland
Matthew, 5th Lord Aylmer	MG	6 June 1815	Unknown
Charles Pratt	Col	29 June 1815	5th Foot

Name	Rank	Date	Reason
Warren Peacocke	MG	27 July 1815	Portuguese Tower and Sword
Thomas Reade	LCol	27 November 1815	DAG, St Helena
Hugh Gough	Col	4 December 1815	Meritorious Service
William Williams	LCol	4 December 1815	Unknown
Robert Arbuthnot	LCol	4 December 1815	Unknown
Benjamin Bloomfield	MG	11 December 1815	Chief Equerry to the Prince Regent
Charles William Doyle	Col	1815	Unknown
Robert Trench	Col	22 December 1815	74th Foot
Joseph Carncross	LCol	22 December 1815	Royal Artillery

Order of the Bath 1815

Most officers received the Most Honourable Order of the Bath. Originally of one class only 'Knight of the Bath' (KB), it was expanded into two divisions (Military and Civil) of three classes on 2 January 1815: 1st Class or Knight Grand Cross of the Bath (GCB), 2nd Class or Knight Commander of the Bath (KCB) and 3rd Class or Companion of the Bath (CB). Only the first two classes carried the title of Sir. Before 1815, it was reflected in the army lists as, for instance, Sir Robert Abercromby, KB and subsequently as Sir Robert Abercromby, GCB, Sir Gordon Drummond, KCB and Lord Frederick Bentinck, CB. The tables list the name of the recipient (in order of appointment), his rank and the date awarded or gazetted. German officers, with some exceptions, are listed either as Baron or with 'de' in lieu of 'von' in their name. Officers of foreign armies and those of the Honourable East India Company are not included. Those marked * were Knights of the Bath before 1815 and were made Knights of the 1st Class (i.e. GCB) upon the expansion of the Order. Those marked † are Honourary Knights. Source for the June dates of the award of the CB is *Monthly Army List* August 1850.

The decision as to who would receive the award of a CB for the Peninsula and other services was still being discussed, and therefore not announced in the London Gazette, when the battles of 16 and 18 June were fought. Then recommendations for the award of a CB for those dates were received and this resulted in some officers' names being duplicated on both lists of recommendations. When the names were announced in the Gazette they were published as initially recommended and so award dates of 4 June and 22 June were mixed in both lists depending upon which service was being recognised.

Table 7.5 Knight Grand Cross of the Bath

Recipient	Rank	Date	KB Date
Prince Frederick, Duke of York*	FM	2 January 1815	30 December 1767
Robert Abercromby*	Gen	2 January 1815	15 June 1792
Alured Clarke*	Gen	2 January 1815	14 January 1797
John, Lord Hutchinson*	Gen	2 January 1815	28 May 1801
Eyre Coote*	Gen	2 January 1815	19 May 1802
John Cradock*	Gen	2 January 1815	16 February 1803
David Dundas*	Gen	2 January 1815	28 April 1803
Arthur, 1st Duke of Wellington*	FM	2 January 1815	28 August 1804
George, 3rd Earl Ludlow*	Gen	2 January 1815	26 September 1804
John Stuart*	LG	2 January 1815	13 September 1806
David Baird*	Gen	2 January 1815	21 April 1809
George Beckwith*	Gen	2 January 1815	24 April 1809
John, Lord Niddry*	LG	2 January 1815	21 April 1809
Brent Spencer*	LG	2 January 1815	21 April 1809
John Sherbrooke*	LG	2 January 1815	16 September 1809
William, Lord Beresford*	LG	2 January 1815	16 October 1810
Thomas, Lord Lynedoch*	LG	2 January 1815	22 February 1812
Rowland, Lord Hill*	LG	2 January 1815	22 February 1812
Samuel Auchmuty*	LG	2 January 1815	22 February 1812
Edward Paget*	LG	2 January 1815	12 June 1812
Stapleton, Lord Combermere*	LG	2 January 1815	21 August 1812
George Nugent*	Gen	2 January 1815	1 February 1813
William Keppel*	Gen	2 January 1815	1 February 1813
John Doyle*	LG	2 January 1815	1 February 1813
Lord William Bentinck*	LG	2 January 1815	1 February 1813
James Leith*	LG	2 January 1815	1 February 1813
Thomas Picton*	LG	2 January 1815	1 February 1813
Galbraith Lowry Cole*	LG	2 January 1815	1 February 1813
Charles, Lord Stewart*	LG	2 January 1815	1 February 1813
Alexander Hope*	LG	2 January 1815	29 June 1813
Henry Clinton*	LG	2 January 1815	29 June 1813
George, 9th Earl of Dalhousie*	LG	2 January 1815	11 September 1813
William Stewart*	LG	2 January 1815	11 September 1813
George Murray*	MG	2 January 1815	11 September 1813
Edward Pakenham*	MG	2 January 1815	11 September 1813
William, Prince of Orange*	Gen	2 January 1815	14 August 1814
Prince Edward, Duke of Kent	FM	2 January 1815	

Recipient	Rank	Date
Prince Ernest, Duke of Cumberland	FM	2 January 1815
Prince Adolphus, Duke of Cambridge	FM	2 January 1815
Prince William, 2nd Duke of Gloucester	FM	2 January 1815
Henry, 2nd Earl of Uxbridge	LG	2 January 1815
Robert Brownrigg	Gen	2 January 1815
Harry Calvert	LG	2 January 1815
Thomas Maitland	LG	2 January 1815
William Clinton	LG	2 January 1815
John Abercromby	LG	7 April 1815
Charles Colville	MG	7 April 1815
James Kempt	MG	22 June 1815

Table 7.6 Knight Commander of the Bath

Recipient	Rank	Date
Gordon Drummond	LG	2 January 1815
John Abercromby	LG	2 January 1815
Ronald Ferguson	LG	2 January 1815
Henry Warde	LG	2 January 1815
William Houston	LG	2 January 1815
William Lumley	LG	2 January 1815
Wroth Palmer Acland	LG	2 January 1815
Miles Nightingall	LG	2 January 1815
Henry Frederick Campbell	LG	2 January 1815
Alan Cameron	MG	2 January 1815
Charles Colville	MG	2 January 1815
Henry Fane	MG	2 January 1815
George Anson	MG	2 January 1815
Kenneth Howard	MG	2 January 1815
Henry Bell, Royal Marines	MG	2 January 1815
John Oswald	MG	2 January 1815
William Anson	MG	2 January 1815
Edward Howorth	MG	2 January 1815
Charles Wale	MG	2 January 1815
John Ormsby Vandeleur	MG	2 January 1815
Edward Stopford	MG	2 January 1815
George Walker	MG	2 January 1815
James Kempt	MG	2 January 1815

Table 7.6 continued

Recipient	Rank	Date
Robert Rollo Gillespie	MG	2 January 1815
William Henry Pringle	MG	2 January 1815
Frederick Robinson	MG	2 January 1815
Edward Barnes	MG	2 January 1815
William Ponsonby	MG	2 January 1815
John Byng	MG	2 January 1815
Thomas Brisbane	MG	2 January 1815
Denis Pack	MG	2 January 1815
Lord Edward Somerset	MG	2 January 1815
Thomas Bradford	MG	2 January 1815
John Lambert	MG	2 January 1815
James Gordon	MG	2 January 1815
Manley Power	MG	2 January 1815
Samuel Gibbs	MG	2 January 1815
Matthew, 5th Lord Aylmer	MG	2 January 1815
Colquhoun Grant	MG	2 January 1815
Thomas S. Beckwith	MG	2 January 1815
Robert O'Callaghan	MG	2 January 1815
John Keane	MG	2 January 1815
Colin Halkett	MG	2 January 1815
Henry Bunbury	MG	2 January 1815
Richard Hussey Vivian	MG	2 January 1815
Henry Torrens	MG	2 January 1815
John Elley	Col	2 January 1815
Charles Belson	Col	2 January 1815
William Howe De Lancey	Col	2 January 1815
Benjamin D'Urban	Col	2 January 1815
George Bingham	Col	2 January 1815
Charles Greville	Col	2 January 1815
Hoylet Framingham	Col	2 January 1815
Andrew Barnard	Col	2 January 1815
William Robe	Col	2 January 1815
Henry Ellis	Col	2 January 1815
John Cameron	Col	2 January 1815
Robert Trench	Col	2 January 1815
Charles Pratt	Col	2 January 1815
Edward Blakeney	Col	2 January 1815
John McLean	Col	2 January 1815
Richard Jackson	Col	2 January 1815
William Douglas	Col	2 January 1815

Sovereign's Honours Awarded for Merit

Recipient	Rank	Date
Colin Campbell	Col	2 January 1815
John Colborne	Col	2 January 1815
Archibald Campbell	Col	2 January 1815
Thomas Arbuthnot	Col	2 January 1815
Henry Bouverie	Col	2 January 1815
William Williams	LCol	2 January 1815
Henry Hollis Bradford	LCol	2 January 1815
Alexander Leith	LCol	2 January 1815
Robert Lawrence Dundas	LCol	2 January 1815
Robert Arbuthnot	LCol	2 January 1815
Charles Sutton	LCol	2 January 1815
James Dawes Douglas	LCol	2 January 1815
Henry Hardinge	LCol	2 January 1815
George Berkeley	LCol	2 January 1815
Jeremiah Dickson	LCol	2 January 1815
John Milley Doyle	LCol	2 January 1815
Thomas Noel Hill	LCol	2 January 1815
Robert Macara	LCol	2 January 1815
Alexander Gordon	LCol	2 January 1815
Henry Carr	LCol	2 January 1815
Charles Broke	LCol	2 January 1815
Lord Fitzroy Somerset	LCol	2 January 1815
James Wilson	LCol	2 January 1815
Alexander Dickson	LCol	2 January 1815
John May	LCol	2 January 1815
George Scovell	LCol	2 January 1815
William Gomm	LCol	2 January 1815
Ulysses Burgh	LCol	2 January 1815
Francis D'Oyley	LCol	2 January 1815
Richard Williams, Royal Marines	LCol	2 January 1815
James Malcolm, Royal Marines	LCol	2 January 1815
James Hope	LCol	2 January 1815
Augustus Frazer	LCol	2 January 1815
Hew Dalrymple Ross	LCol	2 January 1815
Edmund Kenyton Williams	LCol	2 January 1815
Maxwell Grant	LCol	2 January 1815
Frederick Stovin	LCol	2 January 1815
Joseph Carncross	LCol	2 January 1815
Robert Gardiner	LCol	2 January 1815
John Dyer	LCol	2 January 1815
Charles, Baron Linsingen†	LG	2 January 1815

Table 7.6 continued

Recipient	Rank	Date
Sigismund, Baron Low†	MG	2 January 1815
Charles, Baron Alten†	MG	2 January 1815
Henry de Hinüber†	MG	2 January 1815
William de Dornberg†	MG	2 January 1815
Frederick, de Arentsschildt†	Col	2 January 1815
Julius Hartmann†	Col	2 January 1815
Moore Disney	LG	7 April 1815
William Inglis	MG	7 April 1815
James Lyon	MG	7 April 1815
George Cooke	MG	20 June 1815
Peregrine Maitland	MG	22 June 1815
Frederick Adam	MG	22 June 1815

Trivia: Both LG John Moore and MG Isaac Brock had been made Knights of the Bath on 26 September 1804 and 12 October 1812, respectively. They died from wounds before the expansion of the Order or they would have been made GCBs on 2 January 1815.

Table 7.7 Companion of the Bath

Recipient	Rank	Date*
Lord Frederick Bentinck	Col	4 June 1815
Arthur Brooke	Col	4 June 1815
Henry S. Keating	Col	4 June 1815
John McNair	Col	4 June 1815
Alexander Wallace	Col	4 June 1815
Hastings Fraser	Col	4 June 1815
Robert, 11th Lord Blantyre	Col	4 June 1815
James Campbell	Col	4 June 1815
Charles Harcourt	Col	4 June 1815
William Prevost	Col	4 June 1815
John Meade	Col	4 June 1815
William Kelly	Col	4 June 1815
John McLeod	Col	4 June 1815
John Taylor	Col	4 June 1815
Robert D'Arcy	Col	4 June 1815
Thomas St George	Col	4 June 1815
John Murray	Col	4 June 1815
Loftus Otway	Col	4 June 1815

* Announced in *London Gazette* 16 September 1815.

Sovereign's Honours Awarded for Merit

Recipient	Rank	Date
Hamlet Wade	Col	4 June 1815
Edward Kerrison	Col	4 June 1815
George Madden	Col	4 June 1815
John Guise	Col	4 June 1815
James Bathurst	Col	11 June 1815
Paul Anderson	Col	4 June 1815
Hugh Mitchell	Col	4 June 1815
James Watson	Col	4 June 1815
John Lemoine	Col	4 June 1815
Christopher Myers	Col	22 June 1815
Richard Bourke	Col	4 June 1815
John Deane	Col	4 June 1815
Henry Brand	Col	4 June 1815
James Barns	Col	4 June 1815
George D. Robertson	Col	4 June 1815
John Nugent	Col	4 June 1815
Henry Dolphin	Col	4 June 1815
Charles Turner	Col	4 June 1815
Arthur Upton	Col	4 June 1815
Francis Hepburn	Col	4 June 1815
Henry Askew	Col	4 June 1815
William Stewart	Col	4 June 1815
William Stuart	Col	22 June 1815
Jaspar Nicolls	Col	4 June 1815
George Cuyler	Col	4 June 1815
John Ross	Col	4 June 1815
Henry King	Col	4 June 1815
Alexander Abercromby	Col	4 June 1815
William Thornton	Col	4 June 1815
William Wyatt	Col	4 June 1815
Henry Tolley	Col	4 June 1815
John Macdonald	Col	4 June 1815
Nathaniel Blackwell	Col	4 June 1815
David Stewart	Col	4 June 1815
William Johnstone	Col	4 June 1815
Patrick Doherty	Col	4 June 1815
Lewis Davies	Col	4 June 1815
Edward Copson	Col	4 June 1815
Alexander Bryce	Col	4 June 1815
John Pine Coffin	Col	4 June 1815
Neil Campbell	Col	4 June 1815

Table 7.7 continued

Recipient	Rank	Date
George Quentin	Col	4 June 1815
George Mackie	Col	4 June 1815
John Wilson	Col	4 June 1815
Robert Travers	Col	4 June 1815
Samuel Ford Whittingham	Col	4 June 1815
Alexander Woodford	Col	4 June 1815
Frederick Ponsonby	Col	4 June 1815
Felton Hervey	Col	4 June 1815
John, Lord Burghersh	Col	4 June 1815
William Fenwick	LCol	4 June 1815
Louis, Baron Bussche	LCol	4 June 1815
John Buchan	LCol	4 June 1815
John Bromhead	LCol	4 June 1815
Hugh Gough	LCol	4 June 1815
Lorenzo Moore	LCol	4 June 1815
Andrew Pilkington	LCol	4 June 1815
John Gardiner	LCol	4 June 1815
George Middlemore	LCol	4 June 1815
Joseph Morrison	LCol	4 June 1815
William Davy	LCol	4 June 1815
Charles Maxwell	LCol	4 June 1815
Charles Ashworth	LCol	4 June 1815
Archibald Campbell	LCol	4 June 1815
John F. Brown	LCol	4 June 1815
Charles Hill	LCol	4 June 1815
Amos Norcott	LCol	22 June 1815
Charles Bruce	LCol	4 June 1815
John Fitzgerald	LCol	4 June 1815
Alexander McLeod	LCol	4 June 1815
James Erskine	LCol	22 June 1815
John, Baron Bulow	LCol	4 June 1815
William Eustace	LCol	4 June 1815
Charles, Lord Greenock	LCol	4 June 1815
Rudolphus Bodecker	LCol	4 June 1815
Francis Brooke	LCol	4 June 1815
Edward Acheson	LCol	4 June 1815
John Ross	LCol	4 June 1815
Guy L'Estrange	LCol	4 June 1815
Thomas Pearson	LCol	4 June 1815
Robert Nixon	LCol	4 June 1815

Sovereign's Honours Awarded for Merit

Recipient	Rank	Date
Dugald Gilmour	LCol	4 June 1815
Gregory Way	LCol	4 June 1815
John Waters	LCol	4 June 1815
William MacBean	LCol	4 June 1815
George Elder	LCol	4 June 1815
Christopher Patrickson	LCol	4 June 1815
Henry Thornton	LCol	4 June 1815
John Hicks	LCol	22 June 1815
Patrick Lindesay	LCol	4 June 1815
Charles Napier	LCol	4 June 1815
Luke Alen	LCol	4 June 1815
Lord Charles Manners	LCol	4 June 1815
Octavius Carey	LCol	4 June 1815
Michael McCreagh	LCol	4 June 1815
Henry F. Cooke	LCol	4 June 1815
John Ward	LCol	4 June 1815
John Mansel	LCol	4 June 1815
Christopher Hamilton	LCol	4 June 1815
William Blake	LCol	4 June 1815
Edward Miles	LCol	4 June 1815
Hugh Halkett	LCol	4 June 1815
Adolphus, Baron Beck	LCol	4 June 1815
George Reeves	LCol	4 June 1815
Edward Gibbs	LCol	4 June 1815
Russell Manners	LCol	4 June 1815
George T. Napier	LCol	4 June 1815
John Piper	LCol	4 June 1815
Raymond Pelly	LCol	4 June 1815
Stephen Chapman	LCol	4 June 1815
John Hunt	LCol	4 June 1815
John Rudd	LCol	4 June 1815
Hercules Pakenham	LCol	4 June 1815
Charles Rowan	LCol	4 June 1815
Mathew Shawe	LCol	4 June 1815
Alexander Cameron	LCol	22 June 1815
Alexander Tulloh	LCol	4 June 1815
Harcourt Holcombe	LCol	4 June 1815
John Fox Burgoyne	LCol	4 June 1815
John T. Jones	LCol	4 June 1815
Thomas Burke	LCol	4 June 1815
John Harrison	LCol	4 June 1815

Table 7.7 continued

Recipient	Rank	Date
John Harvey	LCol	4 June 1815
Frederick Newman	LCol	4 June 1815
Thomas Dalmer	LCol	4 June 1815
Gustavus Browne	LCol	4 June 1815
Colin Campbell	LCol	22 June 1815
Leonard Greenwell	LCol	4 June 1815
Robert Dick	LCol	4 June 1815
Richard Church	LCol	4 June 1815
Neil Douglas	LCol	22 June 1815
Archibald Maclaine	LCol	4 June 1815
James Hay	LCol	4 June 1815
Robert Oswald	LCol	4 June 1815
George Robarts	LCol	4 June 1815
James Stewart	LCol	4 June 1815
Charles Plenderleath	LCol	4 June 1815
Edward O'Hara	LCol	4 June 1815
James Ogilvie	LCol	4 June 1815
Serjeantson Prescott	LCol	4 June 1815
Charles Vigoureaux	LCol	4 June 1815
Bryan O'Toole	LCol	4 June 1815
Frederick Hartwig	LCol	4 June 1815
Daniel Dodgin	LCol	4 June 1815
Alexis du Hautoy	LCol	4 June 1815
Henry Worsley	LCol	4 June 1815
Dudley St Leger Hill	LCol	4 June 1815
George, 8th Marquess of Tweeddale	LCol	4 June 1815
John P. Hawkins	LCol	4 June 1815
John Woodford	LCol	4 June 1815
Howard Elphinstone	LCol	4 June 1815
William White	LCol	4 June 1815
Richard Armstrong	LCol	4 June 1815
Richard G. Hare	LCol	4 June 1815
Charles F. Smith	LCol	4 June 1815
John H. E. Hill	LCol	4 June 1815
Charles Ellicombe	LCol	4 June 1815
Henry Goldfinch	LCol	4 June 1815
James Webber Smith	LCol	4 June 1815
William Mein	LCol	4 June 1815
William Cross	LCol	4 June 1815

Sovereign's Honours Awarded for Merit

Recipient	Rank	Date
Richard Buckner	LCol	22 June 1815
William F. Napier	LCol	4 June 1815
Martin Lindsay	LCol	4 June 1815
John Galiffe	LCol	4 June 1815
William Cowell	LCol	4 June 1815
Joseph Desbarres	LCol	4 June 1815
William Lewin Herford	LCol	4 June 1815
John Beatty	LCol	4 June 1815
John Bell	LCol	4 June 1815
Samuel B. Auchmuty	LCol	4 June 1815
Thomas Lightfoot	LCol	4 June 1815
Robert Macpherson	LCol	4 June 1815
Francis Eddins	LCol	4 June 1815
Henry Pynn	LCol	4 June 1815
Alured Dodsworth Faunce	LCol	4 June 1815
Miller Clifford	LCol	4 June 1815
Philip, Baron Gruben	LCol	22 June 1815
George Krauchenberg	LCol	4 June 1815
John Campbell	LCol	4 June 1815
Charles Aly	LCol	4 June 1815
Thomas Reade	Maj	4 June 1815
Thomas Evans	Maj	4 June 1815
George Macleod	Maj	4 June 1815
Robert Lawson	Maj	4 June 1815
James Hughes	Maj	4 June 1815
George Lewis, Royal Marines	Maj	4 June 1815
George Marlay	Maj	4 June 1815
Samuel Mitchell	Maj	4 June 1815
Samuel Hext	Maj	4 June 1815
Augustus Heise	Maj	4 June 1815
Alexander Anderson	Maj	4 June 1815
Henry Thomas	Maj	4 June 1815
Thomas Bell	Maj	4 June 1815
Kenneth Snodgrass	Maj	4 June 1815
Victor von Arentsschildt	Maj	4 June 1815
John Rolt	Maj	4 June 1815
John Gomersall	Maj	22 June 1815
William Rowan*	Maj	4 June 1815

* Incorrectly included in the *London Gazette* of 16 September 1815. Corrected in the *London Gazette* 23 September 1815. Rowan would have to wait until 19 July 1838 to receive his CB.

Table 7.7 continued

Recipient	Rank	Date
George Zulke	Maj	4 June 1815
Thomas Adair, Royal Marines	Maj	4 June 1815
Robert Douglas	Maj	4 June 1815
Stewart Maxwell	Maj	4 June 1815
William Robinson, Royal Marines	Maj	4 June 1815
Thomas Reynell	Col	4 June 1815
William Nicolay	Col	22 June 1815
William Harris	Col	22 June 1815
George A. Wood	Col	4 June 1815
Joseph Muter	Col	22 June 1815
James Macdonnell	LCol	22 June 1815
James Sleigh	LCol	22 June 1815
Charles de Jonquieres	LCol	22 June 1815
Arthur Clifton	LCol	22 June 1815
Lord Robert Manners	LCol	22 June 1815
Alexander Hamilton	LCol	22 June 1815
John Hammerton	LCol	22 June 1815
Richard Cooke	LCol	22 June 1815
Robert C. Hill	LCol	22 June 1815
Henry Murray	LCol	22 June 1815
de Lancey Barclay	LCol	22 June 1815
Henry Rooke	LCol	22 June 1815
Frederick de Wissell	LCol	22 June 1815
William, Baron Linsingen	LCol	22 June 1815
George O'Malley	LCol	22 June 1815
Francis Tidy	LCol	22 June 1815
Isaac Clarke	LCol	22 June 1815
Andrew Brown	LCol	22 June 1815
Guy Campbell	LCol	22 June 1815
William Elphinstone	LCol	22 June 1815
Samuel Rice	LCol	22 June 1815
George Fead	LCol	22 June 1815
Leighton Dalrymple	LCol	22 June 1815
Charles Gold	LCol	22 June 1815
Douglas Mercer	LCol	22 June 1815
Alexander, 16th Lord Saltoun	LCol	22 June 1815
Alexander Macdonald	LCol	22 June 1815
Augustus de Wissell	LCol	22 June 1815
James Mitchell	LCol	22 June 1815
George Muttlebury	LCol	22 June 1815

Sovereign's Honours Awarded for Merit

Recipient	Rank	Date
John Fremantle	LCol	22 June 1815
Duncan Cameron	LCol	22 June 1815
Shapland Boyse	LCol	22 June 1815
Morris W. Bailey	LCol	22 June 1815
Fiennes S. Miller	LCol	22 June 1815
Philip Dorville	LCol	22 June 1815
Archibald Money	LCol	22 June 1815
Robert Torrens	LCol	22 June 1815
Goodwin Colquitt	LCol	4 June 1815
John Williamson	LCol	22 June 1815
Stephen Adye	LCol	4 June 1815
Edward Lygon	LCol	22 June 1815
Henry Percy	LCol	22 June 1815
Frederick Reh	LCol	22 June 1815
Frederick de Lutterman	LCol	22 June 1815
Hans, Baron Bussche	LCol	22 June 1815
Frederick de Robertson	LCol	22 June 1815
Dawson Kelly	LCol	22 June 1815
Robert Bull	LCol	22 June 1815
Edward Cheney	LCol	22 June 1815
Richard Llewellyn	LCol	22 June 1815
Donald Macdonald	LCol	22 June 1815
James P. Bridger	LCol	22 June 1815
George H. Murray	LCol	22 June 1815
Augustus, Baron Reitzenstein	LCol	22 June 1815
John Hare	LCol	22 June 1815
George Baring	LCol	22 June 1815
John Leach	LCol	22 June 1815
John Cutliffe	LCol	22 June 1815
John Parker	LCol	22 June 1815
George D. Willson	LCol	22 June 1815
George Miller	LCol	22 June 1815
Charles Beckwith	LCol	22 June 1815
John Campbell	LCol	22 June 1815
William Campbell	LCol	22 June 1815
Charles de Petersdorff	LCol	22 June 1815
John Keyt	LCol	22 June 1815
Augustus Sympher	LCol	22 June 1815
Fielding Brown	LCol	22 June 1815
Lawrence Arguimbeau	LCol	22 June 1815
Henry G. Smith	LCol	22 June 1815

Table 7.7 continued

Recipient	Rank	Date
William Staveley	LCol	22 June 1815
Alexander Wylly	LCol	22 June 1815
George Muller	LCol	22 June 1815
Peter Latour	LCol	22 June 1815
Percy Drummond	Maj	22 June 1815
Leslie Walker	Maj	22 June 1815
Robert Macdonald	Maj	22 June 1815
George Hoste	Maj	22 June 1815
James Fullarton	Maj	22 June 1815
Thomas Rogers	Maj	22 June 1815
Frederick Breymann	Maj	22 June 1815
John Jessop	Maj	22 June 1815
Henry Kuhlmann	Maj	22 June 1815
William Percival	LCol	4 June 1815*
James P. Murray	LCol	8 December 1815†
Hugh Arbuthnot	LCol	8 December 1815
William Woodgate	LCol	8 December 1815
Charles Cother	LCol	8 December 1815
Thomas Downman	LCol	8 December 1815
George Wilkins	LCol	8 December 1815
Charles de Bosset	LCol	8 December 1815
Arthur Jones	LCol	8 December 1815

* Announced in the *London Gazette* 23 September 1815.
† All announced in the *London Gazette* 9 December 1815.

Trivia: *The Duke of Wellington had championed an increase in the status and pay of sergeants in the army. Although they were not recognised with sovereign's awards, on 25 June 1813, a new rank, colour sergeant, was instituted to reward deserving NCOs. A General Order dated 6 July and circulated by the War Office 27 July authorised every company, in every unit, to have one sergeant promoted for distinguished/meritorious service. These newly promoted colour sergeants would be paid 2s 4d per day, while those in the Foot Guards would receive 2s 6d per day.*

Chapter Eight

Campaign Medals for Meritorious or Honourable Service

During the Napoleonic Wars army officers who distinguished themselves were given a variety of awards, including gold medals for meritorious service in battle. Junior officers and enlisted soldiers rarely received any form of recognition because the prevailing attitude at the time was that doing their duty was a reward in itself. It was only in 1815, when the Waterloo Medal was authorised for all who participated in the campaign, that junior officers and enlisted soldiers receive recognition. For many years the thousands of soldiers who fought in the Peninsular War received nothing. This lack of recognition for their services caused many of the Peninsula Army veterans to be disgruntled. In 1847, the Military General Service Medal 1793–1814, was authorised for any soldier who could verify that he had served in one of twenty-nine official campaigns or battles. For many, it was too late. It should be noted that all medals were given for either meritorious service or as a campaign medal. Unlike modern times, no medals were given for valour.

Note that names of the battles are spelled as they appear on the medals and clasps. There is some variation from the modern spelling of the names. The names of the German recipients of the medals are spelled as they appeared in the *London Gazette*. In many cases, Baron was used in place of Von; for example, Charles, Baron Alten instead of Charles Von Alten.

Army Gold Medal and Gold Cross
The British government began issuing Gold Medals for deserving officers in early 1808, when a medal for Maida was awarded. In September 1810 medals were given to 107 senior officers, who had participated in one of the following battles: Roleia, Vimiera, Sahagun, Benevente, Corunna and Talavera. By 1815 a total of twenty-six different medals had been authorised, but less than 1500 of them were ever awarded. The medals came in two sizes. General officers received medals that were 2.1 inches

in diameter, while the medal for other officers was 1.3 inches in diameter. Both were hung from a red ribbon with a blue border. On the front or obverse of the medal was 'Britannia seated on a globe, holding in her right hand a laurel wreath, and in her left, which rests upon a Union shield resting against the globe, a palm leaf; at her feet to her right, a lion. Reverse: A wreath of laurel, encircling the name of the battle or operations for which the medal was granted.'[1]

Initially only commanding officers of battalions and above were eligible to receive the award. In October 1813, the regulations were changed to allow the AG, the QMG, and their deputies and assistants, who were field grade officers, to receive the medal. Not all eligible officers at a battle received the medal, however. Unlike the Waterloo and Army General Service Medals which were campaign medals, the Gold Medal was given for meritorious service. An officer had to be recommended by his commander. In 1813 Lieutenant Colonel William Bunbury was forced to resign in lieu of a court martial for alleged cowardice at the battle of Nive. He did not receive the Gold Medal for the battle.

It was not too long before officers became eligible for multiple medals. Instead of issuing medals for each action to them, they were authorised to wear a clasp with the name of the action above the medal. Once an officer had received a medal and three clasps, it would be replaced by a Gold Cross, in the shape of a Maltese cross. Engraved on the arms of the cross, were the names of the battles for which it was awarded. After receiving the Army Gold Cross, recipients of additional awards would receive a gold clasp to place on its ribbon. In all 469 Gold Medals and Crosses were awarded, and 103 three officers received at least one clasp to their Gold Cross. Two officers received seven clasps, while the Duke of Wellington received nine clasps!

Of the 847 Gold Medals and Gold Crosses awarded, only 143 (17 per cent) were given to captains. Of these 50 (35 per cent) were artillery officers. It was even rarer for a lieutenant to receive one. Only four lieutenants received a medal.

Battles, sieges and campaigns for which Army Gold Medals were awarded

Maida, Roleia & Vimiera, Sahagun & Benevente*, Corunna, Martinique, Guadaloupe, Talavera, Busaco, Barrosa, Fuentes d'Onor, Albuhera , Java, Ciudad Rodrigo, Badajoz, Salamanca, Fort Detroit, Vittoria, Pyrenees, St Sebastian, Chateauguay, Nivelle, Chrystler's Farm, Nive, Orthes, Toulouse.

---

1   Swinburn, 'Medals,' p. 8.

Campaign Medals for Meritorious or Honourable Service

Note that for Roleia and Vimiera only one Gold Medal was issued. If an officer was awarded the Army Gold Cross, he would have the name of the specific battle or campaign he fought in on the cross. If he fought in both of the battles or campaigns, he would have both on the same arm of the cross. For example, if an officer fought at both Roleia and Vimiera, he would not have two arms on the Army Gold Cross. He would have 'Roleia & Vimiera' on one arm. If the officer only fought at Vimiera, he would have 'Vimiera' on the arm of the Army Gold Cross.

Table 8.1 Gold Medals and number of recipients

Gold Medal	No. of recipients
Maida	17
Roleia & Vimiera	31
Roleia	3
Vimiera	14
Sahagun & Benevente	4
Sahagun	1
Benevente	3
Corunna	58
Martinique	34
Guadaloupe	29
Talavera	81
Busaco (also spelled Buzaco)	58
Barrosa	24
Fuentes d'Onor	59
Albuhera	59
Java	33
Ciudad Rodrigo	37
Badajoz	85
Salamanca	167
Fort Detroit	11
Vittoria	200
Pyrenees	108
St Sebastian	61
Chateauguay	2
Nivelle	125
Chrystler's Farm	7
Nive	139
Orthes	138
Toulouse	114

Trivia: *An officer, who received a Gold Medal for a battle was not entitled to receive a clasp to the Military General Service Medal for the same action. It was rare for a senior general officer to receive the Military General Service Medal, since most would qualify for the Gold Medal if they were at the battle. Lieutenant General William Beresford, however, received the Army Gold Cross with seven clasps and the Military General Service Medal with two clasps – Egypt and Ciudad Rodrigo.*

Table 8.2 Number of recipients of a Gold Medal or a Gold Cross

Medal or Army Gold Cross	No. of recipients
Gold Medal	469
Gold Medal with one clasp	143
Gold Medal with two clasps	72
Army Gold Cross	61
Army Gold Cross with one clasp	46
Army Gold Cross with two clasps	18
Army Gold Cross with three clasps	17
Army Gold Cross with four clasps	8
Army Gold Cross with five clasps	7
Army Gold Cross with six clasps	3
Army Gold Cross with seven clasps	2
Army Gold Cross with nine clasps	1

Source: Swinburn, 'Medals', p. 9.

Wellington's Army Gold Cross
The Duke of Wellington's Army Gold Cross consisted of the following:
On the limbs of the medal were:
   Roleia & Vimiera, Talavera, Busaco, Fuentes d'Onor.
On the ribbon were nine clasps:
   Ciudad Rodrigo, Badajoz, Salamanca, Vittoria, Pyrenees, Nivelle, Nive, Orthes, Toulouse[2]

Table 8.3 Officers who had six or more clasps on their Army Gold Cross

Officer	Clasps	Battles and sieges
William Beresford	7	Corunna, Busaco, Albuhera, Badajoz, Salamanca, Vittoria, Pyrenees, Nivelle, Nive, Orthes, and Toulouse

---

2 Swinburn, 'Medals,' p. 9.

Campaign Medals for Meritorious or Honourable Service

Officer	Clasps	Battles and sieges
Denis Pack	7	Roleia & Vimiera, Corunna, Busaco, Cuidad Rodrigo, Salamanca, Vittoria, Pyrenees, Nivelle, Nive, Orthes, Toulouse
Colin Campbell	6	Talavera, Busaco, Fuentes de Onor, Badajoz, Salamanca, Vittoria, Pyrenees, Nivelle, Nive, and Toulouse
Alexander Dickson	6	Busaco, Albuhera, Ciudad Rodrigo, Badajoz, Salamanca, Vittoria, St Sebastian, Nivelle, Nive, Toulouse
George Murray	6	Corunna, Talavera, Busaco, Fuentes de Onor, Vittoria, Pyrenees, Nivelle, Nive, Orthes, Toulouse

Source: Swinburn, 'Medals,' p. 9; Challis, 'The Peninsula Roll Call'.

Note

In most cases in the tables below the individual's rank and position or regiment are those he held at the time of the battle, not those he held when the medal or cross was awarded.

Trivia: On 5 November 2003 General Denis Pack's Army Gold Cross with seven clasps, his Peninsula Gold Medal (which was replaced by the Army Gold Cross), his Waterloo Medal, and his Badge and Star of the Order of the Bath were sold at auction for £115,000!

Table 8.4   Gold Medal recipients for Maida

Name	Rank	Unit or position
John Stuart	MG	Commander of the Forces
Wroth Palmer Acland	BG	Brigade Commander
Galbraith Lowry Cole	BG	Brigade Commander
John Oswald	Col	Brigade Commander
Henry Bunbury	LCol	DQMG
Louis de Watteville	LCol	de Watteville's Regiment
George Johnson	LCol	58th Foot
James Kempt	LCol	Commander of the Light Infantry
John Lemoine	LCol	RA
Patrick Macleod	LCol	78th Foot
Robert O'Callaghan	LCol	Commander of the Grenadiers
Robert Ross	LCol	20th Foot
Haviland Smith	LCol	27th Foot
James MacDonell	Maj	78th Foot

Table 8.4 continued

Name	Rank	Unit or position
John McCombe	Maj	Royal Corsican Rangers
George D. Robertson	Maj	35th Foot
David Stewart	Maj	Left Battalion 78th Foot

Source: Tancred, *Historical Record of Medals*, p. 71.

Table 8.5 Gold Medal recipients for Roleia and Vimiera

Name	Rank	Unit or position	Medal or clasp
Duke of Wellington	LG	Commander of the Forces	Roleia & Vimiera
Ronald Craufurd Ferguson	MG	2nd Brigade	Roleia & Vimiera
Rowland Hill	MG	1st Brigade	Roleia & Vimiera
Brent Spencer	MG	2nd in command	Roleia & Vimiera
Wroth Palmer Acland	BG	8th Brigade	Vimiera
Robert Anstruther	BG	7th Brigade	Vimiera
Barnard Foord Bowes	BG	4th Brigade	Roleia & Vimiera
James Catlin Craufurd	BG	5th Brigade	Roleia & Vimiera
Henry Fane	BG	6th Brigade	Roleia & Vimiera
Miles Nightingall	BG	3rd Brigade	Roleia & Vimiera
Robert Burne	Col	36th Foot	Roleia & Vimiera
James Kemmis	Col	40th Foot	Roleia & Vimiera
George Townsend Walker	Col	50th Foot	Vimiera
James Bathurst	LCol	DQMG	Roleia & Vimiera
Thomas S. Beckwith	LCol	95th Foot	Vimiera
John Cameron	LCol	9th Foot	Vimiera
Henry Craufurd	LCol	9th Foot	Roleia & Vimiera
John Thomas Deane	LCol	38th Foot	Roleia & Vimiera
Henry S. Eyre	LCol	82nd Foot	Roleia & Vimiera
Charles Greville	LCol	38th Foot	Roleia & Vimiera
William Guard	LCol	45th Foot	Roleia & Vimiera
Samuel Venables Hinde	LCol	32nd Foot	Roleia & Vimiera
William Iremonger	LCol	2nd Foot	Vimiera
George A. F. Lake	LCol	29th Foot	Roleia
James Lyon	LCol	97th Foot	Vimiera
John B. Mackenzie	LCol	5th Foot	Roleia & Vimiera
Denis Pack	LCol	71st Foot	Roleia & Vimiera
James Ramsay	LCol	2nd Foot	Vimiera
William Robe	LCol	RA	Vimiera
John Ross	LCol	52nd Foot	Vimiera
John Stewart	LCol	9th Foot	Roleia

Name	Rank	Unit or position	Medal or clasp
Charles D. Taylor	LCol	20th Light Dragoons	Roleia & Vimiera
Henry Torrens	LCol	Military Secretary	Roleia & Vimiera
George James Tucker	LCol	DAG	Roleia & Vimiera
Daniel White	LCol	29th Foot	Roleia & Vimiera
Thomas Arbuthnot	Maj	AAG	Roleia & Vimiera
William Williams Blake	Maj	20th Light Dragoons	Roleia & Vimiera
Thomas Carnie	Maj	6th Foot	Roleia & Vimiera
Andrew Creagh	Maj	95th Foot	Roleia & Vimiera
William Davy	Maj	60th Foot	Roleia & Vimiera
John Rainey	Maj	AQMG	Roleia & Vimiera
Robert Travers	Maj	95th Foot	Roleia & Vimiera
James Viney	Maj	RA	Roleia & Vimiera
William Granville Elliott	Capt	RA	Vimiera
Howard Elphinstone	Capt	RE	Roleia
George Landmann	Capt	RE	Vimiera
William Morrison	Capt	RA	Vimiera
Richard T. Raynsford	Capt	RA	Vimiera

Source: *London Gazette*, 8 September 1810, 13 September 1814; Challis, 'The Peninsula Roll Call'.

Table 8.6 Gold Medal recipients for Sahagun and Benevente

Name	Rank	Unit or position	Medal or clasp
Henry, Lord Paget	LG	Commander	Sahagun & Benevente
Charles Stewart	BG	Cavalry Brigade	Sahagun & Benevente
John Elley	LCol	AAG	Sahagun & Benevente
Colquhoun Grant	LCol	15th Light Dragoons	Sahagun
Oliver Thomas Jones	LCol	18th Light Dragoons	Benevente
George Leigh	LCol	10th Light Dragoons	Sahagun & Benevente
Richard Hussey Vivian	LCol	7th Light Dragoons	Benevente
Ernest von Burgwedel	Maj	3rd KGL Hussars	Benevente

Source: *London Gazette*, 8 September 1810, 5 October 1813; Challis, 'The Peninsula Roll Call'.

Table 8.7 Gold Medal recipients for Corunna

Name	Rank	Unit or position
John Moore	LG	Commander of the Forces
David Baird	LG	1st Division
John Hope	LG	2nd Division
Alexander Mackenzie Fraser	LG	3rd Division
Lord William Bentinck	MG	2nd Brigade 1st Division
William Carr Beresford	MG	1st Brigade 3rd Division
Rowland Hill	MG	1st Brigade 2nd Division
James Leith	MG	2nd Brigade 2nd Division
Coote Manningham	MG	3rd Brigade 1st Division
Edward Paget	MG	Reserve Division
Henry Warde	MG	Guards Brigade 1st Division
James Catlin Craufurd	BG	3rd Brigade 2nd Division
Moore Disney	BG	1st Brigade Reserve Division
Henry Fane	BG	2nd Brigade 3rd Division
John Slade	BG	Cavalry Brigade
William Anson	Col	1st Foot Guards
Robert Cheney	Col	1st Foot Guards
John Harding	Col	RA
Andrew Hay	Col	1st Foot
Paul Anderson	LCol	DAAG
Robert Barclay	LCol	52nd Foot
James Bathurst	LCol	AQMG
Thomas S. Beckwith	LCol	95th Foot
Charles P. Belson	LCol	28th Foot
Thomas Bradford	LCol	AAG
Robert Burne	LCol	36th Foot
John Cameron	LCol	9th Foot
Philips Cameron	LCol	79th Foot
Ralph Darling	LCol	51st Foot
William Howe De Lancey	LCol	AQMG
William Douglas	LCol	91st Foot
John Elley	LCol	AAG
Charles Fane	LCol	59th Foot
Charles Greville	LCol	38th Foot
Samuel Venables Hinde	LCol	32nd Foot
Edward Hull	LCol	43rd Foot
William Iremonger	LCol	2nd Foot
William Maxwell	LCol	26th Foot
George Murray	LCol	QMG
Alexander Napier	LCol	92nd Foot

Campaign Medals for Meritorious or Honourable Service

Name	Rank	Unit or position
Jasper Nicolls	LCol	14th Foot
Denis Pack	LCol	71st Foot
Robert Ross	LCol	2nd Brigade Reserve Division
James Stirling	LCol	42nd Foot
William Edgell Wyatt	LCol	23rd Foot
James Wynch	LCol	4th Foot
Thomas Arbuthnot	Maj	AAG
George Blaquiere	Maj	AQMG
John Colborne	Maj	Military Secretary
John Covell	Maj	76th Foot
Thomas Emes	Maj	5th Foot
George St Leger Gordon	Maj	6th Foot
Chichester Macdonnell	Maj	82nd Foot
Charles Napier	Maj	50th Foot
James Viney	Maj	RA
William Williams	Maj	81st Foot
Edward Wilmot	Capt	RA

Source: *London Gazette*, 8 September 1810, 13 September 1814; Challis, 'The Peninsula Roll Call'.

Trivia: *Although BG Henry Clinton was the adjutant general with the army, he did not receive a Gold Medal for Coruña. He was absent sick during the battle and so was not under fire in order to be recommended for it.*

Table 8.8   Gold Medal recipients for Martinique

Name	Rank	Unit or position
George Beckwith	LG	Commander of Forces
George Prevost	LG	1st Division
Frederick Maitland	MG	2nd Division
Charles Colville	BG	2nd Brigade
Albert Gledstanes	BG	QMG
Daniel Hoghton	BG	1st Brigade
Robert Nicholson	BG	Reserve Brigade
George Ramsay	BG	AG
Charles Shipley	BG	RE
Edward Stehelin	BG	RA
Edward Barnes	LCol	3rd Brigade
Nathaniel Blackwell	LCol	4th West India Regiment
Neil Campbell	LCol	DAG

263

The British Army Against Napoleon

Table 8.8   continued

Name	Rank	Unit or position
Henry Walton Ellis	LCol	23rd Foot
Samuel Fairtlough	LCol	63rd Foot
Gabriel Gordon	LCol	DQMG
John Keane	LCol	13th Foot
George Mackie	LCol	60th Foot
John McNair	LCol	5th Brigade
Edward Pakenham	LCol	7th Foot
John Prevost	LCol	8th West India Regiment
Phineas Riall	LCol	4th Brigade
Peter Thomas Roberton	LCol	8th Foot
Francis Streicher	LCol	York Light Infantry
Henry Tolley	LCol	1st West India Regiment
Luke Alen	Maj	3rd West India Regiment
Archibald Campbell	Maj	Light Battalion
Andrew Davidson	Maj	15th Foot
Patrick Henderson	Maj	Royal York Rangers
Bryce Maxwell	Maj	8th Foot
John M. Nooth	Maj	7th Foot
Richard Payne	Maj	46th Foot
Thomas Wright	Maj	90th Foot
George T. Napier	Capt	52nd Foot

Table 8.9   Gold Medal recipients for Guadaloupe

Name	Rank	Unit or position
George Beckwith	LG	Commander of Forces
Thomas Hislop	MG	1st Division
Thomas Barrow	BG	2nd Brigade
Albert Gledstanes	BG	QMG
George Harcourt	BG	2nd Division
Fitzroy Maclean	BG	3rd Brigade
George Ramsay	BG	AG
Charles Shipley	BG	RE
John Skinner	BG	4th Brigade
Charles Wale	BG	5th Brigade
John R. Burton	Col	RA
Edward Barnes	LCol	46th Foot
Nathaniel Blackwell	LCol	4th West India Regiment
Edward Blakeney	LCol	7th Foot
John Buchan	LCol	4th West India Regiment

Campaign Medals for Meritorious or Honourable Service

Name	Rank	Unit or position
Neil Campbell	LCol	DAG
Henry B. Dolphin	LCol	6th West India Regiment
Gabriel Gordon	LCol	DQMG
John Prevost	LCol	8th West India Regiment
Phineas Riall	LCol	1st Brigade
David Stewart	LCol	Royal West India Rangers
John Stewart	LCol	25th Foot
William Stewart	LCol	8th West India Regiment
Luke Alen	Maj	3rd West India Regiment
Francis Frye Brown	Maj	6th West India Regiment
Francis Eddins	Maj	4th West India Regiment
Patrick Henderson	Maj	Royal York Rangers
Mark Napier	Maj	90th Foot
Edward O'Hara	Maj	York Light Infantry

Source: *Army List*, October 1852.

Trivia: Although the crossing of the Douro River and the liberation of Oporto in May 1809 were considered worthy enough for a Battle Honour to be awarded to some of the units involved, they were not considered worthy enough for either an Army Gold Medal or a Clasp.

Table 8.10 Gold Medal recipients for Talavera

Name	Rank	Unit or position
Duke of Wellington	LG	Commander of the Forces
William Payne	LG	Commander of the Cavalry
John Sherbrooke	LG	1st Division
Christopher Tilson	MG	1st Brigade 2nd Division
Stapleton Cotton	MG	2nd Cavalry Brigade
Rowland Hill	MG	2nd Division
John Randoll McKenzie	MG	3rd Division
George Anson	BG	Cavalry Brigade
Alan Cameron	BG	2nd Brigade 1st Division
Alexander Campbell	BG	4th Division
Henry Frederick Campbell	BG	1st Brigade 1st Division
Henry Fane	BG	Cavalry Brigade
Edward Howorth	BG	RA
Ernst, Baron Langwerth	BG	3rd Brigade 1st Division
Sigismund, Baron Low	BG	4th Brigade 1st Division
Charles William Stewart	BG	AG
Richard Stewart	BG	2nd Brigade 2nd Division

Table 8.10 continued

Name	Rank	Unit or position
Rufane Shaw Donkin	Col	1st Brigade 3rd Division
Samuel Hawker	Col	14th Light Dragoons
James Kemmis	Col	2nd Brigade 4th Division
George Murray	Col	QMG
John Stratford Saunders	Col	61st Foot
Edward Stopford	Col	1st Brigade 1st Division
Matthew, 5th Lord Aylmer	LCol	AAG
James Bathurst	LCol	Military Secretary
George Ridout Bingham	LCol	53rd Foot
Johann Brauns	LCol	2nd KGL Line
William Henry Bunbury	LCol	1st Battalion of Detachments
Granby Thomas Calcraft	LCol	3rd Dragoon Guards
Philips Cameron	LCol	79th Foot
Colin Campbell	LCol	AAG
Edward Copson	LCol	2nd Battalion of Detachments
William Windham Dalling	LCol	3rd Foot Guards
Frederick de Arentsschildt	LCol	1st KGL Hussars
William Howe De Lancey	LCol	DQMG
Charles Donnellan	LCol	48th Foot
Archibald Drummond	LCol	3rd Foot
George Duncan Drummond	LCol	24th Foot
George Henry Duckworth	LCol	48th Foot
John Elley	LCol	AAG
Richard Fletcher	LCol	RE
Hoylet Framingham	LCol	RA
Joseph Fuller	LCol	Coldstream Guards
Alexander Gordon	LCol	83rd Foot
William Guard	LCol	45th Foot
Richard Hulse	LCol	Coldstream Guards
James Lyon	LCol	97th Foot
James Muter	LCol	3rd Foot
William Myers	LCol	1st Brigade 4th Division
William Robe	LCol	RA
Henry Seymour	LCol	23rd Light Dragoons
Lord Edward Somerset	LCol	4th Dragoons
Daniel White	LCol	29th Foot
James Wynch	LCol	4th Foot
Adolphus, Baron Beck	Maj	1st KGL Line
Rudolphus Bodecker	Maj	1st KGL Line
Thomas Chamberlain	Maj	24th Foot

Campaign Medals for Meritorious or Honourable Service

Name	Rank	Unit or position
James R. Coghlan	Maj	61st Foot
William G. Davy	Maj	60th Foot
Carl de Belleville	Maj	2nd KGL Line
Robert L. Dundas	Maj	Royal Staff Corps
Hugh Gough	Maj	87th Foot
William Gwyn	Maj	45th Foot
Julius Hartmann	Maj	King's German Artillery
Robert Lawson	Maj	RA
George Middlemore	Maj	48th Foot
Lincoln Stanhope	Maj	16th Light Dragoons
Henry Thornton	Maj	40th Foot
Richard Vandeleur	Maj	88th Foot
August Von Berger	Maj	7th KGL Line
Carl Von Thalmunn	Maj	7th KGL Line
John Williams Watson	Maj	31st Foot
Adolphus, Baron Wurmb	Maj	Light Battalion
Aretas W. Young	Maj	97th Foot
Alexander Andrews	Capt	60th Foot
Henry Baynes	Capt	RA
August Heise	Capt	2nd KGL Light
Richard Kelly	Capt	66th Foot
Georg Muller	Capt	2nd KGL Line
Charles Boyne Sillery	Capt	RA
Charles Von Rettberg	Capt	King's German Artillery

Source: *London Gazette*, 8 September 1810, 13 September 1814; *Army List*, October 1852.

Trivia: *The Hill brothers of Hawkstone, Shropshire (Rowland, Robert and Thomas Noel) received fourteen Army Gold Crosses, Medals and Clasps for the Peninsular War! General Rowland Hill earned an Army Gold Cross with four Clasps for Roleia and Vimiera, Corunna, Talavera, Vittoria, the Pyrenees, Nivelle, Nive, and Orthes. Colonel Thomas Noel Hill earned an Army Gold Cross with one clasp for Busaco, Cuidad Rodrigo, Salamanca, Vittoria, and San Sebastian. Lieutenant Colonel Robert Hill received the Army Gold Medal for Vittoria. Robert Hill also received the Military General Service Medal. Rowland, Thomas, and Robert were all awarded the Waterloo Medal along with younger brother Clement.*

Table 8.11   Gold Medal recipients for Busaco

Name	Rank	Unit or position
Duke of Wellington	LG	Commander of the Forces
William Carr Beresford	LG	Portuguese Troops
Brent Spencer	LG	1st Division
James Leith	MG	5th Division
Thomas Picton	MG	3rd Division
Charles William Stewart	MG	AG
Francis John Colman	BG	Portuguese Brigade
Robert Craufurd	BG	Light Division
Edward Howorth	BG	RA
Matthew, 5th Lord Aylmer	Col	AAG
Benjamin D'Urban	Col	QMG, Portuguese Troops
George Murray	Col	QMG
Henry MacKinnon	Col	1st Brigade 3rd Division
Denis Pack	Col	1st Portuguese Brigade
Robert Arbuthnot	LCol	Portuguese Staff
Robert Barclay	LCol	2nd Brigade Light Division
James S. Barns	LCol	1st Brigade 5th Division
James Bathurst	LCol	Military Secretary
Thomas S. Beckwith	LCol	1st Brigade Light Division
George Berkeley	LCol	AAG
John Cameron	LCol	9th Foot
Colin Campbell	LCol	AAG
Henry Crawford	LCol	45th Foot
Frederick de Arentsschildt	LCol	1st KGL Light Dragoons
William Howe De Lancey	LCol	DQMG
James Douglas	LCol	8th Portuguese Line
George Elder	LCol	3rd Caçadores
Richard Fletcher	LCol	RE
Hoylet Framingham	LCol	RA
Thomas Noel Hill	LCol	1st Portuguese Line
Henry King	LCol	5th Foot
William McBean	LCol	19th Portuguese Line
Charles McLeod	LCol	43rd Foot
John Meade	LCol	45th Foot
Robert Nixon	LCol	2nd Caçadores
John Nugent	LCol	38th Foot
William Robe	LCol	RA
Robert Le Poer Trench	LCol	74th Foot
Alexander Wallace	LCol	88th Foot

Campaign Medals for Meritorious or Honourable Service

Name	Rank	Unit or position
Hugh Arbuthnot	Maj	52nd Foot
Richard Armstrong	Maj	16th Portuguese Line
Robert Henry Dick	Maj	42nd Foot
Alexander Dickson	Maj	Portuguese Artillery
Dugald L. Gilmour	Maj	95th Foot
John Gordon	Maj	1st Foot
Henry Hardinge	Maj	DQMG, Portuguese Troops
Hercules Pakenham	Maj	AAG
William Smith	Maj	50th Foot
John Stewart	Maj	95th Foot
Charles Sutton	Maj	9th Portuguese Line
Victor Von Arentsschildt	Maj	Portuguese Artillery
Edmund Keynton Williams	Maj	4th Caçadores
Robert Bull	Capt	RA
Hans, Baron Busche	Capt	1st KGL Light
Stephen Chapman	Capt	RE
Robert Lawson	Capt	RA
Hew Ross	Capt	RA
Charles Von Rettberg	Capt	King's German Artillery

Trivia: The spelling of Busaco was not standardised on all medals and clasps. Gold medals, crosses, and claps were 'individually cast and produced very much to order the spelling depended upon whether the individual at the Mint decided Busaco should be spelt with an 's' or a 'z'.' Major General Denis Pack's Army Gold Cross had it spelled 'Buzaco', as was Colonel Henry Hardinge's clasp on the ribbon of his Army Gold Cross. Others had the spelling of 'Busaco'.[3]

Table 8.12   Gold Medal recipients for Barrosa

Name	Rank	Unit or position
Thomas Graham	LG	Commander of the Forces
William Thomas Dilkes	BG	Guards Brigade
Charles Philip Belson	Col	28th Foot
William Wheatley	Col	2nd Brigade
Sambrook Anson	LCol	1st Foot Guards
Andrew F. Barnard	LCol	95th Foot
John Frederick Brown	LCol	28th Foot
Richard Bushe	LCol	20th Portuguese Line

---

3 Personal communication, Oliver Pepys, Medals Department of Spink and Sons Ltd, 28 October 2009.

The British Army Against Napoleon

Table 8.12 continued

Name	Rank	Unit or position
Charles Murray Cathcart	LCol	AQMG
Richard Downes Jackson	LCol	Coldstream Guards
John MacDonald	LCol	DAG
Amos Godsill Norcott	LCol	95th Foot
Thomas Cranley Onslow	LCol	3rd Foot Guards
Frederick Cavendish Ponsonby	LCol	AAG
William Prevost	LCol	67th Foot
Edward Sebright	LCol	1st Foot Guards
Edward Acheson	Maj	67th Foot
Alexander Duncan	Maj	RA
Hugh Gough	Maj	87th Foot
John Ross	Maj	95th Foot
Augustus, Baron Bussche	Maj	2nd KGL Light Dragoons
Robert Gardiner	Capt	RA
Phillip James Hughes	Capt	RA
William Roberts	Capt	RA

Source: London Gazette, 5 October 1810.

Trivia: *In 1825, a monument was erected to Lieutenant General Thomas Picton in Caermarthen, Wales. Beneath the monument were place 'specimens of all the gold, silver, and copper British coins of the present reign'*[4] *and Lieutenant General Picton's Waterloo Medal.*

Table 8.13   Gold Medal recipients for Fuentes d'Onor

Name	Rank	Unit or position
Duke of Wellington	LG	Commander of the Forces
Brent Spencer	LG	1st Division
Stapleton Cotton	LG	Commander of the Cavalry
Charles Colville	MG	2nd Brigade 3rd Division
William Houston	MG	7th Division
Thomas Picton	MG	3rd Division
John Slade	MG	Cavalry Brigade
Charles William Stewart	MG	AG
George Murray	BG	QMG
Matthew, 5th Lord Aylmer	Col	AAG
Edward Howorth	Col	RA

---

4   *Annual Register*, 1825, p. 119.

Campaign Medals for Meritorious or Honourable Service

Name	Rank	Unit or position
Henry MacKinnon	Col	1st Brigade 3rd Division
Edward Michael Pakenham	Col	DAG
Clement Archer	LCol	16th Light Dragoons
George Berkeley	LCol	AAG
Robert, Lord Blantyre	LCol	42nd Foot
Henry Cadogan	LCol	71st Foot
Philips Cameron	LCol	79th Foot
Colin Campbell	LCol	AAG
James Campbell	LCol	94th Foot
Arthur Benjamin Clifton	LCol	1st Dragoons
Frederick de Arentsschildt	LCol	Cavalry Brigade
William Howe De Lancey	LCol	DQMG
John Milley Doyle	LCol	19th Portuguese Line
Mark Joseph Dufaure	LCol	Chasseurs Britanniques
George Elder	LCol	3rd Caçadores
John Elley	LCol	AAG
William Cornwallis Eustace	LCol	Chasseurs Britanniques
Hoylet Framingham	LCol	RA
John Wright Guise	LCol	3rd Foot Guards
Felton Bathurst Hervey	LCol	14th Light Dragoons
Richard Downes Jackson	LCol	AQMG
William Kelly	LCol	24th Foot
Robert Nixon	LCol	2nd Caçadores
William Offeney	LCol	7th KGL Line
Henry Pynn	LCol	18th Portuguese Line
Charles Sutton	LCol	9th Portuguese Line
Robert Le Poer Trench	LCol	74th Foot
John Alexander Wallace	LCol	88th Foot
William Williams	LCol	60th Foot
Carl August Aly	Maj	5th KGL Line
Robert Bull	Maj	RA
Henry William Carr	Maj	83rd Foot
Robert Henry Dick	Maj	42nd Foot
Dugald L. Gilmour	Maj	95th Foot
Leonard Greenwell	Maj	45th Foot
Dudley St Leger Hill	Maj	8th Caçadores
Russell Manners	Maj	74th Foot
Archibald McDonnell	Maj	92nd Foot
Aeneas McIntosh	Maj	79th Foot
Peter O'Hare	Maj	95th Foot
Carl Otto	Maj	1st KGL Hussars

Table 8.13 continued

Name	Rank	Unit or position
Hercules Robert Pakenham	Maj	AAG
Alexander Petrie	Maj	79th Foot
Charles Albert Vigoureux	Maj	38th Foot
Victor von Arentsschildt	Maj	Portuguese Artillery
William Woodgate	Maj	60th Foot
Robert Lawson	Capt	RA
Lord Fitzroy Somerset	Capt	Military secretary

Source: London Gazette, 5 October 1810, 15 September 1814.

Table 8.14 Gold Medal recipients for Albuhera

Name	Rank	Unit or position
William Carr Beresford	LG	Commander of the Forces
Charles, Baron Alten	MG	KGL Brigade
Galbraith Lowry Cole	MG	4th Division
John Hamilton	MG	Portuguese Division
Daniel Hoghton	MG	2nd Brigade 2nd Division
William Lumley	MG	Commander of the Cavalry
William Stewart	MG	2nd Division
Archibald Campbell	BG	2nd Brigade Portuguese Division
Benjamin D'Urban	BG	QMG, Portuguese Troops
William M. Harvey	BG	3rd Brigade 4th Division
William Carroll	Col	Regiment of Hibernia of the Spanish Army
Richard Collins	Col	2nd Portuguese Independent Brigade
George de Grey	Col	Heavy Cavalry Brigade, Cavalry Division
Colin Halkett	Col	1st Brigade 7th Division
William Inglis	Col	57th Foot
Thomas William Stubbs	Col	23rd Portuguese Line
Alexander Abercromby	LCol	3rd Brigade 2nd Division
Robert Arbuthnot	LCol	Military Secretary to General Beresford
Edward Blakeney	LCol	7th Foot
Allan William Campbell	LCol	4th Portuguese Line
John Colborne	LCol	1st Brigade 2nd Division
George Duckworth	LCol	48th Foot
Henry Walton Ellis	LCol	23rd Foot
William Fenwick	LCol	34th Foot

Name	Rank	Unit or position
Edward Hawkshaw	LCol	7th Caçadores
Ernst Ludwig Leonhart	LCol	1st KGL Light
Michael McCreagh	LCol	5th Caçadores
Donald McDonnell	LCol	11th Portuguese Line
William Myers	LCol	1st Brigade 4th Division
John Charles Rooke	LCol	AAG
William Stewart	LCol	3rd Foot
Charles Broke	Maj	AQMG
William Brooke	Maj	48th Foot
Alexander Dickson	Maj	Portuguese Artillery
Peter Fearon	Maj	7th Caçadores
George Leigh Goldie	Maj	66th Foot
Hugh Halkett	Maj	2nd KGL Light
Henry Hardinge	Maj	DQMG, Portuguese Troops
Julius Hartman	Maj	King's German Artillery
Burgh Leighton	Maj	4th Dragoons
Guy G. L'Estrange	Maj	31st Foot
Patrick Lindesay	Maj	39th Foot
John M. Nooth	Maj	7th Foot
Charles Paterson	Maj	28th Foot
Thomas Pearson	Maj	23rd Foot
William Collis Spring	Maj	57th Foot
Frederich Von Hartwig	Maj	1st KGL Light
Gregory H. B. Way	Maj	29th Foot
Conway Benning	Capt	66th Foot
William Braun	Capt	Portuguese Artillery
Gilbert Cimitiere	Capt	48th Foot
Andrew Cleeves	Capt	King's German Artillery
William Despard	Capt	7th Foot
Thomas Gell	Capt	29th Foot
James Hawker	Capt	RA
William Keith	Capt	23rd Foot
William Parry	Capt	48th Foot
James Wilson	Capt	48th Foot
William Mann	Lieut	57th Foot

Source: *London Gazette*, 5 October 1810, 15 September 1814; Dempsey, *Albuera 1811*, pp. 261–4.

Trivia: *Thomas Pearson received the Army Gold Medal for Albuhera with a clasp for Chrystler's Farm. This combination made them very rare among the medals earned during the wars. Pearson had been so* *badly wounded in the Peninsula that he was placed upon the staff in Canada as an Inspecting Field Officer of Militia in early 1812, not really expecting to see active service again!*

Table 8.15   Gold Medal recipients for the Java expedition

Officer	Rank	Unit or position
Samuel Auchmuty	LG	Commander of the Forces
Patrick Alexander Agnew	MG	AG, Madras Establishment
William Eden	MG	QMG
Frederick A. Wetherall	MG	Division Commander
George Wood	MG	Reserve Division, Bengal Establishment
Alexander Adams	Col	Brigade Commander
Samuel Gibbs	Col	Brigade Commander
Robert Rollo Gillespie	Col	Advanced Brigade
Nathaniel Burslem	LCol	DQMG
William Campbell	LCol	78th Foot
Alexander McLeod	LCol	59th Foot
William McLeod	LCol	69th Foot
Colin Mackenzie	LCol	Engineers, Madras Establishment
James Watson	LCol	14th Foot
Patrick Vans Agnew	Maj	DAG, Madras Establishment
Richard Butler	Maj	89th Foot
Alexander Caldwell	Maj	Bengal Artillery
Dennis Herbert Dalton	Maj	Bengal Light Infantry Volunteer Battalion
James Dewar	Maj	3rd Bengal Volunteer Battalion
James Fraser	Maj	78th Foot
Peter Grant	Maj	4th Bengal Volunteer Battalion
Martin Lindsay	Maj	78th Foot
George Miller	Maj	14th Foot
William Raban	Maj	6th Bengal Volunteer Battalion
Walter Syms	Maj	69th Foot
Robert Travers	Maj	22nd Light Dragoons
Udney Yule	Maj	Flank Battalion, Bengal Establishment
Richard Bunce	Capt	Royal Marines
David Forbes	Capt	78th Foot
George Herbert Gall	Capt	Governor General's Body Guard, Bengal Establishment
Hugh Griffiths	Capt	5th Bengal Volunteer Battalion

Name	Rank	Unit or position
John Noble	Capt	Madras Horse Artillery
George Sayer	Capt	Royal Navy

Source: *London Gazette*, 27 August 1814; Swinburn, 'Medals', p. 9.

Trivia: Only one Royal Navy officer received an Army Gold Medal. Captain George Sayer, captain of the *Leda*, received the Gold Medal for Java. He commanded a detachment of 500 sailors in the attack on Fort Cornelis.

Table 8.16 Gold Medal recipients for the siege of Ciudad Rodrigo

Name	Rank	Unit or position
Duke of Wellington	Gen	Commander of the Forces
Thomas Graham	LG	1st Division
Thomas Picton	LG	3rd Division
William Borthwick	MG	RA
Robert Craufurd	MG	Light Division
Henry MacKinnon	MG	1st Brigade 3rd Division
John Ormsby Vandeleur	MG	2nd Brigade Light Division
Denis Pack	BG	1st Portuguese Brigade
Andrew Francis Barnard	Col	1st Brigade Light Division
Neil Campbell	Col	16th Portuguese Line
John Milley Doyle	Col	19th Portuguese Line
William, Prince of Orange	Col	ADC to Commander of the Forces
Alexander Cameron	LCol	95th Foot
James Campbell	LCol	94th Foot
John Colborne	LCol	52nd Foot
John Henry Dunkin	LCol	77th Foot
George Elder	LCol	3rd Caçadores
Richard Fletcher	LCol	RE
Thomas Noel Hill	LCol	1st Portuguese Line
Charles McLeod	LCol	43rd Foot
Bryan O'Toole	LCol	2nd Caçadores
Hercules Robert Pakenham	LCol	AAG
Henry Ridge	LCol	5th Foot
William Williams	LCol	13th Foot
Henry William Carr	Maj	83rd Foot
Alexander J. Dickson	Maj	Portuguese Artillery
Edward Gibbs	Maj	52nd Foot
John Thomas Jones	Maj	RE
Russell Manners	Maj	74th Foot

Table 8.16 continued

Name	Rank	Unit or position
George Thomas Napier	Maj	52nd Foot
Peter O'Hare	Maj	95th Foot
Charles Rowan	Maj	AAG
Joseph Thompson	Maj	88th Foot
Charles Anderson	Capt	94th Foot
George Langlands	Capt	74th Foot
George Miles Milnes	Capt	45th Foot
William Percival	Capt	95th Foot

Source: *London Gazette*, 5 October 1810, 15 September 1814

Table 8.17 Gold Medal recipients for the siege of Badajoz, 1812

Name	Rank	Unit or position
Duke of Wellington	Gen	Commander of the Forces
James Leith	LG	5th Division
Thomas Picton	LG	3rd Division
Charles Stewart	LG	AG
Barnard Foord Bowes	MG	2nd Brigade 4th Division
Charles Colville	MG	4th Division
James Kempt	MG	1st Brigade 3rd Division
George T. Walker	MG	2nd Brigade 5th Division
Benjamin D'Urban	BG	QMG, Portuguese Troops
William M. Harvey	BG	Portuguese Brigade
Robert Arbuthnot	Col	Portuguese Staff
William Howe De Lancey	Col	DQMG
Hoylet Framingham	Col	RA
Charles Amedee Harcourt	Col	40th Foot
William, Prince of Orange	Col	ADC to Wellington
Andrew Francis Barnard	LCol	Light Division
George Henry Berkeley	LCol	AAG
Edward Blakeney	LCol	7th Foot
John Bromhead	LCol	77th Foot
Francis Brooke	LCol	4th Foot
Colin Campbell	LCol	AAG
James Campbell	LCol	2nd Brigade 3rd Division
George Carleton	LCol	44th Foot
William Howe De Lancey	LCol	DQMG
George Elder	LCol	3rd Caçadores
Henry Walton Ellis	LCol	23rd Foot
James Erskine	LCol	48th Foot

Campaign Medals for Meritorious or Honourable Service

Name	Rank	Unit or position
William Howe Erskine	LCol	27th Foot
John Forster Fitzgerald	LCol	60th Foot
Richard Fletcher	LCol	RE
Thomas Forbes	LCol	45th Foot
Edward Gibbs	LCol	52nd Foot
George Grey	LCol	30th Foot
Henry Hardinge	LCol	DQMG, Portuguese Troops
Russell Manners	LCol	74th Foot
Donald McDonnell	LCol	11th Portuguese Line
Charles McLeod	LCol	43rd Foot
John Nugent	LCol	38th Foot
William Robe	LCol	RA
Charles Sutton	LCol	9th Portuguese Line
Robert Le Poer Trench	LCol	74th Foot
John Richard Ward	LCol	27th Foot
John Waters	LCol	AAG
William Williams	LCol	60th Foot
John Henry Algeo	Maj	1st Caçadores
Alexander Anderson	Maj	11th Portuguese Line
John Fox Burgoyne	Maj	RE
Alexander Cameron	Maj	95th Foot
Henry William Carr	Maj	83rd Foot
Alexander Dickson	Maj	Portuguese Artillery
John Duffy	Maj	43rd Foot
John Gillies	Maj	40th Foot
William Gomm	Maj	AQMG
Leonard Greenwell	Maj	45th Foot
Dudley St Leger Hill	Maj	8th Caçadores
Harcourt Forde Holcombe	Maj	RA
John Philip Hunt	Maj	52nd Foot
John May	Maj	RA
James Miller	Maj	23rd Portuguese Line
Peter O'Hare	Maj	95th Foot
Hercules Robert Pakenham	Maj	AAG
Henry Ridge	Maj	5th Foot
Hew Dalrymple Ross	Maj	RA
Charles Rowan	Maj	95th Foot
William Cardon Seton	Maj	88th Foot
John Squire	Maj	RE
Lord Fitzroy Somerset	Maj	Military Secretary
Alexander Tulloh	Maj	Portuguese Artillery

Table 8.17 continued

Name	Rank	Unit or position
Joseph Wells	Maj	43rd Foot
James Wilson	Maj	48th Foot
Richard Bishop	Capt	5th Foot
James Bogle	Capt	94th Foot
Fielding Browne	Capt	40th Foot
James Fergusson	Capt	43rd Foot
Robert William Gardiner	Capt	RA
Samuel Hext	Capt	83rd Foot
John Thomas Jones	Capt	RE
George King	Capt	7th Foot
George Langlands	Capt	74th Foot
John Thomas Leahy	Capt	23rd Foot
John Haskings Mair	Capt	7th Foot
William Percival	Capt	95th Foot
James Singer	Capt	7th Foot
Charles von Rettberg	Capt	King's German Artillery
George D. Willson	Capt	4th Foot

Source: London Gazette, 5 October 1810, 15 September 1814.

Table 8.18 Gold Medal recipients for Salamanca

Name	Rank	Unit or position
Duke of Wellington	Gen	Commander of the Forces
William Carr Beresford	LG	Portuguese Troops
Galbraith Lowry Cole	LG	4th Division
Stapleton Cotton	LG	Commander of the Cavalry
James Leith	LG	5th Division
Charles, Baron Alten	MG	Light Division
Victor, Baron Alten	MG	Cavalry Brigade
George Anson	MG	Cavalry Brigade
William Anson	MG	1st Brigade 4th Division
George, Baron Bock	MG	2nd Brigade Cavalry Division
Henry Frederick Campbell	MG	1st Division
Henry Clinton	MG	6th Division
John H. C. de Bernewitz	MG	2nd Brigade 7th Division
John Hope	MG	7th Division
Richard Hulse	MG	1st Brigade 6th Division
John G. Le Marchant	MG	Cavalry Brigade
Sigismund, Baron Low	MG	3rd Brigade 1st Division
Edward M. Pakenham	MG	3rd Division

Name	Rank	Unit or position
William Henry Pringle	MG	2nd Brigade 5th Division
John Ormsby Vandeleur	MG	2nd Brigade Light Division
Willliam Wheatley	MG	2nd Brigade 1st Division
Thomas Bradford	BG	10th Portuguese Brigade
Richard Collins	BG	6th Portuguese Brigade
Benjamin D'Urban	BG	QMG, Portuguese Troops
Denis Pack	BG	1st Portuguese Brigade
Manley Power	BG	8th Portuguese Brigade
William Frederick Spry	BG	3rd Portuguese Brigade
Neil Campbell	Col	16th Portuguese Line
Henry John Cumming	Col	Cavalry Brigade
James Douglas	Col	8th Portuguese Line
John Elley	Col	AAG
Thomas William Fermor	Col	1st Brigade 1st Division
Colin Halkett	Col	1st Brigade 7th Division
Thomas Noel Hill	Col	1st Portuguese Line
Samuel Venables Hinde	Col	2nd Brigade 6th Division
Georg Heinrich Klingsöhr	Col	5th KGL Line
William McBean	Col	24th Portuguese Line
William Ponsonby	Col	5th Dragoon Guards
William, Prince of Orange	Col	ADC to the Duke of Wellington
Lord Edward Somerset	Col	4th Dragoons
James Stirling	Col	42nd Foot
Thomas William Stubbs	Col	23rd Portuguese Line
John Henry Algeo	LCol	1st Caçadores
Alexander Anderson	LCol	11th Portuguese Line
Frederick Barlow	LCol	Coldstream Guards
Andrew Francis Barnard	LCol	2nd Brigade Light Division
James Stevenson Barns	LCol	1st Foot
George Henry Berkeley	LCol	AAG
George Ridout Bingham	LCol	53rd Foot
Rudolph Bodecker	LCol	1st KGL Line
Henry Frederick Bouverie	LCol	AAG
Henry Hollis Bradford	LCol	AAG
Henry Otway Brand	LCol	Coldstream Guards
Gustavus Braun	LCol	9th Caçadores
Charles Broke	LCol	AQMG
Francis Brooke	LCol	4th Foot
Johann, Baron Bulow	LCol	1st KGL Dragoons
John Fox Burgoyne	LCol	RE
Alexander Cameron	LCol	95th Foot

Table 8.18 continued

Name	Rank	Unit or position
John Cameron	LCol	9th Foot
Colin Campbell	LCol	AAG
James Campbell	LCol	2nd Brigade 3rd Division
Henry William Carr	LCol	83rd Foot
Charles Murray Cathcart	LCol	AQMG
Arthur C. Crookshank	LCol	12th Portuguese Line
George Cuyler	LCol	11th Foot
Lewis Davies	LCol	36th Foot
Frederick de Arentsschildt	LCol	1st KGL Hussars
Frederick de Hertzberg	LCol	Brunswick Light Infantry
Carl Frederich de Jonquieres	LCol	2nd KGL Dragoons
William Howe De Lancey	LCol	DQMG
Alexander Dickson	LCol	Portuguese Artillery
Robert Lawrence Dundas	LCol	Royal Staff Corps
Henry Watson Ellis	LCol	2nd Brigade 4th Division
William Cornwallis Eustace	LCol	Chasseurs Britanniques
John Forster Fitzgerald	LCol	60th Foot
Hoylet Framingham	LCol	RA
Robert Fulton	LCol	79th Foot
John Gomersall	LCol	16th Portuguese Line
Alexander Gordon	LCol	ADC to the Duke of Wellington
Charles James Greville	LCol	1st Brigade 5th Division
John Wright Guise	LCol	3rd Foot Guards
Hugh Halkett	LCol	7th KGL Line
Alexander Hamilton	LCol	30th Foot
George Harding	LCol	44th Foot
Henry Hardinge	LCol	DQMG, Portuguese Troops
Felton Bathurst Hervey	LCol	14th Light Dragoons
John Philip Hunt	LCol	52nd Foot
Richard Downes Jackson	LCol	AQMG
William Johnston	LCol	68th Foot
William Kelly	LCol	24th Foot
Henry King	LCol	5th Foot
John Kingsbury	LCol	2nd Foot
Ernst Ludwig Leonhart	LCol	1st KGL Light
Guy G. L'Estrange	LCol	31st Foot
John MacLean	LCol	27th Foot
John May	LCol	AAG
John Mansel	LCol	53rd Foot
Michael McCreagh	LCol	5th Caçadores

Name	Rank	Unit or position
Edward Miles	LCol	38th Foot
Hugh Henry Mitchell	LCol	51st Foot
Frederick Newman	LCol	11th Foot
John Nugent	LCol	38th Foot
Bryan O'Toole	LCol	2nd Caçadores
Frederick Ponsonby	LCol	12th Light Dragoons
Henry Ridewood	LCol	45th Foot
William Robe	LCol	RA
Charles Rowan	LCol	52nd Foot
Lord Fitzroy Somerset	LCol	Military Secretary
Charles Sutton	LCol	9th Portuguese Line
Robert Le Poer Trench	LCol	74th Foot
John Alexander Wallace	LCol	1st Brigade 3rd Division
John Richard Ward	LCol	27th Foot
John Waters	LCol	AAG
Henry Watson	LCol	1st Portuguese Dragoons
Edmund Keynton Williams	LCol	4th Caçadores
William Williams	LCol	13th Foot
James Wilson	LCol	48th Foot
John Wood	LCol	32nd Foot
Alexander George Woodford	LCol	Coldstream Guards
Peter Adamson	Maj	4th Caçadores
Richard Archdall	Maj	40th Foot
John William Beatty	Maj	24th Portuguese Line
Thomas Bell	Maj	48th Foot
Robert Bull	Maj	RA
Colin Campbell	Maj	1st Foot
Joseph Hugh Carncross	Maj	RA
William Leigh Clowes	Maj	3rd Dragoons
Thomas Dalmer	Maj	23rd Foot
Robert Henry Dick	Maj	42nd Foot
Thomas Downman	Maj	RA
Francis D'Oyley	Maj	AAG
Thomas Evans	Maj	38th Foot
Alured Dodsworth Faunce	Maj	4th Foot
Robert William Gardiner	Maj	RA
William Maynard Gomm	Maj	AQMG
Henry C. E. Vernon Graham	Maj	2nd Foot
Philip, Baron Gruben	Maj	1st KGL Hussars
Julius Hartmann	Maj	King's German Artillery

Table 8.18 continued

Name	Rank	Unit or position
Dudley St Leger Hill	Maj	8th Caçadores
John Humphrey Hill	Maj	5th Caçadores
Thomas Lloyd	Maj	94th Foot
William Napier	Maj	43rd Foot
Frederick Newman	Maj	11th Foot
Francis Needham Offley	Maj	23rd Foot
John Piper	Maj	4th Foot
Hew Dalrymple Ross	Maj	RA
William Cardon Seton	Maj	88th Foot
James Stewart	Maj	AQMG
Frederick Stovin	Maj	ADC to General Picton
Frederick Sympher	Maj	King's German Artillery
George Wilkins	Maj	95th Foot
David Williamson	Maj	4th Foot
Adolph Wilhelm, Baron Wurmb	Maj	Light Battalion
Marcus Annesley	Capt	61st Foot
Richard Bishop	Capt	5th Foot
Edward de Daubraya	Capt	8th Caçadores
Heinrich La Roche de Starkenfels	Capt	1st KGL Line
Robert Douglas	Capt	RA
William Greene	Capt	RA
Robert Haddock	Capt	12th Caçadores
Joseph Hawtyn	Capt	23rd Foot
Robert Lawson	Capt	RA
Robert Macdonald	Capt	RA
George Home Murray	Capt	16th Light Dragoons
William Percival	Capt	95th Foot
Charles Western	Capt	8th Caçadores

Source: *London Gazette*, 5 October 1810, 15 September 1814

Table 8.19 Gold Medal recipients for Fort Detroit

Name	Rank	Unit or position
Isaac Brock	MG	Commander of the Forces
Matthew Elliot	LCol	Indian Department
John Macdonell	LCol	ADC to General Brock
Robert Nichol	LCol	QMG, Upper Canadian Militia
Thomas St George	LCol	Inspecting Field Officer of Militia

Campaign Medals for Meritorious or Honourable Service

Name	Rank	Unit or position
Peter Chambers	Maj	Brigade Commander
Adam Muir	Maj	41st Foot
Joseph Tallon	Maj	Brigade Commander
Matthew Charles Dixon	Capt	RE
John B. Glegg	Capt	ADC to General Brock
Felix Troughton	Lieut	RA

Source: Personal communication from Don Graves.

Trivia: Three gold medals were given for battles of the War of 1812. The first was for Fort Detroit. Although Colonel Henry Procter, 41st Foot, commanded the infantry under MG Brock, during the battle, he was not included in the list of medal recipients compiled by the Governor-General of Canada. This was most likely due to the fact that he was in disgrace for his conduct at the battle of the Thames when the list was compiled in early 1814. Colonel Procter would be tried by a court martial later in 1814 and be sentenced to a public reprimand and loss of rank and pay for six months. He died in 1822 and does not appear to have applied for the award of the medal.

Gold Medal recipients for Vittoria

Many officers were promoted to higher rank in the General Brevet of 4 June 1813, but notice only arrived after Vittoria. To avoid confusion, the ranks are those the officer held at the battle.

Table 8.20 Gold Medal recipients for Vittoria

Name	Rank	Unit or position
Duke of Wellington	Gen	Commander of the Forces
William Beresford	LG	Portuguese Troops
Galbraith Lowry Cole	LG	4th Division
Thomas Graham	LG	Corps Commander
Rowland Hill	LG	Corps Commander
Thomas Picton	LG	3rd Division
George, Earl of Dalhousie	LG	7th Division
William Stewart	LG	2nd Division
Charles, Baron Alten	MG	Light Division
Victor, Baron Alten	MG	Cavalry Brigade
George Anson	MG	Cavalry Brigade
William Anson	MG	1st Brigade 4th Division
George, Baron Bock	MG	2nd Brigade Cavalry Division
Charles Colville	MG	2nd Brigade 3rd Division

Table 8.20 continued

Name	Rank	Unit or position
Henry Fane	MG	Cavalry Brigade
Andrew Hay	MG	1st Brigade 5th Division
Kenneth Alexander Howard	MG	1st Division
James Kempt	MG	1st Brigade Light Division
Robert Ballard Long	MG	Cavalry Brigade
George Murray	MG	QMG
John Oswald	MG	5th Division
Edward Stopford	MG	Guards Brigade 1st Division
John Ormsby Vandeleur	MG	2nd Brigade Light Division
Archibald Campbell	BG	Portuguese Brigade
Benjamin D'Urban	BG	QMG, Portuguese Troops
Denis Pack	BG	1st Portuguese Brigade
Manley Power	BG	8th Portuguese Brigade
William Frederick Spry	BG	3rd Portuguese Brigade
Charles Ashworth	Col	Portuguese Brigade
Matthew, 5th Lord Aylmer	Col	DAG
Edward Barnes	Col	1st Brigade 7th Division
Thomas Brisbane	Col	1st Brigade 3rd Division
John Buchan	Col	7th Portuguese Line
John Byng	Col	2nd Brigade 2nd Division
Henry Cadogan	Col	1st Brigade 2nd Division
John Milley Doyle	Col	19th Portuguese Line
Colquhoun Grant	Col	Cavalry Brigade
William Grant	Col	2nd Brigade 7th Division
John Wright Guise	Col	3rd Foot Guards
Colin Halkett	Col	2nd Brigade 1st Division
Thomas Noel Hill	Col	1st Portuguese Line
John Keane	Col	60th Foot
Duncan McDonald	Col	57th Foot
Robert O'Callaghan	Col	3rd Brigade 2nd Division
William Ponsonby	Col	Cavalry Brigade
William, Prince of Orange	Col	ADC to the Duke of Wellington
Frederick Robinson	Col	2nd Brigade 5th Division
John B. Skerrett	Col	2nd Brigade 4th Division
Lord Edward Somerset	Col	4th Dragoons
Alexander Abercromby	LCol	AQMG
John Henry Algeo	LCol	1st Caçadores
Alexander Anderson	LCol	11th Portuguese Line
Richard Armstrong	LCol	10th Caçadores
Andrew Francis Barnard	LCol	95th Foot

Campaign Medals for Meritorious or Honourable Service

Name	Rank	Unit or position
Charles Philip Belson	LCol	28th Foot
George Henry Berkeley	LCol	AAG
George Ridout Bingham	LCol	2nd Provisional Battalion
Edward Blakeney	LCol	7th Foot
Rudolphus Bodecker	LCol	1st KGL Line
Henry Frederick Bouverie	LCol	AAG
Henry Hollis Bradford	LCol	AAG
Charles Broke	LCol	AQMG
Francis Brooke	LCol	4th Foot
Charles Bruce	LCol	39th Foot
Johann, Baron Bulow	LCol	1st KGL Dragoons
Ulysses Burgh	LCol	Assistant Military Secretary
John Fox Burgoyne	LCol	RE
Louis, Baron Bussche	LCol	2nd KGL Line
John Cameron	LCol	9th Foot
John Cameron	LCol	92nd Foot
Allan William Campbell	LCol	4th Portuguese Line
Archibald Campbell	LCol	6th Foot
Colin Campbell	LCol	1st Foot
Colin Campbell	LCol	AAG
James Campbell	LCol	94th Foot
Henry William Carr	LCol	83rd Foot
Charles Murray Cathcart	LCol	AQMG
Arthur Benjamin Clifton	LCol	1st Dragoons
Charles Cother	LCol	71st Foot
Thomas Dalmer	LCol	23rd Foot
Frederick de Arentsschildt	LCol	1st KGL Hussars
Frederick de Hertzburg	LCol	Brunswick Light Infantry
William Howe De Lancey	LCol	DQMG
Alexander Dickson	LCol	Portuguese Artillery
Jeremiah Dickson	LCol	AQMG
Richard Diggens	LCol	6th Portuguese Cavalry
Patrick Doherty	LCol	13th Light Dragoons
Francis D'Oyley	LCol	AAG
Robert Lawrence Dundas	LCol	Royal Staff Corps
Thomas Dursbach	LCol	11th Caçadores
John Elley	LCol	AAG
Henry Walton Ellis	LCol	23rd Foot
William Fenwick	LCol	34th Foot
John Forster Fitzgerald	LCol	60th Foot
Richard Fletcher	LCol	RE

Table 8.20 continued

Name	Rank	Unit or position
Edward Gibbs	LCol	52nd Foot
John Gomersall	LCol	16th Portuguese Line
William Gomm	LCol	AQMG
Alexander Gordon	LCol	ADC to the Duke of Wellington
Hugh Gough	LCol	87th Foot
Maxwell Grant	LCol	6th Portuguese Line
Charles James Greville	LCol	38th Foot
Henry Hardinge	LCol	DQMG, Portuguese Troops
Julius Hartmann	LCol	King's German Artillery
James Hay	LCol	16th Light Dragoons
Daniel James Hearn	LCol	43rd Foot
Francis Hepburn	LCol	3rd Foot Guards
Felton Bathurst Hervey	LCol	14th Light Dragoons
Charles Hill	LCol	50th Foot
Dudley St Leger Hill	LCol	8th Caçadores
Robert Chambre Hill	LCol	Household Cavalry Brigade
George Holmes	LCol	AAG
William Johnston	LCol	68th Foot
William Kelly	LCol	3rd Provisional Battalion
Henry King	LCol	82nd Foot
Alexander Leith	LCol	1st Provisional Battalion
Thomas Lloyd	LCol	94th Foot
John MacDonald	LCol	14th Portuguese Line
Lord Charles Manners	LCol	3rd Dragoons
John May	LCol	AAG
Michael McCreagh	LCol	5th Caçadores
John McLean	LCol	27th Foot
James Miller	LCol	23rd Portuguese Line
Christian, Baron Ompteda	LCol	1st KGL Light
Bryan O'Toole	LCol	7th Caçadores
Charles Paterson	LCol	28th Foot
Frederick Cavendish Ponsonby	LCol	12th Light Dragoons
Charles Pratt	LCol	5th Foot
George James Robarts	LCol	10th Light Dragoons
John Rolt	LCol	17th Portuguese Line
John Charles Rooke	LCol	AAG
John Ross	LCol	95th Foot
George Scovell	LCol	AQMG
Lord Fitzroy Somerset	LCol	Military Secretary

Name	Rank	Unit or position
James Stewart	LCol	AAG
Charles Sutton	LCol	9th Portuguese Line
Robert Le Poer Trench	LCol	74th Foot
Alexander Tulloh	LCol	Portuguese Artillery
Arthur Percy Upton	LCol	AQMG
Hamlet Wade	LCol	95th Foot
James Wilson	LCol	48th Foot
Alexander George Woodford	LCol	Coldstream Guards
Richard Buckner	Maj	RA
John Camac	Maj	1st Life Guards
Charles Stuart Campbell	Maj	3rd Portuguese Line
Joseph Hugh Carncross	Maj	RA
Frederick de Zeigesar	Maj	2nd KGL Dragoons
Daniel Dodgin	Maj	66th Foot
Alexis du Hautoy	Maj	Chasseurs Britanniques
Augustus Frazer	Maj	Royal Horse Artillery
Peter Fraser	Maj	1st Foot
John Galiffe	Maj	60th Foot
Robert William Gardiner	Maj	RA
Henry Goldfinch	Maj	RE
Edwin Griffith	Maj	15th Light Dragoons
John P. Hawkins	Maj	68th Foot
James Archibald Hope	Maj	AAG
James Hughes	Maj	18th Light Dragoons
Heinrich Peter Hurtzig	Maj	2nd KGL Light
Robert Kelly	Maj	47th Foot
Edward Knight	Maj	11th Portuguese Dragoons
Robert Lawson	Maj	RA
Thomas Lightfoot	Maj	45th Foot
Maxwell MacKenzie	Maj	71st Foot
Robert Barclay MacPherson	Maj	88th Foot
John McPherson	Maj	92nd Foot
Samuel Mitchell	Maj	6th Caçadores
Robert Christopher Packe	Maj	Royal Horse Guards
John Parker	Maj	RA
Serjeantson Prescott	Maj	5th Dragoon Guards
David Roberts	Maj	51st Foot
Archibald Ross	Maj	9th Portuguese Line
Hew Dalyrmple Ross	Maj	RA
Charles Felix Smith	Maj	RE

Table 8.20 continued

Name	Rank	Unit or position
Frederick Stovin	Maj	AAG
Frederick Sympher	Maj	King's German Artillery
George, Marquess of Tweeddale	Maj	AQMG
Charles Albert Vigoureux	Maj	30th Foot
Robert Waller	Maj	AQMG
William Grove White	Maj	48th Foot
Edmund Kenyton Williams	Maj	4th Caçadores
George Henry Zulke	Maj	2nd Caçadores
George Bean	Capt	RA
Joseph Bradbey	Capt	28th Foot
Robert Cairnes	Capt	RA
Robert Douglas	Capt	RA
Saumarez Dubourdieu	Capt	RA
Arthur Rowley Heyland	Capt	40th Foot
Charles Jackson	Capt	2nd Life Guards
Alexander Kyle	Capt	94th Foot
Charles Edwards Livesay	Capt	47th Foot
Stewart Maxwell	Capt	RA
Charles Cornwallis Michell	Capt	Portuguese Artillery
John O'Flaherty	Capt	45th Foot
William Norman Ramsay	Capt	RA
Francis Scott	Capt	59th Foot
James Webber-Smith	Capt	RA
Hans von Hattorf	Capt	1st KGL Dragoons
Friederich von Uslar-Gleichen	Capt	1st KGL Dragoons

Source: *London Gazette*, 13 April 1814.

Table 8.21 Gold Medal recipients for the Pyrenees

Name	Rank	Unit or position
Duke of Wellington	FM	Commander of the Forces
William Beresford	LG	Portuguese Troops
Galbraith Lowry Cole	LG	4th Division
George, Earl of Dalhousie	LG	7th Division
Rowland Hill	LG	Corps Commander
Thomas Picton	LG	3rd Division
William Stewart	LG	2nd Division
William Anson	MG	1st Brigade 4th Division

Campaign Medals for Meritorious or Honourable Service

Name	Rank	Unit or position
Edward Barnes	MG	1st Brigade 7th Division
Thomas Brisbane	MG	1st Brigade 3rd Division
John Byng	MG	2nd Brigade 2nd Division
Charles Colville	MG	2nd Brigade 3rd Division
William Inglis	MG	2nd Brigade 7th Division
George Allan Madden	MG	Portuguese Brigade
George Murray	MG	QMG
Denis Pack	MG	6th Division
Edward M. Pakenham	MG	AG
William Henry Pringle	MG	3rd Brigade 2nd Division
Robert Ross	MG	2nd Brigade 4th Division
Charles Ashworth	BG	Portuguese Brigade
John Buchan	BG	Portuguese Brigade
Archibald Campbell	BG	Portuguese Brigade
Benjamin D'Urban	BG	QMG, Portuguese Troops
Thomas William Stubbs	BG	Portuguese Brigade
Charles Philip Belson	Col	28th Foot
George Ridout Bingham	Col	2nd Provisional Battalion
James Douglas	Col	8th Portuguese Line
John Milley Doyle	Col	19th Portuguese Line
William Grant	Col	82nd Foot
Samuel Venables Hinde	Col	32nd Foot
John Keane	Col	60th Foot
William Kelly	Col	3rd Provisional Battalion
Haviland Le Mesurier	Col	12th Portuguese Line
Duncan McDonald	Col	57th Foot
Robert O'Callaghan	Col	39th Foot
William, Prince of Orange	Col	ADC to the Duke of Wellington
James Stirling	Col	1st Brigade 6th Division
Alexander Abercromby	LCol	AQMG
Alexander Anderson	LCol	11th Portuguese Line
Thomas Arbuthnot	LCol	AQMG
Richard Armstrong	LCol	10th Caçadores
Edward Blakeney	LCol	7th Foot
Henry Hollis Bradford	LCol	AAG
Charles Broke	LCol	AQMG
Gustavus Browne	LCol	9th Caçadores
Ulysses Burgh	LCol	Assistant Military Secretary
Colin Campbell	LCol	AAG
James Robert Coghlan	LCol	61st Foot
Frederick de Hertzburg	LCol	Brunswick Light Infantry

Table 8.21 continued

Name	Rank	Unit or position
Jeremiah Dickson	LCol	AQMG
Daniel Dodgin	LCol	66th Foot
Neil Douglas	LCol	79th Foot
William Douglas	LCol	91st Foot
Francis D'Oyley	LCol	AAG
Alexis du Hautoy	LCol	Chasseurs Britanniques
Robert Lawrence Dundas	LCol	Royal Staff Corps
John Dyer	LCol	RA
Henry Walton Ellis	LCol	23rd Foot
Charles Fane	LCol	59th Foot
John Forster Fitzgerald	LCol	1st Brigade 2nd Division
Alexander Gordon	LCol	ADC to the Duke of Wellington
Maxwell Grant	LCol	6th Portuguese Line
Henry Hardinge	LCol	DQMG, Portuguese Troops
John Bacon Harrison	LCol	50th Foot
John P. Hawkins	LCol	68th Foot
John Hicks	LCol	32nd Foot
Alexander Leith	LCol	1st Provisional Battalion
Robert Macara	LCol	42nd Foot
John MacDonald	LCol	14th Portuguese Line
John MacLean	LCol	27th Foot
James Miller	LCol	23rd Portuguese Line
Frederick Newman	LCol	11th Foot
Bryan O'Toole	LCol	7th Caçadores
Ralph Ouseley	LCol	8th Portuguese Line
Henry Pynn	LCol	18th Portuguese Line
David Roberts	LCol	51st Foot
John Charles Rooke	LCol	AAG
George Scovell	LCol	Royal Staff Corps
Lord Fitzroy Somerset	LCol	Military Secretary
Robert Le Poer Trench	LCol	74th Foot
John Richard Ward	LCol	36th Foot
John Waters	LCol	AAG
Andrew Wauchope	LCol	20th Foot
Henry Worsley	LCol	34th Foot
John Bell	Maj	AQMG
Thomas Alston Brandreth	Maj	RA
Guy Campbell	Maj	6th Foot
Joseph Hugh Carncross	Maj	RA
August Heise	Maj	AAG

Name	Rank	Unit or position
Martin Leggatt	Maj	36th Foot
Thomas Lightfoot	Maj	45th Foot
John Scott Lillie	Maj	7th Caçadores
Donald McNeill	Maj	91st Foot
Samuel Mitchell	Maj	6th Caçadores
Robert Ray	Maj	2nd Portuguese Line
Alexander Rose	Maj	20th Foot
Charles Steevens	Maj	20th Foot
Frederick Stovin	Maj	AAG
Frederick Sympher	Maj	King's German Artillery
Charles Tryon	Maj	AAG
William Grove White	Maj	48th Foot
George Henry Zulke	Maj	2nd Caçadores
Thomas Bell	Capt	48th Foot
Robert M. Cairnes	Capt	RA
Duncan Campbell	Capt	39th Foot
William Campbell	Capt	36th Foot
Robert Douglas	Capt	RA
James Seaton	Capt	92nd Foot
Sempronius Stretton	Capt	40th Foot

Source: *London Gazette*, 13 April 1814.

Trivia: *Thomas William Stubbs and Francis John Colman, serving in the Portuguese army, were both awarded the Army Gold Medal with clasps although neither were officers in the British army. Stubbs had retired by sale of his commission in the 50th Foot in 1800 and Colman had retired by sale of his commission in the 38th Foot in 1805. Colman had retired under the mistaken idea that he had to leave the army to accept an appointment as sergeant-at-arms of parliament. A request to reinstate Colman with his previous rank in the British army was not decided upon before his death in 1811.*

Table 8.22 Gold Medal recipients for the siege of St Sebastian

Name	Rank	Unit or position
Thomas Graham	LG	Commander of the Forces
James Leith	LG	5th Division
Thomas Bradford	MG	10th Portuguese Brigade
Andrew Hay	MG	1st Brigade 5th Division
John Oswald	MG	5th Division
Frederick Robinson	MG	2nd Brigade 5th Division

Table 8.22 continued

Name	Rank	Unit or position
William Frederick Spry	MG	3rd Portuguese Brigade
John Wilson	BG	Portuguese Troops
William Howe De Lancey	Col	DQMG
Charles J. Greville	Col	38th Foot
Thomas Noel Hill	Col	1st Portuguese Line
Michael McCreagh	Col	3rd Portuguese Line
James S. Barns	LCol	1st Foot
George F. H. Berkeley	LCol	AAG
Henry F. Bouverie	LCol	AAG
Francis Brooke	LCol	4th Foot
John Fox Burgoyne	LCol	RE
Richard Cooke	LCol	1st Foot Guards
Henry Craufurd	LCol	9th Foot
John Cameron	LCol	9th Foot
John Thomas Deane	LCol	38th Foot
Alexander Dickson	LCol	Portuguese Artillery
John Dyer	LCol	RA
Charles Ellicombe	LCol	RE
Richard Fletcher	LCol	RE
Augustus Frazer	LCol	Royal Horse Artillery
Johann Gerber	LCol	5th KGL Line
William Gomm	LCol	AQMG
Julius Hartman	LCol	King's German Artillery
John Humphrey Hill	LCol	5th Caçadores
Dudley St Leger Hill	LCol	8th Caçadores
John Philip Hunt	LCol	60th Foot
John May	LCol	AAG
William McBean	LCol	24th Portuguese Line
Edward Miles	LCol	38th Foot
John Piper	LCol	4th Foot
Alexander Thomson	LCol	Assistant Engineer
Edmond K. Williams	LCol	4th Caçadores
Robert Anwyll	Maj	4th Foot
Richard Buckner	Maj	RA
Charles Stuart Campbell	Maj	3rd Portuguese Line
Robert Campbell	Maj	52nd Foot
George Halford	Maj	59th Foot
George H. Henderson	Maj	RE
Timothy Jones	Maj	4th Foot
Robert Kelly	Maj	47th Foot

Campaign Medals for Meritorious or Honourable Service

Name	Rank	Unit or position
John Murray	Maj	20th Foot
Henry Oglander	Maj	47th Foot
Alexander Rose	Maj	20th Foot
Charles Smith	Maj	RE
Kenneth Snodgrass	Maj	13th Portuguese Line
Frederick Sympher	Maj	King's German Artillery
Alexander Thomson	Maj	Assistant Engineer
James Webber-Smith	Maj	RA
John Williamson	Maj	4th Foot
Francis Fuller	Capt	59th Foot
William Gordon	Capt	1st Foot
William Gordon	Capt	24th Portuguese Line
Charles E. Livesay	Capt	47th Foot
Francis Scott	Capt	59th Foot
Thomas Power	Lieut	47th Foot

Source: *London Gazette*, 13 April 1814.

Trivia: *Lieutenant William Mann, adjutant of the 57th Foot, was the senior surviving officer of his regiment after it was cut down at Albuhera by French cavalry. On 31 August 1813, Lieutenant Thomas Power, 47th Foot, earned his gold medal by taking command of the storming party during the assault on the breach at St Sebastian, after its commander was wounded. Lieutenant Power was severely wounded in the attack. For his gallantry, he was mentioned in dispatches and promoted to captain in the 60th Foot, on 6 November 1813. Lieutenant William L. Robe, RA, commanded a three-gun brigade of mountain guns and earned two gold medals for commanding them at Nivelle and Nive. He would be killed at Waterloo. Lieutenant Robe was the son of Lieutenant Colonel William Robe, RA, who had earned a Gold Cross with a clasp. Lieutenant William Bace, 61st Foot, received his gold medal for his actions at the battle of Toulouse. He led his regiment after every senior officer had been killed or wounded.*

Table 8.23 Gold Medal recipients for Chateauguay

Name	Rank	Unit or position
Charles-Michel d'Irumberry de Salaberry	LCol	Canadian Voltigeurs
George McDonnell	LCol	Glengarry Light Infantry Fencibles

Source: Graves, *Field of Glory.* Page 365

Trivia: *The battle of Chateauguay was fought with Canadian fencibles, volunteers and militia. No British line regiments were involved. Only the two commanding officers, both British regular officers serving with the Canadian units, were awarded Gold Medals. Lieutenant Colonel de Salaberry, was the commander of the force and Lieutenant Colonel McDonnell was the second in command.*

Table 8.24   Gold Medal recipients for Nivelle

Name	Rank	Unit or position
Duke of Wellington	FM	Commander of the Forces
William Beresford	LG	Portuguese Troops
Henry Clinton	LG	6th Division
Galbraith Lowry Cole	LG	4th Division
John Hamilton	LG	Portuguese Division
Rowland Hill	LG	Corps Commander
William Stewart	LG	2nd Division
Charles, Baron Alten	MG	Light Division
William Anson	MG	1st Brigade 4th Division
Edward Barnes	MG	1st Brigade 2nd Division
Thomas Brisbane	MG	1st Brigade 3rd Division
John Byng	MG	2nd Brigade 2nd Division
Charles Colville	MG	3rd Division
William Inglis	MG	2nd Brigade 7th Division
James Kempt	MG	1st Brigade Light Division
John Lambert	MG	2nd Brigade 6th Division
George Murray	MG	QMG
Denis Pack	MG	1st Brigade 6th Division
Edward M. Pakenham	MG	AG
Manley Power	MG	8th Portuguese Brigade
William Henry Pringle	MG	3rd Brigade 2nd Division
Charles Ashworth	BG	Portuguese Brigade
John Buchan	BG	Portuguese Brigade
Archibald Campbell	BG	Portuguese Troops
Benjamin D'Urban	BG	QMG, Portuguese Troops
Andrew Francis Barnard	Col	95th Foot
Charles Philip Belson	Col	28th Foot
George Ridout Bingham	Col	2nd Provisional Battalion
Alexander Dickson	Col	Portuguese Artillery
James Douglas	Col	7th Portuguese Brigade
Henry Hardinge	Col	DQMG, Portugese Troops
John Keane	Col	2nd Brigade 3rd Division

Name	Rank	Unit or position
Duncan McDonald	Col	57th Foot
Robert O'Callaghan	Col	39th Foot
William, Prince of Orange	Col	ADC to the Duke of Wellington
Charles Sutton	Col	9th Portuguese Line
John Taylor	Col	88th Foot
Alexander Anderson	LCol	11th Portuguese Line
Thomas Arbuthnot	LCol	AQMG
William Beatty	LCol	12th Portuguese Line
Walter Birmingham	LCol	21st Portuguese Line
Henry Hollis Bradford	LCol	AAG
Gustavus Browne	LCol	9th Caçadores
Charles Bruce	LCol	39th Foot
Ulysses Burgh	LCol	Assistant Military Secretary
Colin Campbell	LCol	AAG
Charles Fox Canning	LCol	ADC to the Duke of Wellington
Henry William Carr	LCol	83rd Foot
James Robert Coghlan	LCol	61st Foot
John Colborne	LCol	2nd Brigade Light Division
Frederick de Hertzburg	LCol	Brunswick Light Infantry
Jeremiah Dickson	LCol	AQMG
Neil Douglas	LCol	79th Foot
William Douglas	LCol	91st Foot
Francis D'Oyley	LCol	AAG
Robert Lawrence Dundas	LCol	Royal Staff Corps
Thomas Dursbach	LCol	11th Caçadores
Howard Elphinstone	LCol	RE
Peter Fearon	LCol	6th Caçadores
Thomas Forbes	LCol	45th Foot
Augustus Frazer	LCol	Royal Horse Artillery
John Gardiner	LCol	6th Foot
John Gomersall	LCol	2nd Portuguese Line
Alexander Gordon	LCol	ADC to the Duke of Wellington
Hugh Gough	LCol	87th Foot
Maxwell Grant	LCol	6th Portuguese Line
Richard Goddard Hare	LCol	AAG
John P. Hawkins	LCol	68th Foot
John Hicks	LCol	32nd Foot
John Humphrey Hill	LCol	5th Caçadores
James Archibald Hope	LCol	AAG
Richard Downes Jackson	LCol	AQMG
Alexander Leith	LCol	1st Provisional Battalion

Table 8.24 continued

Name	Rank	Unit or position
Robert Macara	LCol	42nd Foot
John Maclean	LCol	27th Foot
John May	LCol	AAG
James Miller	LCol	23rd Portuguese Line
Frederick Newman	LCol	11th Foot
Charles Pratt	LCol	5th Foot
John Rolt	LCol	17th Portuguese Line
John Charles Rooke	LCol	AAG
Hew Dalrymple Ross	LCol	Royal Horse Artillery
George Scovell	LCol	Staff Corps of Cavalry
Kenneth Snodgrass	LCol	1st Caçadores
Lord Fitzroy Somerset	LCol	Military Secretary
Frederick Stovin	LCol	AAG
Henry Thornton	LCol	40th Foot
Robert Le Poer Trench	LCol	74th Foot
Alexander Tulloh	LCol	Portuguese Artillery
John Waters	LCol	AAG
John George Woodford	LCol	AAG
Henry Worsley	LCol	34th Foot
Dudley Acland	Maj	57th Foot
William Balfour	Maj	40th Foot
John Bell	Maj	AQMG
Thomas Bell	Maj	48th Foot
James Bogle	Maj	94th Foot
Richard Buckner	Maj	RA
Patrick Campbell	Maj	52nd Foot
William Campbell	Maj	36th Foot
Joseph Hugh Carncross	Maj	RA
William Cowell	Maj	42nd Foot
William Cross	Maj	36th Foot
Joseph F. Desbarres	Maj	87th Foot
John Galiffe	Maj	60th Foot
Augustus Heise	Maj	AAG
John Scott Lillie	Maj	7th Caçadores
George Marlay	Maj	AAG
William Napier	Maj	43rd Foot
Samuel Rice	Maj	51st Foot
James Holmes Schoedde	Maj	60th Foot
Frederick Sympher	Maj	King's German Artillery
Henry Thomas	Maj	27th Foot

Name	Rank	Unit or position
John Walmsley	Maj	82nd Foot
William Balvaird	Capt	95th Foot
Charles Cameron	Capt	3rd Foot
Robert Douglas	Capt	RA
Joseph Felix de Prevôt	Capt	Chasseurs Britanniques
Thomas Laing	Capt	94th Foot
Joseph Marke	Capt	57th Foot
Hector McLaine	Capt	57th Foot
George Miller	Capt	95th Foot
Robert Nickle	Capt	88th Foot
Bayntum Stone	Capt	3rd Provisional Battalion
William Livingstone Robe	Lieut	RA

Source: *London Gazette*, 13 September 1814; *Army List*, October 1852.

Trivia: *George Allan Madden was another former British officer serving in the Portuguese army. Major Madden had to retire by sale of his commission in 1802 after being court-martialled for misconduct in the 12th Light Dragoons (Cornet Madden had replaced a certain Arthur Wellesley as a lieutenant in the regiment in 1791). After serving with distinction in the Peninsular War, a request was made to reinstate him in his rank in the British army. This was done in 1812 and Madden was promoted a lieutenant colonel (ante-dated to 1805), a brevet colonel in 1813 and a major general in 1819. Therefore, unlike Thomas Stubbs and Francis Colman, he was a British officer when awarded his Gold Medal for the Pyrenees.*

Table 8.25   Gold Medal recipients for Chrystler's Farm

Name	Rank	Unit or position
Joseph W. Morrison	LCol	Commander of the Forces
John Harvey	LCol	DAG
Thomas Pearson	LCol	Inspecting Field Officer of Militia
Charles Plenderleath	LCol	49th Foot
Miller Clifford	Maj	89th Foot
Fred George Heriot	Maj	Canadian Voltigeurs
Henry G. Jackson	Capt	RA

Source: Graves, *Field of Glory*, p. 365.

Table 8.26 Gold Medal recipients for Nive

Name	Rank	Unit or position
Duke of Wellington	FM	Commander of the Forces
William Carr Beresford	LG	Portuguese Troops
Henry Clinton	LG	6th Division
John Hope	LG	Corps Commander
Rowland Hill	LG	Corps Commander
William Stewart	LG	2nd Division
Charles, Baron Alten	MG	Light Division
Matthew, 5th Lord Aylmer	MG	Independent Brigade
Edward Barnes	MG	1st Brigade 2nd Division
Thomas Bradford	MG	10th Portuguese Brigade
John Byng	MG	2nd Brigade 2nd Division
Henry de Hinuber	MG	KGL Brigade 1st Division
Andrew Hay	MG	5th Division
Kenneth Howard	MG	1st Division
James Kempt	MG	1st Brigade Light Division
John Lambert	MG	2nd Brigade 6th Division
George Murray	MG	QMG
Denis Pack	MG	1st Brigade 6th Division
Edward Michael Pakenham	MG	AG
William Henry Pringle	MG	3rd Brigade 2nd Division
Frederick Robinson	MG	2nd Brigade 5th Division
Edward Stopford	MG	2nd Brigade 1st Division
John Ormsby Vandeleur	MG	3rd Cavalry Brigade
Charles Ashworth	BG	Portuguese Brigade
John Buchan	BG	2nd Portuguese Brigade
Archibald Campbell	BG	Portuguese Brigade
Benjamin D'Urban	BG	QMG, Portuguese Troops
Robert Arbuthnot	Col	Military secretary to General Beresford
Charles Philip Belson	Col	28th Foot
William Howe De Lancey	Col	DQMG
Alexander Dickson	Col	Portuguese Artillery
James Douglas	Col	7th Portuguese Brigade
Charles James Greville	Col	1st Brigade 5th Division
John Wright Guise	Col	3rd Foot Guards
Colin Halkett	Col	2nd KGL Light
Henry Hardinge	Col	DQMG, Portuguese Troops
Peregrine Maitland	Col	1st Brigade 1st Division
William McBean	Col	9th Portuguese Brigade

Campaign Medals for Meritorious or Honourable Service

Name	Rank	Unit or position
Michael McCreagh	Col	3rd Portuguese Line
Robert O'Callaghan	Col	39th Foot
Christian, Baron Ompteda	Col	5th KGL Line
Henry Askew	LCol	1st Foot Guards
James Stevenson Barns	LCol	1st Foot
William Beatty	LCol	12th Portuguese Line
Adolphus, Baron Beck	LCol	5th KGL Line
George Henry Berkeley	LCol	AAG
Walter Birmingham	LCol	21st Portuguese Line
Nathaniel S. Blackwell	LCol	62nd Foot
Rudolph Bodecker	LCol	1st KGL Line
Henry Frederick Bouverie	LCol	AAG
Charles Broke	LCol	AQMG
Gustavus Browne	LCol	9th Caçadores
Charles Bruce	LCol	39th Foot
Ulysses Burgh	LCol	Assistant Military Secretary
John Fox Burgoyne	LCol	RE
Louis, Baron Bussche	LCol	2nd KGL Light
John Cameron	LCol	9th Foot
John Cameron	LCol	92nd Foot
Colin Campbell	LCol	AAG
Charles Fox Canning	LCol	ADC to the Duke of Wellington
James Robert Coghlan	LCol	61st Foot
John Colborne	LCol	2nd Brigade Light Division
William Cross	LCol	36th Foot
John Thomas Deane	LCol	38th Foot
Neil Douglas	LCol	79th Foot
William Douglas	LCol	91st Foot
Robert Lawrence Dundas	LCol	Royal Staff Corps
Howard Elphinstone	LCol	RE
Augustus Frazer	LCol	Royal Horse Artillery
Dugald Little Gilmour	LCol	95th Foot
Henry Goldfinch	LCol	RE
William Maynard Gomm	LCol	AQMG
Alexander Gordon	LCol	ADC to the Duke of Wellington
Maxwell Grant	LCol	6th Portuguese Line
Richard Goddard Hare	LCol	DAQMG
John Bacon Harrison	LCol	50th Foot
Julius Hartmann	LCol	King's German Artillery
Francis Hepburn	LCol	3rd Foot Guards
John Hicks	LCol	32nd Foot

Table 8.26 continued

Name	Rank	Unit or position
John Humphrey Hill	LCol	4th Portuguese Line
Francis Wheeler Hood	LCol	AAG
James Archibald Hope	LCol	AAG
Richard Downes Jackson	LCol	AQMG
Alexander Leith	LCol	1st Provisional Battalion
Richard Lloyd	LCol	84th Foot
Robert Macara	LCol	42nd Foot
John Macdonald	LCol	AAG
George Marlay	LCol	AAG
John May	LCol	RA
William Mein	LCol	52nd Foot
William Napier	LCol	43rd Foot
Charles Nicol	LCol	66th Foot
Frederick Newman	LCol	11th Foot
Amos Godsill R. Norcott	LCol	95th Foot
Christian, Baron Ompteda	LCol	1st KGL Light
John Piper	LCol	4th Foot
Frederick C. Ponsonby	LCol	12th Light Dragoons
John Rolt	LCol	13th Portuguese Line
Hew Dalrymple Ross	LCol	RA
George Scovell	LCol	Cavalry Staff Corps
Kenneth Snodgrass	LCol	1st Caçadores
Lord Fitzroy Somerset	LCol	Military Secretary
Thomas Staunton St Clair	LCol	5th Caçadores
William Stuart	LCol	1st Foot Guards
William Thornton	LCol	85th Foot
Alexander Tulloh	LCol	Portuguese Artillery
Arthur Percy Upton	LCol	AQMG
Friederich Von Hartwig	LCol	1st KGL Light
John Wardlaw	LCol	76th Foot
John Waters	LCol	AAG
James Dawson West	LCol	1st Foot Guards
Edmund Keynton Williams	LCol	4th Caçadores
Alexander G. Woodford	LCol	Coldstream Guards
John George Woodford	LCol	AQMG
Henry Worsley	LCol	34th Foot
William Balvaird	Maj	95th Foot
Charles Cameron	Maj	3rd Foot
Archibald Campbell	Maj	15th Portuguese Line
Patrick Campbell	Maj	52nd Foot

Campaign Medals for Meritorious or Honourable Service

Name	Rank	Unit or position
Joseph Carncross	Maj	RA
Richard Chetham	Maj	47th Foot
Peter Deshon	Maj	85th Foot
John Dyer	Maj	RA
William Alexander Gordon	Maj	50th Foot
James Hay	Maj	16th Light Dragoons
August Heise	Maj	AAG
Frederick W. Hoystead	Maj	59th Foot
William Norman Ramsay	Maj	RA
Jacob Tonson	Maj	84th Foot
Lewis Carmichael	Capt	RA
Charles Dashwood	Capt	DAAG
William Greene	Capt	61st Foot
James Jenkin	Capt	84th Foot
John Easton Kipping	Capt	4th Foot
Joseph Marke	Capt	57th Foot
Stewart Maxwell	Capt	RA
Charles Mosse	Capt	RA
William Wilkinson	Capt	59th Foot
William Livingstone Robe	Lieut	RA

Source: *Army List*, October 1852.

Table 8.27 Gold Medal recipients for Orthes

Name	Rank	Unit or position
Duke of Wellington	FM	Commander of the Forces
William Carr Beresford	LG	Portuguese Troops
Henry Clinton	LG	6th Division
Galbraith Lowry Cole	LG	4th Division
Stapleton Cotton	LG	Commander of the Cavalry
Rowland Hill	LG	Corps Commander
Thomas Picton	LG	3rd Division
William Stewart	LG	2nd Division
Charles, Baron Alten	MG	Light Division
William Anson	MG	1st Brigade 4th Division
Edward Barnes	MG	1st Brigade 2nd Division
Thomas Makdougall Brisbane	MG	1st Brigade 3rd Division
John Byng	MG	2nd Brigade 2nd Division
Henry Fane	MG	Cavalry Brigade
William Inglis	MG	2nd Brigade 7th Division

Table 8.27 continued

Name	Rank	Unit or position
James Kempt	MG	1st Brigade Light Division
John Lambert	MG	2nd Brigade 6th Division
George Murray	MG	QMG
Denis Pack	MG	1st Brigade 6th Division
Edward Michael Pakenham	MG	AG
Manley Power	MG	8th Portuguese Brigade
Robert Ross	MG	2nd Brigade 4th Division
Lord Edward Somerset	MG	8th Cavalry Brigade
George Townsend Walker	MG	7th Division
Robert Arbuthnot	Col	Military Secretary to General Beresford
Andrew Francis Barnard	Col	95th Foot
James Douglas	Col	7th Portuguese Brigade
John Milley Doyle	Col	19th Portuguese Line
John Elley	Col	AAG
Henry Hardinge	Col	DQMG, Portuguese Troops
John Keane	Col	2nd Brigade 3rd Division
Edward Kerrison	Col	7th Light Dragoons
Robert O'Callaghan	Col	3rd Brigade 2nd Division
John Taylor	Col	88th Foot
Richard Hussey Vivian	Col	5th Cavalry Brigade
Hamlet Wade	Col	95th Foot
Alexander Abercromby	LCol	AQMG
Alexander Anderson	LCol	11th Portuguese Line
Thomas Arbuthnot	LCol	AAG
William Beatty	LCol	12th Portuguese Line
Walter Birmingham	LCol	21st Portuguese Line
Henry Frederick Bouverie	LCol	AAG
Henry Hollis Bradford	LCol	AAG
Charles Broke	LCol	AQMG
Charles Bruce	LCol	39th Foot
Ulysses Burgh	LCol	Assistant Military Secretary
John Cameron	LCol	92nd Foot
Francis Campbell	LCol	3rd Provisional Battalion
Charles Fox Canning	LCol	ADC to the Duke of Wellington
Joseph Carncross	LCol	RA
Henry William Carr	LCol	83rd Foot
James Robert Coghlan	LCol	61st Foot
John Colborne	LCol	2nd Brigade Light Division
William Cross	LCol	36th Foot

Name	Rank	Unit or position
George Cuyler	LCol	11th Foot
Friederich de Hertzberg	LCol	Brunswick Light Infantry
Jeremiah Dickson	LCol	AQMG
Daniel Dodgin	LCol	66th Foot
Patrick Doherty	LCol	13th Light Dragoons
William Douglas	LCol	91st Foot
Francis D'Oyley	LCol	AAG
Alexis du Hautoy	LCol	Chasseurs Britanniques
Henry Walton Ellis	LCol	23rd Foot
Thomas Forbes	LCol	45th Foot
John Gardiner	LCol	1st Brigade 7th Division
Henry Goldfinch	LCol	RE
Alexander Gordon	LCol	ADC to the Duke of Wellington
Maxwell Grant	LCol	6th Portuguese Line
Leonard Greenwell	LCol	45th Foot
John Bacon Harrison	LCol	50th Foot
Robert John Harvey	LCol	AQMG, Portuguese Troops
Felton Bathurst Hervey	LCol	14th Light Dragoons
John Hicks	LCol	32nd Foot
Francis Wheeler Hood	LCol	AAG
James Archibald Hope	LCol	AAG
Richard Downes Jackson	LCol	AQMG
William Johnston	LCol	68th Foot
Charles Kilsha	LCol	11th Caçadores
Alexander Leith	LCol	1st Provisional Battalion
Robert Macara	LCol	42nd Foot
John Maclean	LCol	27th Foot
Russell Manners	LCol	74th Foot
Charles Pratt	LCol	5th Foot
Henry Pynn	LCol	18th Portuguese Line
George Edward Quentin	LCol	10th Light Dragoons
John Rolt	LCol	17th Portuguese Line
John Ross	LCol	95th Foot
Hugh Maurice Scott	LCol	6th Foot
Kenneth Snodgrass	LCol	1st Caçadores
Lord Fitzroy Somerset	LCol	Military Secretary
Frederick Stovin	LCol	AAG
Henry Thornton	LCol	40th Foot
John Waters	LCol	AAG
John George Woodford	LCol	AQMG
Henry Worsley	LCol	34th Foot

Table 8.27 continued		
Name	Rank	Unit or position
George Henry Zulke	LCol	2nd Caçadores
Samuel Benjamin Auchmuty	Maj	7th Foot
John Beatty	Maj	7th Foot
John Bell	Maj	AQMG
Thomas Bell	Maj	48th Foot
James Bent	Maj	20th Foot
John Blaquiere	Maj	83rd Foot
Henry Bright	Maj	87th Foot
Charles Edward Conyers	Maj	82nd Foot
William Cowell	Maj	42nd Foot
George D'Arcy	Maj	39th Foot
Joseph Frederick Desbarres	Maj	87th Foot
John Dyer	Maj	RA
John William Fremantle	Maj	ADC to the Duke of Wellington
John Galiffe	Maj	60th Foot
Robert William Gardiner	Maj	RA
Edwin Griffith	Maj	15th Light Dragoons
Philip, Baron Gruben	Maj	1st KGL Hussars
Samuel Hext	Maj	83rd Foot
James Hughes	Maj	18th Light Dragoons
William Lewin Herford	Maj	23rd Foot
George Jenkinson	Maj	RA
John Scott Lillie	Maj	7th Caçadores
Robert Barclay Macpherson	Maj	88th Foot
George Marlay	Maj	AAG
James Mitchell	Maj	92nd Foot
Edward Mullens	Maj	28th Foot
Henry Roberts	Maj	3rd Foot
Frederick Sympher	Maj	King's German Artillery
Henry Thomas	Maj	27th Foot
William Vincent	Maj	DAQMG
George Bean	Capt	RA
John Campbell	Capt	42nd Foot
Lewis Daniel	Capt	King's German Artillery
Gilbert Elliot	Capt	83rd Foot
Thomas Hilton	Capt	45th Foot
John Grant King	Capt	Brig. Major, 9th Portuguese Brigade
Thomas Laing	Capt	94th Foot
Stewart Maxwell	Capt	RA
John Michell	Capt	RA

Name	Rank	Unit or position
William Russell	Capt	20th Foot
George Turner	Capt	RA

Table 8.28 Gold Medal recipients for Toulouse

Name	Rank	Unit or position
Duke of Wellington	FM	Commander of the Forces
William Carr Beresford	LG	Portuguese Troops
Henry Clinton	LG	6th Division
Galbraith Lowry Cole	LG	4th Division
Stapleton Cotton	LG	Commander of the Cavalry
Thomas Picton	LG	3rd Division
Charles, Baron Alten	MG	Light Division
William Anson	MG	1st Brigade 4th Division
Thomas Makdougall Brisbane	MG	1st Brigade 3rd Division
James Kempt	MG	1st Brigade Light Division
John Lambert	MG	2nd Brigade 6th Division
George Murray	MG	QMG
Denis Pack	MG	1st Brigade 6th Division
Edward Michael Pakenham	MG	AG
Manley Power	MG	8th Portuguese Brigade
Robert Ross	MG	2nd Brigade 4th Division
Lord Edward Somerset	MG	8th Cavalry Brigade
Benjamin D'Urban	BG	QMG, Portuguese Troops
Robert Arbuthnot	Col	Military Secretary to General Beresford
Andrew Francis Barnard	Col	95th Foot
Frederick de Arentsschildt	Col	Cavalry Brigade
Alexander Dickson	Col	Portuguese Artillery
James Douglas	Col	7th Portuguese Brigade
John Milley Doyle	Col	19th Portuguese Line
John Elley	Col	AAG
John Keane	Col	2nd Brigade 3rd Division
Charles Sutton	Col	9th Portuguese Line
John Taylor	Col	88th Foot
Hamlet Wade	Col	95th Foot
Alexander Anderson	LCol	11th Portuguese Line
William Beatty	LCol	12th Portuguese Line
Walter Birmingham	LCol	21st Portuguese Line
Henry Hollis Bradford	LCol	AAG

Table 8.28 continued

Name	Rank	Unit or position
Charles Broke	LCol	AQMG
Johann, Baron Bulow	LCol	1st KGL Dragoons
Ulysses Burgh	LCol	Assistant Military Secretary
Colin Campbell	LCol	AAG
Charles Fox Canning	LCol	ADC to the Duke of Wellington
James Robert Coghlan	LCol	61st Foot
John Colborne	LCol	2nd Brigade Light Division
William Cross	LCol	36th Foot
George Cuyler	LCol	11th Foot
Leighton Cathcart Dalrymple	LCol	15th Light Dragoons
Jeremiah Dickson	LCol	AQMG
Neil Douglas	LCol	79th Foot
William Douglas	LCol	91st Foot
Robert Lawrence Dundas	LCol	Royal Staff Corps
Henry Walton Ellis	LCol	23rd Foot
Thomas Forbes	LCol	45th Foot
Augustus Frazer	LCol	Royal Horse Artillery
John Galiffe	LCol	60th Foot
Robert William Gardiner	LCol	RA
Dugald Little Gilmour	LCol	95th Foot
Henry Goldfinch	LCol	RE
Alexander Gordon	LCol	ADC to the Duke of Wellington
Maxwell Grant	LCol	6th Portuguese Line
William Lewin Herford	LCol	23rd Foot
James Archibald Hope	LCol	AAG
Robert Macara	LCol	42nd Foot
John Maclean	LCol	27th Foot
Lord Charles Manners	LCol	2nd Cavalry Brigade
John Mansel	LCol	2nd Provisional Battalion
John May	LCol	RA
John Oke	LCol	61st Foot
Christopher Patrickson	LCol	43rd Foot
Charles Pratt	LCol	5th Foot
Serjeantson Prescott	LCol	5th Dragoon Guards
George Augustus Quentin	LCol	10th Light Dragoons
John Rolt	LCol	17th Portuguese Line
John Ross	LCol	95th Foot
George Scovell	LCol	Cavalry Staff Corps
Lord Fitzroy Somerset	LCol	Military Secretary
Frederick Stovin	LCol	AAG

Name	Rank	Unit or position
Henry Thornton	LCol	40th Foot
Robert Le Poer Trench	LCol	74th Foot
Victor Von Arentsschildt	LCol	Portuguese Artillery
John Waters	LCol	AAG
James Wilson	LCol	48th Foot
John George Woodford	LCol	AAG
James Allen	Maj	94th Foot
Samuel Benjamin Auchmuty	Maj	7th Foot
John Welwyn Beatty	Maj	7th Foot
Charles Beckwith	Maj	DAQMG
John Bell	Maj	AQMG
Thomas Alston Brandreth	Maj	RA
Joseph Frederick Desbarres	Maj	87th Foot
John Dyer	Maj	RA
August Friederichs	Maj	2nd KGL Light Dragoons
Philip, Baron Gruben	Maj	1st KGL Hussars
Samuel Hext	Maj	83rd Foot
James Hughes	Maj	18th Light Dragoons
James Hugonin	Maj	4th Dragoons
Thomas Hutchins	Maj	3rd Dragoons
Martin Leggatt	Maj	36th Foot
Thomas Lightfoot	Maj	45th Foot
John Scott Lillie	Maj	7th Caçadores
George Marlay	Maj	AAG
George Henry Murphy	Maj	23rd Portuguese Line
William Russell	Maj	20th Foot
Benjamin Sullivan	Maj	8th Portuguese Line
Frederick Sympher	Maj	KGL Artillery
Henry Thomas	Maj	27th Foot
John Campbell	Capt	Light Companies
Edward Charleton	Capt	61st Foot
Lewis Daniel	Capt	King's German Artillery
Bartholomew Vigors Derenzy	Capt	7th Caçadores
Philipp de Sichart	Capt	1st KGL Light Dragoons
Henry Bowyer Lane	Capt	RA
Alexander Martin	Capt	45th Foot
Charles Cornwallis Michell	Capt	Portuguese Artillery
John Michell	Capt	RA
Ernst Poten	Capt	1st KGL Hussars
George Turner	Capt	RA
William Bace	Lieut	61st Foot

The Waterloo Medal

On 28 June 1815, the Duke of Wellington proposed in a letter to the Duke of York

> I would likewise beg leave to suggest to your Royal Highness the expediency of giving to the noncommissioned officers and soldiers engaged in the battle of Waterloo, a medal. I am convinced it would have the best effect in the army; and, if that battle should settle our concerns, they will well deserve it.[5]

Three months later, on 17 September 1815, he wrote to Lord Bathurst, the Secretary of State for the War Department, expanding on his idea:

> I have long intended to write to you about the medal for Waterloo. I recommend that we should all have the same medal, hung to the same ribband as that now used with the medals.[6]

Wellington's proposal was unique, because it was the first medal that would be given to all participants in a battle, regardless of the individual's rank. On 10 March 1816 the Prince Regent authorised a medal for '. . . every officer, non-commissioned officer, and soldier of the British Army, present upon that memorable occasion.'[7] For the first time, an enlisted soldier would be recognised! To receive the medal, the awardee had to have fought at Quatre Bras, the subsequent retreat, or at Waterloo. Unfortunately, not all units understood the instructions on who was eligible to receive the medal. Most regiments included everyone who fought in the battles. There are some notable omissions, though. Charles Fox Canning, the Duke of Wellington's aide-de-camp, did not receive one. The 1st Dragoon Guards and the 2nd Battalion 69th Foot, only provided the names of those who survived, while the 1st KGL Hussars only sent in the names of their officers, although four enlisted soldiers also received the medal. According to Gareth Glover, the Royal Mint's Waterloo Medal Roll showed that names were still being added ten years later.[8] The Waterloo Medal was silver with a bust of the Prince Regent with laurel leafs around head and the inscription George P. Regent on the obverse. On the reverse was a seated figure of a winged Victory. In her left hand was an olive branch, while in her right a palm branch. Around the top of the medal's reverse was the word 'Wellington'. Below the figure of Victory were the words 'Waterloo June 18, 1815'. Engraved in the edge of the medal was the soldier's name, rank, and regiment. The ribbon was crimson with blue borders.

---

5 Carter, *Medals of the British Army*, p. 197.
6 Ibid.
7 Ibid., p. 198.
8 Personal communication from Gareth Glover, 21 May 2009.

The following list is derived from the *The Waterloo Medal Roll* (ed. C.J. Buckland). It provides a good idea of how many medals were issued, but it is not definitive. Those units in italics in the tables only sent in the names of the survivors.

Trivia: Over 35,000 soldiers received the Waterloo Medal. Of these, ninety-five officers were also recipients of a gold medal from the Peninsular War.

Table 8.29 Recipients of the Waterloo Medal

Regiment or position	No. of recipients
Generals, Staff Officers and NCOs	164
Royal Waggon Train	276
RA	2277
RE	11
RA Drivers	1213
Royal Staff Corps	11
1st Life Guards	261
2nd Life Guards	179
Royal Horse Guards	251
1st Dragoon Guards	573
1st Dragoons	358
2nd Dragoons	368
6th Dragoons	359
7th Light Dragoons	456
10th Light Dragoons	438
11th Light Dragoons	462
12th Light Dragoons	404
13th Light Dragoons	437
15th Light Dragoons	452
16th Light Dragoons	459
18th Light Dragoons	433
23rd Light Dragoons	409
1st Foot Guards	2141
Coldstream Guards	907
3rd Foot Guards	1061
1st Foot	615
4th Foot	629
14th Foot	639
23rd Foot	712
27th Foot	589

Table 8.29 continued

Regiment or position	No. of recipients
28th Foot	507
30th Foot	595
32nd Foot	646
33rd Foot	520
35th Foot	564
40th Foot	790
42nd Foot	575
44th Foot	455
51st Foot	604
52nd Foot	1158
54th Foot	607
59th Foot	511
69th Foot	347
71st Foot	799
73rd Foot	496
78th Foot*	4
79th Foot	691
91st Foot	860
92nd Foot	595
95th Foot	1316
1st KGL Light Dragoons	558
2nd KGL Light Dragoons	470
1st KGL Hussars	39
3rd KGL Hussars	696
1st KGL Light Battalion	513
2nd KGL Light Battalion	385
1st KGL Line Battalion	494
2nd KGL Line Battalion	436
3rd KGL Line Battalion	581
4th KGL Line Battalion	396
5th KGL Line Battalion	436
7th KGL Line Battalion (Detachment)	25
8th KGL Line Battalion	536
King's German Artillery	621

* The 78th Foot was in Nieuport as part of the garrison.

Trivia: *Private Robert Burnham of Captain Thoyts's troop of the Royal Horse Guards received a Waterloo Medal.*

The Military General Service Medal 1793–1814

The Military General Service Medal was authorised on 1 June 1847. It is often erroneously called the Peninsula Medal, but it includes battles and campaigns that were not part of the Peninsular War. The original medal was awarded for any of twenty-nine different battles, sieges and campaigns. Although there were many battles and actions during the years 1793 to 1814, only those battles and campaigns that a Gold Medal was given to senior officers were authorised as clasps. A clasp would be worn on the ribbon with each battle or campaign the soldier had participated in. On 12 February 1850 a clasp for Egypt was also authorised. Only soldiers who were still alive when the medal was issued were to receive it. If the soldier died between the times it was authorised and when it was awarded, the family would receive it. Over 26,000 medals were awarded. This was far fewer than the number who would have received it if the government had awarded it sooner than thirty years after the Peninsular War ended, however. The typical recipient would have been in his late fifties or sixties. Incredibly, considering the rough conditions that the soldiers lived in during a campaign, over 300 soldiers were recipients of ten or more clasps! The spelling of the battle or campaign shows the style on the bar on the ribbon.

Table 8.30   Bars to the Military General Service Medal

Battle or campaign	Date
Egypt	1801
Maida	4 July 1806
Roleia	17 August 1808
Vimiera	21 August 1808
Sahagun	20 December 1808
Benevente	29 December 1808
Sahagun & Benevente	20 & 29 December 1808
Corunna	16 January 1809
Martinique	24 February 1809
Talavera	27–28 July 1809
Guadaloupe	6 February 1810
Busaco	27 February 1810
Barrosa	5 March 1811
Fuentes d'Onor	5 May 1811
Albuhera	16 May 1811
Java	August 1811
Ciudad Rodrigo	19 January 1812
Badajoz	6 April 1812
Salamanca	22 July 1812

Table 8.30 continued

Battle or campaign	Date
Fort Detroit	August 1812
Vittoria	21 June 1813
Pyrenees	28 July–8 August 1813
St Sebastian	9 September 1813
Chateauguay	26 October 1813
Nivelle	10 November 1813
Chrystler's Farm	11 November 1813
Nive	9–13 December 1813
Orthes	27 February 1814
Toulouse	10 April 1814

Trivia: Private Jean-Baptiste LaPierre of the Lower Canadian Militia was the only individual to receive clasps for all three battles of the War of 1812: Fort Detroit, Chateauguay and Chrystler's Farm.

Table 8.31   Military General Service Medal – number of clasps

Recipients with ten or more clasps

No. of clasps	No. of recipients	No. of clasps	No. of recipients
15	2	12	77
14	13	11	184
13	40	10	314
Total			630

Recipients with seven or more clasps

No. of clasps	No. of recipients	No. of clasps	No. of recipients
15	0	10	36
14	2	9	58
13	4	8	90
12	9	7	114
11	12		
Total			325

Source: Swinburne, 'Medals: Army General Service'.

Trivia: In March 1889, Captain James Gammell, 59th Foot, forwarded his claim for the Military General Service Medal for Nive, 75 years after the battle! He had left the army shortly after the battle and never got around to submitting his claim.[9]

---

9   Carter, *Medals of the British Army*, p. 170.

Table 8.32 Military General Service Medal – recipients

Fourteen or more clasps

Name	Rank	Regiment	No. of clasps
Daniel Loochstadt	Private	60th Foot	15
James Talbot	Private	45th Foot	15
James Campbell	Major	50th Foot	14
John Hardy	Sergeant	7th Foot	14
Gleen John	Drum Major	45th Foot	14
Edward Kean	Private	45th Foot	14
James Nixon	Sergeant	45th Foot	14
Patrick Haggerty	Private	52nd Foot	14
James Morris	Private	52nd Foot	14
James Schoedde	Major	60th Foot	14
Joseph Hindle	Sergeant	95th Foot	14
John Hughes	Private	RA Drivers	14

Thirteen clasps

Name	Rank	Regiment
Montague Mahoney	Surgeon	7th Foot
Dennis Haworth	Sergeant	7th Foot
Ingham William	Private	7th Foot
Patrick Callaghan	Private	27th Foot
James Coates	Corporal	40th Foot
John Davis	Corporal	40th Foot
John Tanner	Sergeant	40th Foot
James Wolfe	Private	40th Foot
Charles Barnwell	Lieutenant	45th Foot
Philip Gleeson	Private	45th Foot
Thomas Griffiths	Corporal	45th Foot
Thomas Johnson	Private	45th Foot
Hugh Leslie	Private	45th Foot
Patrick Mitchell	Quartermaster	45th Foot
Jonas Neep	Private	45th Foot
William Poole	Private	45th Foot
Patrick Trimmons	Private	45th Foot
Jepson Vickars	Private	45th Foot
William Vines	Private	45th Foot
Richard Wharton	Private	45th Foot
Edward Byrne	Private	52nd Foot
Alexander Devie	Private	52nd Foot
John Faloon	Private	52nd Foot
David Hetherwisk	Private	52nd Foot

Table 8.32 continued

Name	Rank	Regiment
Hugh McCurrie	Sergeant	52nd Foot
John McFarlane	Private	52nd Foot
David McNish	Private	52nd Foot
Richard Morginson	Private	52nd Foot
Francis Watts	Private	52nd Foot
Alexander James Wolfe	Ensign	60th Foot
William Lyons	Sergeant	88th Foot
James Cooke	Private	95th Foot
Alex Eason	Sergeant	95th Foot
John Lamont	Private	95th Foot
William Twigg	Private	Royal Waggon Train
Henry Backfeld	Corporal	1st KGL Hussars
Henry Fellersmann	Gunner	King's German Artillery
Robert Rollands	Private	RA
John Fitton	Private	RA Drivers
George Legg	Private	RA Drivers
Thomas Wilson	Private	RA Drivers

Source: Mullen, *The Military General Service Roll.*

Trivia: Sergeant John Hardy had fourteen clasps to his medal and Private John Hardy had twelve clasps to his. Both served in the 7th Foot.

The Rarest Clasp – Benevente

The Benevente Clasp is so rare that some authorities claim that it was never given out. Most soldiers eligible for the clasp also fought at Sahagun and thus would receive the Benevente and Sahagun Clasp. The records of the War Office state that it was given to three soldiers, but even then there is some controversy about whether William Lyne (7th Light Dragoons) received it.

Table 8.33 Recipients of the Military General Service Medal with Benevente clasp

Name	Regiment	Other clasps received
Henry Evelegh	Royal Horse Artillery	None
William Lyne	7th Light Dragoons	None
Michael Gilmore	18th Light Dragoons	None

Source: Mullen, *The Military General Service Roll.*

References

Official papers
General orders. Spain and Portugal, vol.1, 27 April to 28 December 1809, T. Egerton, [London] 1811
General Regulations and Orders for the Army, Adjutant General's Office, Horse-Guards, 12 August, 1811. W. Clowes, London 1811
British Minor Expeditions 1746–1814, Intelligence Division, HMSO, London 1884,
House of Commons Parliamentary Papers (HCPP)
  Accounts and Estimates, Army Returns, etc.
  Sessional Papers
Return of the Names of the Officers in the Army Who Received Pensions for the Lost of Limbs; or for Wounds, House of Commons, 1816, reprinted by Naval & Military Press, Heathfield 2002 (new edn)
Secretaria dos Negocios da Guerra [Ministry of Foreign Affairs and War], *Order for the Day*, 25 December 1820

Serials
Annual Register, or a View of the History, Politics, and Literature, of the Year, 1825
Army Lists, C. Roworth, London
London Gazette
Monthly Army List
Journal of the Society for Army Historical Research
Journal of the Statistical Society of London, October 1842, p. 309
Royal Military Chronicle, vol. VI, J. Davis, London 1813
United Service Journal and Naval and Military Magazine, Henry Colburn and Richard Bentley, London 1831, pt II, pp. 281–2

General
Adkin, Mark   *The Waterloo Companion*, Stackple Press, Mechanicsburg 2001
Adye, Richard W.   *The Bombardier and Pocket Gunner*, 7th edn, T. Egerton, London 1813
Anon.   *The Waterloo Medal Roll*, ed. C. J. Buckland, Naval and Military Press, Dallington 1992

References

Army Officers Awards of the Napoleonic Period, Savannah Paperback Classics, London 2002

Baker, Anthony   *Battle Honours of the British and Commonwealth Armies, I*, Allan, London 1986

Bamford, Andrew   'The British Army in the Low Countries, 1813–1814', *The Napoleon Series*, www.napoleon-series.org/military/battles/c_lowcountries1814.html

Barnes, Major R. Money   *A History of the Regiments & Uniforms of the British Army*, Sphere Books, London 1972

Beamish, North Ludlow   *History of the King's German Legion*, 2 vols, Thomas and William Boone, London 1832–7

Bell, George   *Soldier's Glory: Being Rough Notes of an Old Soldier*, Spellmount, Tunbridge Wells 1991

Blackman, John L.   *'It All Culminated at Hougoumont': the Letters of Captain John Lucie Blackman, Coldstream Guards 1812–1815*, Gareth Glover (ed.), Ken Trotman, Godmanchester 2009

Booth, John   *The Battle of Waterloo, with Those of Ligny and Quatre Bras*, L. Booth, London 1852

Brett-James, Anthony   *Life in Wellington's Army*, Tom Donovon, London 1994

Brown, William   *With the 45th at Badajoz, Salamanca, and Vittoria*, Napoleonic Archive, Darlington, (no date, about 2003)

Burke, John   *A General and Heraldic Dictionary of the Peerage and Baronetage of the British Empire*, 2 vols H. Colburn and R. Bentley, London 1832

Burnham, Robert and Ron McGuigan   'The Impeccable Timing of Sir George Brown', *The Napoleon Series*, www.napoleon-series.org/military/Warof1812/2008/Issue10/c_ElegantExtracts.html

Calvert, Michael and Peter Young   *A Dictionary of Battles (1715–1815)*, Mayflower Books, New York 1979

Carew, Tim   *How the Regiments got their Nicknames*, Leo Cooper, London 1974

Carter, Thomas   *Medals of the British Army: and How They Were Won*, Groombridge and Sons, London 1861

Chaby, Cláudio de   *Excerptos historicos e collecçao de documentos relativos a guerra denominada na peninsula e as anteriores de 1801, e do Roussilon e Cataluna*, 6 vols, Imprensa Nacional, Lisboa 1863–82

Challis, Lionel   'The Peninsula Roll Call', *The Napoleon Series*, www.napoleon-series.org/research/biographies/GreatBritain/Challis/c_ChallisIntro.html

Chartrand, René   *British Forces in North America 1793–1815*, Men-at-Arms Series 319, Osprey, Oxford 1998

—   *British Forces in the West Indies 1792–1815*, Men-at-Arms Series 294, Osprey, Oxford 1996

—   *Émigré & Foreign Troops in British Service (2) 1803–15*, Men-at-Arms Series 335, Osprey Oxford 2000

Chichester, Henry Manners and George Burges-Short   *The Records and Badges of the British Army*, Frederick Muller, London 1970

Cocks, Edward C.   *Intelligence Officer in the Peninsula: Letters & Diaries of Major the Hon. Edward Charles Cocks 1786–1812*, Julia Page (ed.), Hippocrene Books, New York 1986

Cooper, John S. *Rough Notes of Seven Campaigns: 1809–1815*, Spellmount Library, Staplehurst 1996.
Costello, Edward *The Peninsular and Waterloo Campaigns*, Archon Books, Hamden 1968
Cotton, Edward *A Voice from Waterloo*, EP Publishing, Wakefield 1974
Dalton, Charles *The Waterloo Roll Call*, reprint of the 1904 edition, Arms and Armour Press, London 1978
De Flonblanque, Edward Barrington *Title Treatise on the Administration and Organization of the British Army: with Especial Reference to Finance and Supply*, Longman, Brown, Green, Longmans and Roberts, London 1858
Dempsey, Guy *Albuera 1811*, Frontline Books, Barnsley 2008
Dickson, Alexander *The Dickson Manuscripts: Being Diaries, Letters, Maps, Account Books, with Various Other Papers of the Late Major-General Sir Alexander Dickson*, John H. Leslie (ed.), 5 vols, Ken Trotman, Cambridge 1987
Dumas, Samuel and K. O. Vedel-Petersen *Losses of Life Caused by War*, Clarendon Press, Oxford 1923
Duncan, Major Francis *History of the Royal Regiment of Artillery*, 3rd edn, 2 vols, John Murray, London 1879
Elliott, James E. *Strange Fatality: the Battle of Stoney Creek, 1813*, Robin Brass Studio, Toronto 2009
Farmer, George *The Light Dragoon*, Ken Trotman, Cambridge 1999
Fletcher, Ian *The Waters of Oblivion: the British Invasion of the Rio de la Plata 1806–07*, Spellmount, Brimscombe Port 2006
Fortescue, John W. *A History of the British Army*, Macmillan and Co., 1912–20
— *The County Lieutenancies and the Army: 1803–1814*, Macmillan, London 1909
Fosten, Bryan *Wellington's Heavy Cavalry*, Men-at-Arms Series 130, Osprey Publishing, London 1982.
— *Wellington's Infantry (1)*, Men-at-Arms Series 114, Osprey Publishing, London 1981
— *Wellington's Infantry (2)*, Men-at-Arms Series 119. Osprey Publishing, London 1982
— *Wellington's Light Cavalry*, Men-at-Arms Series 126, Osprey Publishing, London 1982
Fraser, Edward *The Soldiers Whom Wellington Led*, Methuen, London 1913
Frederick, J. M. B. *Lineage Book of the British Army*. Hope Farm Press, Cornwallville 1968
Gazeta de Lisboa, no. 116, published in *Investigador Portuguez em Inglaterra*, March 1818
'General Statement of the Distribution of the Prize Money granted for the Battle of Waterloo and the Capture of Paris in 1815', in *Wellington's Supplementary Despatches*, vol. 10, p. 750
Glover, Michael *The Napoleonic Wars: an Illustrated History 1792–1815*, Hippocrene Books, New York 1979
— *The Peninsular War 1808–1814*, David & Charles, London 1974
— *Wellington as Military Commander*, Sphere Books, London 1973
— *Wellington's Army in the Peninsula 1808–1814*, Hippocrene Books, New York 1977

References

Grattan, William *Adventures with the Connaught Rangers: 1809–1814*, Napoleonic Library, Greenhill Books, London 1989

Graves, Donald E. *Field of Glory: the Battle of Crysler's Farm, 1813*, Robin Brass Studio, Toronto 1999

Graves, Donald E. *Where Right and Glory Lead! The Battle of Lundy's Lane, 1814*, Robin Brass Studio, Toronto 2003

Hall, John A. *The Biographical Dictionary of British Officers Killed and Wounded 1808–1814*, vol. VIII to Charles Oman, *History of the Peninsular War*, Greenhill Books, London 1998

Haydn, Joseph *The Book of Dignities: Containing Rolls of the Official Personages of the British Empire ... from the Earliest Periods to the Present Time ... together with the Sovereigns of Europe, from the Foundation of their Respective States; the Peerage of England and Great Britain*, Longmans, Brown, Green and Longmans, London 1851

Haythornthwaite, Philip J. *The Armies of Wellington*, Arms & Armour Press, London 1994.

Hodge, William B. 'On the Mortality Arising from Military Operations', *Journal of the Statistical Society of London*, XIX, 1856 pp. 219–65

Hook, Theodore Edward *The Life of General, the Right Honourable Sir David Baird, Bart*, 2 vols, R. Bentley, London 1832

Horsman, Reginald *The War of 1812*. Alfred A. Knopf, New York 1969

Irving, L. Homfray *Officers of the British Forces in Canada During the War of 1812–15*, Welland Tribune Print, [Welland, Ont.] 1908

James, Charles *The Regimental Companion*, T. Egerton, London 1800.

Jones, John Thomas *Journals of Sieges Carried on by the Army Under the Duke of Wellington, in Spain, between the Years 1811 and 1814: With Notes*, 2 vols, 2nd edn, T. Egerton, London 1827

Kane, John *List of Officers of the Royal Regiment of Artillery from the Year 1716 to the Year 1899*, 4th edn, William Clowes & Sons, London 1900

Kincaid, John *Adventures in the Rifle Brigade and Random Shots from a Rifleman*, Richard Drew, Glasgow 1981

Kinloch, Charles 'A Hellish Business: the Horrors of War Coupled with the Complexities of the "Purchase" and "Staff Appointment" Systems', in *Letters of Captain Charles Kinloch 52nd Foot 1806–1816*, ed. Gareth Glover, Ken Trotman, Godmanchester 2007

Kitzmiller II, John M. *In Search of the 'Forlorn Hope': a Comprehensive Guide to Locating British Regiments and Their Records (1640–WWI)*, 2 vols, Manuscript Publishing Foundation, Salt Lake City 1988

Larpent, Francis S. *The Private Journal of Francis Seymour Larpent, Judge Advocate General of the British Forces in the Peninsula*, 3 vols, Richard Bentley, London 1853

Lawrence, William *A Dorset Soldier: The Autobiography of Sergeant William Lawrence 1790–1869*, ed. Eileen Hathaway, Spellmount, Tunbridge Wells 1993

Laws, Lt Col. M. E. S. *Battery Records of the Royal Artillery*, Royal Artillery Institute, Woolwich 1952

Lee, Sidney (ed.) *Supplement to the Dictionary of National Biography*, Smith, Elder and Co., London 1901

Leslie, N. B. *The Battle Honours of the British and Indian Armies 1695–1914*, Leo

Cooper, London 1970
— *The Succession of Colonels of the British Army from 1660 to the Present Day*, Gale & Polden, London 1974
Lord, Walter   *The Dawn's Early Light*, W. W. Norton, New York 1972
Mackerlie. P. H. (compiler)   *An Account of the Scottish Regiments, with the Statistics of each from 1808 to March 1861*, William P. Nimmo, Edinburgh 1862
Mathews H. C. G. and Brian Harrison (eds)   *Oxford Dictionary of National Biography*, Oxford University Press, Oxford 2004
Maxwell, Herbert Eustace   *The Life of Wellington. The Restoration of the Martial Power of Great Britain*, 4th edn, 2 vols, S. Low, Marston and Co., London 1900
Maxwell, W. H.   *Life of Field-Marshal His Grace the Duke of Wellington*, 3 vols, H. G. Bohn, London 1845–6
— *The Victories of Wellington and the British Armies*, G. Bell & Daldy, London 1868
Michell, John Edward and Caroline A. Michell   *Records of the Royal Horse Artillery: From Its Formation to the Present Time, Being a Revised Edition of 'The Records of the Horse Brigade'*, W. Mitchell & Co., London 1888
Milne, Samuel   *The Standards and Colours of the Army from the Restoration 1661 to . . . 1881*, Goodall and Suddick, Leeds 1893
Moore, James Carrick   *The Life of Lieutenant-General Sir John Moore, K.B.*, vol. II, J. Murray, London 1834
Muir, Rory   *Salamanca 1812*, Yale University, New Haven 2001
Muir, Rory, Robert Burnham, Howie Muir and Ron McGuigan   *Inside Wellington's Peninsular Army 1808–1814*, Pen & Swords Books, Barnsley 2006
Mullen, A. L. T.   *The Military General Service Roll*, London: Stamp Exchange, London 1990
Nevill, Ralph   *British Military Prints*, Connoisseur Publishing, London 1909
Nicolas, Nicholas H.   *The History of the Orders of British Knighthood*, 4 vols, J. Hunter, London 1842
Oman, Sir Charles   *A History of the Peninsular War*, Greenhill Books, London 1995
— *Studies in the Napoleonic Wars*, Greenhill Books, London 1987
— *Wellington's Army 1808–1814*, Greenhill Books, London 1986
Patterson, John   *Camps and Quarters; Scenes and Impressions of Military Life, Interspersed with Anecdotes of Various Well-known Characters Who Flourished in the War*, vol. 1, Saunders, London 1843
Philippart, John   *The Royal Military Calendar or Army Service & Commissions Book*, 5 vols, 3rd edn, A. J. Valpy, London 1820
Pickles, Tim   *New Orleans 1815*, Campaign Series 28, Osprey, Oxford Publishing 1993
Pivka, Otto von   *The King's German Legion*, Men-at-Arms Series, Osprey Publishing, Oxford 1974
Playford, Thomas   *The Memoirs of Sergeant-Major Thomas Pickford 1810–1830*, ed. Gareth Glover, Ken Trotman, Godmanchester 2006
Reid, Stuart   *Wellington's Army in the Peninsula 1809–14*, Battle Orders Series, Osprey Publishing, Oxford 2004
— *Wellington's Officers*, vol. 1, Partizan Press, Leigh-on-sea 2008.
Reide, Thomas   *A Treatise on Military Finance Containing the Pay and Allowances in*

References

Camp, Garrison, and Quarters of the British Army, 2 vols, T. Egerton, London 1803

Reilly, Robin   *The British at the Gates: the New Orleans Campaign in the War of 1812*. G. P. Putnam's Sons, New York 1974

Rous, John   *A Guards Officer in the Peninsula: the Peninsular War Letters of John Rous, Coldstream Guards, 1812–1814*, ed. Ian Fletcher, Spellmount, Tunbridge Wells 1992

Shaw, W. E.   *The Knights of England*, 2 vols, Genealogical Publishing, Baltimore 1971

Siborne, Herbert   *Waterloo Letters*   Greenhill Books, London 1993

Siborne, William   *History of the War in France & Belgium in 1815*, 2nd edn, 2 vols, T. and W. Boone, London 1844

Smith, Digby   *The Greenhill Napoleonic Wars Data Book*, Greenhill, London: 1998

Smith, Sir Harry   *The Autobiography of Sir Harry Smith*, 1787–1819. Constable, London 1999

Sorando, Luis Muzás   'Trophies of Albuera', *The Napoleon Series*, www.napoleon-series.org/military/battles/c_albueraflags.html

Stanhope, 5th Earl of (Philip Henry)   *Notes of Conversations with the Duke of Wellington: 1831–1851*, John Murray, London 1888

Stephen, Leslie (ed.)   *Dictionary of National Biography*. London: Smith, Elder and Co., 1895.

Swinburne, H. L.   'Medals: Army General Service, 1793–1814', *Encyclopædia Britannica* 1911 edn

Swinson, Arthur   *A Register of the Regiments and Corps of the British Army*, Archive Press, London 1972

Tancred, George and John Murray   *Historical Record of Medals and Honorary Distinctions Conferred on the British Navy, Army, and Auxiliary Forces: from the Earliest Period*, Spink & Son, London 1891

Thomas, George   *The Local Military Paymaster*, T. Egerton, Whitehall: 1812

Thorne, R. G.   *The House of Commons 1790–1820*, Secker and Warburg, London: 1986

Vivian, Richard H.   *Richard Hussey Vivian: A Memoir*, ed. Claud Vivian, Ken Trotman, Cambridge 2003

Wellington, 1st Duke of   *The Dispatches of Field Marshal The Duke of Wellington During His Various Campaigns. From 1799 to 1818*, new edn, ed. John Gurwood, London: John Murray, 1837

—   *General Orders, Portugal, Spain & France, 1809–1815*, T. Egerton, London 1810–16

—   *The General Orders of Field Marshal the Duke of Wellington in Portugal, Spain, and France, from 1809 to 1814: in the Low Countries and France in 1815; and in France, Army of Occupation, from 1816 to 1818*, ed. John Gurwood, 2nd edn, W. Clowes and Sons, London 1837

Wellington, 1st Duke of   *Supplementary Despatches, Correspondence and Memoranda of Field Marshal Arthur Duke of Wellington, KG*, ed. 2nd Duke of Wellington, John Murray, London 1858–65

Wood, William (ed.)   *Select British Documents of the Canadian War of 1812*, 3 vols, Champlain Society, Toronto 1920–28

Index

The index consists only of key names, of principal officers with the rank of general officer, as well as principal events and terms. Individual regiments are not listed.

Abercromby, John 46, 47, 99, 226, 243
Acland, Wroth Palmer 25, 26, 31, 43, 99, 243, 259, 260
Adam, Frederick 56, 246
agents, regimental 93, 128–35
Agnew, Patrick A. 47, 48, 274
Albuera (Albuhera) xii, xiii, xv, xxv, 117, 123, 125, 126, 170, 182, 209, 214, 217, 221, 222, 225, 227, 230, 233, 237, 256, 257, 258, 259, 272, 273, 293, 311
Almaraz 118, 182, 214, 237
Alten, Charles Baron 16, 23, 28, 30, 32, 35, 37, 44, 55, 207, 246, 255, 272, 278, 283, 294, 298, 301, 305
Alten, Victor Baron 35, 37, 53, 55, 107, 278, 283,
Anglesey, Marquess of *see* Paget, Henry, Lord
Anson, George 35, 37, 96, 243, 265, 278, 283
Anson, William 35, 37, 262, 278, 283, 288, 294, 301, 305
Anstruther, Robert 32, 231, 260
Arabia 117
Arroyo dos Molinos 117, 182, 214
Ashworth, Charles 248, 284, 289, 294, 298
Auchmuty, Samuel 25, 26, 47, 48, 101, 102, 105, 239, 242, 274
Aylmer, Matthew Lord 36, 39, 240, 244, 266, 268, 270, 284, 298

Bace, William 293, 307
Badajoz xiii, xv, 118, 171, 201, 209, 214, 218, 256, 257, 258, 259, 276, 311

Baird, David 14, 23, 24, 25, 26, 27, 31, 97, 99, 236, 242, 262
Baltic, 1807, 1808 27, 29
Barnes, Edward 35, 38, 40, 53, 55, 57, 244, 263, 264, 289
baronets 235–6
Barossa (Barosa) xii, xxv, 117, 128, 214, 218, 221, 256, 257, 269, 311
barracks ix, x, xviii, 14, 59, 79, 84, 141, 142, 193, 202, 207
Barrow, Thomas 44, 264
Barsse, Adolphus Baron 23, 28, 34, 37, 52, 107
Bath, Order of the 235, 241–54
battle honours 115–21
Bayly, Henry 35, 38
Baynes, Edward 50, 104
Beckwith, Charles 179, 253, 307
Beckwith, George 40, 44, 102, 105, 242, 263, 264
Beckwith, Thomas S. 39, 244, 260, 262, 268
Bell, George x, 159
Benevente xiii, 214, 255, 256, 257, 261, 311, 314
Bentinck, Lord William 15, 31, 51, 52, 95, 242, 262
Beresford, Lord George 56
Beresford, William Carr 24, 25, 26, 31, 33, 34, 36, 101, 220, 226, 227, 237, 242, 258, 262, 268, 272, 278, 283, 288, 294, 298, 301, 302, 305
de Bernewitz, John 35, 38, 278
Blackman, John Lucie 160, 163
Bladensburg 120, 217

Index

Blomefield, Thomas 27, 109, 236
Blunt, Richard 35, 38
Bock, George 34, 37, 107, 232, 278, 283
Borthwick, William 32, 35, 38, 109, 275
Bourbon vii, 15, 45, 46, 74, 104, 114, 117, 216
Bowes, Barnard Foord 32, 34, 37, 230, 260, 276
Bradford, Thomas 26, 36, 39, 55, 57, 244, 262, 279, 291, 298
Brisbane, Thomas Makdougall 36, 39, 49, 55, 57, 244, 284, 289, 294, 305
Briscall, Samuel 14
Brock, Isaac 49, 230, 231, 246, 282, 283
Brodrick, John 24, 25, 31, 103, 105
Brooke, William 35, 38, 227, 273
Browne, Gore 26, 44, 105
Brown, George 151
Brownrigg, Robert 7, 43, 97, 100, 243
Buchan, John 248, 264, 284, 289, 294, 298
Buenos Aires 25, 26, 217, 218, 226, 227, 233
Burgoyne, John Fox 29, 30, 50, 249, 277, 279, 285, 292, 299
Burne, Robert 35, 38, 260, 262
Burrard, Harry 27, 31, 236
Busaco xii, xiii, xv, 117, 214, 220, 256, 257, 258, 259, 267, 268, 269, 311
Byng, John 36, 39, 55, 108, 244, 284, 289, 294, 298, 301

Cameron, Alan 30, 32, 34, 37, 101, 243, 265
Cameron, John (LCol 9th Foot) 50, 56, 244, 260, 262, 268, 280, 285, 292, 299, 302
Campbell, Alexander 34, 37, 97, 98, 101, 108, 185, 236, 239, 265
Campbell, Archibald 185, 240, 245, 248, 264, 272, 284, 285, 289, 294, 298, 300
Campbell, Charles 49
Campbell, Henry 32, 34, 37, 243, 265, 278
Campbell, James 33, 34, 36, 42,
Campaign of 1815 54–6, 182–3
Cape of Good Hope vii, 4, 5, 13, 14, 15, 23, 24, 25, 61, 62, 63, 64, 65, 77, 116, 155, 215
Cathcart, William Lord 14, 22, 27, 94, 237, 270, 280, 285, 306
chaplains 13, 14, 154, 174, 178, 180
Chateauguay xiii, 217, 256, 257, 293, 294, 312
Chatham, John Pitt, Earl of 7, 42, 43, 96, 109

Chowne, Christopher *see* Tilson, Christopher
Chrystler's Farm xiii, 256, 257, 273, 297, 312
Ciudad Rodrigo xiii, 118, 171, 178, 209, 218, 230, 256, 257, 258, 259, 275, 311
Clinton, Henry 30, 32, 34, 37, 53, 55, 57, 96, 99, 242, 263, 278, 294, 298, 301, 305
Clinton, William 33, 34, 37, 99, 243
Cocks, Edward Charles 161
Cole, Galbraith Lowry 25, 55, 57, 33, 34, 36, 100, 102, 242, 259, 272, 278, 283, 288, 294, 301, 305
Collins, Richard 232, 272, 279
Colman, Francis John 232, 268, 291
Colville, Charles 34, 37, 40, 55, 57, 102, 105, 243, 263, 270, 276, 283, 289, 294
Combermere, Lord *see* Cotton, Stapleton
Commissariat 11–13
Conran, Henry 49
Cooke, George 35, 38, 51, 53, 55, 101, 178, 226, 232, 246
Coote, Eyre 42, 43, 98, 100, 101, 242
Coruña (Corunna) x, xiii, 13, 29, 30, 76, 77, 116, 119, 157, 183, 214, 230, 231, 255, 256, 257, 258, 259, 262, 263, 267, 311
Cotton, Stapleton 31, 33, 36, 55, 57, 96, 237, 242, 265, 270, 278, 301, 305
Cradock, John 31, 43, 242
Craufurd, James Catlin 32, 37, 231, 260, 262
Craufurd, Robert 4, 25, 26, 32, 35, 38, 157, 226, 230, 268, 275

Dalhousie George, Earl of 33, 34, 36, 43, 98, 105, 242, 283, 288
Darroch, Duncan 49
Dalrymple, Hew 29, 31, 97, 98, 99
Decken, Frederick, Baron 28, 107
De Lancey, William Howe 56, 244, 262, 266, 268, 271, 276, 280, 285, 292, 298
Detroit xiii, 118, 256, 257, 282, 283, 312
Dickson, Alexander 32, 50, 159, 245, 259, 269, 273, 275, 277, 280, 285, 292, 294, 298, 305
Dilkes, William Thomas 35, 37, 269
Disney, Moore 31, 34, 37, 43, 97, 246, 262
Dominica xii, 116, 236, 238
Don, George 22, 42, 43, 102, 103
Donkin, Rufane Shaw 35, 38, 266
de Dornberg, William 55, 107, 108, 246
Douglass, Robert 58

322

Index

Douro 15, 117, 170, 209, 265
Doyle, John 101, 235, 236, 242
Doyle, John Milley 240, 245, 271, 275, 284, 289, 302, 305
Drechsel, Frederick, Baron 27
de Drieberg, George 28, 30, 32, 37, 107
Drummond, George Duncan 38, 231, 266
Drummond, Gordon 49, 102, 241, 243
Dundas, David 6, 94, 95, 102, 242
Dundas, Francis 23, 100, 102
Dunlop, James 34, 37
D'Urban, Benjamin 244, 268, 272, 276, 279, 284, 289, 294, 298, 305
Dyott, William 31, 43

Eden, William 47, 48, 51, 274
Egypt vii, 4, 20, 28, 126, 183, 201, 215, 230, 231, 236, 258, 311
El Bodon xv, 117, 214
Elphinstone, Howard 39, 236, 250, 261, 295, 299
Erskine, James 33, 34, 36
Erskine, William 34, 37, 43, 105, 232

facings, regimental 109–115
Fane, Henry 32, 35, 37, 94, 96, 243, 260, 262, 265, 284, 301
Ferguson, Dugald 159, 160
Ferguson, Ronald Craufurd 24, 31, 51, 108, 243, 260
Finch, Edward 23, 27, 97, 99
Fisher, George 32
Fletcher, Richard 39, 218, 236, 239, 266, 268, 275, 277, 285, 292
flogging, *see under* punishment
Forbes, James, Lord 41, 99, 102, 105
Fort Detroit xiii, 256, 257, 282, 283, 312
Framingham, Hoylet 32, 185, 244, 266, 268, 271, 276, 280
Fraser, Alexander Mackenzie 23, 28, 30, 31, 43, 101, 231, 262
Fuentes de Oñoro (Fuentes de Onor) xii, xiii, xv, xxv, 117, 170, 209, 214, 221, 256, 257, 258, 259, 270, 311
Gammell, James 312
Garcia Hernandez 118
Genoa viii, 51, 52, 77, 216
Gibbs, Samuel 47, 48, 50, 51, 230, 232, 244, 274
Gillespie, Robert Rollo 48, 230, 244, 274

Glasgow, George 49
Gledstanes, Albert 40, 44, 104, 240, 263, 264
Göhrde 119
Goldie, Alexander 35, 38
Gordon, James 6, 7, 13, 36, 39, 101, 103, 244
Gore, Arthur 51, 230, 232
Gosselin, Gerard 49, 52
Gower, John Leveson 26, 104
Graham, Thomas 15, 32, 33, 36, 43, 50, 51, 53, 101, 232, 237, 242, 269, 275, 283, 291
Grant, Colquhoun 39, 55, 57, 227, 244, 261, 284
de Grey, George 35, 38, 272
Grosvenor, Thomas 27, 28, 43, 100, 102
Guadeloupe (Guadaloupe) vii, viii, xiii, xxv, 13, 15, 44, 45, 58, 117, 216, 238, 256, 257, 264, 311

half pay x, 12, 16, 172, 173, 175
Halkett, Colin 39, 51, 53, 56, 107, 244, 272, 279, 284, 298
Hamilton, John 34, 37, 103, 185, 236, 239, 272, 294
Hanover vii, xvii, 13, 14, 22, 53, 61, 62, 63, 65, 66, 68, 77, 78
Harcourt, George 44, 264
Hardinge, Henry 245, 269, 273, 277, 280, 286, 290, 294, 298, 302
Harding, John 32, 262
Harvey, William M. 39, 232, 272, 276
Hay, Andrew 35, 38, 44, 103, 230, 262, 284, 291, 298
Hill, Rowland 33, 36, 55, 57, 100, 102, 105, 237, 239, 242, 260, 262, 265, 267, 283, 288, 294, 298, 301
Hindoostan 120, 121
de Hinüber, Henry 35, 37, 42, 53, 55, 107, 246, 298
Hislop, Thomas 44, 103, 226, 236, 264
Hoghton, Daniel 34, 37, 40, 41, 230, 263, 272
Honstedt, Augustus 34, 37, 42, 52, 107
Hope, John 23, 28, 34, 37, 278,
Hope, John (Niddry) 29, 31, 32, 33, 36, 43, 100, 102, 158, 226, 227, 231, 237, 239, 242, 262, 298
Hopetoun, Earl of *see* Hope, John (Niddry)
Houston, William 34, 37, 43, 97, 105, 243, 270

323

Index

Howard, Kenneth Alexander 35, 37, 55, 243, 284, 298
Howorth, Edward 32, 35, 38, 243, 265, 268, 270
Hulse, Richard 35, 38, 232, 266, 278
Huntly, George Gordon, Marquess of 43

Inglis, William 36, 38, 246, 272, 289, 294, 301
Irwin, William 182, 183

Java viii, xiii, 47, 48, 73, 117, 216, 256, 257, 274, 275, 311
Johnston, William 58
Johnstone, George 56

Keane, John 39, 50, 56, 57, 232, 244, 264, 284, 289, 294, 302, 305
Kemmis, James 35, 38, 260, 266
Kempt, James 25, 35, 38, 49, 55, 57, 100, 243, 259, 276, 284, 294, 298, 302, 305
Kenah, Thomas 52
Kincaid, John 178
Kinloch, Charles 158
Knights Bachelor xii, 235, 239

Lambert, John 36, 39, 49, 55, 57, 244, 294, 298, 302, 305
Langwerth, Ernest 23, 30, 32, 37, 107, 230, 265
LaPierre, Jean-Baptiste 312
Leith, James vi, 31, 33, 34, 36, 43, 58, 103, 105, 242, 262, 268, 276, 278, 291
Le Marchant, John G. 35, 37, 230278
Lemoine, John 25, 42, 52, 247, 259
Lightburne, Stafford 33, 34, 37
Linsingen, Charles Baron 23, 27, 43, 107, 245,
Londonderry, Marquess of *see* Stewart, Charles
Long, Robert Ballard 32, 35, 38, 44, 284
Loochstadt, Daniel 313
Low, Sigismund, Baron 34, 37, 107, 246, 265, 278
Lowe, Hudson 54, 56, 108, 240
Ludlow, George 23, 27, 98, 102, 242
Lumley, William 26, 34, 37, 42, 103, 104, 243, 272
Lynedoch, Lord *see* Graham, Thomas
Lyon, James 56, 57, 246, 260, 266

Macdougall, Duncan 158
Macfarlane, Robert 27, 42, 52
Mackenzie, Alexander 42
Mackenzie-Fraser, Alexander *see* Fraser, Alexander Mackenzie
MacKenzie, John 34, 37
Mackenzie, John Randoll 31, 34, 36, 230
Mackenzie, Kenneth 35, 38, 51, 53, 55
Mackinnon, Henry 35, 38, 230
Maclean, Fitzroy 44, 264
Macleod, John 43, 109
Madden, George Allan 39, 247, 289, 297
Maida vi, vii, xii, xiii, 24, 25, 41, 116, 215, 219, 255, 256, 257, 259, 311
Maida, John Stuart, Count of 24, 25, 41, 97, 100, 102, 242, 259
Maitland, Frederick 33, 34, 36, 40, 103, 263
Maitland, Peregrine 53, 56, 57, 246, 298
Mann, William 273, 293
Manningham, Coote 31, 102, 231, 262
Martinique vii, xiii, 13, 15, 40, 44, 58, 117, 119, 216, 256, 257, 263, 311
Mauritius viii, 5, 13, 15, 45–7, 70, 72, 77, 216, 259
Meade, Robert 29
Miami 118
Moncrieffe, George 43, 104
Montevideo (Monte Video) 25, 116
Montresor, Henry 43, 52
Moore, Francis 49
Moore, John xv, xvi, 4, 29, 31, 32, 99, 150, 219, 220, 230, 231, 246, 262
Mulgrave Henry Phipps, Lord 7, 98, 109, 237
Murray, George 13, 23, 28, 30, 35, 38, 49, 55, 57, 100, 242, 259, 262, 266, 268, 270, 284, 289, 294, 298, 302, 305
Murray, John (LG) 30, 31, 33, 36, 103,
Murray, John (MG) 58

Napier, George T. 178, 249, 264
Naples, Bay of 41, 216
Nepean, Nicholas 49
Netherlands 1813–14 50–1
— 1815 53–4
Niagara 48, 118–20, 217
Nicholson, Robert 40, 263
nicknames 119, 121–8
Niddry, Lord *see* Hope, John (Niddry)
Nightingall, Miles 31, 34, 37, 103, 243, 260

324

Index

Nive 119, 182, 256–9, 267, 293, 298–300, 312
Nivelle 182, 183, 214, 223, 256–9, 267, 293–6, 312
Nobility 15–17

Oakes, Hildebrand 99, 102, 104, 109, 236
O'Callaghan, Robert 39, 56, 57, 244, 259, 284, 289, 295, 299, 302
O'Loghlin, Terence 35, 38
Orange, Prince William of 16, 53, 54, 126, 242, 275, 276, 279, 284, 289, 295
Orthez (Orthes) xii, xiii, xxv, 182, 120, 215, 218, 223, 224, 256, 257, 258, 259, 267, 301, 312
Oswald, John 25, 29, 35, 37, 42, 108, 243, 259, 284, 291

Pack, Denis 36, 39, 55, 57, 244, 259, 260, 263, 268, 269, 275, 279, 284, 289, 294, 298, 302, 305
Paget, Edward 16, 23, 30, 31, 33, 36, 98, 101, 226, 227, 242, 262
Paget, Henry, Lord 16, 31, 43, 55, 95, 237, 243, 261
Pakenham, Edward Michael 35, 38, 49, 103, 158, 230, 231, 232, 242, 264, 271, 278, 289, 294, 298, 302, 305
Patterson, John 148–50
pay, half *see under* half pay
pay, officers 143–6
pay, soldiers 196–7
pay, stoppages 146–50
Payne, William 33, 36, 95, 96, 236, 265
Peacocke, Warren 35, 38, 241
Pearson, Thomas 248, 273, 297
peerages 236–7
pensions, widows' 179–80
pensions, for wounded 175–9
Picton, Thomas 33, 34, 36, 43, 55, 101, 230, 242, 268, 270, 275, 276, 282, 283, 288, 301, 305
Ponsonby, William 36, 38, 55, 230, 244, 279, 284
Power, Manley 36, 39, 50, 55, 57, 244, 279, 284, 294, 302, 305
Power, Thomas 293
Prevost, George 40, 49, 97, 100, 101, 236, 238, 263
Pringle, William Henry 35, 38, 104, 244, 279, 289, 294, 298

prize money xxiv, 169–72, 209–10
Proby, John, Lord 51
Procter, Henry 49, 283
punishment 168–9, 204–8
Pyrenees xiii, xvi, 118, 119, 227, 256, 257, 258, 259, 267, 288, 297, 312

Queenston Heights (Queenstown) 118

Ramsay, George 40, 44, 263, 264
Rebow, Francis 35, 38
Riall, Phineas 40, 45, 49, 50, 226, 264, 265
Robe, William 244, 260, 266, 268, 277, 281, 293
Robe, William L. 293, 297, 301
Robinson, Frederick 35, 38, 49, 105, 244, 284, 291, 298
Roliça (Roleia) xii, xiii, xxv, 116, 124, 182, 214, 219, 255, 256, 257, 258, 259, 260, 261, 267, 311
Ross, Andrew 35, 38, 232
Ross, Hew Dalyrmple 240, 269, 287
Rosslyn, James St Clair-Erskine, Earl of 27, 43, 95
Ross, Robert 36, 39, 49, 158, 230, 231, 259, 263, 289, 302, 305
Rottenburg, Francis, Baron 44, 49, 108
Rous, John 162

Sahagun xiii, 116, 214, 255, 256, 257, 261, 311, 314
Salamanca xii, xiii, xv, 118, 122, 124, 159, 201, 214, 218, 222, 225, 230, 233, 256, 257, 258, 259, 267, 278, 311
San Sebastian (St Sebastian) xiii, xxv, 119, 215, 218, 256, 257, 259, 267, 291, 293, 312
Saumarez, Thomas 49
Sayer, George 275
Schoedde, James Holmes 183, 296, 313
Scovell, George 245, 286, 290, 296, 300, 306
seniority 21–58
Sheaffe, Roger 49, 236
Sherbrooke, John 23, 28, 29, 31, 33, 36, 49, 98, 100, 103, 104, 108, 239, 242, 265
Shipley, Charles 40, 44, 58, 239, 263, 264
Sicily 4, 13, 14, 15, 24, 25, 28, 41, 42, 51, 52, 61, 62, 63, 64, 65, 67, 77, 78
Simmons, George 179
Skerrett, John B. 36, 39, 51, 104, 230, 232, 226, 284

325

Index

Skinner, John 45, 264
Slade, John 31, 34, 37, 262, 270
Smith, Harry 165
Smith, Haviland 36, 38, 42, 259
Smyth, George S. 49
Somerset, Edward, Lord 36, 39, 55, 57, 244, 266, 279, 284, 302, 305
Somerset, Fitzroy, Lord 245, 272, 277, 281, 286, 290, 296, 300, 303, 306
Sontag, John 30, 32, 34, 37, 43
South America vii, 4, 23, 25, 26, 76, 77, 215
Spencer, Brent 4, 27, 31, 33, 36, 102, 105, 242, 260, 268, 270
Spry, William Frederick 36, 38, 232, 279, 284, 292
Stehelin, Edward 40, 58, 263
Stewart, Charles William 32, 34, 37, 96, 237, 242, 261, 265, 268, 270, 276
Stewart, Richard 28, 30, 32, 34, 37, 231, 265
Stewart, William 29, 33, 34, 37, 43, 102, 242, 247, 265, 272, 273, 283, 288, 294, 298, 301
Stopford, Edward 35, 38, 243, 266, 284, 298
Stovin, Richard 49
Stuart, John *see* Maida, John Stuart, Count of
Stubbs, Thomas William 272, 279, 289, 291
Swayne, Hugh 49

Talavera xii, xiii, xv, 117, 119, 126, 214, 217, 220, 226, 227, 230, 237, 255, 256, 257, 258, 259, 265, 267, 311
Talbot, James 313
Tarifa 117
Taylor, Herbert 51
Tilson, Christopher 31, 33, 34, 36, 101, 265
Torrens, Henry 6, 20, 103, 105, 244, 261
Toulouse xii, xiii, 120, 127, 182, 183, 215, 218, 223, 224, 225, 256, 257, 258, 259, 293, 305, 312

Uxbridge, Earl of *see* Paget, Henry, Lord

Vandeleur, John Ormsby 35, 38, 53, 55, 243, 275, 279, 284, 298

Venta del Pozo 118
Vimeiro (Vimiera) xiii, xxv, 14, 116, 214, 255, 256, 257, 258, 259, 260, 261, 267, 311
Vincent, John 49, 50
Vitoria (Vittoria) xii, xiii, xvi, xxv, 118, 122, 182, 201, 215, 218, 222, 229, 256, 258, 259, 267, 283, 312
Vivian, Richard Hussey 39, 56, 57, 157, 158, 244, 261, 302

Walcheren vii, xii, 3, 42, 43, 76, 77, 216, 229, 231
Wale, Charles 45, 243, 264
Walker, George Townsend 35, 38, 108, 243, 260, 276, 302
Waller, Charles 32
War of 1812 49–50, 216–17, 283, 312
Warde, Henry 31, 47, 100, 243, 262
Waterloo 28, 53, 54, 119, 121, 171, 172, 176, 178, 179, 182, 209, 210, 216, 217, 224, 225, 230, 233, 259, 267, 270, 293, 308–10
Watteville, Louis de 49, 108, 259
Wauchope, Patrick 28, 105, 230, 231
Wellington, Arthur Wellesley, Duke of 14, 15, 17–20, 22, 27, 28, 30–3, 36, 53, 54, 57, 150, 172, 200, 202, 203, 226, 227, 233, 237, 239, 242, 254, 256 260, 265, 268, 270, 275, 278, 283, 288, 294, 297, 298, 301, 305, 308
Wetherall, Frederick A. 48, 104, 274
Wheatley, William 35, 38, 232, 269, 279
Whitelocke, John 25, 26, 101, 103
Wilson, George 39, 232
Wilson, John 239, 248, 292
Wilson, Robert 36, 39
Wood, George 47, 48, 274
Wood, George A. 30, 51, 54, 56, 57, 239, 252
Wynch, James 38, 231, 263, 266

York, Prince Frederick, Duke of 6, 7, 14, 17, 20, 150, 242, 308
Yorke, John Henry 24, 231